Inquisition
and Society in Spain
in the sixteenth and seventeenth centuries

Henry Kamen

Indiana University Press
Bloomington

for Eulàlia

Manufactured in Great Britain

Library of Congress Cataloging in Publication Data

Kamen, Henry Arthur Francis.
    Inquisition and society in Spain in the sixteenth
and seventeenth centuries.

    Bibliography: p.
    Includes index.
    1. Inquisition—Spain.   2. Spain—Church history.
I. Title.
BX1735.K29 1985   272'.2'0946   85–10804

ISBN 0–253–33015–7
ISBN 0–253–22775–5 (pbk.)

1   2   3   4   5 89 88 87 86 85

Contents

Preface

The recent appearance of Emil van der Vekene's *Bibliotheca Bibliographica Historiae Sanctae Inquisitionis* (2 vols, Vaduz 1982–3) testifies to an impressive growth of research into all aspects – social, institutional and literary – of the tribunal, a far cry from the situation that prevailed when my *Spanish Inquisition* first came out in 1965. Interest in the topic has spread: witness the general study in Russian by I.R. Grigulevich, *Istoriya Inkvizitsii* (Moscow 1970), which was translated into German and then reissued as *Inkvizitsiya* (1976). Special mention should be made of the fine exhibition put on by the Spanish Ministry of Culture at the end of 1982 in the Palacio de Velázquez of the Retiro gardens in Madrid. Valuable original research has been presented at international congresses, notably one held at Cuenca in September 1978, whose proceedings were published as *La Inquisición española, Nueva visión, nuevos horizontes* (1980), and one held in New York in April 1983, whose proceedings were published by Angel Alcalá (ed), *Inquisición española y mentalidad inquisitorial* (Barcelona 1984). The result of these and other researches has been incorporated into my present work, which retains much of the text of my earlier study but is in all essentials a new book, both in its archival sources and in its conclusions. The labour of investigation continues, especially in Spain, where the classic and still unreplaceable work of Henry Charles Lea has at last begun to appear in translation, and where an ambitious new *Historia de la Inquisición* (Madrid 1984) has been published by the Biblioteca de Autores Cristianos. The limited dimensions of the present study make it essential that readers seeking further information should consult the above works and also my bibliographical references. Editorial restrictions on space have obliged me to cover only the early modern period: a fuller version that includes the

eighteenth and nineteenth centuries is available in the Spanish
edition.

When Padre Fidel Fita, the father of Inquisition studies, began
his scholarly researches in the 1890s, the field was still a battle-
ground for sectarian prejudices. Today, scientific detachment has
replaced the old attitudes, but we are not necessarily any nearer to
understanding the Inquisition. Indeed, excessive and exclusive attention to the tribunal and its archives, rather than to the broader
social context in which it operated, has frequently threatened to
give us a misleading picture of its role, rather as if one were to
attempt a history of the police without knowing much about the
society, the laws or the institutions within which the police work.

Many friends and colleagues have helped with crucial information. To them all, and specially to my sons Nicholas and Jeffrey, I
owe a debt of gratitude for moral support.

Institute for Research in the Humanities,
Madison, Wisconsin

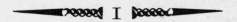

Introduction

In the west: a small but expanding society of under a million people, their energies directed to the sea and the first fruits of trade and colonization in Asia. In the south: a society of half a million farmers and silk-producers, Muslim in religion, proud remnants of a once dominant culture. To the centre and north: a Christian Spain of some six million souls, divided politically into the crown of Castile (with two-thirds of the territory of the peninsula and three-quarters of the population) and the crown of Aragon (made up of the realms of Valencia, Aragon and Catalonia). In the fifteenth century the Iberian peninsula remained on the fringe of Europe, a subcontinent that had been overrun by the Romans and the Arabs and that offered to the curious visitor an exotic symbiosis of images: Romanesque churches and the splendid Gothic cathedral in Burgos, mediaeval synagogues in Toledo, the cool silence of the great mosque in Córdoba and the majesty of the Alhambra in Granada.

In mediaeval times it was a society of uneasy coexistence (*convivencia*), increasingly threatened by the advancing Christian reconquest of lands that had been Muslim since the Moorish invasions of the eighth century. For long periods, close contact between communities had led to a mutual tolerance among the three faiths of the peninsula: Christians, Muslims and Jews. Even when Christians went to war against the Moors, it was (as a thirteenth-century writer argued) 'neither because of the law [of Mohammed] nor because of the sect that they hold to',[1] but solely because of conflict over land. Christians lived under Moorish rule (as Mozárabes) and Muslims under Christian rule (as Mudéjares). The different communities shared a broad culture that blurred racial prejudices, and military alliances were made regardless of religion. St Ferdinand, King of Castile from 1230 to 1252, called himself 'king of the three

religions', a singular claim in an increasingly intolerant age: it was
the very period that saw the birth of the mediaeval papal Inquisition
(c. 1232).

The notion of a crusade was largely absent from the earlier
periods of the Reconquest, and the communities of Spain coexisted
in a relatively 'open' society. At the height of the Reconquest it was
possible for a Catalan philosopher, Ramon Llull (d. 1315), to com-
pose a dialogue in Arabic in which the three characters were a
Christian, a Moor and a Jew. Political links between Christians and
Muslims in the mediaeval epoch are exemplified by the most famous
military hero of the time, the Cid (Arabic *sayyid*, lord). Celebrated
in the *Poem of the Cid* written about 1140, his real name was
Rodrigo Díaz de Vivar, a Castilian noble who in about 1081 transferred his services from the Christians to the Muslim ruler of Saragossa and, after several campaigns, ended his career as independent
ruler of the Muslim city of Valencia, which he captured in 1094.
Despite his identification with the Muslims, he came to be looked
upon by Christians as their ideal warrior. In the later Reconquest,
the ideals of coexistence remained but the reality of conflict was
more aggressive. The Christians cultivated the myth of the apostle
St James (Santiago), whose body was alleged to have been discovered at Compostela; thereafter Santiago Matamoros (the Moor-
slayer) became a national patron saint. In Al-Andalus, the invasion
of militant Muslims from north Africa – the Almorávids in the late
eleventh century; the Almohads in the late twelfth – embittered the
struggle against the Christians.

The tide, however, was turning against Islam. In 1212 a combined Christian force met the Almohads at Las Navas de Tolosa and
shattered their power in the peninsula. By the mid-thirteenth century the Muslims retained only the kingdom of Granada. After its
capture by the Christians (1085), Toledo immediately became the
intellectual capital of Castile because of the transmission of Muslim
and Jewish learning. The School of Translators of Toledo in the
twelfth and thirteenth centuries rendered into Latin the great semitic treatises on philosophy, medicine, mathematics and alchemy.
The works of Avicenna (Ibn-Sina), Al-Ghazali, Averroes (Ibn-
Rushd) and Maimonides filtered through to Christian scholars. Mudejar art spread into Castile. No attempt was made to convert
minorities forcibly. But by the fourteenth century 'it was no longer
possible for Christians, Moors and Jews to live under the same roof,
because the Christian now felt himself strong enough to break down

the traditional custom of Spain whereby the Christian population made war and tilled the soil, the Moor built the houses, and the Jew presided over the enterprise as a fiscal agent and skilful technician'.[2] The division of labour fostered prejudice and discrimination. Mudejars tended to be peasants or menial urban labourers; Jews for the most part kept to the big towns and to small trades; the Christian majority, while tolerating their religion, treated the minorities with disdain.

Mudejars were possibly the least affected by religious tension: they were numerically insignificant in Castile and in the crown of Aragon lived separately in their own communities, so that friction was minimal. Jews, however, lived mostly in urban centres and were more vulnerable to outbreaks of violence. Civil war in both Castile and Aragon in the 1460s divided the country into numberless local conflicts and threatened to provoke anarchy. The accession of Ferdinand and Isabella to the throne in 1474 did not immediately bring peace, but gradually the powerful warlike nobles and prelates fell into line. Their belligerent spirit was redirected into wars of conquest in Granada and Naples. Of the two realms of Spain, Aragon had been the one with an imperial history, but Castile with its superior resources in men and money rapidly took over the leadership. The militant Reconquest spirit was reborn, after nearly two centuries of dormancy. It still retained much of its old chivalric spirit: in the Granada wars, the deeds of Rodrigo Ponce de León, Marquis of Cadiz, seemed to recall those of the Cid. But the age of chivalry was passing. The wars in Italy provoked bitter criticism of the barbarities of the Spanish soldiery,[3] and in Granada the brutal enslavement of the entire population (15,000 people) of Málaga after its capture in 1487 gave hint of a new savagery among the Christians.

Apparent continuity with the old Reconquest is thus deceptive. Military idealism continued to be fed by chivalric novels, notably the *Amadis de Gaula* (1508), but beneath the superficial gloss of chivalry there burned an ideological intolerance typified by the great conquests of Cardinal Cisneros in Africa (Mers-el-Kebir 1505 and Oran 1509), and Hernán Cortés in Tenochtitlán (1521). It is also significant that the new rulers of Spain were willing to pursue an intolerant policy regardless of its economic consequences. In regard to both the Jews and the Mudejars, Isabella was warned that pressure would produce economic disruption, but she was steeled in her resolve by Cisneros and the rigorists. Ferdinand, responding to protests by Barcelona, maintained that spiritual ideals were more important than material considerations about the economy. A 'crusading' spirit thus replaced the spirit of convivencia, and religious exclusivism began to triumph.

There had always been community tensions in a society as divided as mediaeval Spain. Conflicts occurred at both popular and personal levels, between Mudejar and Christian villages, between Christian and Jewish neighbours; but convivencia produced an extraordinary degree of mutual respect. The coexistence of tolerance and conflict, *sol y sombra*, was a unique feature of peninsular society, reflected perhaps only in the Hungarian territories of the Ottoman empire. Communities lived side by side and shared many aspects of language, culture, food and dress, consciously borrowing each other's outlook and ideas. Minority groups, however, accepted fully that there was a persistent dark side, that there was no sun without shadow. Their capacity to survive centuries of sporadic persecution, and to continue to survive well into the seventeenth century under conditions of gross inequality, was based on a long apprenticeship.

The alternation of tolerance and conflict resulted in a remarkable absence of 'heresy' in Spain: the three faiths retained the sharpness and purity of ideologies polished by the rough edge of controversy. Rabbis in 1492, no less than *alfaquis* in 1609, remained utterly sure of their truths. Christianity likewise was so untarnished that the papal Inquisition, active in France, Germany and Italy, was never deemed necessary in Castile and made only a token appearance in Aragon. In the penumbra of the three great faiths there were, it is true, a number of those who, whether through the indifferentism born of tolerance or the cynicism born of persecution, had no active belief in organized religion. The virtual absence of heresy meant that though defections to other faiths were severely punished in Christian law, no machinery was ever brought into existence to deal with these non-believers or with the forced converts of shaky belief: for centuries, society continued to tolerate them, and the policy of burning practised elsewhere in Europe was little known in Spain.

The phenomenon of the Inquisition requires special attention because it had few roots in Spanish history. It was a wholly alien institution transplanted onto Castilian soil, had no precedent in Castilian practice, and aroused a storm of opposition when it began its activities. Not surprisingly, some have tried to argue that its origins were not Christian but semitic.[4] Perhaps even more relevant than its origins, however, is the question of why it was accepted and therefore survived. The breakdown of convivencia and the polarization of Castilian society between the majority Old Christian lords and peasants on one hand, and the minority faiths on the other, was crucial to this process. The unusual degree of social equality in Castile, where feudalism had never existed and there were consequently no rigid status barriers between the classes, favoured the feeling of solidarity among Old Christians. The lower classes shared the priorities and prejudices of their betters. 'Although a peasant and labouring girl', says Dorotea to her noble lover Fernando in Cervantes' *Don Quixote*, 'I consider myself the equal of you who are a lord and knight.'[5] When Francesco Guicciardini went on an embassy to Spain in 1512, he was quick to note that pride in nobility played a big part in the character of the ordinary Spaniard.[6]

In succeeding centuries the situation remained unchanged. Under Philip IV, the diplomat Saavedra Fajardo observed that the distinction between nobility and common people was less marked in Spain than in Germany. As late as the nineteenth century, in the time of Isabella II, Balmes claimed that there was no country in the world where there was more levelling of classes than Spain, and that in Spain a man of the humblest class of society would stop in the road the highest magnate in the land.[7] This familiarity between the classes meant that the lower orders came to accept the ideals of their betters, the nobility; chivalry, and the concept of 'honour' which sprang from this,[8] found a ready home in the imagination of the people. Castilians of Old Christian origin acquired an identity that transcended status barriers. Their prejudices against Jews and Muslims were extended also to New Christians from these minorities. A solid social front, captained by the Old Christian elites, prepared the way for the elimination of a plural, open society. The crown accepted this policy because it seemed to present no threat to stability, but the new developments failed to bring about social unity, and the machinery of the Inquisition served only to intensify and deepen the shadow of conflict over Spain.

The Great Dispersion

You only need to ask:
Is this or that man a threat to us? Then
is he a Jew.

Bertolt Brecht, *Der Jüde, ein Unglück für das Volk*

'The kings and lords of Castile have had this advantage, that their Jewish subjects, reflecting the magnificence of their lords, have been the most learned, the most distinguished Jews that there have been in all the realms of the dispersion; they are distinguished in four ways: in lineage, in wealth, in virtues, in science.'[1] Such was the fully justified boast of a fifteenth-century Castilian rabbi. The Jews in Spain were the largest and most homogeneous of the communities in Europe.[2] Present in the peninsula since well before Roman times,[3] they were a significant and largely urban minority. The first great Christian persecution of Jews occurred in the seventh century, and made them greet with relief the Moorish invasions that established the Muslim caliphate of Córdoba, under whose liberal regime they prospered socially and economically. This came to an end in the twelfth century with the overthrow of the caliphate by the invading Almorávids, who persecuted Christian and Jew alike and destroyed their places of worship. The Jews fled to Christian territory and under the tolerant eye of Christian rulers continued to prosper in their new surroundings. Thus although intermittent persecution did occur, some degree of tolerance was the general rule. 'In the commercial sphere, no visible barriers separated Jewish, Christian and Saracen merchants during the major period of Jewish life in Spain. Christian contractors built Jewish houses and Jewish craftsmen worked for Christian employers. Jewish advocates represented gentile clients in the secular courts. Jewish brokers acted as intermediaries between Christian and Moorish principals. As a by-product, such continuous daily contacts inevitably fostered toler-ance and friendly relationships, despite the irritations kept alive in the name of religion.'[4]

Political rivalry and economic jealousy helped to break down the security of the Jewish minority. From the thirteenth century on-wards, anti-Jewish legislation became common in Europe. The Council of Arles in 1235, for example, ordered all Jews to wear a round yellow patch, four fingers in width, over their hearts as a mark of identification. Such legislation was never enforceable in the Spanish kingdoms, where Jews were a prominent minority, but successive Cortes continued to call for it – in 1371 at Toro and in 1405 at Madrid. The Jewish situation worsened in other countries: in 1290 England expelled all its Jews, and in 1306 France followed suit; but in Spain convivencia managed to hold out. Hostility con-tinued, however, to come from three directions: from the urban elites who were debtors to the Jews, from the ordinary Christian population who lived beside the Jews in the towns but resented their separateness and their apparent success, and from some rural communities which considered the urban Jews as their exploiters. Jews were, of course, culturally different; but they were Spaniards and in no sense a separate race, nor at any time were their numbers augmented by immigration from abroad. Their spoken language was moreover the same. They no longer spoke Hebrew, which was reserved only for religious rituals and for inscriptions.[5] Instead, in the Muslim kingdoms they spoke Arabic (the great Jewish philoso-pher Maimonides wrote all his works in Arabic), and in Castile they spoke Castilian.[6] Certainly they were politically separate, and separ-ateness, accepted as a measure of protection, came to be a divisive force.[7] Each Jewish quarter or *aljama* was a separate society within the towns, with its own officials and its own taxes, exempt from most municipal obligations except the duty to defend the town, and liable to pay taxes only to the crown, under whose direct control it came. In practice, the crown had few resources with which to protect the aljamas against hostile municipalities.

Religious fanaticism, stirred up in southern Spain in 1390 by Ferrant Martínez, Archdeacon of Ecija, lit the spark to this powder-keg. In June 1391, during a hot summer made worse by economic distress, urban mobs rioted, directing their anger against the privi-leged classes and against the Jews.[8] In Seville hundreds of Jews were murdered and the aljama was destroyed. Within days, in July and August, the fury spread across the peninsula: those who were not murdered were compelled to accept baptism. In Córdoba, wrote a Hebrew poet, 'there was not one, great or small, who did not apostasise'. In Valencia during July, some 250 were murdered; in Barcelona during August, some 400. The major aljamas of Spain were wiped out. From this time the conversos came into existence on a grand scale.

Converso (or New Christian) was the term applied to one who had converted from Judaism or Islam. Given the forced nature of the mass conversions of 1391, it was obvious that many conversos could not have been genuine Christians, and they were inevitably regarded with suspicion as a fifth column within the Church. Terms of opprobrium were applied to them, the most common being *marranos*, a word of obscure origin.[9] Though no longer Jews in religion, they continued to suffer the rigours of antisemitism.

Even in the pluralist society of mediaeval Spain, Jews had always suffered discrimination. In the Christian kingdoms their first great era was the thirteenth century, when their science and influence reached heights great enough to justify the claims made by Moses Arragel in the opening lines of this chapter. Jewish scientists and writers distinguished themselves at the court of Alfonso x of Castile.[10] The medical profession was virtually monopolized by Jews, and royal and aristocratic circles relied heavily on this group for physicians: as one historian observes of the kingdom of Aragon, 'there was not a noble or prelate in the land who did not keep a Jewish physician',[11] and a similar situation also existed in Castile. The unfortunate sequel in any critical period was that Jewish doctors were accused of poisoning their patients.

Popular hostility to Jews was based largely on their financial activities. In the fourteenth century they acted as tax-gatherers and fiscal officials to the crown and aristocracy. Henry II told the Cortes of Burgos in 1367 that 'we farmed out the collection of the revenue to Jews because we found no others to bid for it';[12] and in 1469 the Cortes of Ocaña complained to Henry IV that 'many prelates and other ecclesiastics farm to Jews and Moors the revenue and tithes that belong to them; and they enter churches to apportion the tithe among the contributors, to the great offence and injury of the Church.'[13] A direct result of hostility to this situation may be seen in the serious rioting at Toledo in 1449, when murders and sackings marked the resentment of the population against converso tax-gatherers employed by the royal minister Alvaro de Luna.

In the thirteenth century, under Jaime I of Aragon, some bailiffs of royal revenues in the major cities were Jews. In 1369 a Jew, Joseph Pichon, was 'chief treasurer and manager of the revenues of the realm' under Henry II. A century later, under Ferdinand and Isabella, Abraham Senior was treasurer of the Santa Hermandad, David Abulafia was in charge of supplies for the troops at Granada, and Isaac Abrabanel administered the tax on sheep, the *servicio y montazgo*. Not surprisingly, a foreign traveller commented on Queen Isabella that 'her subjects in Catalonia and Aragon say publicly that the queen is a protector of Jews'.

In Saragossa the aljama had become a virtual bank, by the fifteenth century, controlling the greater part of the capital of the Christian population. Municipalities in Aragon used to resort to the aljama for loans and credit, and so great was the dependence of all social classes in Saragossa on it that when it was open for business 'there appeared ... nobles, gentry, clergy, friars from all the religious orders, representatives of nunneries, and parish officials.'[14] So closely identified were the Jews with fiscal administration that at the end of the seventeenth century a writer complained:

> Formerly all who applied themselves to the gathering of taxes were Jews and people of low origin; yet now, when they are not so, people look on them as Hebrews, even though they be Old Christians and of noble descent.[15]

The role of Jews in finance was inevitably exaggerated in the popular mind. The number of Jewish financiers and tax-gatherers was proportionately small, and by the fifteenth century they served in the lower grades of the fiscal system, as tax-gatherers rather than as treasurers. In the period 1440–69 only 15 per cent (seventy-two persons) of tax-farmers serving the crown of Castile were Jews.[16] By this date, however, very many other tax officers were conversos, and in the popular mind these too were looked upon as Jews. A chronicler of the period, Andrés Bernáldez, *cura* of Los Palacios near Seville, summed up the economic role of the Jews in the following way. They were, he said,

> merchants, salesmen, tax-gatherers, retailers, stewards of nobility, officials, tailors, shoemakers, tanners, weavers, grocers, pedlars, silk-mercers, smiths, jewellers, and other like trades; none broke the earth, or became a farmer, carpenter or builder, but all sought after comfortable posts and ways of making profits without much labour.[17]

Though Jews were undoubtedly most active in trade, it was not because they were wealthy but because their marginal position in society forced them logically into the service industries. In practice they were almost never big merchants and were restricted, as Bernáldez's list shows, to the small trades and minor professions. The picture was identical in all the aljamas for which details are available.[18] The Jewish communities were not, on the whole, rich (their annual tax contribution to the royal treasury in 1480 represented only 0.33 per cent of ordinary revenue), and had negligible social status. In size and numbers they had shrunk dramatically since the massacres of 1391, and indeed in some cities aljamas no longer existed. In Barcelona, the mediaeval Jewish *call* (street) was abolished in 1424 because it was deemed unnecessary; in Toledo, the ancient aljama consisted by 1492 of possibly only forty houses. This would seem to indicate that by the end of the fifteenth century Jews were no longer a significant bourgeoisie.[19]

The social profile of Spanish Jewry, in fact, changed to a degree that makes the picture given by Andrés Bernáldez unacceptable. Living in a region where the Jews had preferred the protection of the big towns, Bernáldez commented that

> they never wanted to take jobs in ploughing or digging, nor would they go through the fields tending cattle, nor would they teach their children to do so; all their wish was a job in the town, and earning their living without much labour while sitting on their bottoms.[20]

Other sources appear to support the picture of a totally urbanized Jew.[21] The example of Badajoz, in rural Extremadura, shows that all the 231 conversos punished by the Inquisition between 1493 and 1599 came from the professional and commercial classes. They held posts ranging from that of mayor and municipal official to the lesser occupations of physician, lawyer, trader, shopkeeper and manufacturer.[22] The same is true of Saragossa and other principal cities for which we have details. This picture makes it plausible to explain events in terms of tension between rural Christians and urbanized Jews. However, there is ample evidence to prove that since 1391 the Jews had put less confidence in the cities and had moved out into the countryside, where their relationship with Christians was surprisingly peaceful. By the late fifteenth century, contrary to what Bernáldez asserts, Jewish farmers and peasants could be found throughout Spain. In Aguilar de la Frontera, near

Córdoba, of the sixty *sanbenitos* or penitential garments hung up in local churches in the late sixteenth century, about nineteen belonged to peasant farmers (*labradores*).[23] In Toledo, a considerable proportion of Jews were peasants working their own lands.[24] In Buitrago (Guadalajara), members of the prosperous Jewish community (which in 1492 boasted six rabbis and even a municipal *regidor*) owned 165 fields of flax, 102 meadows, 18 market gardens, a large amount of pasture and a few water rights.[25] In Hita, in the same region, they had two synagogues and nine rabbis; the major investment was in wine, with Jews owning 396 vineyards totalling no less than 66,400 vines.[26] In Sos in Upper Aragon, birthplace of King Ferdinand himself, Jews were 'cultivators of vines, flax and cereals, and their business relations with Christians contributed to fraternal amity', their main callings being as peasants or as moneylenders.[27] There was thus considerable variety in the social position of Jews in the peninsula. In many areas convivencia went on even while the stormclouds were gathering. In Avila, which was untouched by the fury of 1391, the Jews survived as perhaps the biggest aljama in Castile, constituting nearly half the city's population of seven thousand.[28]

The political position of the vulnerable Jewish population was clearly worsening during the early fifteenth century. Antisemitic legislation of 1412, inspired in part by the zealous Valencian saint, Vincent Ferrer (who shares some responsibility for the events of 1391), and the converso Chancellor of Castile, Bishop Pablo de Santa María, deprived them of the right to hold office or possess titles, and prevented them changing their domicile. They were also excluded from various trades such as those of grocer, carpenter, tailor and butcher; they could not bear arms or hire Christians to work for them; they were not allowed to eat, drink, bathe or even talk with Christians; and they were forbidden to wear any but coarse clothes. The legislation was not always enforced and subsequent Cortes of Castile continued the pressure. In 1413–14 Vincent Ferrer helped to organize a top-level debate between Christian and Jewish scholars, which Pope Benedict XIII ordered to be held in his presence at Tortosa. At this famous Disputation of Tortosa[29] the chief star on the Christian side was the recently converted papal physician Joshua Halorqui, who now took the name Jerónimo de Santa Fe. The Disputation brought about more conversions, including members of the prominent Aragonese family de la Caballería, and entire aljamas in Aragon.

Growing pressure on the Jews arose in some measure out of the converso situation. It was well known that many among the neophytes were 'judaizers', practising their Jewish religion in secret while outwardly affecting sincerity in the Catholic faith. The destruction of the old aljamas meant that in many cases there was no longer a physical division between the religions, so that conversos were able to live within the proximity of the Jewish streets. From the 1460s Christian spokesmen – among them the converso general of the Jeronimite order, Alonso de Oropesa – argued that the conversos would be less tempted to maintain their Jewish links if Jews were clearly separated from the rest of the population. Active political and commercial hostility to the conversos had fateful consequences for the Jewish minority.

From the beginning of their reign in 1474, Ferdinand and Isabella determined to maintain between Jews and Christians the same peace that they were trying to establish in the cities and among the nobility. The monarchs were never antisemitic: as early as 1468 Ferdinand had a Catalan Jew from Tárrega, David Abenasaya, as his physician, and both he and Isabella continued to have Jewish doctors and financiers as their closest collaborators. In both Aragon and Castile they followed the policy of their predecessors: taking the Jews under their direct personal control on the same terms as other Christian and Muslim communities which were in the royal jurisdiction. 'All the Jews in my realms', Isabella declared in 1477 when extending her protection to the community in Trujillo, 'are mine and under my care and protection and it belongs to me to defend and aid them and keep justice.' Likewise in 1479 she gave her protection to the fragile Jewish community in Cáceres.[30] Given that Jews were constantly on the defensive against powerful municipal interests, the interventions of the crown in local politics present an impressive picture of the monarchy protecting its Jews. In 1475, for example, the city of Bilbao was ordered to revoke commercial restrictions it had placed on Jews in the town of Medina de Pomar; in 1480 the town of Olmedo was ordered to construct a gate in the wall of the judería to give Jews access to the town square.[31] The monarchs intervened repeatedly against municipalities which tried to eliminate the commercial activity of the Jews.

Royal policy, however, had to contend with mounting antisemitism. In 1476 the Cortes of Madrigal, on the initiative not of the crown but of the towns, passed sumptuary laws against Jews and Mudejars enforcing the wearing of a distinctive symbol, and restricted the practice of usury. Jews were inevitably unhappy (in Avila they refused to lend any money until the regulations on usury were clarified), but it was not until the rigorous legislation of the 1480 Cortes of Toledo, which put into effect a strict policy of separation and restricted Jews to aljamas, that real hardships were suffered. There is no doubt that antisemitic groups in the municipalities were responsible for such measures: in Burgos, in 1484 Jews were not allowed to sell food; in 1485 they were ordered to shut the aljama on all Christian feast-days; in 1486 a limit was put on the number of Jews in the ghetto (the order was subsequently annulled by the Catholic kings).[32] The monarchs, too, were firmly convinced that a separation of Jews from Christians was the most effective answer to the converso problem, and in 1480 they set in motion a body whose entire concern was with judaizers: the Inquisition. Though the Inquisition only had authority over Christians, Jews quickly realized that they too were in the line of fire, and all their worst travails date from 1480.

A policy of partial expulsion of Jews, with the aim of separating them from their converso brethren, was gradually introduced by the Inquisition. At the end of 1482, a partial expulsion of the Jews of Andalucia was ordered.[33] In January 1483 Jews were ordered to be expelled from the dioceses of Seville, Córdoba and Cadiz; the crown delayed implementation and they were not actually driven out from Seville until summer 1484. In 1486 Jews were expelled by royal order from the dioceses of Saragossa, Albarracín and Teruel in Aragon. Meanwhile many towns carried out their own unauthorized expulsions, ignoring the protests of the crown.[34] Though Ferdinand and Isabella intervened repeatedly to protect their Jews from excesses (as late as 1490 they began an enquiry into Medina del Campo's ban on Jews setting up shops in the main square), the monarchs appear to have been thoroughly convinced by Inquisitor General Torquemada of the necessity for the separation of Jews. When the local expulsions had failed, after ten long years, to stem the heresies of the conversos, the crown decided on the most drastic measure of all – a total expulsion of Jews.

It was a decision unprecedented in European history. Jews expelled by other countries in mediaeval times had been tiny minorities; in Spain, by contrast, they had for centuries been a significant, prosperous and integral part of society. The practice of convivencia was by now little more than a memory, as a case of 1490 showed. The Muslims of Guadalajara were accused of converting a Jewish boy to Islam, and though they protested that such conversions 'had been the custom in these realms', the Royal Council ruled that 'hereafter no Jew may turn Moor'; nor indeed could Moors turn Jew.[35] It had, of course, long been impossible (since at least 1255) for Christians to turn Jew or Muslim: when groups of ex-Christians were captured after the fall of Málaga they were immediately put to death.[36] Ferdinand and Isabella hesitated for some time over expulsion: the crown stood to lose revenue from the disappearance of a community whose taxes were paid directly to the crown, and which moreover had helped to finance the war in Granada.

Many people in Spain may have been anxious to get rid of the Jews for social and economic reasons: the Old Christian elites and several municipalities saw in them a source of conflict and competition.[37] The decision to expel, however, was the crown's alone, and it appears to have been taken exclusively for religious reasons: there are no grounds for maintaining that the government stood to profit, and Ferdinand himself admitted that the measure hurt his finances.[38] The king and queen were undoubtedly encouraged in their policy by the fall of Granada in January 1492, which seemed a signal of divine favour. On 31 March, while they were in the city, they issued the edict of expulsion, giving the Jews of both Castile and Aragon until 31 July to accept baptism or leave the country. The decree gave as its main justification 'the great harm suffered by Christians [i.e. conversos] from the contact, intercourse and communication which they have with the Jews, who always attempt in various ways to seduce faithful Christians from our Holy Catholic Faith'. When the news broke, a deputation of Jews led by Isaac Abrabanel went to see the king. Their pleas failed, and at a second meeting they offered the king a large sum of money if he would reconsider his decision. There is a story that when Torquemada heard of the offer he burst into the monarchs' presence and threw thirty pieces of silver on the table, demanding to know for what price Christ was to be sold again to the Jews. At a third meeting which Abrabanel, Senior and the Jewish leaders had with the king, it became clear that Ferdinand was determined to go ahead. In despair they turned to the queen. She, however, explained that the decision, which she firmly supported, came from Ferdinand: 'the Lord has put this thing into the heart of the king'.[39]

It seems, in fact, that the proposal to expel came from the Inquisition, and that the king did no more than support the Holy

Office: there was more than a grain of truth in the story of Torquemada and the pieces of silver. The general expulsion was no more than an extension of the regional expulsions that the Inquisition had been carrying out, with Ferdinand's support, since 1481. Moreover, the king himself, in a letter that he sent to the Count of Aranda on the same day as the expulsion, explained the circumstances concisely:

> The Holy Office of the Inquisition, seeing how some Christians are endangered by contact and communication with the Jews, has provided that the Jews be expelled from all our realms and territories, and has persuaded us to give our support and agreement to this, which we now do, because of our debts and obligations to the said Holy Office; and we do so despite the great harm to ourselves, seeking and preferring the salvation of souls above our own profit and that of individuals.[40]

Though most Jews in Spain were under royal jurisdiction, a few were not; the king therefore had to explain, for example, to the Catalan Duke of Cardona, who had assumed that 'his' Jews were not affected, that the edict was universal. Seigneurs were promised the property of their expelled Jews as compensation. It is possible that the monarchs thought mass conversions would be more likely than mass emigration. The rabbi of Córdoba was baptized in May, with Cardinal Mendoza and the papal nuncio as sponsors. In June the eighty-year-old Abraham Senior, chief rabbi of Castile and principal treasurer of the crown, was baptized in Guadalupe with the king and queen as his sponsors. He and his family adopted the surname Coronel; a week later he was nominated regidor of his home town of Segovia and member of the Royal Council. His colleague Abrabanel took over as rabbi and began to negotiate terms for the emigration.

Public opinion was well prepared for the edict. Stories of Jewish atrocities had been circulating for years. One concerned an alleged ritual murder performed on a Christian child at Sepúlveda (Segovia) in 1468. The converso Bishop of Segovia, Juan Arias Dávila, is reported to have punished sixteen Jews for the crime. The most famous of all the cases concerned the alleged ritual murder of a Christian infant at La Guardia in the province of Toledo, in 1491. Six conversos and as many Jews were said to have been implicated in this plot, in which a Christian child was apparently crucified and had its heart cut out in an attempt to create a magical spell to destroy Christians. Such, at least, was the story pieced together

from confessions extracted under torture, the culprits being executed publicly at Avila in November 1491.[41] The affair received
wide publicity: we find a printed relation of it circulating in Barcelona shortly after. The timing was ominous, and there can be little
doubt that it helped prepare many to accept the expulsion of the
Jews. Atrocity stories of this sort, common in Europe both before
and since – in England there were the cases of William of Norwich
in 1144 and Hugh of Lincoln in 1255 – served to feed the most
vicious antisemitism.

No reliable data exist for the expulsion. It has been suggested
that about 165,000 were expelled from all Spain,[42] and Baer has
proposed equally high totals of 150,000 expelled from Castile and
30,000 from Aragon.[43] As evidence accumulates of the relatively
small size of Jewish communities, it is very likely that the real
figures will turn out to be only half those cited. In any case, not all
Jews emigrated; and of those who did, many returned up to 1499,
after which return was forbidden. Those who went abroad sought
shelter in Christian Italy and Muslim north Africa and Turkey. After
1492 the only peninsular realms tolerating Jews were Portugal and
Navarre. The bulk of refugees therefore went to Portugal, where
they were unmolested until 1497, when all Jews there were ordered
to become Christian as a condition of the marriage between King
Manoel and Isabel, daughter of the Catholic monarchs. Navarre
required its Jews to convert in 1498.

The sufferings of those forced into exile for the sake of religion
are vividly detailed by the chronicler Andrés Bernáldez, in a picture
that has become all too familiar since the fifteenth century.[44] The
richer Jews out of charity helped to pay the costs of the poorer
exiles, while the very poor managed to help themselves in no other
way but by accepting baptism. They were unable to sell their possessions for gold or silver, for the export of these metals was forbidden; so they sold houses and property for the most desperate
substitutes. 'They went round asking for buyers and found none to
buy; some sold a house for an ass, and a vineyard for a little cloth
or linen, since they could not take away gold or silver.' The ships
which met them at the ports were overcrowded and ill-managed.
Once they had put out to sea, storms drove them back, forcing
hundreds to reconcile themselves to Spain and baptism. Others, no
more fortunate, reached their desired haven in north Africa only
to be pillaged and murdered. Hundreds of others staggered back
to Spain by every available route, preferring familiar sufferings to

those of the open sea and road. A rabbi whose father was one of the exiles, wrote:

> Some of them the Turks killed to take out the gold which they had swallowed to hide it; some of them hunger and the plague consumed and some of them were cast naked by the captains on the isles of the sea; and some of them were sold for men-servants and maid-servants in Genoa and its villages and some of them were cast into the sea.[45]

Many writers have assumed that the expulsion was motivated by greed and a wish to rob the Jews, but there is little evidence of this. The crown did not profit and had no intention of profiting. By Ferdinand's own admission, he stood to lose substantial revenue; and sums realized from the sale of goods of the Jews were negligible. Many individuals and corporations that had owed money to the Jews clearly benefited, but this was an incidental consequence of a measure that was primarily religious in motivation. The effects on Spain were probably smaller than is often thought. The sultan of Turkey is reported to have said at a later date that he 'marvelled greatly at expelling the Jews from Spain, since this was to expel its wealth'. But in practice Jews had been allowed to transfer many assets to conversos, and those who returned, such as Samuel Abolafía of Toledo,[46] were given back their property.

Converts were protected: in 1493 the monarchs forbade people in the dioceses of Cuenca and Osma to call baptized Jews *tornadizos* (turncoats).[47] The new converts and the old conversos continued to function in the trades and professions in which the Jews had distinguished themselves, and the purely economic impact of the expulsion was thereby softened. What Spain lost, nevertheless, cannot be estimated merely in economic terms. The State turned its back on the plural society of the past, cut off an entire community that had been an integral part of the nation, and intensified the converso problem without solving it. The Jews had finally been driven into the Christian fold. 'In this way', wrote the curate of Los Palacios, 'was fulfilled the prophecy of David in the psalm *Eripe me*, which says: *Convertentur ad vesperam, et famen patientur, ut canes; et circuibunt civitatem*. Which is to say: "They shall return at evening, and shall suffer hunger like dogs, and shall prowl round the city". Thus these were converted at a late hour and by force and after great suffering.'[48]

3

The Coming of the Inquisition

Sancho Panza: Since I believe firmly and truly in God and in all that the Holy Catholic and Roman Church holds and believes, and am a mortal enemy of the Jews, historians should have mercy on me and treat me well in their writings.

Cervantes, *Don Quixote*, Book II chap. 8

The expulsion of the Jews opened a new and bitter chapter in Spanish history. At one stroke the Catholic monarchs had doubled the number of false converts in the realm. A 'converso danger', which until then may have been little more than a figment of the clerical imagination, now became solid reality. With so many new forced conversions, the proportion of judaizers multiplied and Jewish practices flourished in a vast and ever-growing underground complex of heresy. Ferdinand and Isabella had hoped that the expulsion would shut off the sources of Judaism, but their solution created new problems, provoked social discord and continued to be criticized by Spaniards both then and thereafter. It was the first major step towards the growth of a 'society of conflict'.

In economic terms the expulsion did not cause any serious crisis. Many Jews stayed and retained their property, but they could hardly expect to be favourably accepted in communities where antisemitism had been stirred up. Emigrants had been allowed to transfer their property to New Christians, so that assets continued to remain in converso hands. In the new post-1492 Christian society, the conversos occupied exactly the same social position as the Jews. As before the expulsion, they continued to be a rural and urban population occupied in the same activities as the Jews, whether as merchants or as tax-gatherers, moneylenders, farmers, tailors and cobblers. Like the Jews, they tended to keep a communal existence very similar to life in the ghettos. The populace found it easy enough to identify the New Christians with the old Jews, and this social identification led inevitably to religious identification. Such a process was helped not only by the conservative habits of the conversos and by the survival of Jewish practices and religious observance, but also by the impossibility many genuine converts found in adapting themselves to Christian usages such as the eating of pork.

Conversos had played an active role in Christian Spain for over a century. In the open society of the later Middle Ages, many successful Jewish families had converted and therefore qualified not only to hold public office but also to marry into the Old Christian elite. In the wake of the anti-converso riots in Toledo in 1449, a royal secretary, Fernan Díaz de Toledo, wrote a report or *Instrucción* for the Bishop of Cuenca, in which he argued that all the leading noble lineages of Castile, including the Henríquez (from whom Ferdinand the Catholic descended), could trace their descent from conversos.[1] In Aragon nearly every noble house had Jewish blood, and half the senior posts in the Aragonese government were held by conversos. In Castile under Isabella the Catholic, at least four bishops were of converso origin. Also of known converso blood was Cardinal Juan de Torquemada, uncle of the first Inquisitor General, whose converso ancestry cannot therefore be doubted.

By contrast, there is no reason whatever for supposing – as is often done – that the first Archbishop of Granada, Hernando de Talavera, was of converso origin. Three secretaries of Queen Isabella – Fernando Alvarez, Alfonso de Avila and Hernando del Pulgar – were all New Christians.[2] Individual conversos founded powerful families of their own which contributed not only to the unease of the aristocracy but also to the dismay of the Jews. In Aragon the powerful converso family of de la Caballería contributed, besides a few prominent clergy, the vice-chancellor of the council of Aragon, a treasurer of the kingdom of Navarre, an admiral, a vice-principal of the University of Saragossa, and several others.[3] Don Juan Pacheco, Marquis of Villena and master of the Order of Santiago, was a descendant on both sides of the former Jew, Ruy Capon. His brother, Pedro Girón, was master of the Order of Calatrava, and the Archbishop of Toledo was his uncle.[4] Among the most distinguished of Castilian converts was Salomon Halevi, chief rabbi of Burgos, who was converted along with his brothers in 1390, adopted the name Pablo de Santa María, took holy orders and eventually became in turn Bishop of Cartagena, Bishop of Burgos, tutor to the son of Henry III, and papal legate. His eldest son Gonzalo became Spanish delegate to the Council of Constance and Bishop successively of Astorga, Plasencia and Sigüenza, and also attended the Council of Basel. His second son, Alonso de Cartagena, succeeded his father in the see of Burgos.[5]

Citation of isolated names can exaggerate and distort the significance of conversos in public life, but there can be little doubt that their presence at certain times and places was striking. At the end of the fifteenth century the principal administrators of Aragon were conversos; at the very moment the Inquisition began to function, five conversos – Luis de Santangel, Gabriel Sánchez, Sancho de Paternoy, Felipe Climent and Alfonso de la Caballería – held the five most important posts in the kingdom. In many Castilian cities, such as Burgos (where the Cartagenas and the Maluendas were prominent) and Toledo, conversos were influential on the municipal council. In others, they used their tenure of public office to band together, and thus contributed to the bitter and sometimes bloody clan rivalry that characterized Castilian political life in the later fifteenth century. The converso historian Diego de Valera reported that in Córdoba on the city council 'there was great enmity and rivalry, since the New Christians were very rich and kept buying public offices, which they made use of so arrogantly that the Old Christians would not put up with it'. In Segovia, according to the chronicler Alonso de Palencia, the conversos 'shamelessly took over all the public posts and discharged them with extreme contempt for the nobility and with grave harm to the State'. The conversos acted, says Palencia, 'as a nation apart, and nowhere would they agree to act together with the Old Christians; indeed, as though they were a people of totally opposed ideas, they openly and brazenly favoured whatever was contrary to the Old Christians, as could be seen by the bitter fruit sown throughout the cities of the realm'.[6] It is very likely that converso participation in public life was never as dominant as some modern writers have suggested, but there is no mistaking the intensity of the faction struggles in cities with a significant New Christian elite.

It is no surprise to find that converso families were as capable as Old Christians of contributing to the cultural and social life of Spain. A few distinguished sixteenth-century names – Juan Luis Vives, Juan de Avila, Luis de León, Teresa of Avila, Diego Laínez – were of known converso origin. Until quite recently it was a fashion among some scholars to identify creative genius in Spain almost exclusively with converso blood,[7] but the extremely frail supports for this view have tended to collapse as the historical evidence for the Jewish origins of Fernando de Rojas, Hernando de Talavera, Bartolomé de las Casas and many others has failed to materialize. Like all disadvantaged minorities, Jews and conversos certainly made their presence felt in areas where they had some freedom of movement. The small independent professions attracted them. Of a sample of 1,641 Toledo conversos who were involved with the Inquisition in 1495, the majority were in modest occupations, but there were a significant number of jewellers and silversmiths (59), traders (38), tax-farmers (15) and money-changers (12).[8]

Finance was a well-known area in which Jews and conversos excelled. It is memorable that, but for converso finance, Columbus' first voyage in 1492 would not have been carried out: it was the Aragonese conversos Luis de Santangel and Gabriel Sánchez who protected and financed the expedition; Jews and conversos, including a Jewish interpreter, formed part of the crew; and it has been argued that Columbus himself was descended from a family of Catalan conversos.[9] A high proportion of the great financiers of the seventeenth century were conversos, mainly of Portuguese origin thanks to the flight of conversos from the persecution in Portugal; the more distinguished of these we shall encounter later. Several Spaniards were later to regret the expulsion of Jewish financiers in 1492, and in the seventeenth century we first meet suggestions by native writers that the growing wealth of countries like Holland was due in great measure to the help of Jewish capital flowing into Amsterdam. At a later date, the decline of Spain and the triumph of its enemies was blamed on the international Jewish conspiracy. Among the first writers to take this line was the otherwise distinguished poet Francisco de Quevedo, who claimed that Jewish elders from all over Europe had held a secret meeting at Salonika, where they drew up their secret plans against Christendom.[10] The Count Duke of Olivares was similarly obsessed with the power of Jewish finance, and entertained serious plans to invite the Jews back into Spain and so undo all the harm of 1492.

The other notable occupation of the conversos was medicine.[11] As with the financiers, their numbers and importance should not be exaggerated. Untypical examples can inflate their significance. The Inquisition in Logroño (Navarre) at the end of the sixteenth century found itself in need of a doctor, but could find no Old

Christian with the necessary qualifications; finally it had to appoint a converso. The Inquisition in Madrid was consulted and decreed that the tribunal should keep him but give him no official status, in the hope that an Old Christian might some day be found. An equally embarrassing case occurred in Llerena, where the Inquisition in 1579 reported that for lack of Old Christian doctors the town authorities had appointed as their official doctor 'a man who was imprisoned by this Inquisition as a judaizer for three and a half years'.[12]

Even the crown had conversos in attendance: Doctor Francisco López Villalobos was court physician to both Ferdinand the Catholic and Charles v. Among other famous conversos should be mentioned Doctor Andrés Laguna (1499–1560), naturalist, botanist and physician, a native of Segovia and one of the great luminaries of Spanish science. The outstanding services of conversos to medicine are amply illustrated by the number of doctors who appear in the records of the Inquisition during the sixteenth and seventeenth centuries. Why they should have played so great a part in the liberalprofessionsitisdifficulttosay,buttherewasnodifficultyinspreading the rumour that Jews became physicians because this gave them a greater opportunity to carry on their nefarious deeds.

Following a long tradition, converso families gave many sons and daughters into the hands of the Church, to be brought up in the religious orders. While this policy would have been followed only by sincere converts, no doubt many other young conversos chose the clerical life because it gave them the easiest chance of advancement. Converso students were consequently to be seen in ever growing numbers in the universities of Spain, and choice benefices and even episcopal sees went to them in preference to Old Christians.

By the mid-sixteenth century it was reported that most of the Spanish clergy resident in Rome in search of preferment were of Jewish origin. Anti-converso publicists in the mid-fifteenth century had already suggested that the New Christians were infiltrating the Church and threatening to take it over. Conversos, it was argued, had worked their way into the heart of Christian society, into the ranks of the aristocracy and the Church, and were planning to destroy it from within.

The infiltration of the aristocracy was proved by two sixteenth-century publications. In Aragon an assessor of the Inquisition of Saragossa drew up what became known as the *Libro verde de*

Aragón,[13] a genealogical table tracing the origins of the nobility, from which it became clear that the most prominent families in the kingdom had not escaped converso infiltration. This document, which was set down in manuscript in the first decade of the six-teenth century, was soon to become a source of major scandal, for copies were passed from hand to hand, added to and distorted, until the government could no longer tolerate so vicious a slander against the leading nobles of the realm. In 1623, therefore, the extreme measure was taken of ordering all available copies of these *libros verdes* to be burnt. But already a far more powerful libel had been circulating in secret. In 1560 the Cardinal Francisco Mendoza y Bobadilla, angered by a refusal to admit two members of his family into a military order, presented to Philip II a memorandum, later to be known as *Tizón de la Nobleza de España*, or *Blot on the Nobility of Spain*, in which he claimed to prove that virtually the whole of the nobility was of Jewish descent.[14] The proofs he offered were so incontrovertible that the *Tizón* was reprinted many times down to the nineteenth century, almost always as a tract against the power and influence of the nobility. At no time was even the slightest attempt at a rejoinder to these two publications made.

The implications for a social class that affected to despise the Jews and conversos could not fail to be serious. On the one hand the nobility was claiming for itself a privileged position in return for its long services to the crown, and on the other it was being morally undermined by a racial dilution which tended to bring it into con-tempt. If the nobles were no longer truly Old Christians, then they had no right to true nobility. The dangerous point was obviously approaching at which membership of the nobility was in itself grounds for suspicion of debased blood, and only membership of non-noble classes provided any guarantee against Jewish descent. In an important memoir upon the royal council presented by the historian Lorenzo Galíndez de Carvajal to the Emperor Charles V, it was significantly reported that several of the most important mem-bers were of converso origin; among the exceptions, however, was Dr Palacios Rubios, 'a man of pure blood because he is of labouring descent'.[15] The 'because' represented a threat to the claim of the Old Christian elite to be free of Jewish contamination, and intensi-fied the struggle to purify Christian society of converso blood.

Converso writers joined the controversy.[16] Many genuine Chris-tians of converso origin were hostile to the judaizers among their number and impatient with what seemed to be the subversive activities of the Jews. Their works were directed principally to demonstrating the falsity of Judaism. Among these writers was Bishop Pablo de Santa María, with his *Scrutinium scripturarum, dialogus Sauli et Pauli contra Judaeos*, written in 1432 but published posthumously in 1591 at Burgos. Another distinguished author was the former rabbi Joshua Halorqui, who adopted the name Jerónimo de Santa Fe, founded a powerful converso family and produced his anti-Jewish polemics in the form of a work called *Hebraeomastix*. A member of a third great converso family, Pedro de la Caballería, wrote in 1450 a treatise known in Latin as *Zelus Christi contra Judaeos*. These three converso productions were distinguished by learned theological arguments and a profound factual knowledge of Jewish rites, so that although they were full of hostility they did not contain falsifications and slanders. The same cannot be said for the work of a friar named Alonso de Espina, whose *Fortalitium fidei contra Judaeos* was written in 1458 and published in 1460.

Espina, a well-known Franciscan friar and confessor to Henry IV of Castile, used his position to stir up hatred against Jews and conversos. Though described by most historians as a converso, he was almost certainly not one:[17] the deliberate distortions and fabrications in his work betray a complete ignorance of semitic society. In the 1450s he was exceptionally busy in a campaign to bring about the forced conversion of the Jews, and his tract helped by its themes and language to contribute to the general detestation of the race. For Espina, the crimes of Jews against Christians were all too well known: they were traitors, homosexuals, blasphemers, child-murderers, assassins (in the guise of doctors), poisoners, usurers, and so on. Such accusations clearly sprang from fanaticism rather than knowledge, and it is little wonder if they served to stir up similar fanaticism in Spanish audiences. What differentiates Espina from the converso apologists, however, is the fact that his accusations were clearly racialist in character and purpose, whereas the anger of Santa María and the others was more explicitly directed against the stubborn unbelief of their unconverted brethren. Espina's tract was little more than Jew-baiting, while the others were concerned about the cause of religion. His book has been viewed as a draft proposal which influenced the structure of the Spanish Inquisition,[18] but in reality there was no significant difference between his ideas and those of the mediaeval French Inquisition on which the Spanish Holy Office was eventually modelled.

The first great defence raised by Old Christians against conversos was to try and exclude them from any part in public administration. This occurred as a result of the memorable disturbances at Toledo in 1449. As a result of the riots that year, the Old Christians held a court to determine whether the conversos should be allowed to continue holding public office. Pedro Sarmiento, a leader of the Old Christians, proposed a special statute (known as the *Sentencia-Estatuto*) which, despite the opposition of the Bishop of Cuenca, was passed by the city council on 5 June 1449. In this it was resolved 'that no converso of Jewish descent may have or hold any office or benefice in the said city of Toledo, or in its territory and jurisdiction', and that the testimony of conversos against Old Christians was not to be accepted in the courts.[19]

The immediate result of this was a bull issued by Pope Nicholas V on 24 September 1449 under the significant title *Humani generis inimicus* (Enemy of the human race), in which he denounced the idea of excluding Christians from office simply because they came from a particular race. 'We decree and declare', the pope went on, 'that all Catholics are one body in Christ according to the teaching of our faith.' Another bull of the same date excommunicated Sarmiento and his colleagues for alleged rebellion against the Spanish crown. Other Spanish ecclesiastical authorities followed the pope in declaring that baptized converts were entitled to all the privileges of the Christian community. But the *Sentencia-Estatuto* represented powerful forces which could not easily be suppressed. The state of civil war then reigning in Castile made the crown all too willing to win friends by conciliation, and in 1450 the pope was asked by King Juan II to suspend his excommunication of those practising racialism. A year later, on 13 August 1451, the king formally gave his approval to the *Sentencia-Estatuto*. This meant a victory for the Old Christian party – a victory repeated once more when, on 16 June 1468, in the year after the Toledo riots of 1467, King Henry IV confirmed in office in the city all holders of posts formerly held by conversos. The same king on 14 July of the same year conceded to the city of Ciudad Real the privilege of excluding conversos from all municipal office.[20]

The fact that two of the chief cities in Castile had succeeded in excluding conversos from public office meant that a new and dangerous turning point had been reached in the struggle between Old and New Christians. This was serious enough in its consequences for political stability in the kingdom, but a few conscientious clergy were also worried about the effect on the unity of the

Christian body. It was after some deliberation, therefore, that in about 1468 the Archbishop of Toledo, Alonso Carrillo, condemned the existence in Toledo of guilds organized on racial lines, some of them excluding conversos and others excluding Old Christians. The archbishop stated:

> Divisions bring great scandal and schism and divide the seamless garment of Christ, who, as the Good Shepherd, gave us a command to love one another in unity and obedience to Holy Mother Church, under one Pontiff and vicar of Christ, under one baptism, formed under the law into one body, so that whether Jew, Greek or Gentile we are regenerated by baptism and made into new men. From which it is obvious how culpable are those who, forgetting the purity of the law of the gospel, create different lineages, some calling themselves Old Christians and others calling themselves New Christians or conversos ... what is evil is that in the city of Toledo, as in the other cities, towns and places of our see, there are many guilds and brotherhoods of which some under pretence of piety do not receive conversos and others do not receive Old Christians ...[21]

The archbishop, therefore, by his authority dissolved the said guilds and forbade any similar racial associations under pain of excommunication. Unhappily his good intentions bore no fruit. The racial split between conversos and Old Christians had grown too wide for one prelate alone to heal. By constant propaganda and petty persecution the mood of the populace had been whipped into one of fury against the conversos.

Of the thousands of Jews who in the course of the preceding century had been forced by persecution and massacre to accept baptism, few embraced Catholicism sincerely. Many, if not most, of them continued to practise the Jewish rites both secretly and openly, so that the authorities were faced with a large minority of pseudo-Christians who had neither respect nor love for their new faith. Throughout the provinces of Toledo, Extremadura, Andalucia and Murcia, according to a polemic written in 1488, of all the conversos 'hardly any are true Christians, as is well known in all Spain'.[22] The chronicler and royal secretary Hernando del Pulgar, himself a prominent converso, vouched for the existence of secret judaizers among the New Christians of Toledo. Church authorities understandably took alarm at the large numbers of false Christians who were mocking God and the true religion. No attempts seem to have been made to deal with the problem by missionary preaching rather than persecution.

Within Spanish Catholicism there thus existed a core of those who had never accepted the validity of their baptism. Despised by the Old Christians for their race, scorned by the Jews for their apostasy, the conversos lived in a social atmosphere they had never willingly chosen. Many of them lived close to the Jewish quarter, to which they still felt a cultural affinity; they retained traditional characteristics in dress and food which were difficult to shake off; some returned actively to the practice of Judaism. Pulgar reports that within the same converso household some members might be sincere Christians and others active Jews; his experience was that many 'lived neither in one law nor the other', retaining key Jewish customs while practising formal Christianity. As we shall see, the Inquisition speedily and efficiently identified the various forms of judaizing, and punished ruthlessly: evidence soon accumulated of a vast range of Jewish practices which the conversos perpetuated and which the authorities regarded as heretical. Blanket suspicion fell on all conversos and inquisitors began to treat them all as judaizers.

But were the conversos Jews? Antisemitic writers at the time of the Inquisition were unanimous that conversos were secret Jews and must be purified ruthlessly. Many modern writers, some of them in no way antisemitic, have consistently identified the conversos as Jews. The dominant school in modern Jewish historiography has likewise ironically insisted that the Inquisition was right and that all conversos were aspiring Jews: Yitzhak Baer states uncompromisingly that 'the conversos [Hebrew, *anusim*] and Jews were one people, united by destiny'.[23] '*Every* converso', writes another Israeli historian, 'did his best to fulfil Mosaic precepts, and one should regard as sincere the aim they *all* set themselves: to live as Jews'.[24] If this view is accepted, not only does it appear to justify the establishment of the Inquisition but it also contradicts the testimony of many conversos of the late fifteenth century.

The primary evidence used by historians to call in doubt the Christianity of the conversos is the documentation of the Holy Office, a huge mass of often unsolicited and damning testimony to the errors of thousands of conversos. Rejecting this source as being tainted, however, some modern Jewish historians have looked elsewhere for their evidence.[25] Netanyahu in particular has relied on Jewish opinion of the fifteenth century, as given in the *responsa* (dogmatic interpretations) of rabbis, which held that conversos were Jews neither in belief nor in practice.[26] In his view, the 'converso danger' was invented by Church and State as an excuse to justify their spoliation of both conversos and Jews; the harvest of heretics reaped by the early Inquisition owed its success to deliberate falsification or to the completely indiscriminate way in which residual Jewish customs were interpreted as being heretical; and active Judaism among some conversos was caused primarily by the awakening of their consciousness under persecution and the consequential reversion to the faith of their ancestors.

The controversy over the Jewishness of the *anusim* is largely an internal dispute among Jewish historians, while serving also to raise broader fundamental questions about the reliability of contemporary evidence. Certainly the most plausible conclusion is that held by very many at the time, namely that some were practising Christians and others were practising Jews. Simply to be of Jewish origin did not mean that one felt Jewish. The *consellers* (city councillors) of Barcelona expressed this opinion firmly to their new inquisitor in 1486: 'we do not believe that all the conversos are heretics, or that to be a converso makes one a heretic'.[27] Pulgar, in a controversy which he entered into over the methods used by the Inquisition,[28] spoke for generations of conversos when he admitted that the religious practice of many New Christians was confused; this he attributed solely to lack of preaching. It is, by the same token, impossible to deny all validity to the evidence of widespread judaizing, which was no myth nor solely a response to the establishment of the Inquisition: twenty years before the Holy Office came into being, the extent of the problem had already led to calls for an Inquisition.

At every level, opponents of the conversos used allegations of false religion against them. During the 1449 disturbances in Toledo, Hebrew books were found in the library of one of the New Christian regidors and accusations of heresy were made. The allegations, whether true or false, embittered political struggles among the rival clans. There were civic riots in 1470 in Valladolid, and in 1473 converso groups were expelled from Córdoba after a murderous struggle which prepared the way for further killings in Jaén. Though the direct instrument of violence in all these cases was the populace, we must go beyond it to get at the real culprits: the Old Christians with a prominent part in both municipal and Church administration, who resented sharing power with men of mixed blood and dubious orthodoxy. Because of them, antisemitism had come to stay.

Anti-converso publicists exploited cases which served their pur-

pose. Events such as the discovery and immediate burning at Llerena in September 1467 of two conversos for practising Judaism
were visible proof of the religious insincerity of many New Christians. Preachers under Ferdinand and Isabella made the most of
cases like this. Among them was Alonso de Hojeda, a Dominican
prior of Seville, who devoted all his energies to making the crown
aware of the reality of the danger from Jews and false converts. His
opportunity came when Queen Isabella arrived in Seville in July
1477 and stayed until October 1478. Historians are unanimous in
citing Hojeda's preaching as one of the immediate influences on the
queen in her final decision about the conversos. Soon after Isabella's
departure from Seville, Hojeda uncovered evidence of a secret meeting of judaizing conversos in the city, and with this in hand he
went to demand the institution of measures against the heretics.
The evidence seems to have impressed the government, which
asked for a report on the situation in Seville. The report, supported
by the authority of Pedro González de Mendoza, Archbishop of Seville, and that of Tomás de Torquemada, prior of a Dominican convent in Segovia, revealed that not only in Seville but throughout
Andalucia and Castile the conversos were practising Jewish rites in
secret. Faced with this situation, Ferdinand and Isabella consented
to introduce the machinery of an Inquisition into Castile, and sent
orders to Rome for the bull of institution to be obtained.

The Inquisition as such was not unknown in Spain. Since 1232
papal commissions for inquisitors had been issued in the crown of
Aragon, as part of the campaign against Catharism then being
conducted in Languedoc.[29] By the fifteenth century, these inquisitors had lapsed into almost total inactivity. Castile, on the other
hand, had never known the existence of an Inquisition, that is, of
a body which concerned itself solely with rooting out heresy. The
bishops and their Church courts had so far sufficed to deal with the
punishment of heretics. The unusual nature of the converso problem, however, led to demands for a special 'inquisition' well before
the reign of Ferdinand and Isabella. In 1461 a group of Franciscans
led by Alonso de Espina approached the converso general of the
Jeronimite Order with a view to 'setting up in this realm an inquisition into heretics such as they have in France'.[30] The general,
Alonso de Oropesa, supported the move warmly, and Henry IV
applied to Rome petitioning that an Inquisition be set up.[31] Nothing
more is heard of the proposal.

Nearly twenty years later, the argument used by Hojeda and

others was that the converso problem was of such great and grave dimensions that only the introduction of a full-time Inquisition would be adequate to meet the threat. Consequently, the bull which was finally issued by Pope Sixtus IV on 1 November 1478 provided for the appointment of two or three priests over forty years of age as inquisitors: powers of appointment and dismissal were granted to the Spanish crown.[32] After this, no further steps were taken for two years. This long interlude would seem to contradict Hojeda's argument about the urgency of the converso danger. What seems a likely explanation is that Ferdinand and Isabella favoured a cautious period of leniency before going on to severe measures, and that this policy may have been influenced in part by the large number of conversos in prominent positions at court. Finally, Ferdinand grew convinced of the need; as he explained several years later, 'We could do no less, because we were told so many things about Andalucia.'[33] On 27 September 1480, at Medina del Campo, commissions as inquisitors in accordance with the papal bull were issued to the Dominicans Juan de San Martín and Miguel de Morillo, with Juan Ruiz de Medina as their assessor or adviser. With these appointments the Spanish Inquisition came into definitive existence.

The new body had clearly been set up as the result of agitation against the New Christians. Its immediate purpose, therefore, was to ensure religious orthodoxy in Spain. It is important to observe here that the Inquisition had authority only over baptized Christians, and the unbaptized were completely free from its disciplinary measures. This meant that Ferdinand and Isabella were not at the moment attempting to enforce unity of faith in the peninsula: they were merely attempting to solve the problem of social and racial dissidence which was aggravated above all by the doubtful orthodoxy of the conversos. This policy was all too obviously supported by Old Christians and by religious zealots, among whom conversos were prominent. Opposition to the new institution was inevitable. Immediately after their appointment the inquisitors were sent to work in Seville, where the spotlight had first been put on the converso danger. By mid-October 1480, operations had begun in Seville.

The first result was a mass exodus of conversos. In Seville and Córdoba and the towns of Andalucia, according to the chronicler Hernando del Pulgar, more than four thousand households took to flight, women and children included:

and since the absence of these people depopulated a large part of the country, the Queen was informed that commerce was declining; but setting little importance on the decline in her revenue, and prizing highly the *limpieza* [purity] of her lands, she said that the essential thing was to cleanse the country of that sin of heresy, for she understood it to be in God's service and her own. And the representations which were made to her about this matter did not alter her decision.[34]

Refugees who fled to the lands of neighbouring aristocrats, in the hope that feudal jurisdictions would protect them from the Inquisition, were speedily disillusioned when the nobles complied with an order to hand over all refugees within a fortnight, under pain of excommunication. Not all the conversos thought flight the best solution. In Seville the wealthy Diego de Susán – one of the city's leading citizens and father to a beautiful daughter Susanna, famous as the *fermosa fembra* – called together a group of converso colleagues, including prominent ecclesiastics and magistrates, for a meeting in the church of San Salvador. With them, according to a contemporary source, were

> many other rich and powerful men from the towns of Utrera and Carmona. These said to one another, 'What do you think of them acting thus against us? Are we not the most propertied members of this city, and well loved by the people? Let us collect men together ...' and thus between them they allotted the raising of arms, men, money and other necessities. 'And if they come to take us, we, together with armed men and the people will rise up and slay them and so be revenged on our enemies'.[35]

The rising might well have succeeded but for the *fermosa fembra* who, anxious about the possible fate of her Old Christian lover, betrayed the plot to the authorities. All those implicated were arrested and the occasion was made the excuse for the arrest of the richest and most powerful conversos of Seville. With this prize catch the first auto de fe of the Spanish Inquisition was celebrated on 6 February 1481, when six people were burnt at the stake and the sermon at the ceremony was preached by Fray Alonso de Hojeda. Hojeda's triumph was short-lived, for within a few days the plague which was just beginning to ravage Seville numbered him among its first victims. According to Bernáldez:

> A few days after this they burnt three of the richest leaders of the city, namely Diego de Susán, who was said to be worth ten million maravedis and was a chief rabbi, and who apparently died as a Christian; Manuel Sauli; and Bartolomé de Torralva. They also arrested Pedro Fernández

Benadeba, who was one of the ringleaders and had in his house weapons to arm a hundred men, and Juan Fernández Abolasia, who had often been chief magistrate and was a great lawyer; and many other leading and very rich citizens, who were also burnt.[36]

When Susanna saw the result of her betrayal, she is said to have first retired to a convent, and then to have taken to the streets, remorse eating into her soul until she died in poverty and shame, her last wishes being that her skull should be placed over the door of her house as a warning and example to others.

The heretics brought to light by the establishment of an Inquisition at Seville justified the introduction of other tribunals throughout the country. The emergency, for it was seen as such, meant that more bulls would have to be obtained from Rome. Accordingly, a papal brief of 11 February 1482 appointed seven more inquisitors, all Dominican friars, among them being the well-known name of Tomás de Torquemada. New tribunals were set up at Córdoba in 1482, and at Ciudad Real and Jaén in 1483. The tribunal at Ciudad Real was only temporary, and was permanently transferred to Toledo in 1485. By 1492 the kingdom of Castile had tribunals at Avila, Córdoba, Jaén, Medina del Campo, Segovia, Sigüenza, Toledo and Valladolid, though not all these had a permanent existence, and the southern tribunals were far more active than those in the north. Opposition to the Inquisition inevitably took a violent form after the first despairing pleas and flights. In Toledo, one of the most important converso centres in the realm, a plot against the inquisitors was planned for the feast of Corpus Christi 1484: the outcome followed the pattern of Seville, with betrayal, arrest and execution. The despair of the conversos at this time is amply revealed by their tame subjection to arrest and execution during what a modern apologist for the Inquisition concedes was 'a period of imprisonments and trials whose like has perhaps never been equalled by any other tribunal.'[37] In the first eight years of life of the Seville tribunal alone, according to Bernáldez, 'more than seven hundred persons were burnt and over five thousand punished.'[38]

The machinery of the Inquisition was regulated in accordance with the needs of the administration. Isabella was at this time engaged in reforming the councils which controlled central government in Castile, so that when in 1480 at the Cortes of Toledo it was decided to reform the governing councils, it seemed natural to follow this up with a separate council for the increasingly important affairs of the Inquisition. Accordingly, in 1483 the *Consejo de la Suprema y General Inquisición* (or *Suprema* for short) came into existence. The new council consisted initially of three ecclesiastical members, and a fourth member as president of the council, with the title (this came into existence slightly later) of Inquisitor General. The first Inquisitor General was Fray Tomás de Torquemada. By 1483, then, the Inquisition had taken firm root in Castile, and had been given its essential administrative organization. The problem now was whether the Castilian Inquisition should be extended to the kingdom of Aragon.

Resistance to the introduction of the Inquisition into Castile had been meagre and abortive. Popular opinion had been prepared for it and racial rivalry welcomed it. The only serious setback to royal policy occurred on 29 January 1482 when Pope Sixtus IV, responding to protests from Spanish clergy about abuses committed by the inquisitors of Seville, revoked the powers granted by the bull of foundation and allowed the Seville inquisitors to continue only if subjected to their bishop. The appointment of seven new inquisitors on 11 February 1482, far from being a surrender by the pope to the king, was accompanied by firm gestures by the pontiff in favour of the conversos. Ferdinand in May 1482 protested bitterly to Rome, particularly since a further conflict had now arisen over the Inquisition of Aragon. The mediaeval Inquisition had existed in Aragon since the 1230s but had become almost defunct by the fifteenth century. As part of his vigorous new policy, Ferdinand took steps in 1481 and 1482 to assert royal control over the appointment and payment of inquisitors. His aim was to resurrect the old papal Inquisition but also to subject it to his own control so as to come into line with practice in Castile. In Aragon, therefore, the new Inquisition was simply a continuance of the old tribunal, with the difference that the crown now controlled appointments and salaries, so that the tribunal became effectively more dependent on Ferdinand than on the pope.

The first activities of this reformed tribunal, with its main centres in the cities of Barcelona, Saragossa and Valencia, were directed against the conversos, who took alarm at developments and prepared for mass emigration. But differences with the pope, supplemented no doubt by pressure on Rome from conversos, brought activities to a temporary stop. On 18 April 1482 Sixtus IV issued what Lea calls 'the most extraordinary bull in the history of the Inquisition'. In this remarkable bull the pope protested

that in Aragon, Valencia, Mallorca and Catalonia the Inquisition has for
some time been moved not by zeal for the faith and the salvation of
souls, but by lust for wealth, and that many true and faithful Christians,
on the testimony of enemies, rivals, slaves and other lower and even less
proper persons, have without any legitimate proof been thrust into
secular prisons, tortured and condemned as relapsed heretics, deprived
of their goods and property and handed over to the secular arm to be
executed, to the peril of souls, setting a pernicious example, and causing
disgust to many.[39]

Accordingly, in future episcopal officers should act with the inquisitors: the names and testimony of accusers should be given to the
accused, who should be allowed counsel; episcopal gaols should be
the only ones used; and appeals should be allowed to Rome. The
bull was extraordinary because, in Lea's words, 'for the first time
heresy was declared to be, like any other crime, entitled to a fair
trial and simple justice'.[40] Besides, there is little doubt that the pope
welcomed the chance to assert once more his authority over an
Inquisition that had once been papal and had now slipped entirely
into the hands of the King of Aragon. So favourable was the bull to
converso claims that their influence in obtaining it cannot be
doubted. Ferdinand was outraged by the papal action and pretended
to disbelieve in the authenticity of the bull on the grounds that no
sensible pontiff would have issued such a document. On 13 May
1482 he wrote to the pope:

> Things have been told me, Holy Father which, if true, would seem to
> merit the greatest astonishment. It is said that Your Holiness has granted
> the conversos a general pardon for all the errors and crimes they have
> committed ... To these rumours, however, we have given no credence,
> because they seem to be things which would in no way have been
> conceded by Your Holiness, who have a duty to the Inquisition. But if
> by chance concessions have been made through the persistent and cun-
> ning persuasion of the said conversos, I intend never to let them take
> effect. Take care therefore not to let the matter go further, and to revoke
> any concessions and entrust us with the care of this question.[41]

Before this resolution, Sixtus IV wavered, and in October 1482
announced that he had suspended the bull. The way lay completely
open to Ferdinand. Papal co-operation was definitively secured by
the bull of 17 October 1483, which appointed Torquemada as Inquisitor General of Aragon, Valencia and Catalonia, thus uniting
the Inquisitions of the Spanish crown under a single head. The new
tribunal came directly under the control of the crown and was the

only institution whose authority ran in all the territories of Spain, a fact of great importance for future occasions when the ruler of Castile wished to interfere in other provinces where his sovereign authority was not recognized. This was not the end of papal interference, however, and the next half century or so witnessed several attempts by Rome to interfere in questions of jurisdiction and to reform abuses which might give the Inquisition a bad name. Besides this, the conversos in Spain never gave up their struggle to modify the practices of the tribunal, which they rightly considered a threat, not just to judaizers, but to the whole race of New Christians. Because of their representations to Rome, papal intervention was continued on their behalf, and thus led to several minor quarrels between crown and papacy.

Within the crown of Aragon there was bitter opposition to the introduction of the Castilian tribunal. Though Castile and Aragon had been joined by the marriage of the Catholic monarchs, they remained politically separate and each kingdom preserved its individual administration and liberties. In the eastern realms the *fueros* (laws) vested supreme authority less in the king alone, as was the case in Castile, than in the king acting together with the Cortes; when the latter was not in session its standing committee, the Diputación, watched over the laws. The resurrection of the old papal Inquisition posed a threat to the conversos but was no innovation and aroused little criticism. It was a different matter when Castilian inquisitors were appointed to realms where the fueros stipulated that senior officials must be native-born. The converso elite found that they had a constitutional argument to support their hostility.

Although the mediaeval Inquisition was moribund in Catalonia, the city of Barcelona had in 1461 received papal approval to have its own local inquisitor, Joan Comes. The Catalans therefore saw no need for a new tribunal. When the Cortes of the crown of Aragon met at Tarazona in April 1484, Catalonia refused to send deputies to approve the new Inquisition. In May Torquemada took the step of nominating two new inquisitors for Catalonia and at the same time revoked the commission held by Comes. The Catalans exploded into anger. The appointment of the new inquisitors, they wrote to Ferdinand, was 'against the liberties, constitutions and agreements solemnly sworn by Your Majesty'; in Barcelona both legal and Church authorities ruled that Comes was the only rightful inquisitor of the city.[42] In reply, Ferdinand affirmed that 'no cause nor interest, however great, will make us suspend the Inquisition'.

The conflict dragged on, and conversos began to emigrate in large numbers from the city. Fearing for the economic life of Barcelona, the consellers complained to Ferdinand in December 1485 of the 'losses and disorder caused in this land by the Inquisition that Your Highness wishes to introduce.... The few remaining merchants have ceased to trade.... Foreign realms are growing rich and glorious through the depopulation of this country.' In May 1486, they warned Ferdinand that the city would be 'totally depopulated and ruined if the Inquisition were introduced'. It was already too late. In February 1486 Pope Innocent VIII found a way out of the dilemma by sacking all the existing papal inquisitors in the crown of Aragon and securing the simultaneous withdrawal of the Castilian nominees. The initiative was handed back to Torquemada, who appointed a new inquisitor for Catalonia, Alonso de Espina, a Dominican prior from Castile. Not until June 1487 did Espina succeed in entering the city, but his entry was boycotted by the Diputación and the consellers. The latter protested subsequently that the inquisitors were acting 'against the laws, practice, customs and liberties of this city'. The Holy Office was now firmly implanted, but little fruit remained for it to pluck. Throughout 1488 it burnt only seven victims, and in 1489 only three. There was never any doubt as to whom the Inquisition was directed against: of 1,199 people it tried between 1488 and 1505 – most in their absence since they had fled – all but eight were conversos.[43] Among the distinguished refugees was Antoni de Bardaxi, regent of the Chancillería, whose task it had been to give legal approval to the establishment of the Holy Office.

In Valencia, opposition was based similarly on the fueros. There were two existing inquisitors with papal commissions, the Dominicans Juan Cristóbal de Gualbes and Juan Orts, who from 1481 represented the revived mediaeval tribunal, but they seem to have done little. In March 1484 they were removed and Torquemada nominated, as representatives of the new Inquisition, the Aragonese Juan de Epila and the Valencian Martín Iñigo. Since the Cortes of Tarazona in 1484 had approved the new Inquisition, the nominees should have had no problems in Valencia. From July to October, however, the three estates of the Valencian Cortes kept up a stream of protests, asking 'not that the Inquisition be suspended but that it be in the hands of natives of this realm';[44] and detailing other requests, such as an end to secret testimony. Opposition crumbled before the obduracy of Ferdinand, who recalled that no protest had been made by the Valencians at Tarazona, and that the fueros must never be used to shield heresy. Even after the inquisitors began work in November 1484, opposition continued and the king was obliged to alternate threats with arguments. 'If there are so few heretics in the realm', his representatives commented acridly, 'one wonders why people should be afraid of the Inquisition.'[45]

In the kingdom of Aragon, converso families had long played a prominent role in politics and finance. Regardless of inevitable opposition, on 4 May 1484 Torquemada appointed the first two inquisitors for Aragon, Gaspar Juglar and Pedro Arbués de Epila. According to Lea, the inquisitors set to work immediately, holding autos de fe on 10 May and 3 June 1484. These dates, however, are not only excessively early, but they also sin against the inquisitorial rule which allowed a term of grace, usually about a month, to elapse before taking action against heretics. It is therefore more likely that the autos in question were held in 1485. This activity of the new tribunal deeply disturbed not only conversos but all those whose loyalty was to the fueros of Aragon. As the chronicler of Aragon, Jerónimo de Zurita, reported:

> Those newly converted from the Jewish race, and many other leaders and gentry, claimed that the procedure was against the liberties of the realm, because for this offence [of heresy] their goods were confiscated and they were not given the names of witnesses who testified against them.
>
> As a result [continued Zurita] the conversos had all the kingdom on their side, including persons of the highest consideration, among them Old Christians and gentry.[46]

When public opposition grew so great that there was a move to summon the four estates of the realm, Ferdinand hastily sent a circular letter to the chief nobles and deputies, justifying his position:

> There is no intention of infringing the fueros but rather of enforcing their observance. It is not to be imagined that vassals so Catholic as those of Aragon would have demanded, or that kings so Catholic would have granted, fueros and liberties adverse to the faith and favourable to heresy. If the old inquisitors had acted conscientiously in accordance with the canons there would have been no cause for bringing in the new ones, but they were without conscience and corrupted with bribes.
>
> If there are so few heretics as is now asserted, there should not be such dread of the Inquisition. It is not to be impeded in sequestrating and confiscating and other necessary acts, for be assured that no cause

or interest, however great, shall be allowed to interfere with its proceeding in future as it is now doing.[47]

Whatever the motives, whether personal dread or constitutional opposition, resistance continued. The most remarkable case of resistance in the whole of Spain occurred in 1484 at the city of Teruel, a hundred miles to the south of Saragossa.[48] In that year the tribunal of Saragossa sent two inquisitors to the city to establish a tribunal there, but the magistrates refused them permission to enter the city gates. The inquisitors thereupon withdrew to the neighbouring town of Cella, from which they issued an excommunication and interdict against the city and its magistrates. The clergy of Teruel promptly obtained papal letters releasing the city from these censures. The Inquisition thereupon decreed in October 1484 that all the public offices in Teruel were confiscated to the crown and their present holders deprived of them; this was followed by an appeal to the king to carry out the decree. Ferdinand replied with an order in February 1485 to all his officials in Aragon, asking them to raise arms and help the inquisitors. The response to this was not adequate, so Ferdinand also called on troops from the borders of Castile to help in the enterprise. Faced with such massive coercion the city was easily reduced to obedience, and with its submission in the spring of 1485 the Inquisition seemed to have triumphed everywhere in Aragon. The reasons for Teruel's resistance seem to have lain almost exclusively in the great influence exercised there by conversos, so that here there was little pretence of defending the fueros of Aragon. By 1485, indeed, the fueros were a dead issue.

But converso opposition had by no means been destroyed. On the one hand it was growing in strength with the passive support of Old Christians who resented the introduction of the new tribunal into Aragon, and on the other it was becoming more desperate because of the obvious failure of resistance as shown by the example of Teruel. In the highest converso circles the idea of the assassination of an inquisitor gained currency, and was supported by people as eminent as Gabriel Sánchez, treasurer of the king, and Sancho Paternoy, the royal treasurer (*maestre racional*) in Aragon. The climax came on the night of 15 September 1485, as the inquisitor Pedro Arbués was kneeling in prayer before the high altar of Saragossa cathedral. Beneath his gown the inquisitor wore a coat of mail and on his head a steel cap, because of warnings about threats against his life. On the night in question, eight conspirators hired by conversos entered the cathedral by the chapter door and stole up behind the inquisitor; after verifying that this was indeed Arbués, one of them stabbed him in the back with a stroke that went through his neck and proved to be his death wound. As Arbués staggered away, two of the others also inflicted wounds on him. The murderers made their escape and the canons of the cathedral rushed in to find the inquisitor dying: Arbués lingered for twenty-four hours and died on 17 September.

The shock of this murder led to developments which the conversos should certainly have foreseen.[49] When it was discovered that the assassins were judaizers the whole mood of the city of Saragossa, and with it that of Aragon, changed. Arbués was declared to be a saint,* miracles were worked with his blood, mobs roamed the streets in search of conversos, and a national assembly voted to suspend the fueros while the search for the assassins went on. In this atmosphere the inquisitors came into their own. Autos of the reformed Inquisition were held on 28 December 1485, and the murderers of Arbués expiated their crime in successive autos de fe lasting from 30 June 1486 to 15 December the same year. One of them had his hands cut off and nailed to the door of the Diputación, after which he was dragged to the market-place, beheaded and quartered, and the pieces of his body suspended in the streets of the city. Another committed suicide in his cell the day before his ordeal, by breaking a glass lamp and swallowing the fragments; he too suffered the same punishment, which was inflicted on his dead body.

More than these initial measures was needed in order to uproot the whole conspiracy, which involved so many and such eminent people that individuals were being punished for it as late as 1492. The heads that now rolled came from the highest families in Aragon. Whether they were judaizers or not, members of the leading converso houses had connived at the murder and were sooner or later destroyed by the Inquisition, which remained in full control of all the judicial measures taken. A study of the list of victims shows the constant appearance of the great names of Santa Fe, Santangel, Caballería, and Sánchez. Francisco de Santa Fe, son of the famous converso Jerónimo and a counsellor of the governor of Aragon,

* He was popularly venerated as *el Santo martyr*, and was assigned a feast day in Spain in the sixteenth century. But a reluctant Rome did not canonize him until 1867.

committed suicide by jumping from a tower and his remains were burnt in the auto of 15 December 1486. Sancho Paternoy was tortured and condemned to perpetual imprisonment. Luis de Santangel, who had been personally knighted by Juan II for his military prowess, was beheaded and burnt in the market-place of Saragossa on 8 August 1487; his cousin Luis, whose money loans made possible the voyages of Columbus, was made to do penance in July 1491. Altogether, over fifteen members of the Santangel family were punished by the Inquisition before 1499; and between 1486 and 1503 fourteen members of the Sánchez family suffered a similar fate. This immense sweep of conversos into the nets of the tribunal was effective in destroying for ever the political and social grip of New Christians on the Aragonese administration. Not for the first time, a cause triumphed through one useful martyrdom. For the conversos one murder, cheaply achieved at a total cost of six hundred gold florins (which included the wages of the assassins), turned out to be an act of mass suicide which annihilated all opposition to the Inquisition for the next hundred years.

In Mallorca, where the old Inquisition had already begun activities against judaizers in 1478, the new tribunal was introduced without incident in 1488 and began operations immediately. The inquisitors, Pedro Pérez de Munebrega and Sancho Martín, found enough work to keep them occupied in the hundreds of cases that filled the years 1488 to 1491.[50] Politically, the island was undisturbed, and no outbreaks against the tribunal occurred until a generation later under Charles V when a rising led by the converso Bishop of Elna in 1518 led to the temporary expulsion of the inquisitors from the city of Palma. The acceptance by Mallorcans of the activities of the tribunal is all the more unusual since conversos formed a considerable part of the population, thanks to the riots of 1391 in Palma, the preaching of Saint Vincent Ferrer in 1413 and 1414, and the final forcible conversion of the Jews in 1435. The large number of conversos in the autos de fe between 1488 and 1499 – 347 in all, excluding the hundreds who were pardoned for confessing voluntarily – proves that here also existed a minority problem of important dimensions.

The Spanish Inquisition was thus established everywhere in Spain several years before the final decision to expel the Jews. In those twelve terrible years, conversos and Jews alike suffered from the rising tide of antisemitism: while the latter were being harassed and then expelled from dioceses in Aragon and Andalucia, the former were being purged of those who retained vestiges of their ancestral Judaism. Many conversos, aware of the pitiless and undiscriminating persecution that awaited them, fled abroad without necessarily intending thereby to defect from the Catholic faith. Refugees therefore feature prominently among those condemned in the early years. In the first two years of the tribunal at Ciudad Real, fifty-two victims were burnt alive but 220 had to be condemned to death in their absence. In the Barcelona auto de fe of 10 June 1491, three persons were burnt alive but 139 were condemned *in absentia*. In Mallorca the same process was repeated when the auto of 11 May 1493 witnessed only three burnings in person but forty-seven burnings of the effigies of absent fugitives.[51]

The purpose of the Inquisition emerges unequivocally from the figures: 99.3 per cent of those tried by the Barcelona tribunal between 1488 and 1505, and 91.6 per cent of those tried by that of Valencia between 1484 and 1530, were conversos of Jewish origin.[52] The savagery of the onslaught against the conversos was without equal in the history of any tribunal in the western world; set beside it, the mediaeval Inquisition appears a model of moderation. Never before had Spaniard so relentlessly been set against Spaniard in a civil conflict that endured from generation to generation. Hernando del Pulgar estimated that up to 1490 the Inquisition in Spain had burnt two thousand people and reconciled fifteen thousand others under the edicts of grace.[53] His contemporary, Andrés Bernáldez, estimated that in Seville alone between 1480 and 1488 the tribunal had burnt over seven hundred people and reconciled more than five thousand, without counting all those who were sentenced to 'perpetual' imprisonment.[54] A later historian, the annalist Diego Ortiz de Zúñiga, claimed that in Seville between 1481 and 1524 over twenty thousand heretics had abjured their errors, and over a thousand obstinate heretics had been sent to the stake.[55]

Thanks to the edicts of grace, in the early years suspects flocked to the Inquisition in the hope that voluntary confession might clear their record: thousands were 'reconciled' to the Catholic faith, in Toledo alone some 4,300 persons in 1486–7.[56] The mass reconciliations were no proof of mildness, for they were accompanied by terrifying and – for Spain – unprecedented displays of religious ferocity. In the great auto de fe at Ciudad Real on 23 February 1484, thirty people were burnt alive and forty in effigy; in the auto at Valladolid on 5 January 1492, thirty-two were burnt alive. In some tribunals the proportion of burnings was extraordinarily high.

In Guadalupe in 1485, nearly 44 per cent of those arrested were burnt; in Avila in 1490–1500, nearly 41 per cent.[57] In Valencia the tribunal seems to have meted out the death penalty to about 38 per cent of the two thousand early cases whose outcome we know; and by 1530 it had despatched four-fifths of all death sentences passed before 1592.[58] In rounded terms, it is likely that over three-quarters of all those who perished under the Inquisition in the three centuries of its existence, did so in the first twenty years.

Because documentation for the early years has not usually survived, it is difficult to arrive at reliable figures for the activity of the Inquisition. Some data, and figures for later periods, are offered below.

Tribunal	Period	Relaxations		Other
		Person	Effigy	victims
Ciudad Real[59]	1483–1485	52	220	183
Toledo[60]	1485–1501	250	500	5,400
Toledo[61]	1575–1610	11	15	904
Toledo[61]	1648–1794	8	63	1,094
Saragossa[62]	1485–1502	124	32	458
Valencia[63]	1484–1530	754	155	1,076
Barcelona[64]	1488–1498	23	445	421
Mallorca[65]	1488–1729	120	496	664
Canaries[66]	1504–1820	11	107	2,145

Since conversos occupied a significant place in administration, the professions and trade, diminishing numbers through persecution and emigration must have had a considerable impact on areas of Spain where they had been numerous. In Barcelona, according to the consellers in 1485, the refugees 'have transferred to other realms all the money and goods they have in this city'.[67] In 1510 the few conversos who remained there claimed that they had once been a flourishing group of 'over six hundred families, of whom over two hundred were merchants', and that they now numbered only fifty-seven families, close to ruin.[68] In Valencia, we know the professions of 736 conversos tried by the Inquisition: 34 per cent were in commerce and 43 per cent were artisans, principally in textiles.[69] The conversos of Spain were in no way the cream of the population, but their ruin could not fail to cause concern to the civic authorities; this, indeed, even more than constitutional reasons, was the main cause of non-converso resistance to the Inquisition in Teruel. It is likely that the persecution of the conversos was far more damaging to the economy than the later and more spectacular expulsion of the Jews, who because of their marginal status played a smaller role in key sectors of public life and possibly controlled fewer economic resources.

The establishment of the Inquisition has often been taken as evidence to support the view that the Catholic monarchs desired to impose uniformity of religion on Spain; the expulsion of the Jews would seem to confirm this hypothesis. Though the monarchs, as fervent Catholics, would have preferred the nation to be united in faith, there is in fact no evidence of a deliberate policy to impose uniformity. Throughout the first decade of the Inquisition's career, Ferdinand and Isabella did not cease to protect their Jews while simultaneously trying to eliminate judaizing among the conversos. Even after the expulsion of the Jews, the Mudejars remained in full enjoyment of their freedom of religion – in Castile for another decade, in Aragon for another thirty years. The drive against heresy pursued so ruthlessly by Ferdinand, far from being part of a policy of unification, was no more than the culmination of a long period of official anxiety over the religion of the conversos, anxiety that had already in 1461 led to early plans for an Inquisition and that eventually in the 1480s gave birth to the tribunal.

4

The Roots of Opposition

There were differing opinions.

Juan de Mariana S.J., *Historia General de España*

'What we cannot doubt', writes a modern Spanish apologist for the Inquisition, 'is that in the fifteenth and sixteenth centuries the immense majority of the Spanish people, with their kings, magistrates and bishops leading them, gave their decisive support to the proceedings of the Inquisition.'[1] This is a fact that no reputable historian would care to deny. Even the great Llorente, last secretary and first historian of the tribunal, was staggered by the lack of evidence for any opposition to it in Spain. As he declared in 1811 in a discourse read to the Royal Academy of History, meeting in Madrid at the height of the Peninsular War:

> If in investigating what a nation thought about a certain institution we were to be guided solely by the testimony of public writers, there is no doubt that the Spanish people had as much love as hate for the Inquisition. ... You will find hardly a book printed in Spain from the time of Charles the Fifth to our own days in which the Inquisition is not cited with praise.[2]

The apparent support given by the Spanish people to the Inquisition has inevitably created problems of interpretation. Partisans of the Holy Office have maintained that its popularity was based on its unswerving sense of justice, and that it responded to a profound religious need. Critics, by contrast, have presented it as a tyranny imposed by the State upon the free consciences of Spaniards. Both extremes of opinion can be supported by contemporary evidence, but neither is wholly plausible. The primitive state bureaucracies of fifteenth-century Castile and Aragon were ill-equipped to impose a tyranny on the mass of the people and in reality never attempted to do so. If the Inquisition was popular, on the other hand, we need to examine why this came about. Its support among the masses arose out of the bitter social struggles of the late fifteenth century, and it represented the interests of the vast majority of the population – the Old Christians – against those of a small converso minority. Though popular support always remained the basis of the Inquisition's power, such support was seldom more than passive; the Inquisition, as we shall see, was accepted but never loved.

There can be little doubt that the introduction of the Inquisition was a shock. The Aragonese had never fully activated their mediaeval one and were in no mood to accept another. The Castilians were in an even more sensitive position: never in all their history had they institutionalized the persecution of heresy. It had traditionally been a tolerant, open society, with no sectarian movements of the type that had arisen in England, France and Germany. Judaizers had occasionally been condemned by episcopal courts prior to the establishment of the Inquisition, but in accord with existing law.[3] How, then, did Spaniards come to accept a tribunal that was not only alien to their own traditions[4] but which from the first violated every established principle of justice? The most eloquent testimony to the initial mood of revulsion comes from the pen of the sixteenth-century Jesuit Juan de Mariana. According to him, inquisitorial procedure

> at its inception appeared very oppressive to Spaniards. What caused the most surprise was that children paid for the crimes of their parents, and that accusers were not named or made known, nor confronted by the accused, nor was there publication of witnesses: all of which was contrary to the practice followed of old in other tribunals. Besides this, it appeared an innovation that sins of that sort should be punished by death. And what was most serious was that because of these secret investigations they were deprived of the liberty to listen and talk freely, since in all the cities, towns and villages there were persons placed to give information of what went on. This was considered by some to be the most wretched slavery and equal to death.[5]

Despite the strong language in which it is phrased, this opinion was not apparently shared by Mariana, who also presents as 'better and more correct' a contrary view in favour of the Inquisition. Significantly, he nowhere gives the impression that the critical view was held only by conversos. The specific points quoted, on innovations in judicial procedure, the death sentence for judaizing, and the practice of spying, were indeed questions that Old Christians raised in Castilian and Aragonese Cortes over the next few years. Fully aware of the novelty of inquisitorial practice, Mariana admitted that the new harsh measures were a deviation from the normal charitable procedure of the Church; but, he says, it was held 'that at times the ancient customs of the Church should be changed in conformity with the needs of the times'.

'The needs of the times': it is the clue to the survival of the Inquisition. While urban factions in Toledo, Ciudad Real and other cities were struggling to dislodge conversos from power, in the 1480s Ferdinand and Isabella, fresh from the civil wars and the constitutional settlement achieved at the Cortes of Toledo (1480), were beginning a military crusade against the Moors of Granada. In 1486 they sought blessing for their cause at the shrine of St James in Compostela. Crisis times required crisis measures: the message was implicit in every major directive issued by Ferdinand in these years, and helps to explain the unusual co-operation he obtained throughout Spain. It may also help to explain the totally uncompromising firmness with which he insisted that the Inquisition be accepted everywhere, regardless of consequences. We have his remarkable statement to the consellers of Barcelona in 1486, that

> before we decided on introducing this Inquisition into any of the cities of our realms, we carefully considered and looked at all the harm and ill that could follow from it and that could hit our taxes and revenue. But because our firm intention and concern is to prefer the service of God to our own, we wish the Inquisition to be established regardless, putting all other interests aside.[6]

The deliberate stimulation of a feeling of crisis (aggravated by converso plots, by the murder of Arbués, by the episode of the La Guardia infant), and the universal response to the great twelve-year-long crusade against Granada pressurized public authorities to conform and stilled the protests of individuals. Because the Inquisition was a crisis instrument, it may be that Ferdinand never intended it to be permanent (no steps, for example, were taken to give it a regular income). This certainly was the feeling of the Toledo writer who commented in 1538 that 'if the Catholic kings were still alive, they would have reformed it twenty years ago, given the change in conditions'.[7] The unprecedented activities of the Holy Office were deemed to be acceptable only as an emergency measure, until the crisis had passed.

Critics remained uneasy that harsh penalties should be imposed on those who had never been properly Christianized. Were judaizers wholly to blame? Had they ever been catechized after their forced baptism? And were the penalties not extreme? Mariana testifies to a great deal of dissent in Spain:

> At the time there were differing opinions. Some felt that those who sinned in this way should not suffer the death penalty; but apart from this they admitted that it was just to inflict any other kind of punishment. Among others sharing this opinion, was Hernando del Pulgar, a person of acute and elegant genius.[8]

Nowhere does Mariana claim that the 'better and more correct' contrary opinion was a majority one, and we may conjecture that Pulgar's view was widely held in higher circles. Many Spaniards were indeed appalled at the tide of bloodshed. 'We are all aghast', the consellers of Barcelona informed Ferdinand bluntly in 1484, 'at the news we receive of the executions and proceedings that they say are taking place in Castile.'[9] Pulgar was no less horrified. Denouncing the resort to coercion at a time when evangelization had not been tried, the royal secretary informed the Archbishop of Seville that tens of thousands of converso children in Andalucia

> had never been out of their homes or heard and learned any other doctrine but that which they had seen their parents practise at home. To burn all these would be not only cruel but difficult to carry out.
>
> I do not say this, my lord, in favour of the evildoers, but to find a solution, which it seems to me would be to put in that province outstanding persons who by their exemplary life and teaching of doctrine would convert some and bring back others. Of course [the inquisitors] Diego de Merlo and doctor Medina are good men; but I know very well that they will not produce such good Christians with their fire as the Bishops Pablo [de Santa María] and Alonso [de Cartagena] did with water.[10]

While agreeing that heresy should be repressed, Pulgar objected to capital punishment. His principal authority for this position was Saint Augustine, who had advocated the use of force but not the death penalty against the Donatist heretics of north Africa in the fifth century. The testimony of the liberal and humane secretary is important evidence that the temper of contemporaries was not entirely in favour of bloody measures, and that the more extreme actions of the Inquisition were not necessarily in conformity with the standards of the age.

His contemporary Juan de Lucena, a noted humanist and servant of the crown, entered, like Pulgar, into public controversy over the methods of the Inquisition. At one time royal emissary to Rome and then a member of the Royal Council, Lucena was apparently a converso and, according to his adversary canon Alonso Ortiz of Toledo, not only 'attempted with his sophistries to defend the conversos' but also 'insisted to the king and queen that there should be no Inquisition'. Lucena claimed, says Ortiz, that Jews 'baptized through fear did not receive the sacrament properly, and should therefore be treated not as heretics but as infidels', and that 'conversos ought to be convinced with reasons and inducements, not with coercion and punishments'.[11]

Further evidence of opposition to the persecution of Jews and conversos comes from an official of the Holy Office itself. The Sicilian inquisitor Luis de Páramo wrote that many learned Spaniards, both before and after 1492, thought the expulsion wrong in principle, as well as harmful to the Church, for two main reasons: firstly, because those who had been baptized by force had not received the sacrament properly and therefore remained essentially pagan;[12] secondly, because the expulsion was an implicit invitation to annihilate the Jews, which would be contrary to Scripture. The first reason was, of course, of paramount importance, for if Jews had been forced into conversion their baptism was invalid and the Inquisition had no jurisdiction over them. The standard reply to this argument was simple: the mere fact that the Jews had *chosen* baptism as an alternative to death or exile meant that they had exercised the right of free choice: there was therefore no compulsion, and the sacrament was valid.

Throughout the subsequent period, criticisms were made of the treatment of conversos. Fray José de Sigüenza, sixteenth-century historian of the Jeronimite Order, lamented that there had been no other prelates in Spain like the saintly Hernando de Talavera, Archbishop of Granada and confessor to Queen Isabella. In his treatment of New Christians, says Fray José, Talavera

> would not allow anyone to harm them in word or deed, or burden them with new taxes and impositions, for he detested the evil custom prevalent in Spain of treating members of the sects worse after their conversion than before it ... so that many refused to accept a Faith in whose believers they saw so little charity and so much arrogance.
>
> And if [continues Fray José] there had been more prelates who walked in this path, there would not have been so many lost souls stubborn in the sects of Moses and Mahommed within Spain, nor so many heretics in other nations.[13]

Testimony as powerful as this, penned a full century after the protests of Pulgar, bears witness to the continued existence in Spain of a responsible body of opinion which condemned not only the practices of the Inquisition but also the atmosphere reigning in a society which had lost its conscience.

Talavera's position was stated most clearly in his *Católica impugnación*, a sharp attack which he directed against a 'heretical leaflet' issued in 1480 by a pro-Jewish converso of Seville. Deflating the pretensions of the Jews and conversos to be a specially gifted nation ('the Greeks were much more so, and the Romans, and even the Arabs'), Talavera supported the traditional death penalty for heresy; on the other hand, he attacked the antisemitism to which conversos were subjected, and stated firmly that reason rather than persecution was the way of bringing conversos back to the fold: 'heresies need to be corrected not only with punishments and lashes, but even more with Catholic reasoning'.[14] It was the policy he later adopted towards the Moriscos of Granada. His tract, possibly because of its controversial nature, was placed on the Index of forbidden books in 1559.

At times the protests cut so deep as to strike at the very basis of the Inquisition. These dissentient voices abhorred the racial persecution, the methods of coercion and dishonesty, the abdication of Christian responsibility and charity. The fact that men like these existed in an age where heresy was regarded as the worst of all social crimes is a tribute to the pluralist society that had once existed in Spain. At the same time, it makes nonsense of the claims that the excesses committed in this period, whether by the Inquisition or by other bodies, can be excused because of the standards of the age. The few who differed are proof that no uniform standards existed in that age.

In the initial period, opposition was invariably promoted by conversos. Unable to secure support in Spain they turned to Rome. Thus a bull issued by Sixtus IV on 2 August 1483, and almost certainly obtained by converso money, ordered greater leniency to be exercised in the tribunal of Seville and revoked all appeal cases to Rome. Only eleven days later, however, the pope withdrew the bull, after pressure from the Spanish rulers. Sixtus IV died in 1484, to be succeeded by Innocent VIII, a pontiff who followed his policy of intervening in favour of the conversos while taking care not to anger the Catholic monarchs. The bulls issued by Innocent on 11 February and 15 July 1485, asking for more mercy and leniency and for greater use of the practice of secret reconciliation[15] are typical of the efforts made by the Holy See to avoid lasting infamy falling on the tribunal's victims. Yet even if we see the hand of the conversos in all these attempts to mitigate the worst aspects of inquisitorial procedure, it is impossible to maintain that conversos alone constituted the opposition.

Hostility to the practice of sanbenitos, for example, was shared by Old and New Christian alike. These penitential garments were ordered to be worn in public by the condemned, causing them public humiliation and bringing ill-fame to the towns where they lived. It was this that Mariana singled out as being 'very oppressive to Spaniards'. In Andalucia, according to Bernáldez, people were allowed to cease wearing them 'so that the disrepute of the territory should not grow'.[16] Spying would have been objected to in any community and, as we shall see, aroused appropriate reactions. Prior to 1492 the Jews themselves were asked to spy on conversos. At Toledo in 1485 the inquisitors collected the rabbis and made them swear to anathematize in their synagogues those Jews who did not denounce judaizers.[17] In practice, ex-Jews rather than Jews appear to have been the active delators: in Ciudad Real in 1483-5 a former rabbi, Fernan Falcón, was the chief witness used against most of those arrested for judaizing.[18]

Although conversos in Castile were notoriously hostile to the new tribunal, we hear little of opposition by Old Christians during the first two decades of the Inquisition's existence. Yet this was, as we have seen, by far the most bloody period of its history: tens of thousands of Christians of Jewish origin had been executed, ruined or driven into exile in a campaign without precedent in Spanish or European history, and through all this few Old Christians had bestirred themselves to raise their voices in protest. Only when the officers of the tribunal in Castile began to extend their activities to non-conversos did the murmurs of discontent become audible.

In 1499 the inquisitor of Córdoba was replaced after being found guilty of fraud and extortion. His successor, appointed in September that year, was Diego Rodríguez Lucero. Within a short time Lucero began his own bizarre career of extortion, arresting leading citizens on trifling or false pretexts in order to seize their property in confiscations. His actions were protected against exposure by the complicity of a secretary of the king, Juan Roiz de Calcena. Prominent members of Old Christian families soon became ensnared in Lucero's net, and an atmosphere of terror gripped the community. To justify his actions Lucero invented tales of a Jewish conspiracy to subvert Spain. An annalist of Córdoba reports that

> to gain credit as a zealous minister of the faith and to gain higher dignities, he began to treat the accused in prison with extreme rigour, forcing them to declare their accomplices, which resulted in the denunciation of so great a number of people, both conversos and Old Christians, that the city was scandalized and almost burst into rioting.[19]

Converso witnesses testified that they had been forced to teach Jewish prayers to Old Christian prisoners so that Lucero could accuse the latter of judaizing. A report from the cathedral chapter and city council in December 1506 accused Lucero of 'killing and robbing and defaming any and everybody'. An independent enquiry by the Córdoba authorities in November concluded that Lucero's evidence against his victims was 'all fabricated'; that Fray Diego Deza, Archbishop of Seville and Inquisitor General, had failed to respond to petitions against the inquisitor; that four hundred innocent prisoners were currently in the cells; and that Lucero had deliberately burnt as many of his victims as possible (107 were burnt alive in one auto in December 1504; twenty-seven in another in May 1505) to stop them complaining to the new King of Castile, Philip the Fair.[20]

One of the inquisitor's last victims was the eighty-year-old Jeronimite Archbishop of Granada, Hernando de Talavera. Accusing Talavera of having a synagogue in his palace, Lucero arrested the archbishop and all his household (which included his sister, two nieces and their daughters, and the servants). Both relatives and servants were tortured, and duly produced denunciations against Talavera. The papacy opportunely intervened, the archbishop was acquitted of all charges in April 1507, and he and his family were set free.[21] It came too late to benefit the old man. Walking barefoot and bareheaded through the streets of Granada in the procession on Ascension Day, 13 May, he was seized by a violent fever which the following day ended his life. This great and holy man, whose care for his flock, regardless of race, had left him no time to care for himself, died in perfect poverty; his household, for which he had not provided, had to resort to the charity of the Bishop of Málaga. Nearly a century later, Fray José de Sigüenza claimed that his like had not since been seen in Spain.

On 16 July the same year Gonzalo de Ayora, captain general and chronicler, wrote a letter of protest to the king's secretary Miguel de Almazán.

The government had failed to exercise effective control over its ministers. As for the Inquisition, the method adopted was to place so much confidence in the Archbishop of Seville and in Lucero ... that they were able to defame the whole kingdom, to destroy, without God or justice, a great part of it, slaying and robbing and violating maids and wives to the great dishonour of the Christian religion ...

The damages which the wicked officials of the Inquisition have wrought in my land are so many and so great that no reasonable person on hearing of them would not grieve.[22]

The redress so urgently demanded began with the resignation of Deza under pressure, and the appointment on 5 June 1507 of Francisco Jiménez de Cisneros, Cardinal Archbishop of Toledo, as the Inquisitor General. In May 1508 the Suprema eventually voted to arrest Lucero, who was taken in chains to Burgos, while his victims in the prison of Córdoba were all released. The ex-inquisitor received no punishment for his crimes, but was allowed to retire to Seville, where he died in peace.

At the same time as the troubles in Córdoba, complaints were raised in Llerena (Extremadura) against the activities of the new inquisitor, a man named Bravo, who had for a time been an assistant of Lucero in Córdoba. So many wealthy prisoners were thrown into the cells by Bravo, despite the protests of one of his colleagues, that the relatives of the condemned finally gathered enough courage to petition the crown:

We the relatives and friends of the prisoners in the cells of the Inquisition of Llerena kiss the royal hands of Your Highness and testify that the inquisitors of that province, together with their officials, have persecuted and persecute both the prisoners and ourselves with great hatred and enmity, and have carried out many irregularities in the procedure of imprisonment and trial, and have maltreated not only the said prisoners but their wives and children and property.[23]

There is no record of any censure of Bravo's policy, and it appears likely that he was allowed to pursue his career unchecked. Lucero's malign influence also seems to have haunted the tribunal at Jaén, where a professional 'witness' who had formerly served the inquisitor now extended his activities. The man's name was Diego de Algeciras, and for a reasonable pittance he was ready to perjure himself in testifying to the judaizing activities of any number of conversos. Thanks to his assistance, the richest conversos of the city were soon in gaol on suspicion of heresy. Those who still remained free petitioned the crown to restore jurisdiction over heresy to the Bishop of Jaén, whose mercy they trusted more than the abuses of the officials of the Inquisition.[24]

Most abuses probably originated not with the inquisitors themselves but with their subordinate officials. Among the more notorious cases was the notary at Jaén, who locked a young girl of fifteen in a room, stripped her naked, and whipped her until she agreed to testify against her mother.[25] A deposition drawn up by witnesses at Toledo and dated 26 September 1487 asserts that the receiver of confiscated goods in that tribunal, Juan de Uría, had defrauded sums amounting to 1.5 million maravedis, enough to set himself up in comfort.[26] There were opportunities for lining one's pockets even at the bottom of the ladder. In 1588, the inquisitor from Madrid who carried out the inspection of the tribunal at Córdoba reported that both the door-keeper and the messenger of the tribunal were criminals and profiteers, and that this was well known throughout the city, although apparently not to the inquisitors of Córdoba.[27]

In the crown of Aragon, too, Old Christians who had condoned the persecution of conversos now began after the death of Queen Isabella to rally to the defence of the fueros. Meeting together at Monzón in 1510, the representatives of Aragon, Catalonia and Valencia raised the question of reform in jurisdiction. No further steps were taken until their next meeting at Monzón in 1512, when a comprehensive list of reforms was drawn up: to this list Ferdinand put his signature, thus agreeing to the first of the many *concordias* made between the Inquisition and the individual provinces of Spain. Among other things, the concordia of 1512 stipulated that the number of familiars in the kingdom should be limited; that the Inquisition should not be exempt from local taxes; that officials of the tribunal who committed crimes should be tried by a secular court; that in cases of confiscation, property which had formerly belonged to the condemned should not be included in the confiscation; and that trade with conversos should not be prohibited, since this depressed commerce. Moreover, the tribunal was not to exercise jurisdiction over usury, bigamy, blasphemy and witchcraft unless heresy were involved. The fact that pressure had to be put on the king through the Cortes proves how serious were some of the objections raised in Aragon against inquisitorial procedure. Yet the demands made in 1512 are relatively mild when compared with some of those made at a later date.

At the death of Ferdinand on 23 January 1516 the crown passed to his grandson Charles, who was in Flanders at the time. Since the death of Isabella on 26 November 1504 Ferdinand had been King of Aragon only, and Castile had been under the rule of their daughter Juana (the Mad), widow since 1506 of Philip the Fair of Austria. The death of Ferdinand would normally have meant the acceptance of Juana as queen, but her mental dislocation made her obviously unfitted to rule, so that her son Charles was everywhere accepted as rightful sovereign.

While awaiting the arrival of Charles in Spain, Cisneros maintained control of the Inquisition. In his will the Catholic King had called upon his successor to preserve the Inquisition. This Charles had every intention of doing. But the new reign aroused hopes of reform, particularly in converso hearts, and Cisneros was greatly alarmed by a rumour that Charles intended to allow the publication of the names of witnesses in inquisitorial trials. In a letter which the now ageing cardinal wrote to Charles, apparently in March 1517, he asserted that the Inquisition was so perfect a tribunal 'that there will never be any need for reform and it would be sinful to introduce changes'.[28] The publication of witnesses' names would lead inevitably to their murder, as had happened recently in Talavera de la Reina when an accused converso, on learning the name of his denouncer, went out to waylay him and assassinated him. Cisneros was not, however, unalterably opposed to reforms, as his own life and career had demonstrated. During his tenure of the post of Inquisitor General, he had taken care to dismiss the more notorious inquisitors, including the secretary of the Suprema. He wrote to Charles in December 1576 advising him that the royal secretary Calcena and others should have nothing further to do with the Inquisition, in view of their excesses. Lea's very fair verdict is that 'we may feel assured that he showed no mercy to those who sought to coin into money the blood of the conversos'.[29]

Whatever Cisneros' views may have been, many contemporaries thought that some reform in the judicial procedure of the Inquisition was essential, even if they did not question its actual existence. The arrival of the seventeen-year-old king from Flanders set off a train of requests and demands which constituted the last chapter in the struggle to subject the Inquisition to the rule of law. When Charles, after his arrival in Spain in September 1517, held the first Cortes of his reign at Valladolid in February 1518, the procuradores petitioned that Your Highness provide that the office of the Holy Inquisition proceed in such a way as to maintain justice, and that the wicked be punished and the innocent not suffer.

They asked moreover that the forms of law be observed, and that the inquisitors be chosen from reputable and learned men. The main result of this was the series of instructions for the Inquisition drawn up principally on the initiative of Jean le Sauvage, chancellor of the king, a man who was accused of being in the pay of the conversos. The preamble to these proposed instructions claims that

> accused people have not been able to defend themselves fully, many innocent and guiltless have suffered death, harm, oppression, injury and infamy ... and many of our vassals have absented themselves from these realms; and (as events have shown) in general these our realms have received and receive great ill and harm; and have been and are notorious for this throughout the world.

The proposed reforms, therefore, included provisions that prisoners be placed in open, public prisons, be able to receive visitors, be assigned counsel, be presented with an accusation on arrest, and be given the names of witnesses; in addition, goods of the accused should not be taken and sold before their actual condemnation, nor should the salaries of inquisitors be payable out of confiscations. Prisoners should be allowed recourse to mass and the sacraments while awaiting trial, and care should be taken not to let those condemned to perpetual prison die of hunger. If torture were used, it should be in moderation, and there should be no 'new inventions of torture as have been used until now'.[30] Each of these clauses points to the existence of evils which the new pragmatic was supposed to remedy. Whether the document was inspired by conversos or not is obviously irrelevant. The important thing was that serious abuses had crept into the practice of the Inquisition, and that a concern for justice demanded some reform.

Had the instructions ever been approved, a totally different tribunal would have come into existence. The burden of secrecy would have been completely lifted, and opportunities for abuses would have correspondingly diminished. Happily for those who supported the Inquisition, the new Inquisitor General appointed by Charles on the death of Cisneros, Cardinal Adrian of Utrecht, Bishop of Tortosa, firmly opposed any innovation. Shortly after this, early in July 1518, Sauvage died. With him collapsed any hope of fundamental alterations in the structure of the Inquisition. Adrian, who as a

Netherlander appears not to have had any close knowledge of Spanish problems, even reversed some of the reforms of Cisneros, by reappointing Calcena to a post of authority as secretary to the Suprema.

Meanwhile Charles had gone to Aragon, where he accepted the allegiance of the kingdom in the Cortes which opened at Saragossa in May 1518. Surprisingly, when these Cortes offered to advance him a large sum of money in exchange for Charles' agreement to a list of thirty-one articles which were substantially the same as those drawn up by Sauvage, the king agreed. It soon became clear that he had no intention of observing the agreement, for a subsequent message to the Spanish ambassador in Rome asked him to secure from the pope revocation of the articles and a dispensation from his oath to observe them. However, the Cortes had already taken the step of having Charles' signature to the articles authenticated by Juan Prat, the notary of the Cortes. All the relevant papers were then sent to Rome in the hands of Diego de las Casas, a converso from Seville. After the dissolution of the Cortes in January 1519, the Inquisition stepped in to arrest Prat on the charge of having falsified the articles drawn up at the Cortes. The accusation was obviously false, but both ecclesiastical and secular authorities in Castile acted as though it were true. The new chancellor, Mercurino Gattinara, urgently drew up papers which he sent to Rome in April, claiming that these were genuine and that the official copy was a forgery. By now a serious constitutional quarrel had arisen inside Aragon, and the deputies and nobility of the realm, meeting in conference in May, sent a request to Charles for the release of Prat, threatening not to grant any money until their demands were met. They summoned the Cortes and refused to disperse until justice had been done.

At this stage Pope Leo x intervened in favour of the Aragonese. In July 1519 he issued three briefs, one to Charles, one to the Inquisitor General and one to the tribunal of Saragossa, reducing the powers of the Inquisition to the bounds of ordinary canon law and revoking all special privileges granted by his predecessors. Charles and his officials refused to allow the publication of the briefs in Spain, and instead a firm protest was sent to Rome. The pope now shifted his position and suspended the briefs without revoking them. At this the Aragonese immediately discontinued payment of any grants to the crown. Finally, in December 1520 the pope confirmed the concordia of 1518, but in terms which did not specify whether it was Prat's or Gattinara's version that was the correct one. A compromise was eventually reached in 1521, when Cardinal Adrian accepted the Aragonese version for the time being, and released Prat. The victory of the Aragonese was an unsubstantial one. The Inquisition at no time afterwards admitted the validity of the concordias of 1512 and 1518, so that the struggles of these years were after all in vain.

At the Castilian Cortes of Coruña in 1520, the requests made at Valladolid for a reform in the procedure of the Inquisition were repeated, but to no avail. Later that same year, while Charles was away in Flanders, another plan for reform was presented to him, but this and subsequent proposals were in vain. On his return to Spain, a Cortes was held at Valladolid in 1523. Again the old suggestions for reform were brought up, fortified by a request that the salaries of inquisitors should be paid by the crown and not be drawn from confiscations. Failure was again the result. In 1525 the Cortes which met at Toledo complained of abuses committed by both inquisitors and familiars, but they achieved nothing beyond a promise that wrongs would be righted if they really existed. In 1526 in Granada the king was presented with a memorial demonstrating the evils of the secret procedure of the Inquisition, and asking for prisoners to be kept in public gaols instead of the secret cells of the tribunal.[31] To this there is no recorded reply. Almost annually such requests had been presented to the crown, and as regularly refused. Quite obviously a persistent stream of opposition was in continuous existence, dedicated not so much to the suppression of the Inquisition as to the cure of abuses. Against a stubborn Charles, however, no impact could be made. In April 1520 the king observed to a correspondent that 'in the Cortes of Aragon and Catalonia the Holy Office has been criticized and attacked by some people who do not care much for its preservation'.[32] The reference to Aragon should not divert us from the fact that, as we have seen, criticism had been raised just as frequently in the realm of Castile. Throughout Spain, then, the organs of constitutional government became the last channels of protest available to opponents of the Holy Office.

From 1519 to 1521 the energies of the peninsula were occupied in the famous revolt of the Comuneros, a confusing and complex struggle waged partly by town oligarchies against the royal authorities who had the support of the nobility, and partly by rival factions against each other in the great cities. Inevitably some conversos, with their known activity in many municipalities, could be found on the rebel side: among the leading Comuneros were a Coronel in Segovia, a Zapata in Toledo, a Tovar in Valladolid. Rumour, seasoned in part with malice, tended to exaggerate their role, however. The Constable of Castile informed Charles v in 1521 that the 'root cause of the uprising in these realms has been the conversos'; and after the rebel defeat at Villalar on 23 April 1521, according to the emperor's jester, 'many dead were found without foreskins'.[33] A generation later the Archbishop of Toledo, Siliceo, could claim that 'it is common knowledge in Spain that the Comunidades were incited by descendants of Jews'. In practice there seems to have been no significant identification of the converso cause with that of the Comuneros, and many known conversos fought on the royalist side. It is certain that some rebels hoped to modify or abolish the Inquisition: the Admiral of Castile claimed early in 1521 that 'the Comuneros say there will be no Inquisition', and hostility to the tribunal is recorded in various parts of the realm. But the Junta that headed the Comunidad was scrupulously careful to cause no offence to the Holy Office, and not a single reference to the Inquisition occurs among the demands made to the government.[34] The tribunal survived this critical period with its functions intact: indeed in Valencia, where a parallel revolt of Germanías (brotherhoods) was taking place, its functions were reinforced by the compulsory mass baptisms carried out on the Mudejars by the rebels.

In the years after the Comunidades, objections to the activities of the Inquisition continued to be made in both Castile and Aragon. A typical example is the memorial drawn up on 5 August 1533 and read to Charles at the Aragonese Cortes in Monzón.[35] The sixteen articles included complaints that 'some inquisitors of the Holy Office, in the voice and name of the Inquisition, have arrested and imprisoned people for private offences in no way touching the Holy Office'; that inquisitors were taking part in secular business; that they had extended their jurisdiction illegitimately by prosecuting cases of sodomy, usury and bigamy – questions which had nothing to do with heresy; that the inquisitors of Aragon, Catalonia and Valencia had an excessive number of familiars, whose identity was kept concealed, thus provoking numerous abuses. As for the Moors, said the protest, addressing itself to the Inquisitor General, 'Your Reverence knows well the way in which they were "converted", and the little or no teaching or instruction in our Holy Catholic

Faith which has been given them, and the lack of churches in the places where they live. Yet despite this lack of teaching and instruction, they are being proceeded against as heretics.' Worse still, the Inquisition was illegitimately seizing the land they had confiscated from the Moorish converts. To all these complaints Alonso Manrique, the Inquisitor General, gave a firm, negative reply. The protests were shelved.

Complaints along these lines were to play an important part in future controversies over the Inquisition. Inquisitorial jurisdiction in moral matters, for instance, was considered then, as later, a wrongful extension of its powers. But sweeping appeals like the protest of 1533 were growing fewer as the position of the Holy Office became stronger. Not only did the existence of the Inquisition become almost wholly unquestioned, but toleration of its attendant abuses became more widespread and pronounced. As papal and royal favour confirmed it in its position as one of the key institutions of the realm, it grew to overwhelm all opposition and criticism.

By the mid-sixteenth century the tribunal was invulnerable. In part this had happened because of the implicit support of the Old Christian majority, who had tolerated two decades of blood-letting directed against the conversos because it suited their own interests and who, too late, attempted to restrain the Inquisition when it appeared to be working against them. By then, in the new social atmosphere of the 'closed' society, the Holy Office had become essential to the maintenance of established attitudes. In part, also, the Inquisition survived because of the unswerving support of the crown, which could ill afford to lose so useful an institution. Like Ferdinand before him, Charles v was wholly dedicated to it, and introduced a similar tribunal into the Netherlands in 1520. When the Aragonese disputes over Juan Prat occurred in 1518, Charles informed the Cortes: 'you can be sure that we would rather agree to lose part of our realms and states than permit anything to be done therein against the honour of God and against the authority of the Holy Office'.[36] During the Comunidades, Charles exhorted his viceroys in Spain to resist any attack on the Inquisition.[37] In subsequent years, therefore, the monarchy had at its disposal a unique institution upon which it could call in case of need. This continued to have repercussions in the crown of Aragon, where the activities of the tribunal were always regarded as unconstitutional.[38]

Popular – as against political – resistance to the Inquisition is difficult to assess. In a recent analysis (see below, p. 185) of prosecutions by the Holy Office, it would appear that during the sixteenth century about a tenth of the people arrested were guilty of verbal or physical hostility to the tribunal, with the rate falling to about half that level in the seventeenth century. Not only was the Inquisition very concerned to protect its own authority but it was also quick to detect 'heresy' in hostile statements made about it: the result is that the archives contain thousands of examples of apparent 'opposition', ample material with which to prove the hostility of the Spanish people. A little reflection must show, however, that the excessive zeal of the Inquisition in taking note of every little expletive reported to it has helped to deform reality and may mislead us. 'I don't give a damn for God or for the Inquisition!' 'I care as much for the Inquisition as for the tail of my dog!' 'What Inquisition? I know of none!' 'I could take on the whole Inquisition!' 'The Inquisition exists only to rob people!' These are among the thousands of recorded oaths, yet they no more prove hostility to the Inquisition than the absence of oaths in the documentation during the late eighteenth century proves support for the Inquisition. There were certainly many individual examples of enmity to the tribunal, but very many others were little more than oaths uttered out of habit or when drunk or in moments of anger or stress. There are likewise hundreds of recorded cases of conflicts at a popular level with inquisitors, familiars and every aspect of the functioning of the Holy Office. The brawling and the swearing may demonstrate a lack of love and respect, but otherwise prove little more than that Spaniards have never inertly accepted the political or religious systems imposed on them. In *ancien régime* Spain, no popular movements ever attacked the Inquisition and no rioters ever laid a finger on its property.

Although Spaniards supported the Inquisition, they never accepted it unquestioningly. Conversos were normally hostile to it. In 1528 in Catalonia the tribunal arrested a man for distributing a manuscript which accused the Inquisition of lies, perjury, murder, robbery and raping women in prison; in 1567 in Badajoz the inquisitors seized a notice that had been posted up in public and stated that 'the property of every New Christian is at risk, six years from today not a single one will be left to arrest'.[39] Both documents were clearly converso in origin. Old Christians also had their grievances, especially in rural areas where they resented the prying and spying of inquisitors from the city. In sixteenth-century Galicia, a parish priest begged his congregation to be deaf and dumb when the inquisitors visited: 'let us be very careful tomorrow', he said, 'when the inquisitor comes here. For the love of God, don't go telling things about each other or meddle in things touching the Holy Office.'[40] In seventeenth-century Catalonia the parish priest of Aiguaviva publicly rebuked the commissaries of the Inquisition when they came to check the baptismal records in order to carry out a proof of limpieza: 'he told them not to write lies, and that it would not be the first time they had done so, by falsifying signatures and other things'.[41]

The Inquisition was not the imposition of a sinister tyranny on an unwilling people. It was an institution brought into being by a particular socio-religious situation, impelled and inspired by a decisively Old Christian ideology, and controlled by men whose outlook reflected the mentality of the mass of Spaniards. The dissenters were a few intellectuals, and others whose blood alone was sufficient to put them outside the pale of the new society being erected on a basis of triumphant and militant conservatism.

5

'Silence has been imposed'

> It was a sad state when virtuous men, because of their great achievements, had to undergo hostility, accusations and injuries from those who should have been their defenders.
>
> Juan de Mariana S.J., *Pro Editione Vulgata*

'We live in such difficult times that it is dangerous either to speak or be silent', protested the great Spanish humanist Juan Luis Vives to Erasmus in 1534.[1] The ill wind of controversy was tearing down all the hopes of liberals in Europe, and Christian humanism was being forced to choose between an old world it disliked and a new one it mistrusted. Those who were not wise enough to conform went to the wall. In writing to Erasmus, Vives was only informing him of what the former knew was bound to happen. That year the English statesman and saint, Sir Thomas More, was taken into custody for denying royal supremacy over the Church; while the hope of humanists in Spain, Doctor Juan de Vergara, was condemned to confinement in the cells of the Inquisition. The problem faced by these two men was a European one, intimately related to the political and religious issues that had been provoked by the revolt of Martin Luther. It was the reaction to this revolt, in Spain as in other countries, that led to a narrowing of intellectual frontiers until little room remained for the humanists and Spain withdrew into the confines of the 'closed' society.

Yet the reaction had been preceded by a dawn full of promise. At the beginning of the sixteenth century the great centres of humanism were in Italy and in northern Europe, where the name of Erasmus held sway. In 1509 a talented Renaissance prince ascended the throne of England, and Erasmus greeted in him the beginning of triumphs for the New Learning. The Spanish peninsula was no less open to all that was best and learned in Europe. Native genius mingled with imported erudition to produce the beginnings of a cultural Renaissance. The wellsprings of this new learning were in Italy. It was there that the young Andalucian Antonio de Nebrija went in 1463 to complete his university education at Bologna, returning twelve years later to the halls of his own Salamanca, from which he was subsequently transferred to become the brightest luminary of Cisneros' new university at Alcalá de Henares. And it was from Italy that Peter Martyr of Anghiera came in 1488 to educate the young nobles of Spain, preceded four years before by Lucio Marineo Siculo, who joined the ranks of the illustrious professors at Salamanca. The learning they promoted was diffused throughout the realm by the introduction of the printing press, which was to be found in most of the major cities by the 1480s. By 1501 over eight hundred titles had been published in Spain. In 1480 all duties on the import of books were removed.

The triumphs of Spanish humanism were inevitably exaggerated by contemporaries. No more than a fraction of the elite (notable among them the grandee Mendoza family) were active patrons of the arts, and only a restricted number of clergy and scholars were devoted to classical studies. Few advances were made in education or literacy, and the popular tradition in literature (represented for example by the *Celestina* of 1499) was still predominant. The Florentine ambassador Guicciardini took a sardonic Italian view in 1512 when he observed that the Spaniards 'are not interested in letters, and one finds very little knowledge either among the nobility or in other classes, and few people know Latin'. Regular contact with the Netherlands and Italy, however, had by the turn of the century accustomed Spaniards to the art and spirituality of the north and the literature of the Renaissance. The accession of Charles v in 1516 committed Spain still further to cultural interchange.

A key figure in the advancement of learning was Cisneros, Archbishop of Toledo from 1495 and Inquisitor General from 1507. Renowned for the holiness of his life and the severity of his discipline, he began reforming the religious orders in the Church and upheld the norms of conduct in the Holy Office. His outstanding cultural achievement was the University of Alcalá, which became the centre of humanist studies in Spain. Its first chancellor, Pedro de Lerma, had studied at Paris. Nebrija was, as Erasmus wrote to Luis Vives in 1521, its 'principal ornament'. Among its brilliant professors were the converso brothers Juan and Francisco de

Vergara, the latter of whom was described by Marineo Siculo as the greatest classical scholar in Spain. The breadth of the university syllabus, particularly in its faculty of theology, set it apart from the other centres of learning in Spain, and very soon its popularity rivalled that of Salamanca. Over and above this was the task which Cisneros set the professors of the university – to produce a critical edition of the Bible which would remain a classic of contemporary scholarship. The great Polyglot Bible which resulted from this enterprise consisted of six volumes, with the Hebrew, Chaldean and Greek originals of the Bible printed in columns parallel to the Latin Vulgate. The Complutensian (from Compluto, the Latin for Alcalá) Polyglot was finally published in 1522.[2]

Meanwhile the influence of Desiderius Erasmus, dominant in European humanism, began to penetrate the open frontiers of Spain. In 1516 the name of Erasmus was first traced by a Spanish pen, and in 1517 Cardinal Cisneros unsuccessfully invited the famous Dutch scholar to come to Spain. By 1524 a number of intellectuals in the peninsula had rallied to the doctrines of Erasmus, to whom Vives wrote in June 1524, 'Our Spaniards are also interesting themselves in your works.' The wit and satire directed by Erasmus against ecclesiastical abuses, and particularly against lax standards in the mendicant orders, found a ready hearing in a country where the highest Church officials had themselves led the movement in favour of reform. The presence of prominent intellectuals and literary men in the entourage of Charles v ensured protection for Erasmian doctrines at the court. Finally, the two principal prelates in the Church – the Archbishop of Toledo, Alonso de Fonseca, successor to Cisneros, and Alonso Manrique, the Inquisitor General – were enthusiastic followers of Erasmus. The triumph of Erasmianism was confirmed with the translation of Erasmus' *Enchiridion*, undertaken in 1524 by Alonso Fernández, Archdeacon of Alcor. Published towards the end of 1526, it was greeted by immediate and widespread enthusiasm in the peninsula. As the translator himself wrote to Erasmus in 1527:

At the Emperor's court, in the cities, in the churches, in the convents, even in the inns and on the highways, everyone has the *Enchiridion* of Erasmus in Spanish. Till then it had been read in Latin by a minority of Latinists, and even these did not fully understand it. Now it is read in Spanish by people of every sort, and those who had formerly never heard of Erasmus have learned of his existence through this single book.[3]

The publisher of the *Enchiridion*, Miguel de Eguia, was printer to the University of Alcalá and brought out some hundred books of humanist orientation. Erasmus remained by far the best seller, and was informed in 1526 that 'though the printers have produced many thousands of copies, they cannot satisfy the multitude of buyers'. There were also many personal contacts between friends of the humanist who came to Spain and Spaniards who went north to see him. Among the latter the most significant was young Juan de Vergara, who left the peninsula with the emperor in 1520 and spent two years with Erasmus in the Netherlands. On his return, starry-eyed, he wrote to Vives: 'The admiration felt for Erasmus by all Spaniards is astonishing.' This was not quite true. Several Spanish scholars were critical of the northerner's methods of exegesis; others were uneasy at similarities between Erasmus and Luther. Some of the mendicant orders in particular were smarting under the satirical attacks of Erasmus, and pressed for a debate on his heresies. A conference presided over by the Erasmian Inquisitor General Manrique, and including some thirty voting representatives of the orders, eventually met at Valladolid in the summer of 1527.[4] The deliberations were inconclusive, with half the representatives coming out in favour of the Dutchman. The failure of the attack appeared as a victory for the humanists. On 13 December Charles V himself wrote to Erasmus, asking him not to worry over controversy in Spain:

> as though, so long as we are here, one could make a decision contrary to Erasmus, whose Christian piety is well known to us. ... Take courage and be assured that we shall always hold your honour and repute in the greatest esteem.[5]

With the crown, the Inquisition, and the Spanish Church on his side, Erasmus' position was impregnable in Spain, where he enjoyed a popularity greater than in any other country in Europe. This promising start to what might have been a great cultural epoch was shattered by two distinct developments within Spain – the growth of illuminism and the discovery of Protestants – and by the limitations imposed throughout Europe on free thought by political events.

The spiritual and devotional movements in Castile in the late fifteenth century were warmly patronized by Cisneros, and produced a literature of which the most outstanding example was the *Spiritual ABC* (1527) of the Franciscan friar Francisco de Osuna.

Adepts of the Franciscan school believed in a mystical method known as *recogimiento*, the 'gathering up' of the soul to God; those who practised it were *recogidos*.[6] Out of this mystical school, however, there grew up a version (condemned by the general chapter of the Franciscans in 1524) emphasizing the passive union of the soul with God; the method was known as *dejamiento* (abandonment), and adepts were called *dejados* or *alumbrados* (illuminists). Mystical movements and the search for a purer interior religion were common coin in Europe at this time, and in Spain there was powerful patronage of mystics by the great nobility. One alumbrado group was patronized by the Mendoza Duke of Infantado in his palace at Guadalajara: it consisted of the *beata*[7] Isabel de la Cruz, Pedro Ruiz de Alcáraz, and Maria de Cazalla and her Franciscan brother Juan, auxiliary Bishop of Avila. Alcáraz was also connected with another group at Escalona, patronized by the Marquis of Villena. Meanwhile a parallel group of mystics emerged in Valladolid: the chief influence here was the beata Francisca Hernández, whose fame as a holy woman attracted into her circle Bernardino Tovar, a brother of Juan de Vergara, and the Franciscan preacher Francisco Ortiz.

In 1519 Isabel de la Cruz was denounced to the Inquisition by a servant-girl of the Mendozas. There had been fusses before about other beatas – the beata of Piedrahita (1512) was a famous example – and little may have come of this denunciation. But investigations happened to coincide with the appearance of the Lutheran scare, and the inquisitors quickly realized that elements of heresy were involved. One by one, in a slow and patient enquiry that stretched over several years, the illuminist leaders were detained on the orders of Inquisitor General Manrique. Isabel and Alcáraz were arrested in April 1524. On 23 September 1525 Manrique issued an 'edict on the alumbrados', a list of forty-eight propositions which gives a valuable summary of their doctrine and leaves little doubt that their beliefs were indeed heretical.[8] Isabel and Alcáraz were sentenced to appear in an auto de fe at Toledo on 22 July 1529. The attention of the inquisitors now shifted to Valladolid, where Francisca Hernández had gathered around her a group of adepts who practised *recogimiento* in opposition to the method of the Guadalajara mystics. Her most devoted admirer was the well-known Franciscan preacher Francisco Ortiz,[9] and she lived for a while with the rich Cazalla family, relatives of María de Cazalla. Her fame spread: great lords and clergy visited her, and Erasmians such as Eguía and

Tovar frequented the house. Her imperious character brooked no rivalry, however, and she quarrelled first with the Cazallas, then with the Erasmians. When she was arrested by the Inquisition in March 1529, the indignant Francisco Ortiz went into his pulpit and denounced the Inquisition for its 'public and open' sin in detaining her, but was himself immediately arrested and sentenced to reclusion in a monastery.

The year 1529 proved to be a turning point. In August the Erasmian Manrique was disgraced and confined to his see of Seville. At the same time the protecting hand of the emperor was withdrawn: Charles left in July for Italy and took with him some of the most influential Erasmians. This made it possible for the conservatives, who had been biding their time after the defeat at Valladolid, to take the offensive. One of their first victims was an hidalgo of Old Christian origin, Diego de Uceda, chamberlain to a high official in the Order of Calatrava. A deeply religious Catholic, Uceda was also an Erasmian who shared the Dutchman's scepticism about superstitions and miracles. Journeying in February 1528 from Burgos to his native city of Córdoba, he fell in with a travelling companion to whom he talked too earnestly and freely about religion, particularly about Luther. He was denounced to the Inquisition by his companion, arrested, tortured, and condemned despite all the evidence that he was blameless in his religious beliefs and practices. He finally abjured his 'errors' at the Toledo auto de fe of 22 July 1529.[10]

The mingling of mystical, Erasmian and heretical influences made the 1520s a unique period of both freedom and tension. The inquisitors sought Lutheran ideas everywhere, and located them in the views of some of the alumbrados. More significant for them, perhaps, was the fact that nearly every person implicated in the groups of these years was a converso: Isabel, Alcáraz, Hernández, Ortiz, Tovar, the Cazallas. It was as though conversos were seeking to reject formal Catholicism by interiorizing their religion. The tendency had a long history among the conversos. At home neither in Judaism nor in Christianity, many of them at all social levels had demonstrated signs of scepticism, unease and Nicodemism. There was a well-known case at the court of King Juan II of Castile (d. 1454), of the converso Alfonso Fernández Samuel, who in his will had requested that when laid out in his coffin, he should have the cross placed at his feet, the Koran at his breast, and the Torah, 'his life and light', at his head.[11] In the early years of the Inquisition, considerable evidence came to light not simply of judaizing but also of messianism on one hand and irreligious scepticism on the other; many conversos, indeed, were ironically condemned for beliefs that orthodox Judaism would have regarded as heretical, such as denying the immortality of the soul.[12] Dissent among the conversos did not, therefore, necessarily imply any drift towards Judaism. There was nothing remotely Jewish about the beliefs of the alumbrados: the root influence was Franciscan spirituality, the environment was the comfortable patronage afforded by Old Christian nobility.[13]

From the moment she was detained, Hernández attempted to save her skin by incriminating all those against whom she bore a grudge. Tovar had persisted in following her despite the warnings of Vergara. It was no doubt knowledge of Juan de Vergara's hostility that moved Hernández, at her trial in 1530, to denounce him as a Lutheran, a claim which was supported by other disciples of hers. Tovar was already in prison. He was followed there by his brother on 24 June 1530. Finally in April 1532 María de Cazalla was imprisoned and tortured and accused of the various heresies of Lutheranism, illuminism and Erasmianism.[14] Her trial dragged on until December 1534, when she was fined and ordered not to associate again with illuminists. Her brother the bishop had opportunely died in 1530. The Inquisition had not yet finished with their family, however, for from them sprang the circle of Protestants which alarmed Valladolid two decades later. Although the circle had closed round the mystics, they emerged comparatively unscathed: Hernández was by 1532 living in freedom in Medina del Campo; Isabel and Alcáraz, though condemned to perpetual prison, were released after a few years;[15] María de Cazalla was absolved for lack of evidence.

The attack on the alumbrados, though of short duration and with few serious casualties, had consequences of lasting importance. This can be seen clearly in the case of the famous preacher St Juan de Avila. Active in the mission field in Andalucia in the late 1520s, Avila was denounced as an alumbrado and spent nearly a year (1532–3) in the cells of the Inquisition. He used his idle hours to think out the shape of a book of spiritual guidance, the *Audi, Filia*, which was not in fact presented for publication until 1556. An innocent victim of the alumbrado scare in the 1530s (Avila was a converso), in the 1550s he fell foul not only of the Protestant scare but also of an Inquisitor General, Valdés, who was suspicious of all mystical writings 'works of contemplation for artisans' wives' was how he saw them, according to Luis de Granada). Valdés banned the book in his 1559 Index, and Avila in despair burnt a large number of his manuscripts.[16] Though the *Audi, Filia* circulated in manuscript for several years, it was not until after its author's death in 1569 that the Inquisition allowed it to be published, at Toledo in 1574. A whole generation of spirituality – we shall come across the case of Luis de Granada – fell under suspicion because of the supposed danger from illuminism.[17]

The most direct threat, however, seemed to come from Lutheranism. An Old Christian, the Basque priest Juan López de Celaín, who had links with the alumbrados of Guadalajara, was arrested in 1528 and burnt as a Lutheran in July 1530.[18] Lutheranism was also one of the allegations made against Juan de Vergara.[19] This eminent humanist, secretary to Cisneros and later to his successor at Toledo, Alonso de Fonseca, was one of the foremost classical scholars in Spain. He had collaborated in the Polyglot Bible, had held the chair of philosophy at Alcalá, and had proposed offering the chair of rhetoric there to Vives. Arrested in 1530, tried and imprisoned, Vergara was obliged to abjure his errors in an auto at Toledo on 21 December 1535, and to pay a fine of 1,500 ducats. After this he was confined to a monastery, from which he emerged in 1537. Because of his eminence, he was one of the few victims of the Inquisition allowed, even after his disgrace, to resume his old position in society; and we encounter him once more in 1547 at the centre of the great controversy carried on at Toledo over the proposed statutes to exclude conversos from office in the cathedral.

Other arrests followed. Alonso de Virués, a Benedictine and preacher to Charles V, was the first of several eminent preachers of the emperor to be accused of heresy, presumably because of contacts that he, like Vergara, had made abroad. Arrested in 1533 and confined in prison by the Inquisition of Seville for four long years, he pleaded in vain that Erasmus had never been condemned as unorthodox. Finally in 1537 he was made to abjure his errors and condemned to confinement in a monastery for two years, and was banned from preaching for another year. Charles V, however, made strenuous efforts to save Virués, and in May 1538 obtained from the pope a bull annulling the sentence. Virués was restored to favour and appointed in 1542 as Bishop of the Canary Islands, where he died in 1545.

In 1530 Mateo Pascual, professor at the University of Alcalá and a leading Erasmian, was accused of doubting the doctrine of purgatory. He was tried by the Inquisition, sentenced to the confiscation of all his goods and retired abroad to Rome to end his days in peace.[20] Another outstanding victim, sometimes connected with the origins of Protestantism in Spain, was Juan de Valdés, also of the University of Alcalá, who in the fateful year 1529 published his theological study *Diálogo de Doctrina Christiana*, which was closely based on some of Luther's early writings. It was immediately attacked by the Inquisition despite the testimony of Vergara and others. The controversy over the book took so dangerous a turn that in 1530 Valdés fled to Italy, just in time to avoid the trial that was opened against him. His treatise was thereafter distinguished by its appearance in every Index of prohibited books issued by the Inquisition.[21]

A further casualty of the alumbrado trials was the printer to Alcalá University, Miguel de Eguía, denounced by Francisca Hernández for Lutheranism. He was imprisoned in 1531 and spent over two years in the cells of the Inquisition at Valladolid,[22] but was released at the end of 1533 and fully absolved. Less fortunate was Pedro de Lerma. Former chancellor of Alcalá University, former dean of the theological faculty at the Sorbonne, canon of Burgos cathedral, this eminent scholar fell under the influence of Erasmus and publicized this in his sermons. He was denounced to the Inquisition and imprisoned, and finally in 1537 was made to abjure publicly, in the towns where he had preached, eleven propositions he was accused of having taught. In shame and resentment the old man shook the dust of Spain off his feet and fled to Paris where he resumed his position as a dean of the faculty, dying there in August 1541. According to his nephew Francisco Encinas (famous in the history of European Protestantism as Dryander), people in Lerma's home city of Burgos were so afraid of the possible consequences of this event that those who had sent their sons to study abroad recalled them at once.[23] Such a reaction from those who were not directly concerned in the struggle now being waged against the Erasmians, shows that the broader issues at stake were being all too well understood by educated Spaniards. Erasmianism and the new humanism were being identified with the German heresy, and for some the only protection was dissociation.

The 1530s were, in a way, the end of the road. In December 1533 Rodrigo Manrique, son of the Inquisitor General, wrote bitterly from Paris to Luis Vives, on the subject of Vergara's imprisonment:

> You are right. Our country is a land of pride and envy; you may add: of barbarism. For now it is clear that down there one cannot possess any

culture without being suspected of heresy, error and Judaism. Thus silence has been imposed on the learned. As for those who take refuge in erudition, they have been filled, as you say, with great terror. ... At Alcalá they are trying to uproot the study of Greek completely.[24]

Faced by this wave of reaction, the mild goodwill of the humanists was powerless. Erasmus saw his friends in Spain being silenced one by one. His last surviving letter to that country is dated December 1533: beyond that lay silence. Three years later he died, still highly respected in the Catholic world, so much so that in 1535 the pope had offered him a cardinal's hat. But in Spain his cause was snuffed out, and the last hopes vanished with the death of Alonso Manrique in 1538.

The fall from favour of Erasmianism, and the suspicions directed against liberal humanism, seemed to be justified by the apparent links between Erasmus and the growing Protestant menace. Bataillon has shown how the Protestant stream which sprang from illuminism between 1535 and 1555 adapted Erasmianism to its own purposes and moved towards the doctrine of 'justification by faith alone' without ever formally rejecting Catholic dogma.[25] Many leading humanists, such as Juan de Valdés, were Erasmians whose defections from orthodoxy were so significant as to give cause for the belief that they were crypto-Protestants. Vigilance against radical Erasmianism was therefore strengthened. The Lutheran threat, however, took a long time to develop. As late as 1520 Luther had not been heard of in Spain, and the first Spaniards to come into contact with his teachings were those who accompanied the emperor to Germany: some of these, seeing in him only a reformer, were favourable to his ideas. By early 1521 Lutheran books, translated into Spanish by conversos in Antwerp, were entering Spain via the Flanders trade route. The first ban on them was issued by Cardinal Adrian of Utrecht, regent and Inquisitor General, on 7 April 1521. In view of the Comunero revolt, the political no less than the religious implications of Luther were taken seriously in Spain. Books continued to arrive at all the major ports in the peninsula, but the Inquisition was vigilant: a vessel seized at Pasajes had its hold full of books 'of writings by Luther and his followers'. In Burgos Bernardino Tovar was able to purchase Lutheran books imported from Flanders. By 1524, it was reported from the court, 'there is so much awareness of Luther that nothing else is talked about'.[26]

However, a full generation went by and Lutheranism failed to take root in Spain. In the period up to 1558 there were no more than thirty-nine cases of alleged Lutheranism among Spaniards arrested by the Inquisition,[27] and most of these were merely people who had made careless statements which savoured of Lutheranism. There was some curiosity about the heresies Luther was propounding, but no sign of any active interest. What explanation can we offer for this astonishing inability of Protestant ideas to penetrate the peninsula? With its unreformed Church, backward clergy and mediaevalistic religion, Spain was surely ripe for conquest by the Reformation. In one major respect, however, the country was peculiarly unfertile ground: unlike England, France and Germany, Spain had not since the early Middle Ages experienced a single significant popular heresy; all its ideological struggles since the Reconquest had been directed against the minority religions, Judaism and Islam. There were consequently no native heresies (like Wycliffism in England) on which the German ideas could build. Moreover, Spain was the only European country to possess a national institution dedicated to the elimination of heresy. By its vigilance and by co-ordinating its efforts throughout the peninsula, the Inquisition checked the seeds of heresy before they could be sown. In the 1540s, therefore, possibly the only Spaniards to come directly into contact with Lutheranism were those in foreign universities (at Louvain, for example, where Philip II was shocked by the views of some of the Spaniards in 1558; or in France, where Miguel Servet was educated); those accompanying the emperor's court in Germany; and those who, with the opening of the Council of Trent (1546), were obliged to read Lutheran books in order to combat the errors in them. The flow of books was impossible to stop completely ('from one hour to the next', the Inquisition commented in 1532, 'books keep arriving from Germany'), but strict vigilance seemed to have kept the contagion out.

The area most vulnerable to the penetration of foreign ideas was Seville, centre of international commerce. In 1552 alone, the Inquisition there seized some 450 Bibles printed abroad.[28] As Archbishop of Seville, Manrique encouraged the appointment of scholars from Alcalá as canons and preachers of the cathedral. One of these, Juan Gil or Egidio, was nominated by Charles V in 1549 as Bishop of Tortosa, but the appointment was quashed when Egidio was accused of heresy and in 1552 made to retract ten propositions; he died in peace in 1556.[29] Times were changing, both in Spain as a whole and in Seville: in 1546 the city obtained a new archbishop who was also made Inquisitor General, Fernando de Valdés, a ruthless careerist who saw heresy everywhere.[30] In 1556 Valdés objected to the appointment as cathedral preacher of Constantino Ponce de la Fuente, an Alcalá humanist and converso who was chaplain to Charles v in Germany between 1548 and 1555. His writings were examined for heresy; he was arrested by the Inquisition and died in its cells two years later. Neither Egidio nor Constantino can be considered Lutherans: they were humanists who believed in a strongly spiritual religious life and none of their views appears to have been explicitly heretical.[31] There were, however, active Protestants in Seville – a total of around 120 persons, including the prior and members of the Jeronimite monastery of San Isidro, together with several nuns from the Jeronimite convent of Santa Paula. The Seville group managed to exist in security until the 1550s, when some monks from San Isidro opportunely fled: the exiles included Cipriano de Valera, Cassiodoro de Reina,[32] Juan Pérez de Pineda and Antonio del Corro, who played little part in Spanish history but were glories of the European Reformation.

Meanwhile, in northern Castile, another circle of Protestants had come into existence.[33] The founder was an Italian, Carlos de Seso, who had turned to Protestantism after reading Juan de Valdés, and who from 1554 had been *corregidor* (civil governor) of Toro. His missionary zeal soon converted an influential and distinguished circle centred on Valladolid and numbering some fifty-five persons, most of noble status and some with converso origins. The most eminent of the converts was Dr Agustín Cazalla, who had been to Germany as chaplain to Charles v and had also accompanied Philip there. Cazalla was influenced by his brother Pedro – parish priest of Pedrosa, near Valladolid – and with him the whole Cazalla family, led by their mother Leonor de Vivero,[34] fell into heresy. Their beliefs were no simple extension of the illuminist or Erasmian attitudes of the previous generation: in their clear rejection of most Catholic dogma the Valladolid heretics were true Protestants. They also included scions of impeccably Old Christian nobility. A leading member of the group, Fray Domingo de Rojas, son of the Marquis of Poza, recruited young Ana Enríquez, daughter of the Marquis of Alcanices: he told her 'that there were only two sacraments, baptism and communion; that in communion Christ did not have the part attributed to him; and that the worst of all things was to say mass, since Christ had already been sacrificed once and for all'.[35]

The Seville group was exposed in 1557, when Juan Ponce de

León, eldest son of the count of Bailén, was arrested together with others for introducing books from Geneva. His chief accomplice was Julián Hernández, who had spent a considerable time in the Reformed churches of Paris, Scotland and Frankfurt, and who specialized in smuggling Protestant literature into his native country.[36] The Inquisition collected information and in 1558 made a wave of arrests, including the whole Cazalla family in April and Constantino in August. A merciless repression was set in train by Fernando de Valdés, who may have been concerned to exaggerate the menace in order to regain the favour he had recently lost with the emperor. Commenting on the high social origins of many of the accused, Valdés told Charles v that 'much greater harm can follow if one treats them with the benignity that the Holy Office has shown towards Jewish and Mohammedan conversos, who generally have been of lowly origin'.

The emperor did not need to be alerted. The sudden emergence in Spain's two principal cities of a contagion from which everyone felt the country had been free,[37] sent shock waves through the nation. Charles v, in retirement at his villa beside the monastery of Yuste in Extremadura, saw to his horror the rise within Spain of the very menace that had split Germany apart. For him there could be only one response: ruthless suppression. His historic letter of 25 May 1558 to his daughter Juana, regent in Spain during Philip II's absence in the Netherlands, appealed to her to follow the tough policy that he himself had used against heresy in Flanders.

I am very satisfied with what you say you have written to the king informing him of what is happening about the people imprisoned as Lutherans, more of whom are being daily discovered. But believe me, my daughter, this business has caused and still causes me more anxiety and pain than I can express, for while the king and I were abroad these realms remained in perfect peace, free from this calamity, but now that I have returned here to rest and recuperate and serve Our Lord, this great outrage and treachery, implicating such notable persons, occurs in my presence and in yours. You know that because of this I suffered and went through great trials and expenses in Germany, and lost so much of my good health. Were it not for the conviction I have that you and the members of your Councils will find a radical cure to this unfortunate situation, punishing the guilty thoroughly to prevent them spreading, I do not know whether I could restrain myself leaving here to settle the matter. Since this affair is more important for the service of Our Lord and the good and preservation of these realms than any other, and since it is only in its beginnings, with such small forces that they can be easily put down, it is necessary to place the greatest stress and weight on a quick remedy and exemplary punishment. I do not know whether it will be enough in these cases to follow the usual practice, by which according to common law all those who beg for mercy and have their confession accepted are pardoned with a light penance if it is a first offence. Such people, if set free, are at liberty to commit the same offence, particularly if they are educated persons.

One can imagine the evil consequences, for it is clear that they cannot act without armed organization and leaders, and so it must be seen whether they can be proceeded against as creators of sedition, upheaval, riots and disturbance in the state; they would then be guilty of rebellion and could not expect any mercy. In this connection I cannot omit to mention what was and is the custom in Flanders. I wanted to introduce an Inquisition to punish the heresies that some people had caught from neighbouring Germany and England and even France. Everyone opposed this on the grounds that there were no Jews among them. Finally an order was issued declaring that all people of whatever state and condition who came under certain specified categories were to be *ipso facto* burnt and their goods confiscated. Necessity obliged me to act in this way. I do not know what the king my son has done since then, but I think that the same reason will have made him continue as I did, because I advised and begged him to be very severe in dealing with these people.

Believe me, my daughter, if so great an evil is not suppressed and remedied without distinction of persons from the very beginning, I cannot promise that the king or anyone else will be in a position to do it afterwards.[38]

This letter really marks the turning point in Spain. From now on, thanks to the fears of Charles and the policy which was laid down for the Inquisitor General Valdés, heterodoxy was treated as a threat to the State and the religious establishment. Writing to the pope on 9 September the same year, Valdés affirmed that 'these errors and heresies of Luther and his brood which have begun to be preached and sown in Spain, are in the way of sedition and riot.'[39]

Sedition and riot, armed organization and leaders – how far from the dreams of Cazalla and Constantino! Yet once again well-meaning men were prey to the tensions gripping Europe, and the result was a series of autos de fe which burnt out Protestantism in Spain. The first holocaust was held at Valladolid on Trinity Sunday, 29 May 1559. Of the thirty victims, fourteen were burnt, including Cazalla and his brother and sister. The only one to die unrepentant was the *licenciado* Francisco Herrero, from Toro. All the rest died repentant after professing conversion, among them Agustín Cazalla, who blessed the Holy Office and wept aloud for his sins. The next auto at Valladolid was held on 8 October in the presence of Philip II, who had now returned to Spain and for whom an impressive ceremony was mounted. Of the thirty accused, twenty-six were Protestants, and of these twelve (including four nuns) were burnt at the stake. Carlos de Seso was the showpiece. The inquisitors had for days attempted to make him recant and, in fear for his life, he had shown every sign of repentance; but when at last he realized that he was to be executed regardless, he made a full and moving statement of belief: 'in Jesus Christ alone do I hope, him alone I trust and adore, and placing my unworthy hand in his sacred side I go through the virtue of his blood to enjoy the promises that he has made to his chosen'.[40] He and one other accused were burnt alive as impenitents. 'How could you allow this to happen?', the corregidor of Toro called out to the king during the auto. 'If my own son were as wicked as you', Philip replied indignantly, 'I myself would carry the wood with which to burn him!'

It was now the turn of Seville. The first great auto there was held on Sunday, 24 September 1559.[41] Of the seventy-six victims present, nineteen were burnt as Lutherans, one of them in effigy only.* This was followed by the auto held on Sunday, 22 December 1560.[42] Of the total of fifty-four victims on this occasion, fourteen were burnt in person and three in effigy; in all, forty of the victims were Protestants. Egidio and Constantino were two of those burnt in effigy, while those actually burnt included two English sailors, William Brook and Nicholas Burton, and a native of Seville, Leonor Gómez, together with her three young daughters. This auto de fe was followed by one two years later, on 26 April 1562, and by another on 28 October: the whole of that year saw eighty-eight cases of Protestantism punished, including eighteen who were burnt in person, prominent among the latter being the prior of San Isidro and four of his priests.

With these burnings, as we know by hindsight, native Protestantism was almost totally extinguished in Spain. For contemporaries in 1559, however, it was the start to an emergency without precedent in Spanish history. That very August the primate of the Spanish Church, Archbishop Carranza of Toledo, was arrested by the Inquisition on charges arising in part out of allegations made by Cazalla and Seso.[43] Threatened, as it seemed, by the incursions

---

* Dead and absent victims were represented at autos by figures or effigies which were burnt in their stead: hence the need to talk of others being burnt in person.

of heresy, the inquisitors stretched their resources to check the contagion wherever it might appear. In Toledo in September 1559 placards were found posted up on houses and in the cathedral itself, attacking the Catholic Church as 'not the Church of Jesus Christ but the Church of the devil and of Antichrist his son, the Antichrist pope'.[44] The culprit, apprehended in 1560 and burnt, was a priest, Sebastián Martinez. The great autos de fe up to 1562 served to remind the population of the gravity of the crisis and taught them to try and identify Lutherans in their midst. As a consequence the tribunals of the Inquisition in the 1560s devoted themselves to a hunt for Lutheran heresy, and drew into their net scores of Spaniards who in an unguarded moment had made statements praising Luther or attacking the clergy.[45]

The real brunt of the attack on Lutheranism, however, was borne by foreign visitors to Spain, such as traders and sailors. The heresy scare intensified xenophobia among all sections of the population, and made Spain unsafe for foreigners for the best part of a century. In Barcelona the inquisitor in 1560 felt it opportune to hold an auto de fe 'so that people are on their guard against foreigners'.[46] Foreigners indeed constituted the bulk of prosecutions in these years, especially in frontier tribunals.[47] In Barcelona between 1552 and 1578 there were fifty-one alleged Lutherans burnt in person or in effigy, but all were foreign. Nearly all the cases arising at Valencia from 1554 to 1598 involved foreigners, eight of whom were burnt in person or in effigy. In the tribunal of Calahorra (later transferred to Logroño), though there were as many as sixty-eight cases of suspected Lutheranism in 1540–99, the majority of those, 82 per cent, were foreigners.

Protestantism, in part because of the stringent measures taken against it after 1559, never developed into a real threat in Spain. The total number of Spaniards tried by the Inquisition for suspected 'Lutheranism' in the late sixteenth century was about two hundred, but most of these were in no sense Protestants. There were of course a few convinced heretics to be found – among them Gaspar de Centelles, burnt in Valencia in 1564,[48] and Fray Cristóbal de Morales, burnt in Granada in 1571 – but less than a dozen Spaniards were burnt alive for Lutheranism in the later part of the century outside the cases tried at Valladolid and Seville. The Reformation passed Spain by, but continued nevertheless to modify profoundly the sequence of events in the peninsula.

European heresy was too enormous a threat to be ignored; crown and Church therefore combined to preserve Spain from contamination. The harsh policy begun by Charles v, who died in September 1558, was continued by his son. After his return to the Peninsula in 1559, Philip issued an order on 22 November to all Spaniards studying or teaching abroad to return within four months. The exceptions to this were those at particular named colleges at Bologna, Rome, Naples and Coimbra: no Spaniards were in future to be allowed abroad to study except at these. At home a strict check was imposed by the Inquisition on any divergence from orthodoxy in the universities. This was carried out in two main ways: by censorship of all books used for reading and study, and by disciplinary action against rashly outspoken professors. Bishops were encouraged to inspect all libraries in their dioceses, and at Salamanca University a score of the staff went carefully through the library to weed out any dangerous books.

The breaking off of academic contact with other countries (certainly motivated, on Philip's part, by his horror at the novelties which the Spanish students at Louvain were imbibing) was never intended to be total, but its impact was soon felt. Of 228 Spanish scientific authors who flourished in the early sixteenth century, some 11 per cent had been professors in foreign universities and 25 per cent had studied abroad; after 1560 the proportion was negligible. At Montpellier, famous for its medical studies, 310 Spaniards (mostly Aragonese) studied between 1503 and 1558; up to 1565 fourteen more registered; after 1573 no further Spaniards attended.[49] Spain was saved for Catholicism. Erasmianism was extirpated and Protestantism in the peninsula was strangled at birth; the question, still hotly debated, is whether in the process damage was not done to the nation and its culture.

The most effective protection that the government could give to its people was to erect a *cordon sanitaire* of censorship round the country. The first major casualty of this move was Erasmus. The earliest official Index of forbidden books issued in Spain in 1551 included the *Colloquies* of Erasmus. This list was simply a reissue of an Index drawn up by the University of Louvain in the Netherlands. While Louvain was debating whether to condemn Erasmus more fully, the Roman Inquisition under Paul IV came out in 1559 with a general condemnation of all the works of Erasmus. The Jesuits protested strongly against this measure, among the most vociferous being the Dutchman St Peter Canisius. Diego Laínez for his part said openly to the pope that the Index was something 'which re-

stricted many spirits and pleased few, particularly outside Italy'.[50]
The enlightened opposition of the Jesuits to any restriction on liberal
writers came to nothing. The Index of prohibited books issued by
the Spanish Inquisition in 1559 listed sixteen works by Erasmus,
including the *Enchiridion*. Spain was following the lead of Rome.
From this time the name of Erasmus was slowly and methodically
obliterated from the memory of Spain. The Spanish Index of 1612
banned completely all works of Erasmus in Spanish, and classifed
the author in the category of *auctores damnati*. When the famous
theologian Martin de Azpilcueta quoted at about this time from the
works of Erasmus, he cited the author as *quidam*, 'someone': so
completely did the greatest humanist of the century become an
'unperson' in Spain. Knowledge of his writings did not fade so
quickly. It remained in the stream of thought that stretched as far
as Cervantes, but when individuals cited the forgotten name (it was
Francisco Sánchez who in 1595 declared in a lecture, 'Whoever
speaks ill of Erasmus is either a friar or an ass!') they were called to
answer before the Inquisition.

Controls over printing dated back to Ferdinand and Isabella, who
on 8 July 1502 issued a pragmatic by which licences were made
obligatory for the printing of books inside Spain as well as for the
introduction of foreign books. Within Spain, licences could be
granted only by the presidents of the *Chancillerías* (high courts) of
Valladolid and Granada, and by the prelates of Toledo, Seville, Granada, Burgos and Salamanca. There were no existing guides to heretical books, so the Inquisition had to rely at first on foreign direc-
tion. It was a papal order that provoked the first ban on Lutheran
books in Spain, issued by Cardinal Adrian of Utrecht on 7 April
1521 in his capacity as Inquisitor General. Thereafter prohibitions
of individual books were notified through letters (*cartas acordadas*)
sent to the tribunals, and from 1540 regular lists of banned works
were issued by the Holy Office. The first printed Index to be used in
Spain, issued by Inquisitor General Valdés in September 1551, was
no more than a reprint of the Index compiled by the University of
Louvain in 1550, with a special appendix devoted to Spanish
books.[51] Steps were taken to have the Index distributed by the
tribunals.[52] Each tribunal was allowed to modify its local version,
so we know of at least five Indices issued in 1551–2, by the tribunals of Toledo, Valladolid, Valencia, Granada and Seville.[53] Looking
back to the ban on Lutheran books in 1521, we can see in the
1551 Index the fruits of thirty years of censorship: the works of

sixteen authors, mainly the leaders of the Reformation, were condemned in their entirety; but for the rest the Inquisition was content
to ban some 61 works individually, and lay down regulations about
Bibles, books in Hebrew and Arabic, and works printed without
authorization.

Censorship up to the 1550s may be considered moderate. It
changed, however, with the ferocious decree issued on 7 September
1558 by the regent Dona Juana.[54] This measure banned the introduction of all foreign books in Spanish translation, obliged printers
to seek licences from the Council of Castile (which in 1554 had
been granted control over such licences), and laid down a strict
procedure for the operation of censorship. Contravention of any
of these points would be punished by death and confiscation. At
the same time the Inquisition was allowed to issue licences when
printing for its own purpose, thus giving it perfect freedom and
full armament for the battle now under way. According to the
new rules, manuscripts were to be checked and censored both
before and after publication, and all booksellers were to keep by
them a copy of the Index of prohibited books. So thorough and
effective was the decree of 1558 that it remained in force in Spain
until the end of the *ancien régime*. The censorship organized by the
Inquisition existed side by side with this censorship of the State,
and was expressed mainly in the edition of Indices of heretical
works. Inquisitorial censorship graded the books on its Indices
according to the extent of their error: some authors had only a
few words or a few lines deleted from their books, others had all
their works condemned *in toto*. To help carry out the task of censorship many of Spain's most brilliant minds – among them Juan
de Mariana and Melchor Cano – were employed. Censors were
drawn mainly from the religious orders, with Dominicans playing a
major role.[55]

The harsh controls imposed in 1558 were supplemented in 1559
by the Index issued by Fernando de Valdés. In structure the Index
did not innovate, and followed the previous Louvain-based publication of 1551. Books were divided into sections according to language, and forbidden if they fell into the following categories: all
books by heresiarchs; all religious books written by those condemned by the Inquisition; all books on Jews and Moors with an
anti-Catholic bias; all heretical translations of the Bible; all vernacular translations of the Bible, even by Catholics; all devotional
works in the vernacular; all controversial works between Catholics

and heretics; all books on magic; all verse using Scriptural quotations 'profanely'; all books printed since 1515 without details of author and publisher; all anti-Catholic books; all pictures and figures disrespectful to religion.

The Spanish Index was controlled only by the Spanish authorities and had no connection with that of Rome, which also began in the sixteenth century to draw up its own list of prohibited books. While Spain often had on its list works which Rome had prohibited, there was no rule that one Index should follow the lead of the other, and several authors were astonished to find that Spain had forbidden books of theirs which circulated freely in Italy. Alternatively, Rome would ban books which circulated freely in Spain.[56] There was one other important difference between the two. The Roman Index was exclusively a prohibitory one: that is, it banned books without regard to the number of errors in it, and without specifying whether a book could be published if it were expurgated. The Spanish Index, on the other hand, both expurgated and prohibited books, so that some works could circulate if the relevant passages cited in the Index were excised. In this respect the Spanish system was more liberal. When the Indices clashed, reasons were invariably political, as in the case of the Italian Cardinal Baronio, who some years later, in 1594, complained that although the pope had sanctioned his writings there were moves to put him on the Spanish Index. Baronio was certainly not in favour in Spain, but the relevant work by him was banned only by the State and not by the Inquisition.[57]

The co-operation of Church and State in the legislation of 1558–9 should be stressed. The decree of September 1558 put control over all printing firmly in the hands of the State alone, thus confirming the monopoly exercised by the Council of Castile since 1554 and removing from the Inquisition the power that it had exercised in the 1530s to licence books. At the same time, however, the power to prohibit was effectively conceded to the Holy Office. No significant conflict appears to have occurred as a result of this division of powers. Quarrels over jurisdiction took place only at the local level, when inquisitors and secular officials intruded into each other's spheres'. With a free hand over censorship, Valdés launched his hurriedly prepared Index of 1559. He had already issued a general censure of Bibles and New Testaments in 1554, condemning sixty-seven editions of the Scriptures issued in Lyon, Antwerp, Paris and other places. There were at least two notable features of the Index of August 1559. In the first place it greatly extended the list of prohibitions, adding in all 253 new book titles, fourteen editions of the Bible, nine of the New Testament, and fifty-four editions of books of hours. For the first time, Castilian literature was severely hit: in 1551 the Inquisition had only eleven Castilian works on its banned list, this was now inflated by eighty-eight new items. Among the authors now appearing were Gil Vicente, Hernando de Talavera, Bartolomé Torres Naharro, Juan del Encina, Garci Sánchez and Jorge Montemayor.[58] The *Lazarillo de Tormes* was banned and also the *Cancionero General*. Sixteen of Erasmus' works were prohibited, as well as notable works by Juan and Alfonso de Valdés, the *Catechism* of Archbishop Carranza, and Boccaccio in Spanish. The second notable aspect of the Index was its campaign against vernacular works of piety that savoured either of superstition or of illuminism: out of fifty-four books of hours condemned, for example, thirty-four were in Castilian. The most prominent casualties, however, were Juan de Avila's *Audi, Filia*, Luis de Granada's *Libro de la Oración* and St Francis Borja's *Obras del Christiano*.

Granada's *Libro de la Oración*, first published in 1554, became so popular in Spain that it went through twenty-three editions up to 1559 when it was put on the Index (principally at the instance of the famous theologian Melchor Cano, who had been among the first to smell heresy in the *Catechism* of the Archbishop of Toledo). It was in vain that Fray Luis tried to get the ban rescinded. Finding no help in Spain, he succeeded in getting the *Libro* approved by the Council of Trent and the pope. Such approval was not enough for the inquisitors, and it was only when he accepted 'corrections' in his text that the book was allowed to circulate freely.[59] The ban on Borja also emanated from Cano, an open enemy of the Jesuits. Because it was an international order, many in Spain were suspicious of the Company of Jesus; indeed, as a Jesuit from Valladolid wrote, some say 'that the Theatines (which is what they call us here in this Babel) have been the source of Luther's errors'. Valdés' Index fell like a thunderclap on the Company. Borja, Duke of Gandía and former viceroy of Catalonia, was the most distinguished recruit ever to join the society in Spain, and the ban on his work threatened to bring disrepute not only upon him but upon all the Jesuits. St Francis, fearing that he was about to be arrested by the Inquisition, left Spain for Rome in the spring of 1560 and never again returned to his homeland.[60] This was not the end of the travails of the Jesuits. The 1559 Index prohibited devotional works in the vernacular even if they were not printed (at that time many books used to circulate as manuscript copies). The worried rector of the Jesuit college in Seville went to the inquisitors to ask if the ban applied also to Loyola's *Spiritual Exercises*, which was used by the novices in manuscript translation and not published in Castilian until 1615. To his horror he was told that the prohibition did apply; he went back to the college, collected all the copies of the *Exercises*, handed them to the Inquisition, then took to his bed in grief and mortification.

The Index of 1559 has often been taken to represent the beginning of an epoch of repression in Spanish culture. This view needs to be weighed carefully. It was the first but also the only pre-1700 Index to attack notable works of Castilian poetry and literature, all of them antedating the mid-sixteenth century.[61] None of the authors concerned had a serious brush with the Inquisition on account of the work affected. Thereafter, no Index before the eighteenth century went any further in attacks on Spanish literature. Rather than opening a repressive phase, the 1559 Index seems in fact to have been the climax of a specific campaign – one that had begun in 1521 – to keep Spanish writing within the bounds of orthodoxy.

Subsequent Indices, therefore, started from a completely different perspective. The next Index was not issued for a quarter of a century, and in the interim the Inquisition proceeded by *cartas acordadas*, issuing some forty-three orders affecting a total of fifty books.[62] The single most important influence on Catholic thinking about censorship at this period was the Index of Prohibited Books issued by the Council of Trent in 1564. Its premises were accepted as authoritative by all the theologians and inquisitors who helped to prepare the next Spanish Index. Meanwhile Philip II had arranged for the Tridentine Index to be published in Flanders in 1570, and sponsored the preparation there by Benito Arias Montano, the distinguished Hebraist, of a special 'expurgatory' Index (1571), which excised passages from otherwise orthodox books and thus saved them from prohibition.

The Indices of 1564 and 1571 played a fundamental part in the elaboration of Spain's new Index, first discussed at a committee meeting in Salamanca in the latter year. Juan de Mariana apparently devoted considerable time to helping the compilers: 'I worked on it as much as anybody, and for a long time had four secretaries together helping me'.[63] The Index which emerged consisted of two huge volumes – one of prohibited books (1583), the other of expurgated (1584) – issued by the Inquisitor General Gaspar de

Quiroga. The numerical advance on the heretical authors listed by Valdés in 1559 was impressive. In all some six hundred new heretics (most taken from the 1564 and 1571 compilations) made their appearance and were totally prohibited. In addition a total of 682 new books were prohibited, over two-thirds of them in Latin, one-fifth in Dutch or German and one-twelfth in French.[64]

The scope of the 1583 Index was staggering. By its sheer size it drew into its ambit the whole of the European intellectual world, both past and present: editions of classical authors and of fathers of the Church, the collected works of Peter Abelard and of Rabelais, selected works by William of Ockham, Savonarola, Jean Bodin, Machiavelli, Juan Luis Vives, Marsiglio of Padua, Ariosto, Dante and Thomas More (whose *Utopia* was banned until expurgated, although the Index conceded that he was *vir alius pius et catholicus*) were among the casualties. At first glance it would appear that the Inquisition was declaring war against the whole of European culture. In reality the Quiroga Index was so different to the hasty, crude Index of Valdés that its character requires closer examination. The 1559 Louvain-based Index had listed some 670 prohibitions, of which just over a hundred items were in Castilian, and of these possibly about twenty were specifically works of literature. The Quiroga Index totalled five times as many prohibitions as those in the Valdés list, yet the number of Castilian works increased by barely thirty and of these none is readily identifiable as a work of literature. Though it is possible, then, to criticize the Valdés Index for its presumed harm to Spanish literature, the Quiroga Index did little to affect the literary or reading habits of Spaniards: the overwhelming bulk of books it prohibited were unknown to Spaniards and had never entered Spain. It is therefore misleading to regard the 1583 Index as directly repressive: it was a vast intellectual structure that did little to touch the daily reality of readers, students or booksellers.

Among the influences behind the Quiroga Index were Montano, Mariana, Jerónimo de Zurita and other intellectuals. All were zealous upholders of the Counter Reformation who saw in the machinery of censorship a golden opportunity not to repress freedom of learning but actively to *form* the culture of the society in which they lived. The vast borrowing of prohibitions from the Tridentine Index was their gesture to papal authority, but of more direct interest to them than the obvious struggle against heresy was the problem of educating Spaniards. A contemporary of theirs, the Toledo humanist and poet Alvar Gómez de Castro, has left a memoir on principles of censorship.[65] He divides harmful works into two categories; those in Latin and those in the vernacular. Harmful books in the first category may be kept by instructed persons, but should not be used in schools. Of those in the second category, some such as Boccaccio should be carefully expurgated. As for Spanish books in the second category, some are books of romance and chivalry, and 'since they are without imagination or learning and it is a waste of time to read them, it is better to prohibit them, except for the first four books of *Amadis*'. Others in this class are books on love, of which some, such as the *Celestina*, are serious and good, while others are of such poor quality that they should be banned. Also in this class are works of poetry, again including both good and bad: the bad should be expurgated or eliminated. The interesting criterion employed was obviously that of literary merit.

Mariana conceded in 1579 that otherwise excellent books by Borja and others should continue to be banned because of 'the evil times', and was even firmer than Gómez de Castro in his views on the educative role of books. Urging the inclusion in the Spanish rules for the Index of the Tridentine rule banning 'absolutely those books that narrate or teach lascivious and obscene things' (in fact his advice was not followed), Mariana also urged that 'in particular one should ban such books both in Latin and in Castilian, to wit *Celestina*, *Diana de Montemayor*, and books of chivalry, even if it were only to force people to read good books and genuine histories'. Mariana's full list of unworthy literature also included select works by Virgil, Ovid, Catullus, Propertius and other classical authors.[66] The fact that his suggestions were not fully incorporated into the Index is good evidence that he was by no means the dominant influence in its compilation. The scant attention, moreover, paid to Castilian literature in the Index, shows clearly that its function was rather to keep out foreign works than to purge or restrict domestic creativity.

The Indices of the seventeenth century were those of 1612 (with an appendix in 1614), 1632 and 1640. A prominent part in their compilation was played by the distinguished Jesuit Juan de Pineda, aided among others by Francisco Peña, the editor of Eymeric. The Index of 1612, issued under Inquisitor General Sandoval y Rojas, departed from previous practice. Instead of publishing separate volumes for prohibited and expurgated books, as was done in 1583–4, the Cardinal published both together in an *Index librorum prohibitorum et expurgatorum*. The enormous volume resulting from this plan departed in another way from previous practice. Instead of dividing the material simply into Latin and vernacular books, it was now proposed to divide the material into three classes. Into the first class went authors who were completely prohibited; into the second went books that were prohibited, regardless of author; and into the third went books not bearing the names of their authors. For example, all heresiarchs would go into the first class, whereas Dante's *Monarchia* would go into the second. Even this classification, however, was not strictly adhered to. Though Erasmus fell into the first class, and all his works without exception were banned in Spanish translations, several of his Latin works which were clearly beyond suspicion were permitted.

The Index of 1632 was issued by Inquisitor General Zapata, and that of 1640 by Inquisitor General Antonio de Sotomayor. Similar to the 1612 compilation in scope and content, Sotomayor's Index offered a general survey of the intellectual advances of the seventeenth century, and complemented the efforts of the Quiroga Index to exclude European thought from Spain. It is not surprising to find Francis Bacon and other major writers condemned in the first class as heretics. Like the Quiroga Index, that of 1640 had little impact on native literature, apart from the surprising appearance of Mariana, who had to endure expurgations in seven of his works as well as in his *De mutatione monetae* (on the coinage) and his *Tractatus de Morte et Immortalitate*; and the well-known case of Cervantes, who lost by expurgation a sentence in book two, chapter thirty-six, of his *Quixote*, concerning works of charity. Despite its coincidence with the early period of the Scientific Revolution, moreover, the 1640 Index was tolerant towards some aspects of science. Johannes Kepler and Tycho Brahe, as heretics, were classified as *auctores damnati* and therefore appeared in class one; but virtually all their works were permitted in Spain after very minor expurgations. Some were allowed without any expurgation, but with the proviso that a note on the book should state that it was by a condemned author. Into this category fell Kepler's *Astronomia nova* of 1609, his *Epitome Astronomiae Copernicanae* of 1618, and his *Chilias logarithmorum* published at Marburg in 1624.

With these Indices ended the first great period in the censorship of the Inquisition. The great compilations of 1583 and 1640 were not by their nature repressive weapons, and served more to dissuade Spaniards from reading foreign authors whom none but a few could have read anyway. The real weight of censorship in the

country operated, it must be stressed, outside the scope of the Indices: in the various systems of control at the disposal of both State
and Inquisition, and in the *formative* restrictions that the Counter
Reformation introduced into Spain.[67]

The first major control attempted by the Inquisition after 1521
and by the State after 1558 was over the entry of foreign books.
The successful activities of Julián Hernández, who perished in the auto
at Seville in December 1560, were a fraction of the effort made by
Protestants to bring books into the country. In 1556 Margaret of
Parma informed the Council of State that heretics 'intend to send
to Spain through Seville thirty thousand books of Calvin, and I hear
that Marcus Pérez, who is here in Antwerp, is charged with this
task'.[68] Seaports were inevitably the centre of inquisitorial scrutiny,
and foreign sailors were vulnerable to arrest if they happened to be
carrying Protestant devotional literature. Diplomats abroad sent
back regular information on any unusual activity by printers or
traders. The Inquisition began to claim the right to be the first to
visit foreign ships when they entered territorial waters. This provoked continuous conflicts with local officials: in Bilbao the corregidor was ordered by the crown to give precedence to the Inquisition; in the Canaries the diocesan vicars were similarly told to give
way.[69] Although commercial cargo was the usual hiding-place for
books, the ever-zealous Inquisition insisted in 1581 that 'the pack-
ages and the beds of the sailors' should also be examined.[70]

The operation was certainly successful in general terms, but
never completely so. The inquisitors of Barcelona commented on
the problem in 1569: 'the books coming through this frontier are
very numerous and even if there were many inquisitors we would
not be enough to deal with so many volumes; to entrust the work
to friars and experts is not enough to keep people happy, and
annoys the booksellers'. The inquisitors therefore proposed 'a commission of two persons to look at the books, paid by the booksellers,
whose suggestion it is'.[71] Many condemned books filtered into the
country, to judge by the case of Joseph Antonio de Salas, knight of
the Order of Calatrava, whose library was offered for sale to the
public on his death in 1651. It was then found that among the
2,424 volumes in the collection, to quote the censor, 'there were
many books prohibited or unexpurgated or worthy of examination,
either because they were by heretical authors or were newly published abroad by unknown writers'.[72] There were in fact 250 prohibited works in the library – a proportion of one in ten – showing

that foreign books were smuggled regularly and often successfully into Spain, despite the death penalty attached to this crime.

The second major control was at the point of contact between a book and its potential reader. All book shipments into the country, all bookshops and public and private libraries, were regularly examined, and items expurgated or confiscated. Booksellers were regularly visited and checked: as early as 1536 St Thomas de Villanueva was employed by the Inquisitor General to visit bookshops. A lightning check in 1566 in Seville is described thus by an inquisitor: 'at a fixed hour, nine in the morning, all the bookshops of Seville were occupied by familiars of the Holy Office, so that they could not warn each other nor hide nor take out any books, and later we came and made all the shops close and are visiting them one by one'.[73] The task of censorship obviously took many years. One censor reported to the Inquisition that to expurgate a private library in Madrid worth 18,000 ducats he had laboured eight hours daily for four months.[74] Benito Arias Montano, whose task was to check the entire library of the Escorial, took a little longer. Since censorship over printed matter existed in every European country, and had always been accepted in Spain, it would be a mistake to think that Spaniards felt extraordinarily oppressed by the system. On the other hand, it was precisely at this level of daily and ordinary censorship, rather than at the lofty level of the Index, that most of the painful experiences of individuals occurred.[75] Up to the 1540s, for example, it had been common for the Inquisition to allow individuals special licences to read or keep prohibited books, usually for purposes of study (how, for instance, could one refute Luther without first reading him?). After 1559 all such licences were suspended, and not until the 1580s were exceptions made.

Literature collected during searches was sent to the nearest tribunal for further judgment: there it remained until disposed of. Thus in December 1634 the tribunal of Saragossa had in its keeping 116 copies of the Bible, fifty-five copies of various works by Erasmus and eighty-three volumes of the works of Francisco de Quevedo.[76] In earlier periods, when excessive zeal was predominant, books might be consigned to the flames. Torquemada in his day had organized a book-burning in his monastery in Salamanca. A royal decree of October 1501 ordered Arabic books to be burnt in Granada, and a huge bonfire was held under the auspices of Cisneros. From about 1552 the Inquisition began symbolic burnings of books to accompany the disciplinary rites of the autos de fe, and some twenty-seven books were ordered to be burnt at a ceremony in Valladolid in January 1558.[77] Later generations sometimes preferred to store the prohibited books. The Escorial was used regularly as a store, and in 1585 the prior reported that its library possessed 'many prohibited books sent at different times by His Majesty, and kept there by licence from the late Don Gaspar de Quiroga'. Half a century later the practice was still being carried on, for in 1639 the Escorial possessed a total of 932 prohibited books.[78] Laudable as this may have been, it was not practised everywhere, with the result that a great number of works condemned by the Inquisition were all but wiped out of existence. In the early seventeenth century there was a plan, supported by both inquisitors and booksellers, to set up a central store of banned books; but 'none of those in favour of setting it up wished to take on the task of doing it',[79] so nothing was done.

Any institution claiming the right, as the Inquisition did, to control cultural activity, was bound to attract opposition from intellectuals. Though Spaniards accepted the need for controls, they were never so sanguine as to believe that the inquisitors knew best. It was a Spaniard resident in Rome, Bartolomé de Valverde, chaplain to Philip II, who in 1584 protested to Cardinal Sirleto, the then director of the Roman Index, over the poor quality of his censors, 'condemning works they have never handled ... usually nonentities who know not a word either of Greek or of Hebrew, and lack either judgment or capacity. Being paid nothing for reading innumerable books, and to discharge themselves from a task little to their taste, they take the way out which confers on them an air of learning, and suppress the books.'

In Spain conflicts with authoritarian inquisitors began with the notable case of the great humanist Nebrija. The Inquisitor General Diego de Deza confiscated his papers in 1504 because Nebrija had dared to maintain that as a philologist he was capable, no less than theologians like Deza, of determining the texts of Holy Scripture. Deza was subsequently sacked as Inquisitor General and Nebrija was able to rely on the full protection of Cisneros. In an *Apologia* written years later, Nebrija accused Deza of seizing his writings 'not to examine them or condemn them, but to stop me writing. ... That good prelate wanted to wipe out all traces of the two languages on which our religion depends [Hebrew and Greek].' The humanist commented indignantly on the injury to scholarship:

> Must I reject as false what appears to me in every way as clear, true and
> evident as light and truth itself? What does this sort of slavery mean?
> What unjust domination when one is prevented from saying what one
> thinks, although to do so involves no slight or insult to religion![80]

Malicious and ignorant inquisitors were not a rarity – we have
already noted the persecution of Talavera by Lucero – and none
put his personal ambition and malice to greater use than Inquisitor
General Fernando de Valdés, who undermined the career of Juan de
Vergara and destroyed that of Bartolomé Carranza. In general, however, the involvement of the Inquisition in cultural matters was
governed less by the personality or inadequacy of the inquisitors
than by the social climate. In literature, no less than in religious
matters, prosecutions were set in motion largely by denunciations
made by private individuals, so that the Inquisition, although prosecutor, was seldom the initiator. This can be seen in the brush
that Ignatius Loyola had with the Inquisition, when current suspicions of conversos and illuminists caused him to be denounced
because of his religious practices while a student at Alcalá in 1527.[81]
The change in the cultural climate in 1558 had a crucial influence
on the Inquisition, which hardened its attitudes rapidly under
Valdés. Ideas which might in other times have been tolerated were
now discouraged. The idea of a vernacular Bible was one of the
great casualties of these years, in a country which had been second
to none in Biblical scholarship.

Much of the conflict was very simply over language. How could
one distinguish between orthodox and unorthodox piety if both
used the same language? How could one grasp the real meaning of
a religious writing? Dissenting from the tendentious interpretation
put on Carranza's writings by Melchor Cano, his fellow Dominican
Juan de la Peña argued that 'it is impossible to avoid all the methods
of expression used by heretics, unless we learn our speech all over
again'. Yet the inquisitors were, of course, right to suspect – as in
the case of the alumbrados and even more of Juan de Valdés – that
heterodoxy was sheltering behind pious language. This did not stop
many from criticizing the 1559 Index. In September that year, a
Jesuit wrote:

> The faint-hearted have reacted by becoming more faint-hearted and
> those dedicated to virtue are in dismay, seeing that the Inquisitor General
> has published an edict forbidding almost all the books in Spanish that
> have been used up to now by those who try to serve God; and we are in

times when women are told to stick to their beads and not bother about other devotions.[82]

Perhaps the most notorious conflict between intellectuals and the Inquisition originated in the malicious denunciations of some of his colleagues made by a professor at the University of Salamanca, León de Castro. In December 1571 Castro and a Dominican colleague, Bartolomé de Medina, laid before the Inquisition at Valladolid some accusations against three professors at the University of Salamanca. The three in question were Fray Luis de León, of the Order of St Augustine, Gaspar de Grajal and Martín Martínez de Cantalapiedra. The denunciations said that they had taken heretical liberties with their study of scripture and theology. Fray Luis in particular bore the brunt of the attack. Famous as a theologian and immortalized as one of Spain's finest poets, at the age of thirty-four he was elected to a chair at Salamanca. He thereby aroused the hostility of his rivals, who slandered him because of his Jewish descent and accused him of uttering dangerous theological propositions. Among other things, it was said that he had questioned the accuracy of the Vulgate translation of the Bible; had preferred the Hebrew text to the Latin; had translated the Song of Songs as a profane love song instead of a divine canticle; and had held that scholastic theology harmed the study of scripture. Grajal was arrested on similar charges on 22 March 1572. Five days later Luis de León and Martínez were taken into custody. Blind belief in the justice of their cause and in the benevolence of the Holy Office cheered the prisoners, but they were soon disillusioned. For Fray Luis it was to be the beginning of an imprisonment that lasted four years, eight months and nineteen days. Cut off completely from the outside world in the cells of the tribunal at Valladolid, his only consolation was the permission he received to read and write in his cell, out of which emerged his classic devotional treatise *De los Nombres de Cristo*. From the first he was aware of a campaign against himself. On 18 April 1572 he wrote from his cell:

I have great suspicions that false testimony has been laid against me, for I know that in the last two years people have said and still say many things about me that are transparent lies, and I know that I have many enemies.

He awaited justice, yet none was forthcoming, nor was there any promise of an early trial. His constant appeals were of no avail. A year later, on 7 March 1573, he was writing to the inquisitors:

It is now a year since I have been in this prison, and in all this time you have not deigned to publish the names of witnesses in my case, nor have I been given any opportunity of a full defence.

He was finally sentenced to a reprimand which involved retraction of the several propositions he was said to have held. In prison he had suffered despair, fever and humiliation. Release from the cells came in mid-December 1576. Weary but undefeated, he greeted his freedom with characteristic restraint:

> Aqui la envidia y mentira
> Me tuvieron encerrado.
> Dichoso el humilde estado
> del sabio que se retira
> y de aqueste mundo malvado,
> y con pobre mesa y casa,
> en el campo deleitoso,
> con solo Diós se compasa,
> y a solas su vida pasa
> ni envidiado ni envidioso.*

Restored once more to his rostrum at the university, he is said to have begun his first lecture with the words. 'As I was saying last time ...' But for his enemies this was not the last time. In 1582 he was summoned to a second trial for having uttered rash propositions. The Inquisitor General, Gaspar de Quiroga, intervened on his behalf and in 1584 he escaped with a warning to avoid controversial issues in future.[83]

Less fortunate than Fray Luis were his other colleagues at the university. Gaspar de Grajal, who had been arrested five days before, was thrown into the cells of the Inquisition; there his health gave way, and he died before judgment could be passed on him. A colleague from the University of Osuna, Alonso Gudiel, who was professor of Scripture there, was also arrested in the same month on the basis of Castro's accusations. Before this case had been dealt with he also died in prison, in April 1573. The only one to outlast his treatment was Cantalapiedra, who had been professor of Hebrew at Salamanca and whose whole life had been dedicated to the study of Holy Scripture. His term of imprisonment in a Valladolid cell

---

* Here envy and lies held me in prison. Happy the humble state of the scholar who retires from this malicious world and there in the pleasant countryside, with modest table and dwelling, governs his life with God alone, and passes his days all by himself, neither envied nor envying.

exceeded even that of Luis de León. It lasted for over five years, from March 1572 to May 1577, and despite his constant appeals for a quick decision there was no hurry to bring him to trial. Eventually he was liberated but never regained his academic post. 'I have laboured to interpret scripture before the whole world', he told the inquisitors in 1577, 'but my only reward has been the destruction of my life, my honour, my health and my possessions'.[84] The bitter lesson he drew from this was drawn by many other contemporaries: 'it is better to walk carefully and remain prudent' (sapere ad sobrietatem). It was a prudence that severely compromised academic life in every country where the established order silenced speculation.

The work of León de Castro was not yet over. The great Hebrew scholar and humanist Benito Arias Montano had spent several years in collaboration with Netherlandish scholars on the preparation, patronized by Philip II, of a new Polyglot Bible, which was printed and issued in Antwerp in 1571 in eight volumes.[85] Provisional approval was secured from Rome in 1572 and 1576. There was, however, considerable criticism of the project in Spain. In 1575, writing from Rome, Montano complained of

> a great rumour which a certain León de Castro of Salamanca has raised in that university, to criticize and discredit the greatest work of letters that has ever been published in the world, the Royal Bible which His Majesty has for the benefit of Christendom ordered to be printed in Antwerp under my direction.

León de Castro was not the only critic. There were others, wrote Montano in 1579, 'men of letters who seek to find and note some error in my writings, making extraordinary efforts to do so'.[86] The conflict was primarily one between scholars, and the criticisms then made of the Polyglot are now seen to have been in part justified, but the danger was that the Holy Office might be brought into the fray.

Although the storm passed, Montano was the object of further, and this time indirect, attacks. In 1592 he was instrumental in bringing about a profound change in the spiritual life of José de Sigüenza, Jeronimite historian and monk of the Escorial, in the library of which Montano worked. Montano, it has been suggested, had heterodox views on religion which he had picked up in the Netherlands, and which he may have communicated to Sigüenza. No evidence for this thesis has been found, but it is undeniable that Montano had an enormous influence on Sigüenza. In 1592 some of

Sigüenza's malicious colleagues, motivated in part by hostility to Montano's Hebraic studies, denounced Sigüenza to the Inquisition. It was a brief three-month trial, and Sigüenza was completely exonerated by the Inquisition.[87]

Another famous man of letters to fall foul of the Holy Office was Francisco Sánchez, 'el Brocense', professor of grammar at Salamanca. He was denounced in 1584 on charges of loose and presumptuous opinions on theological matters, and summoned before the tribunal of Valladolid. Although the tribunal voted for his arrest and the sequestration of his goods, the Suprema altered this sentence to one of grave reprimand only. Brocense's turbulent and intemperate mind was not put off by this narrow escape, and he returned to the fray, disputing theology with theologians (once again it was a case of conflict between theologians and grammarians) and casting contempt on Aquinas and the Dominicans. In 1593, therefore, at the age of eighty, this excitable old man found himself in trouble once more. Reports of his speeches were relayed to the tribunal of Valladolid, and in 1596 the Inquisition began proceedings against him. But no action was taken until 1600, when he was suddenly seized and put under house arrest, and his papers sequestrated. Among the charges raised against him was that 'he always subjects his understanding to obedience to the faith; but that in matters which are not of faith he has no wish to subject his understanding'.[88] Aged, in ill health and humiliated by his treatment, Sánchez died at the beginning of December 1600. Because of the scandal hanging over his name, he was denied funeral honours by the University of Salamanca.

It is true that these were among the few prominent intellectuals to be directly censured by the Inquisition, and that the circumstances were special ones, involving the vicious slanders of León de Castro and others. Yet it is peculiarly significant that three of the victims – Luis de León, Gaspar de Grajal and Alonso Gudiel – were conversos by origin, and that witnesses claimed that Cantalapiedra was also one. In an academic atmosphere where scholars might be liable to prosecution because of their Jewish origins, academic freedom could be gravely compromised. The importance of the prosecutions lay not in the small number of victims so much as in the repercussions felt by others. One example was sufficient to silence many. When Fray Luis de León heard of the arrest of his colleague Grajal he wrote indignantly to a friend in Granada, 'This fate of the master has scandalized everyone and given just cause for keeping silent out of fear.' On another occasion, Fray Luis informs us, he had been lecturing about the fraternal correction of heretics when

> those students who were furthest from the rostrum signalled that I should speak louder, because my voice was hoarse and they could not hear well. Whereupon I said, 'I am hoarse, and it's better to speak low like this so that the inquisitors don't hear us.' I don't know if this offended anyone.[89]

Fray Luis' own fate inspired a strong reaction in the eminent Jesuit historian Mariana. Commenting in a famous passage on the prosecution of Fray Luis and his colleagues, he said that the case

> caused anxiety to many until they should know the outcome. There was dissatisfaction that persons illustrious for their learning and reputation had to defend themselves in prison from so serious a threat to their fame and good name. It was a sad state when virtuous men, because of their great achievements, had to undergo hostility, accusations and injuries from those who should have been their defenders. ... The case in question depressed the spirits of many who observed the plight of another, seeing how much affliction threatened those who spoke freely what they thought. In this way, many passed over to the other camp, or trimmed their sails to the wind. What else was there to do? The greatest of follies is to exert oneself in vain, and to weary oneself without winning anything but hatred. Those who agreed with current ideas did so with even greater eagerness, and entertained opinions that were approved of and were the least dangerous, without any great concern for the truth.[90]

To build so great a volume of discontent on the prosecution of a handful of academics indicates that what lay at stake in the case of Luis de León and his colleagues was far more than elementary justice and their individual reputations. The issues extended beyond Salamanca to the whole intellectual world of post-Renaissance and Erasmian Spain. Proceedings such as those against the Salamanca professors stand out only because of their infrequency, and there is no evidence of any systematic persecution of academics. But it is certain that the spirit of individual and free enquiry was being subordinated to the political and religious establishment, not only in Spain but in the whole of post-Reformation Europe.

The conflict between humanism and dogmatism was summed up neatly in the complaint of a learned Dominican at Salamanca in 1571, that 'In this university there is great play about novelty and little about the antiquity of our religion and faith'.[91] It is significant that the inquisitorial prosecutor of El Brocense alleged that he was

'a rash, insolent heretic, temerarious and stubborn like all grammarians and Erasmians'.[92] Independent investigation was criticized
because it might lead to error. Why search out a dangerous new
truth if the old one were safer? This was the dilemma faced by the
humanist Pedro Juan Núñez when he wrote to Jerónimo de Zurita in
1556[93] that the inquisitors did not wish people to study humanities

> because of the dangers present in them, for when a humanist corrects
> an error in Cicero he has to correct the same error in Scripture. This and
> other similar problems drive me insane, and often take away from me
> any wish to carry on.

The reaction against humanism was common to much of the
post-Reformation world, and by no means uniquely a consequence
of inquisitorial prejudice. In the same way the reaction against
unorthodox spirituality was common to much of counter-Reformation Europe, and the Inquisition was no innovator in this respect. The continued suspicion of illuminism and of certain types of
popular religion explains the difficulties that St Teresa of Avila had
to suffer. On one occasion, she remarks in her *Life*,

> people came to me in great alarm, saying that these were difficult times,
> that some charge might be raised against me, and that I might have to
> appear before the inquisitors. But this merely amused me and made me
> laugh. I never had any fear on that score.

The optimism she showed at this time was not repeated later. In
1574 her *Life* fell under suspicion and was examined by the Inquisition, which decided not to license it for publication until after
her death (1582). In 1576 denunciations were made to the tribunal
of Seville against her and her reformed Carmelites, but the Inquisition did not press the matter. The saint was seriously worried, but
she told one of her preoccupied advisers, Father Gracián, 'Father,
would that we could all be burnt for Christ', and on another occasion, 'Father, the Holy Inquisition, sent by God to protect his faith,
is hardly likely to harm someone who has such faith as I.'[94] After
her death further denunciations were made against her in 1589–
91 by Alonso de la Fuente, a friar with an obsession about illuminists, but the Inquisition ignored him.

The continuing history of the later alumbrados, with which the
incident of St Teresa is closely related, revolves around the denunciations made by Fray Alonso de la Fuente from 1573 onwards
against groups of adepts in Extremadura and later in Andalucia.
Undoubtedly crazed, with a burning hatred of Jews and of Jesuits,

Fray Alonso was perceptive enough to be able to identify the new illuminism and its leaders, most of whom were clergy. At a big auto de fe in Llerena on 14 June 1579, twenty alumbrados were among the sixty penitents. The group had strange beliefs, rejecting the Church and Christ and centring their devotion on 'God': their leader, Hernando Alvarez, 'said that Jesus Christ was good for nothing except to be a gipsy'. The alumbrados of Andalucia were subsequently hit by an auto held at Córdoba on 21 January 1590.[95]

The famous inquisitorial trials of the sixteenth century constitute a dramatic aspect of intervention by the Holy Office in academic and religious life, but because they were exceptional events it is difficult to gauge their significance. For some historians, the Inquisition probably played a far more negative role in its constant and petty intervention in the working life of writers. Prominent among these were writers of Jewish origin. A striking example is Antonio Enríquez Gomez (d. 1663), whose colourful life as a converso (much of it spent in France) ended with his return to Spain and his quiet death in Seville – where, however, he had the honour of appearing in effigy in two autos de fe, one before (in 1660) and one after (in 1665) his death.[96]

The difficulties faced by converso writers have received particular attention from a whole school of disciples of the scholar Americo Castro. Castro argued in several brilliant essays that the semitic background of Spain, as expressed through the careers of thinkers and writers of Jewish origin, contributed to the formation of a creative but pessimistic mentality. To be a converso became a spur to creativity, but at the same time provoked the risk of conflict with the established order and the Inquisition. Followers of the Castro thesis have thus used racial origins as a tool of literary analysis, and the thought of Luis de León and St Teresa among others has been interpreted in this light. The most notable attempt to use the interpretation has been in studies on the *Celestina*, on the unproven premise that its author, Fernando de Rojas, was a converso.[97] Attempts have also been made – again without historical evidence – to suggest that many other famous liberals such as Hernando de Talavera, Arias Montano and Bartolomé de las Casas were of converso origin.

There can, of course, be no doubt that converso blood could be a serious impediment in the antisemitic society of Spain's Golden Age. The outstanding example is Juan Luis Vives, Spain's most illustrious humanist, who spent his entire career abroad. Born in

Valencia of converso parents who continued to practise their Jewish religion in secret, Vives was sent by his father to study abroad in Paris at the age of sixteen in 1509, a year after the death of his mother in an epidemic. His life and brilliant career were thereafter based in the Netherlands. After Nebrija's death in 1522 Vives was invited to occupy his chair at Alcalá, but refused. Family circumstances combined to make Vives a permanent exile from his homeland: in 1520 his father was arrested by the Inquisition as a judaizer and burnt alive in 1524; four years later his long-dead mother was also prosecuted and her bones disinterred and burnt.[98] To argue from isolated cases like that of Vives, however, that converso thought in Spain represented an undercurrent of dissidence and also created a confrontation between the Inquisition on one side and creativity on the other, is difficult to substantiate. The Inquisition was certainly suspicious of conversos, perhaps logically so in the case of the Hebraists of Salamanca, but in no way did it consistently persecute all writers of semitic origin. St Teresa was notoriously of converso stock, yet the fact was never cited against her.[99]

The continuing discussion over the impact of the Inquisition on culture and literature must come to terms with several uncomfortable facts. It must be conceded, for example, that Menéndez Pelayo was right to assert that 'never was there more written in Spain, or better written, than in the two golden centuries of the Inquisition'.[100] We can go further, and agree with him that the Index of prohibited books probably had little impact on literature and even less on science. For the first half-century of its existence, the Inquisition played no significant part in the literary world, prosecuted no notable writer, and interfered seriously only with some texts of Renaissance theatre.[101] Not until the onset of the Reformation, and many years after repression had been practised in England and France, did the Holy Office begin to operate a system of cultural control. Even then, the Indices were conceived less as mechanisms to crush national creativity than as massive filters through which the culture of Europe might be permitted into Spain in a purified form. The Index of 1559 was indubitably harsh, but later Indices had a limited, even petty role: Góngora had minor problems with the censor in 1627;[102] Cervantes had one line excised from the Quixote in 1632;[103] the expurgations of Francisco de Osuna and Antonio de Guevara in the Index of 1612 are trivial; that of Florián de Ocampo in 1632 ridiculous.[104] Many creative writers had brushes

with the Inquisition,[105] but the total effect of these incidents appears
to have been so slight that no convincing conclusion can be drawn;
indeed, some famous victims such as Lope de Vega, who appeared
on the Index a century after his death, and Mariana, whose treatise
on coinage was banned in his lifetime, were warm supporters of
the Holy Office. The impact of the Inquisition on foreign works was
arguably more important: the entire literature of the Protestant
north was forbidden to Spaniards, assuming that they were capable
of reading it. Its scientific output, however, was not disallowed. The
1583 Quiroga Index had a negligible impact on the accessibility of
scientific works,[106] and Galileo was never put on the list of forbidden
books.

To add to all this, we must bear in mind that at no time was the
peninsula as cut off from the outside world as the decrees of 1558
might lead us to suppose. Under Habsburg rule the armies of Spain
dominated Europe, its ships traversed the Atlantic and Pacific, and
its language was the master tongue from central Europe to the
Philippines. Tens of thousands of Spaniards went abroad every year,
mainly to serve in the armed forces. Cultural and commercial contact with all parts of western Europe, especially the Netherlands
and Italy, continued absolutely without interruption. It is unlikely
that this extensive contact in the great age of empire had no impact
on Spanish attitudes.

The image of Spain as a nation sunk in intellectual torpor and
religious superstition, all of it due to the Inquisition, is one that
Menéndez Pelayo was right to controvert. Spain was in reality one
of the freest nations in Europe, with active political institutions at
all levels. Remarkably free discussion of political affairs was tolerated, and public controversy occurred on a scale paralleled in few
other countries. The national debate held at Valladolid over Erasmus in 1527 was followed a generation later by the great disputation between Las Casas and Sepúlveda before the Royal Council.
Every major topic of importance, from the status of conversos (the
subject of a war of words in 1449) to the expulsion of the Moriscos,
was freely and publicly debated. The historian Antonio de Herrera
confirmed that such free discussion was essential for otherwise 'the
reputation of Spain would fall rapidly, for foreign and enemy nations would say that small credence could be placed in the words
of her rulers, since their subjects were not allowed to speak freely'.
In the seventeenth century the *arbitristas* continued the tradition
of controversy, and the diplomat Saavedra Fajardo commented

approvingly that 'grumbling is proof that there is liberty in the State; in a tyranny it is not permitted'.

How does the Inquisition fit into this picture? It undoubtedly had a negative influence, because its function was by definition negative. The problem remains to measure the limits of its influence and how much responsibility can be attributed to it for the successes and failures of Spanish history.

6

The End of Morisco Spain

Los dos ríos de Granada,
uno llanto y otro sangre.

Lorca, *Baladilla de los Tres Ríos*

Moorish Spain, the Spain of the invaders from north Africa, remained in places under Muslim control for some seven centuries.
Consequently, the peoples who thus entered Spanish history were
no less a part of its structure than the Christian and Jewish population. They intermarried with them, and exchanged ideas and languages, so that the three religions were recognized as part of one
empire.

The Reconquest changed all this. The Christian advance took
Saragossa in 1118, Córdoba in 1236, Valencia in 1238 and Seville
in 1248; finally, after a long interval, Granada fell in 1492. The
end of Moorish power meant that the Moors ceased to exist as a
nation, and became no more than a minority within a Christian
country. As Muslim subjects of a Christian king they were now
'Mudejars'. The terms of the capitulation of Granada were generous
to the vanquished and reflected mediaeval traditions of convivencia.
The Mudejars were guaranteed their customs, property, laws and
religion; they kept their own officials, to be supervised, however, by
Castilian governors; and those wishing to emigrate were allowed to
do so. Many of the elite found life under Christian rule intolerable
and passed over into north Africa. Reorganization of the territory
was entrusted to Iñigo López de Mendoza, second Count of Tendilla
and later first Marquis of Mondéjar. Hernando de Talavera was
appointed first Archbishop, and encouraged conversions by means
of charitable persuasion, respect for Mudejar culture and the use of

Arabic during religious services. But progress was slow and in 1499 Cisneros asked Ferdinand and Isabella, who were then in Granada, for permission to pursue a more vigorous policy. The new phase of compulsory conversion, often with mass baptisms, provoked a brief revolt in December 1499 in the Albaicín, the Mudejar quarter of Granada, which was appeased only through the good offices of Tendilla and Talavera. Isabella continued to give Cisneros her support; after further conversions, he reported in January 1500 that 'there is now no one in the city who is not a Christian, and all the mosques are churches'.

The forced conversions precipitated another revolt in January 1500 in the Alpujarras; it lasted for three months and was put down with difficulty. Cisneros' view now was that by rebellion the Mudejars had forfeited all rights granted by the terms of capitulation and they should be offered a clear choice between baptism or expulsion; his personal preference was 'that they should convert and be enslaved, because as slaves they will be better Christians'. Over the next few months the Mudejars of Granada were systematically converted by force; a few were allowed to emigrate. By 1501 it was officially assumed that the kingdom had become one of Christian Moors – the *Moriscos*. They were granted legal equality with Christians; but were forbidden to carry arms and subjected to growing pressure to abandon their racial culture. A huge bonfire of Arabic books, ordered by a royal decree of October 1501 and not specifically by Cisneros, was held in Granada. It was the end of the capitulations and of Moorish al-Andalus: 'if the king of the conquest does not keep faith,' lamented the former imam of the mosque at Granada, 'what can we expect from his successors?'

With Granada apparently converted, Isabella was not inclined to tolerate Muslims elsewhere in her realms. On 12 February 1502 all Mudejars in Castile were offered the choice between baptism and exile. Virtually all of them, subjects of the crown since the Middle Ages, chose baptism, since emigration was rendered almost impossible by stringent conditions. With their conversion Islam vanished from Castilian territory, and continued to be tolerated only in the crown of Aragon. By repeating a step that had already been taken against the Jews, Isabella abolished plurality of faiths in her dominions but also created within the body of Christian society the wholly new problem of the Moriscos.

Many Mudejars had thought that by accepting baptism they would be left in peace. From about 1511, however, various decrees deliberately attacked their cultural identity in an effort to confirm their abandonment of Muslim practice. These measures culminated in an assembly convoked by the authorities in Granada in 1526, when all the distinctive characteristics of Morisco civilization – the use of Arabic, their clothes, their jewellery, ritual slaughter of animals, circumcision – came under attack; to help combat these, it was decided to transfer the local tribunal of the Inquisition from Jaén to Granada.

In the crown of Aragon there was no comparable pressure on the Mudejars. The principal reason for this was the great power of the landed nobility and the authority of the Cortes. On the estates of the nobles the Mudejars formed a plentiful, cheap and productive source of labour, from which the expression arose 'Mientras más Moros más ganancia' (more Moors, more profit). Whether to placate his nobility or in pursuit of a moderate policy, Ferdinand repeatedly warned the inquisitors of Aragon not to persecute the Mudejar population or resort to forced conversions. The Mudejars therefore continued to lead an independent existence until the revolt of the Comuneros in 1520.

Simultaneously with the uprisings in Castile, Valencia experienced disturbances of its own. Here the rebels, grouped into *Germanías* of brotherhoods, organized an urban revolution directed against the local aristocracy. Valencia had the largest Muslim population of any province in Spain. The Mudejars were almost exclusively a rural community and were subjected to the big landowners of the realm. The Germanía leaders saw that the simplest way to destroy the power of the nobles in the countryside would be to free their vassals, and this they did by baptizing them. The years 1520–22 in Valencia thus witnessed the forcible baptism of thousands of Muslims. The defeat of the rebels by royal troops should in theory have allowed the Mudejars to revert to Islam, since forced baptisms were universally regarded as invalid. But the authorities were not so eager to lose their new converts. The Inquisition in particular was concerned to hold the Mudejars to the letter of their baptism. To the argument that the conversions had taken place under compulsion, the standard answer was once again given that to *choose* baptism as an alternative to death meant the exercise of free choice, which rendered the sacrament of baptism valid.[1] The Inquisition was therefore ordered to proceed on the assumption that all properly executed baptisms were valid.

It now seemed incongruous to tolerate Muslims elsewhere in the

crown of Aragon. In November 1525 Charles v issued a decree
ordering the conversion of all Mudejars in Valencia by the end of
the year, and of those elsewhere by the end of January 1526. From
1526 the Muslim religion no longer existed in Spain officially: all
Mudejars were now Moriscos. Writing to the pope in December that
year, Charles v admitted that 'the conversion was not wholly voluntary among many of them, and since then they have not been
instructed in our holy faith'. Considerable efforts were subsequently
made to evangelize the new 'converts' in the regions of greatest
concentration; among the clergy leading the campaign was the
distinguished humanist Antonio de Guevara, who laboured in Valencia and Granada.[2]

The Morisco problem varied across the peninsula according to
density of population.[3] The highest concentration was in the kingdom of Granada, where Moriscos in the 1560s were some 54 per
cent of the population, and in areas such as the Alpujarra mountains constituted the totality. In Valencia they formed a third of the
population in the late sixteenth century, in Aragon about a fifth. In
Catalonia Moriscos were a tiny group, and in Castile they were
proportionately even less, perhaps a total of some twenty thousand
in 1502,[4] scattered throughout the country in small urban *morerías*,
and living at peace with their Christian neighbours. There were
major differences between the Morisco communities. The Granadans, recently subjugated, included a flourishing upper class, preserved their religion and culture intact, and usually spoke Arabic
(*algarabía*): they were an integral Islamic civilization.[5] The Valencians were largely a rural proletariat, but because they lived quite
separately from the Christian population and were so numerous
they managed to preserve most of their customs, religion and language. Elsewhere in Spain, Arabic was almost unknown among the
Moriscos: all spoke Castilian or *aljamía*, which in the early sixteenth
century was still written in Arabic script.

Until the early years of the reign of Philip ii the efforts of the
Inquisition to keep Moriscos to their nominal Christianity were
little more than a gesture. The largest numbers to be tried were in
the crown of Aragon, but they were only the tip of the iceberg of
unbelief in Morisco Spain. There were two main reasons for the
relative absence of prosecutions: the conviction of both Church and
State that a proper programme of conversion should be undertaken,
and the strong opposition of Christian seigneurs to any interference
with their rights over their Morisco vassals. In January 1526 the

leaders of the Valencian Moriscos succeeded in obtaining from the crown and Inquisitor General Manrique a secret concordia or agreement that if they all submitted to baptism they should be free for forty years from any prosecution by the Holy Office, since it would be impossible for them to shed all their customs at once. In 1528 this concordia was made public, and in that same year the Cortes of Aragon, meeting at Monzón, asked Charles to prevent the Inquisition prosecuting Moriscos until they had been instructed in the faith. Their request was timely, for the guarantee was no more lasting than the one granted to the Mudejars of Granada. The Holy Office interpreted the concordia to mean that it could bring to trial those converts who had slipped back into Islamic practices.

In December of 1526, the year when the Inquisition was transferred from Jaén to Granada, regulations were reissued forbidding Granada Moriscos to use the Arab language, Moorish clothes or Moorish names. Morisco money offered to Charles brought about the suspension of these rules. But the removal of one burden was balanced by the imposition of another in the form of the Inquisition, whose measures the Moriscos spent the next generation in trying to modify. In Aragon, protests raised against the Inquisition in the Cortes of Monzón of 1533 included claims that the tribunal was seizing land confiscated from its victims, to the detriment of the actual feudal owners of the land. Similar complaints were raised in the Cortes of 1537 and 1542. In 1546 the pope intervened and decreed that for a minimum period of ten years the Inquisition should not confiscate any property from the Moriscos.

Only the year after this, however, we find the Cortes of Valencia stating that the tribunal was disregarding such injunctions. It was after great difficulty that finally in 1571 the Inquisition showed itself open to compromise. The resulting concordia was embodied in a decree of October 1571 by which, in return for an annual payment of 2,500 ducats to the Inquisition, the tribunal agreed not to confiscate or sequestrate the property of Moriscos on trial for heresy. Monetary fines could be levied, but with a limit of ten ducats only. The agreement benefited all sides: the Inquisition, since it brought in a regular annual revenue; the Moriscos, since it protected property for members of their families; and the lords of the Moriscos, since it preserved lands they had leased to their Morisco dependants.

The principal problem remained that of converting the Moriscos, who overwhelmingly rejected Christianity. When in Granada in

1526, Charles V was informed that 'the Moriscos are truly Moors: it is twenty-seven years since their conversion and there are not twenty-seven or even seven of them who are Christians'. In Granada and Valencia they held fast to their religion, observing prayers, fasts and ablutions, and strengthened in their faith by their clergy, the *alfaquis*. Had religious practice alone been at issue, social tension might not have been so high. But in the everyday contact with Old Christians there was irritation and conflict over dress, speech, customs and, above all, food: Moriscos slaughtered their animal meat ritually, did not touch pork (the meat most commonly eaten in Spain) or wine, and cooked only with olive oil whereas Christians cooked with butter or lard. They tended also to live apart in separate communities, which could lead to antagonism: for example, in Aragon between highland Christians (the *montañeses*) and Moriscos living in the plains. Even in Castile, where the older Morisco communities were more assimilated, there were cases such as Hornachos (Extremadura), a flourishing and almost entirely Morisco town of 4,800 people which at the expulsion in 1610 emigrated in its entirety to Morocco. Though religious zeal was weaker in Castile and parts of Aragon, where coexistence with Christians had diluted traditional practices, Islam endured because of community solidarity. In general, Moriscos were strongly repelled by the doctrines of the Trinity and the divinity of Jesus, and felt extreme repugnance at the sacraments of baptism (families would wash the chrism off on returning home, and hold a Muslim ceremony), penitence and the Eucharist (Morisco irreverence at mass was proverbial).[6]

There were many attempts to catechize the Moriscos.[7] From 1526, missionary efforts were made in Valencia and Granada. In the 1540s a Franciscan, Fray Bartolomé de los Angeles, missionized Valencia; in the 1560s further campaigns were conducted in Valencia by Jesuits and other clergy. Much of this effort was based on a genuine attempt to come to terms with Arabic culture: in 1566 the Archbishop of Valencia, Martín de Ayala, published his manual *Doctrina Christiana en lengua aráviga y castellana*, and missioners were chosen who could speak Arabic. Juan de Ribera, the saintly prelate who became Archbishop of Valencia in 1568, initiated a financial scheme to increase the stipends of priests and make work among the Moriscos more congenial to the clergy. He also helped to found a seminary and a college for Morisco boys and girls. For the forty-three years that he held this see, Ribera made every

effort to travel round his bishopric and attend to the needs of the
Moriscos.

Considerable opposition to the missionary programme in the
crown of Aragon came, however, from the seigneurs, who had
opposed the forced conversions of 1526 and at every stage fought
the activities of the Inquisition. In 1561 in Valencia the inquisitor
Miranda named members of the rich Morisco family of Abenamir
as familiars of the Inquisition, but the Duke of Segorbe, their over-
lord, ordered them to give up the appointment since his protection
was sufficient for them. It was in the nobles' interest to keep their
Morisco dependants strictly subordinated, since they were a major
source of revenue. By extension, the nobles in various Cortes
pressed continually for Moriscos to be free from the confiscations
levied by the Inquisition, and this led eventually to the 1571 concordia. In 1541 the Admiral of Aragon, Sancho de Moncada, was
tried by the Inquisition for building a mosque for his Moriscos and
telling them 'that they should pretend to be Christians externally
but remain Moors internally'.[8] In 1566 the Inquisition of Aragon
complained that 'the seigneurs daily persecute the commissaries
and familiars that the Holy Office has in their lands, expelling them
and telling them that in their territory they want no Inquisition'.[9]
In 1571 the Grand Master of the Order of Montesa appeared in an
auto de fe for protecting his Moriscos. In 1582 in Aragon when the
lord of Ariza, Jaime Palafox, heard that the Inquisition had arrested
three of his vassals, he and his men burst into the house of a
familiar and beat and stabbed him to death; for this the courts sent
him for life to the north African fortress of Orán.[10]

Even had the nobles been more co-operative, it is unlikely that
the Moriscos would have responded favourably to Christian over-
tures. From the very beginning, legislation had attempted to deprive
them of any cultural identity, but they defiantly maintained and
proclaimed their separateness: María la Monja of Arcos in 1524 said
'that not for all the world would she cease saying that she had
been a Moor, so great a source of pride was it for her'.[11] The
authorities, as the Granada regulations of December 1526 showed,
were convinced that all Morisco customs were obstacles to the
acceptance of Christianity. In 1538 a Morisco of Toledo was arrested by the Inquisition and accused of 'playing music at night,
dancing the zambra [a traditional dance] and eating couscous',
implying that these activities were heretical. In 1544 the synod of
the bishopric of Guadix held that 'it is suspicious to take baths,

especially on Thursday and Friday night'! Even the Morisco manner of sitting – never on seats but always on the ground – could be viewed as Islamic. It was in vain that those who knew these customs for what they were protested. In 1513 Archbishop Talavera, who had encouraged his Moriscos to sing Arabic hymns at mass, complained to the crown. In 1514 the Count of Tendilla attacked Ferdinand's attempt to make Moriscos abandon their clothing: 'What clothing did we use to wear in Spain until the coming of King Henry the Bastard, how did we wear our hair, what sort of food did we eat, if not in the Morisco style?'[12] When all the repressive legislation was repeated in a pragmatic of January 1567 in Granada, Francisco Núñez Muley, a Morisco leader who had once been page to Talavera, drew up a memorial protesting against the injustices done to his people:

> Every day we are mistreated in every way, by both secular officials and clergy, all of which is so obvious that it needs no proof.... How can people be deprived of their natural tongue, in which they were born and raised? The Egyptians, Syrians, Maltese and other Christian people speak, read and write in Arabic, and are still Christians as we are.

Two generations of tension exploded finally into the revolt that began on Christmas Eve of 1568 in Granada and spread to the Alpujarras. It was a savage war, with atrocities on both sides, and military repression was brutal.[13] Thousands of Moriscos died, and over 80,000 were forcibly expelled from the kingdom and made to settle in Castile. The end of the rebellion did little to solve the problem. The Granadans brought into Castilian communities an Islamic presence they had not hitherto known: where Castile had had about 20,000 Mudejars, by the end of the century there were over 100,000, Arabic in tongue and Muslim in culture. Moreover, the military threat was now obvious. Some 4,000 Turks and Berbers had come into Spain to fight alongside the insurgents in the Alpujarras. Morisco banditry in the south reached its peak in the 1560s. There were millennarian hopes of liberation from oppression. Inevitably, seeing the obduracy of the Moriscos, the authorities reverted to a repressive policy.

The Inquisition was particularly active after the 1560s. In the tribunal of Cuenca the arrival of the Granadans quintupled the number of Moriscos prosecuted, strengthened the faith of the Castilian Muslims and provoked a wave of persecution by the Holy Office.[14] In the tribunal of Saragossa 266 Moriscos had been tried over the years 1540–59; between 1560 and 1614 the total shot up to 2,371, a ninefold increase. In Valencia there were eighty-two Morisco prosecutions in the earlier period, but 2,465 in the latter – a thirtyfold increase. In the autos de fe in both tribunals in the 1580s, Moriscos constituted up to 90 per cent of all accused.[15] It is true that the repression of the Moriscos was in no way comparable to the severity meted out to judaizers and Protestants: in Cuenca only seven Moriscos were relaxed in person out of 102 cases in the period 1583–1600, and in Granada only twenty were relaxed out of 917 Moriscos appearing in autos in the years 1550–95.[16] This was because the Moriscos were not usually treated as heretics but rather as infidels to whom patience should be shown. However, there is no doubt that the patience of the Christian missioners had long since run out. Reporting from a visit to the Moriscos of Aragon in 1568, the Bishop of Tortosa wrote: 'There people have me fed up and exasperated.... They have a damnable attitude and make me despair of any good in them.... I have been through these mountains for eight days now and find them more Moorish than ever and very set in their bad ways. I repeat my advice that they should be given a general pardon without insisting on confessions, for there is no other way (unless it be to burn them all).'[17] 'All of them live as Moors, and no one doubts this', the Inquisition of Aragon had affirmed in 1565.[18] Throughout Spain there was ample evidence that most Moriscos were proud of their Islamic religion and fought to preserve their culture: oppression only strengthened their separateness. 'They marry among themselves and do not mix with Old Christians, none of them enters religion nor joins the army nor enters domestic service nor begs alms; they live separately from Old Christians, take part in trade and are rich', runs a report of 1589 made to Philip II on the Moriscos of Toledo.[19] By contrast, for Moriscos the inquisitors were 'thieving wolves whose trade is arrogance and greed, sodomy and lust, tyranny, robbery and injustice'; the Inquisition was 'a tribunal of the devil, attended by deceit and blindness'.[20]

The confrontation between Christian and Islamic civilization in Spain moved towards a climax. In Granada Moriscos were now less than a tenth of the population[21] and the centre of tension moved to the huge Morisco community of Valencia,[22] where the military threat from the Ottoman empire, backed up by piracy and coastal raids, made the authorities take steps to restrict and disarm Moriscos. The Alpujarra crisis of 1568–70 was followed opportunely by victory at Lepanto in 1571, but Lepanto did not end fears of invasion.[23] Morisco banditry in the south worsened after the 1570s. From this decade French Protestant leaders were in touch with Aragonese Moriscos. In 1580 at Seville a conspiracy abetting invasion from Morocco was discovered. In 1602 Moriscos were plotting with Henry IV of France. In 1608 the Valencian Moriscos asked for help from Morocco. The threat was powerful and real: 'Fear entered into the heart of Spain.'[24]

Though Moriscos still retained their identity as a community, their active culture was forced, under the pressure of confrontation, to go underground. Castile seemed determined to uproot Arabic civilization.[25] In order to coexist with a majority religion, Muslims were allowed by their law to practise *taqiya*, 'dissimulation', feigning the established creed but practising their own.[26] Many continued to hold fast to the mediaeval ideal of convivencia (the Inquisition of Toledo tried one for saying 'that every one should be allowed to practise his own religion', another for maintaining 'that the Jew and the Muslim could each be saved in his own law'[27]). In time, however, as language faded and literature deteriorated – the late appearance of the romance *Abencerraje y Jarifa* in 1565, a story of love between Christian and Moor, was a Christian work with no relevance to the social reality of its time – only a few members of the Morisco elite were left to defend the vanished glory of Islamic Spain. It was at this stage in 1595 that the astonishing discovery was made in a cave at Sacromonte, Granada, of a number of tablets engraved in ancient Arabic and claiming to add information to the Christian revelation.[28] A big controversy ensued, with many Christian authorities believing in their genuineness; only in 1682 did Innocent XI pronounce the tablets fraudulent. The fraud had in fact been perpetrated by two prominent Moriscos, Miguel de Luna and Alonso del Castillo, in an attempt to syncretize Islamic culture and Christian faith.

By the 1580s official opinion had moved in favour of a solution similar to that of 1492. In Lisbon in 1581 Philip II convened a special committee to discuss the matter, and in September 1582 the Council of State formally proposed a general expulsion. The decision was approved by both Church and Inquisition. It was warmly supported by Martín de Salvatierra, Bishop of Segorbe, who in 1587 drew up a memorial favouring expulsion,[29] and by Archbishop Ribera who, seeing the failure of his zealous attempts to convert the Moriscos, turned into their most implacable enemy. There was, nevertheless, also opposition to the proposed expulsion.

The Cortes of both Castile and Valencia were silent on the matter, showing their lack of support, and under Philip III both the Duke of Lerma and the king's confessor in 1602 opposed expulsion since 'it would be terrible to drive baptized people into Barbary and thus force them to turn Moor'. As late as 1607 the crown's highest ministers preferred a policy of preaching and instruction. The arbitristas of the period were uniformly opposed to expulsion, and González de Cellorigo in his *Memorial* (1600) denounced the idea. Most powerful of all, the nobility of the crown of Aragon were solidly against any measure that would deprive them of their labour force.

However, by 1609 the Duke of Lerma had changed his mind, after presenting to the Council of State a decision that the lords in Valencia – where his own estates lay – should be compensated by being given the lands of the expelled Moriscos. The conviction also grew that Morisco population growth was uncontrollable: between Alicante and Valencia on one side and Saragossa on the other, a vast mass of 200,000 Moorish souls advanced into the flesh of Christian Spain. In Granada there were further expulsions to counteract the rise in numbers. In Aragon there had been 5,674 Moriscos in 1495, but in 1610 they numbered 14,190 – a fifth of the population. In Valencia the results of censuses made in 1565 and 1609 suggested that the Old Christians might have increased by 44.7 per cent and the Moriscos by a remarkable 69.7 per cent. 'Their aim was to grow and multiply like weeds', claimed a writer of 1612.[30] Castration as a method of control was recommended in 1587 by Martín de Salvatierra.

The expulsion was eventually decreed on 4 April 1609, and took place in stages up to 1614. Operations commenced in Valencia, which contained half the Moriscos in the peninsula and was therefore potentially the most dangerous province. In all, about 300,000 Moriscos were expelled, from a peninsular population of some 320,000.[31] Although the human losses of the expulsion represented little more than 4 per cent of Spain's population, the real impact in some areas was very severe. Where Moriscos had been a large minority, as in Valencia and Aragon, there was immediate economic catastrophe; but even where they were few in number, the fact that they had a minimal inactive population with no gentry or clergy or soldiers meant that their absence could lead to dislocation. Tax returns fell and agricultural output declined. The Inquisition also faced a bleak future. In 1611 the tribunals of Valencia and

Saragossa complained that the expulsion had resulted in their bankruptcy, since they were losing 7,500 ducats a year which they had
formerly received from ground-rents. The tribunal of Valencia at
the same time acknowledged receiving some compensation, but
claimed that a sum of nearly 19,000 ducats was still payable to it
by the government to make up for what it had lost.[32] A statement
of revenue drawn up for the tribunal of Valencia just before the
expulsion of the Moriscos shows that 42.7 per cent of its income
derived directly from the Morisco population. A similar statement
drawn up for the Inquisition of Saragossa in 1612 showed that
since the expulsion its revenue had fallen by over 48 per cent.[33]

Within about a century, with the support of the Inquisition, the
authorities had carried out a radical surgery to excise from Spain
two of the three great cultures of the peninsula. Cardinal Richelieu
in his memoirs described the Morisco expulsions as 'the most barbarous act in human annals'. Cervantes in his Quixote makes a
Morisco character, Ricote, applaud the heroic act of Philip III, 'to
expel poisonous fruit from Spain, now clean and free of the fears in
which our numbers held her'.[34] Writers then and later closed their
ranks and attempted to justify the operation. Virtually all the Valencian nobility at the time opposed expulsion, but Boronat, the
leading historian of the Morisco question, glosses over their universal opposition and praises those few lords 'of pure blood and
Christian heart' whose religion overrode their self-interest and made
them support the measure. For the historian Florencio Janer the
expulsion was the necessary excision of an 'enemy race' from the
heart of Spain.[35]

Such attitudes ignore the complexity of the problem. Opposition
to the hard line was more widespread than is often assumed. The
leading writer Pedro de Valencia, writing before the decision had
been taken, stated that 'expulsion is a harsh penalty and affects
many innocent children, and no unjust course that offends God can
be of benefit to the realm'.[36] Fernández de Navarrete in 1626
attacked the expulsion of both Jews and Moriscos as ill-advised. It
was by no means clear, moreover, that religion was the main motive for the measure. In 1611 when it was proposed to expel the
Moriscos of the valley of Ricote, a community of six towns in Murcia,
a special report pointed out that the 2,500 inhabitants were truly
Christian, but the expulsion still went ahead. Given the enormous
controversy aroused within Spain by the expulsions, it is not surprising that as late as 1690 the Moroccan envoy in Madrid could

report having heard officials denounce the Duke of Lerma's responsibility for the act.[37]

The attitude of the Inquisition, likewise, was neither uniform nor always hard-line. In Valencia, for example, the inquisitors in 1582 were pessimistic about christianizing the Moriscos – 'in the six hundred years that they have lived in Spain we have seen few converted' – and proposed 'to expel all of them from Valencia and settle them in Old Castile, but not to send them to the Levant or Barbary, because after all *they are Spaniards like ourselves*'.[38] By the end of that year the prospect of expulsion had already been broached. The Spanish Inquisition took no active part in the decision to expel, which was arrived at exclusively by a small group of politicians in Madrid. It continued, however, to act with severity against Moriscos accused of offences against religion, and after 1609 those still in its cells were given the unenviable choice of punishment or exile. A small proportion of Moriscos managed to obtain special permission to remain: they consisted in part of the wealthy assimilated elite, and in part of slaves. Almost in its totality, Muslim Spain was rejected and driven into the sea: thousands for whom there had been no other home were expelled to France, Africa, the Levant.[39] It was the last act in the creation of a closed society and completed the tragedy that had been initiated in 1492.

Despite official propaganda, there is little proof that the expulsion was supported by Spaniards. 'It is a most malign policy of state', Fernández de Navarrete commented in 1626, 'for princes to withdraw their trust from their subjects.' Nor was the realm as cleansed from Islamic heresy as the zealots would have wished. Between 1615 and 1700 prosecutions of Moriscos made up about 9 per cent of cases tried by the Inquisition: the frequency in that period varied from only one case in Valladolid to 197 in Valencia and 245 in Murcia.[40] There continued, moreover, to be startling incidents in later years, such as the group of wealthy Morisco families brought to trial in Granada in 1728.[41] Convivencia had vanished from Spain. But had religious peace and unity been achieved?

Racialism and its Critics

Yo soy un hombre,
aunque de villana casta,
limpio de sangre y jamás
de hebrea o mora manchada.

Lope de Vega, *Peribáñez*

Social attitudes in late mediaeval Spain were inevitably conditioned by the political, religious and military environment. The relatively democratic nature of Castilian society meant that social mobility was accompanied by mobility of ideals between upper and lower classes. Thus a 'noble' attitude to life was not necessarily restricted to the noble elite: members of the humblest professions, especially in northern Spain, could claim to be hidalgos and enjoy the privileges attached to rank. Rank demanded respect for one's integrity or 'honour'. In Old Christian society, honour had been earned not simply by personal integrity but also by demonstrating that one had achieved distinction: thus the winning of honour in battle was a sure step upwards. In time the respected ideals of society – valour, virility, piety, honest wealth – became the basis of 'honour' and 'reputation'. At its simplest level in the village, 'honour' was the opinion held of one by neighbours, and to compromise one's honour – by crime, by sexual misconduct – brought disgrace. At the apex of the social pyramid a noble was in danger of compromising his honour in many ways, but society allowed him several avenues of defence, not least because a prominent person was responsible for protecting not only his own personal honour but also that of his kin, his dependants and sometimes his community. The violent methods of protecting honour – assassinating a seducer, duelling with someone who had offered an insult – were punishable by law, but in many cases the law gave way to public opinion and let the perpetrator go free.

The concept of honour discriminated against the unsuccessful. The poor, mean and outcast were deemed incapable of honour. An hidalgo was permitted to obtain wealth, but not through vulgar means such as working for an employer. Those who did not share the same faith were likewise arguably out of the scope of honour. In Reconquest Spain this theoretically applied to Jews and Muslims, but in practice it applied only to the humbler social ranks: there is ample evidence of Jews and Muslims of the elite being treated on equal terms by Christians. By the fifteenth century the deterioration in the social position of Jews and Muslims had decisively affected their capacity to obtain honour. Certainly, the Castilian view that all Old Christians, by the mere fact of not being tainted by semitic blood, were honourable, was becoming widespread. 'Though poor,' says Sancho Panza, 'I am an Old Christian, and owe nothing to anybody.' It was felt that Spain, its traditions and faith, belonged exclusively to Old Christians. The heritage could not be shared with those who were outside the picture, whether Jews or Moors or heretics. What had begun as social discrimination developed into racial antagonism and racialism.

The concept of honour, pride and reputation became chauvinistic and exclusivist.[1] By the fifteenth century it was felt by many that the honour of one's faith and nation could be preserved only by ensuring that one's lineage was preserved free of contamination by Jews and Muslims. Yet what if the highest ranks of the nobility had been penetrated by Jewish blood? It was notorious that the principal families of Aragon and Castile, and even the royal family, could trace their descent through conversos. Old Christian Spain would collapse if this process went on. A few zealous souls therefore considered that now was the time to stop the Jewish fifth column. With this we have the beginnings of a new stress on racial purity and the consequent rise of the cult of *limpieza de sangre* (purity of blood).

The first serious attempt in Castile to discriminate between Christians on the grounds of race alone occurred, as we have seen, in the Toledo disturbances of 1449. There were precedents for the move: in Aragon as early as 1437, complaints were made to the pope that conversos were being excluded from office.[2] An early case in Castile occurred in the town of Villena, which had been granted a royal privilege in February 1446 to exclude conversos from residence. The Toledo troubles encouraged further discrimination. In

1468 the crown granted Ciudad Real the right to exclude conversos from office. In 1473 in Córdoba there were serious disturbances after the formation of a confraternity excluding conversos.

The Toledo riots touched such important issues of principle that an immediate controversy was aroused. One of the first attacks on the 1449 *Sentencia-Estatuto* was made by the distinguished legist Alfonso Díaz de Montalvo,[3] who emphasized the common traditions and inheritance of Jews and Christians, and pointed out that a baptized Jew was no different from a baptized Gentile. The Mother of God and all the Apostles, he said, had been Jews. Those self-styled Christians who had drawn up the *Sentencia* were moved by material greed and were wolves disguised as sheep in the flock of Christ. At the same time the converso royal secretary Fernan Díaz de Toledo drew up his *Instrucción* for his friend Lope de Barrientos, Bishop of Cuenca, in which he doubted whether any noble family in Castile were free of converso origins. Another distinguished intervention came from the Dominican Cardinal Juan de Torquemada, who was also of converso origin, in his *Treatise against Midianites and Ishmaelites* (1449).[4] The most important refutation of the *Sentencia* came from the pen of the Bishop of Burgos, Alonso de Cartagena, son of the converso Pablo de Santa María, his predecessor in the see. In his *Defensorium Unitatis Christianae* (1449–50),[5] he argued that the Catholic Church was properly the home of the Jews, and that Gentiles were the outsiders who had been invited in. His moderate arguments were continued by the General of the Jeronimites, the converso Alonso de Oropesa, who in 1465 completed his *Lumen ad revelationem gentium*, which stressed the need for unity in the Church, and outlined the rightful place held in it by Jews.[6]

The objections raised by these writers, and reflected in the hostility to the *Sentencia* shown both by the pope and the Archbishop of Toledo,[7] were not enough to prevail against political faction, demagogy and prejudice. By 1461 Alonso de Espina was pressing for an Inquisition to be established. It was certainly the Inquisition that, from 1480 onwards, gave a major impetus to the spread of racial discrimination in favour of purity of blood. The social antagonism of which Spaniards had long been aware was now heightened by the spectacle of thousands of judaizers being found guilty of heretical practices and herded to the stake. National security no less than religious purity seemed to depend on the exclusion of conversos from all positions of trust and importance. In 1483 a papal bull ordered that episcopal inquisitors should be Old Christians, and in the same year the Order of Alcántara issued a statute excluding all descendants of Moors and Jews from its ranks. One by one the religious bodies began to insert conditions of limpieza into their statutes.

The Colegio Mayor of San Bartolomé in Salamanca may have been the first university college to adopt a statute of limpieza, shortly after 1482.[8] The Colegio of Santa Cruz at Valladolid had a statute as part of its foundation rules in 1488. Other colleges did not hesitate to contradict the rules of their founders. That of San Ildefonso, founded by Cisneros in 1486, had no statutes against conversos, but after the cardinal's death the college adopted one in 1519. When he founded the great monastery of St Thomas Aquinas at Avila, Torquemada applied to the pope in 1496 for a decree excluding all descendants of Jews. It was not until 1531 that any other Dominican foundation followed Torquemada's lead. The first cathedral chapter to adopt a limpieza statute was that of Badajoz in 1511. The cathedral chapter of Seville in 1515 adopted the same ruling on the initiative of its archbishop, the inquisitor Diego de Deza. The University of Seville, although it had been founded by a converso, in 1537 adopted a statute of limpieza after someone had carefully blotted out of the original charter the clause making the university open to all.[9]

The Inquisition played a leading part in all these events. From the beginning it had been the rule, as set out in Torquemada's instruction issued at Seville in November 1484, that

the children and grandchildren of those condemned [by the Inquisition] may not hold or possess public offices, or posts, or honours, or be promoted to holy orders, or be judges, mayors, constables, magistrates, jurors, stewards, officials of weights and measures, merchants, notaries, public scriveners, lawyers, attorneys, secretaries, accountants, treasurers, physicians, surgeons, shopkeepers, brokers, changers, weight inspectors, collectors, tax-farmers, or holders of any other similar public office.[10]

This practice was upheld by the Catholic monarchs, who issued two decrees in 1501 forbidding the children of those condemned by the tribunal to hold any post of honour or to be notaries, scriveners, physicians or surgeons.

The liberality of the Jeronimites, shown in the writings of Alonso de Oropesa, General of his Order from 1457 and re-elected for four successive terms, appears to have attracted judaizers to become members.[11] Officials resisted pressure to discriminate, but in 1485 a scandal broke over the mother house at Guadalupe, where it was found that a friar, Diego de Marchena, had been accepted as a member though he had never been baptized, and that he continued to practise Judaism within the protection of the monastery. The chapter meeting of the order in 1486 adopted a statute excluding conversos, despite a special appeal from Ferdinand and Isabella that they should not. The decision was unfortunately reinforced by the discovery that year of a nest of judaizers in the Jeronimite monastery of La Sisla in Toledo. The prior, García de Zapata, used to say when elevating the Host at mass, 'Up, little Peter, and let the people look at you', and when in confession would always turn his back on the penitent. The Inquisition of Toledo burnt him and four other monks of the monastery in 1486–7. Though there continued to be very strong opposition within the Order to the statute of exclusion, it was not revoked and indeed in 1552 the exclusion was extended to all those of Moorish origin. Other religious orders were slow to follow the Jeronimite example. Not until 1525 did the Franciscans adopt a statute of limpieza, against strong internal opposition. Shortly after this the Dominicans began discrimination, and a limpieza statute was adopted by them in Aragon. All these measures were crowned by the definitive adoption of a statute by the cathedral chapter of Toledo in 1547.

The Archbishop of Toledo had attempted unsuccessfully in 1539 to introduce a statute of limpieza. His successor in 1546, Juan Martínez Siliceo, did not mean to fail.[12] Born of humble peasant stock, Siliceo had struggled upwards to carve out a brilliant career for himself. He had studied for six years at the University of Paris and later taught there for three. Called home to teach at Salamanca, he soon attracted enough attention to be appointed tutor to Charles v's son, Philip, a post he held for ten years. When the see of Toledo fell vacant in 1546 he was appointed to it. The new archbishop was preoccupied with more than merely his freshly won dignity. He had been haunted all his life by the shadow of his humble origins, and drew his only pride from the fact that his parents had been Old Christians.

In his new post he felt in no mood to compromise with converso Christians whose racial antecedents were in his mind the principal threat to a secure and unsullied Church. When, therefore, in September 1546 he discovered that the pope had just appointed a converso, Doctor Fernando Jiménez, to a vacant canonry in the cathedral, and that the new incumbent's father had once been condemned by the Inquisition as a judaizer, he refused to accept the appointment. Siliceo wrote to the pope protesting against his candidate, and sounding a warning that the first church in Spain was now in danger of becoming a 'new synagogue'. The pope withdrew his man, but Siliceo thought this was not enough and proceeded to draw up a statute to exclude all conversos from office in the cathedral. A chapter meeting was hurriedly convoked on 23 July 1547, and with ten dissentient votes against twenty-four the statute of limpieza was pushed through.

The voting figures show that not all the canons had been present at the meeting. An immediate protest was raised by the Archdeacons of Guadalajara and Talavera, Pero González de Mendoza and Alvaro de Mendoza, both sons of the powerful Duke of Infantado, and both Old Christians. Condemning the injustice and impropriety of the statute, they criticized the archbishop for not calling all the dignitaries of the cathedral to his meeting, and also threatened to appeal to the pope. The controversy that followed gives us an invaluable summary of the views both of opponents and of supporters of the limpieza statutes.

According to the explanatory document drawn up by Siliceo,[13] the policy of limpieza was now practised in Spain by the military orders, by university colleges and by religious orders. The existence of a converso danger was proved by the fact that the Lutheran heretics of Germany were nearly all descendants of Jews. Nearer home, 'the archbishop has found that not only the majority but nearly all the parish priests of his archdiocese with a care of souls ... are descendants of Jews.' Moreover, conversos were not content with controlling the wealth of Spain. They were now trying to dominate the Church. The size of the danger was shown by the fact that in the last fifty years over fifty thousand conversos had been burnt and punished by the Inquisition, yet they still continued to flourish. To emphasize this argument, the archbishop demonstrated that of the ten who had voted against the statute, no less than nine were of Jewish origin, five of them coming from the prolific converso family to which Fray Garcia de Zapata belonged. The opposition to the statute, however, was of greater significance than this might suggest. It is true that among the most hostile to the statute were the dean of the cathedral, Diego de Castilla, and the illustrious humanist Juan de Vergara, both conversos; but at least six other canons who shared their hostility were Old Christians. What distinguished these canons (two of whom were, as we know, of the noble house of Mendoza) and the dean was their irrefutably aristocratic lineage, in contrast to Siliceo, who was of humble origin. In the protest drawn up by the dissentient clergy[14] the complaint was made that, first, the statute was against canon law; secondly, it was against the laws of the kingdom; thirdly, it contradicted Holy Scripture; fourthly, it was against natural reason; and, fifthly, it defamed 'many noble and leading people of these realms'. The sting lay in the fifth article. As Siliceo and his opponents well knew, few members of the nobility had not been tainted with converso blood. By promoting a limpieza statute, therefore, the archbishop was obviously claiming for his own class a racial purity which the tainted nobility could not boast.

Despite all opposition, however, the statute was authoritatively confirmed and the pope ratified it in 1555. Philip II wavered at first in his attitude, but eventually in 1556 came down in favour. A letter written by the king at this time reveals his firm belief that 'all the heresies which have occurred in Germany and France have been sown by descendants of Jews, as we have seen and still see daily in Spain'.[15] When the judgments of the King of Spain and of the leader of the Spanish Church had been so clouded by antisemitic fantasies, it was not surprising to discover the same prejudices rooted in the heart of Spanish society.

Controversy over the question was not exhausted by Siliceo's success. The 1547 statute of Toledo was immediately condemned by the University of Alcalá as a source of 'discord sown by the devil'. In Rome Pope Paul IV had approved the statute, but he did this out of policy and not principle. The same Paul IV in 1565 refused to approve a statute for the cathedral of Seville and condemned limpieza as contrary to canon law and ecclesiastical order. His successor Pius V was a consistent enemy of the statutes,[16] and tried in vain to get a nominee of his who was not limpio elected as Archdeacon of Toledo. The tide of controversy was stemmed by the Inquisition, which in 1572 tried to forbid any writings either for or against the statutes. But as long as limpieza was practised and upheld by Church, State and Inquisition, the dust could not be allowed to settle.

Because the shadow of racialism was slowly extending itself across Spain, there is a danger of exaggerating its extent.[17] Antisemitism was everywhere, but not all institutions or individuals practised it. In 1522, for example, the Inquisition stipulated that the Universities of Salamanca and Valladolid should not grant degrees to conversos.[18] But in 1537 Charles V decreed that in colleges where New Christians were being excluded, 'the constitutions of the founders be respected'.[19] Indeed throughout the period, conversos can be found both as students and as professors in the major universities. Likewise, though the Inquisition was undoubtedly a force for antisemitism, it did not specifically exclude conversos as officials until as late as the 1550s, and only in 1572 were strict rules for entry laid down. Apart from the Inquisition there appear to have been statutes of limpieza[20] in the six Colegios Mayores of Castile, in the Military Orders (the Order of Santiago adopted one only as late as 1555), in some religious orders (Jeronimites, Dominicans and Franciscans), in some cathedrals (Toledo, Seville, Córdoba, Jaén, Osma, León, Oviedo and Valencia), and in various local confraternities and guilds. Private legal arrangements, such as entails (mayorazgos), might also lay down conditions of limpieza. In all these cases, and notably in the universities and the religious orders, the rules were regularly infringed. In international bodies such as the mendicant orders, moreover, it was impossible to operate absolute exclusion. There were, indeed, so many areas where limpieza did not apply, that opponents of the statutes questioned whether it was logical to continue discrimination when it was still possible for a converso to enter most religious orders, become a priest or bishop, enter the army, become a regidor or corregidor, or obtain a noble title.[21]

Though limpieza was practised in only a limited number of public institutions, these were undeniably so important that a serious barrier to status mobility was created. In theory canon law limited the extent to which the sins of fathers could be visited on their sons and grandsons. But limpieza in practice adopted no such limits. If it were proved that an ancestor on any side of the family had been penanced by the Inquisition or was a Moor or Jew, the descendant could be accounted of impure blood and disabled from office. Applicants for many posts had to present genealogical proofs of the purity of their lineage. The fraud, perjury, extortion and blackmail that came into existence because of the need to prove limpieza was widely recognized as a moral evil. If pretendants to office could not offer convincing genealogical proofs, commissioners were appointed to visit the localities concerned and take sworn statements from witnesses about the antecedents of the applicant. The commissioners examined parish records and collected verbal testimony. In an age when written evidence was rare, the reputation of applicants lay wholly at the mercy of local gossip and hostile neighbours, so that bribery became necessary. If an applicant was refused a post with the Inquisition the tribunal never gave any reason, with the result that the family of the man became suspected of impurity even if this was not the case. Some applicants had to go through legal processes which lasted as long as two years, with all the attendant expenses, before a proper genealogy could be drawn up. Others resorted to perjury to obtain posts, thus involving themselves and their witnesses in heavy fines and infamy when the tribunal discovered their offence. Frequently applicants would be disabled from employment simply by the malicious gossip of enemies, because 'common rumour' was generally allowed as evidence.[22] Genealogy became a social weapon, and in a society where the genealogical proof was a principal passport to employment in Church and State, it may safely be said that racialism had been erected into the system of government.

The importance of the concept of 'infamy' cannot be exaggerated. The honour of a Castilian lay in his religion and his race. If either was impugned it would bring shame and disgrace upon both himself and his family and all his descendants. This view was followed by a writer of the time of Philip iv, Juan Escobar de Corro, who in his *Tractatus bipartitus de puritate et nobilitate probanda* equated the words 'purity' and 'honour', and considered death preferable to infamy. For Escobar the stain on an impure lineage was ineffaceable and perpetual.[23] Here was a racialist doctrine of original sin of the most repulsive kind, at least by Christian standards, for it meant that not even baptism was able to wash away the sins of one's fathers. The Inquisition made its own contribution to this attitude. Recalcitrant heretics were burnt in autos de fe, but lesser offenders were given punishments including the wearing of garments called sanbenitos, worn also by victims before they were burnt. Early in the sixteenth century the practice was begun of hanging up the sanbenitos of victims after the period for which the garment had to be worn. This practice was standardized by the official Instructions of 1561, which stipulated that

> all the sanbenitos of the condemned, living or dead, present or absent, be placed in the churches where they used to live ... in order that there may be perpetual memory of the infamy of the heretics and their descendants.[24]

The declared aim of displaying these sanbenitos was therefore to publish and perpetuate the infamy of condemned persons, so that from generation to generation whole families should be penalized for the sins of their ancestors. There is no doubt that this was the deliberate aim, for it became general practice to replace old and decaying sanbenitos with new ones bearing the same names of the offenders. These sanbenitos were widely hated not only by the families concerned but also by the districts on which they brought disrepute. The city of Logroño (Navarre) in 1570 successfully petitioned the Suprema to be allowed to remove from its churches the great number of sanbenitos belonging properly to churches in other regions.[25] The fear in this case was that so many garments would bring disrepute on the whole city and province. In the rising against the Spanish government in Sicily in 1516, the sanbenitos in the churches were torn down and never replaced. In the peninsula, however, the tribunal took every care to ensure that sanbenitos should be exposed ceaselessly, and this was practised diligently everywhere until the end of the eighteenth century. One of the obvious and particular uses of this system was that genealogical proofs could easily be tested against the evidence of the garments. As matters turned out, in the end it mattered not at all whether a man had been burnt or simply made to do penance in an auto de fe. Thanks to the sanbenito, his descendants still laboured under civil disability and public infamy.

Infamy was beyond doubt the worst punishment imaginable in those times. In the ordinary criminal courts, humiliating punishments that brought public shame (*vergüenza*) and ridicule were feared more than the death sentence,[26] since they ruined one's reputation for ever in the local community and brought disgrace on all one's family and relatives. In the Inquisition, similarly, one's 'honour' could be destroyed by humiliating penalties (such as flogging), but the gravest of all punishments was the sanbenito, since its duration was perpetual, bringing shame both on family and local community. When young Ana Enríquez, daughter of the Marquis of Alcanices and sister-in-law of Francisco Borja, was condemned by the Inquisition in 1559 to wear a sanbenito for her part in the Protestant group of Valladolid, Borja used his influence to have the sanbenito part of her sentence annulled: the 'honour' of her family was thereby saved. Though the Holy Office was clearly responsible for perpetuating infamy, from very early on it also tried to restrict the rumour and slander associated with it, and in numerous cases prosecuted those who attempted to defame their neighbours. Ironically, it therefore became an offence, punishable by the Inquisition, to call someone a 'Jew': in 1620, for example, Antonio Vergoños, a familiar and priest of Gerona, was banished for a year from his village for slandering a neighbour as a 'Jueu'.[27]

Spanish concern over infamy extended also to non-Judaic heresy. The violent reaction against the Valladolid Protestants was provoked in part by a curious national pride which did not admit the possibility of Castilians becoming infested by heresy. 'Before that time', commented one contemporary, 'Spain was clean [limpia] of these errors.'[28] When Carlos de Seso and Fray Domingo de Rojas were being brought back to Valladolid, reported the Inquisitor General, 'in all the villages through which they passed, crowds of men, women and children came out to see them, calling for them to be burnt. The friar[29] was very afraid that his relatives would kill him on the journey.'[30] Rojas had good reason to fear. We know of the remarkable case of Juan Díaz – a Spanish disciple and friend of the reformer Bucer – who was assassinated in Germany by his own brother Alfonso, a Catholic who feared that his brother's heresy would bring shame on his family and on all Spain.[31] The Inquisition shared this attitude to the extent of trying to pursue Spanish heretics such as Miguel Servet even beyond the borders of Spain, for fear that their heresies would bring disgrace on the honour of the Spanish nation.[32] The tradition was continued with some energy by the government of Philip II, which employed the heretic-hunter Alonso del Canto in the Netherlands to bring back to Spain those who might bring ill-fame on the country.[33]

The social consequences of the limpieza cult were so corrosive that there was always strong opposition to it, even at the highest levels. It became a continual source of friction between the Society of Jesus and the Inquisition. Ignatius Loyola had first encountered fears of illuminism and Judaism when, as a student at Alcalá in 1527, he fell under suspicion because of his strict religious practices. This was the very year that the province of Guipúzcoa made into law an earlier ordinance of 1483, forbidding entry to conversos. At this time Ignatius indignantly denied any knowledge of Judaism, since he was a noble from a province (Guipúzcoa) which had hardly known Jews. Some years later, however, he declared while dining with friends that he would have considered it a divine favour to be descended from Jews. When asked his reason for saying this, he protested, 'What! To be related to Christ Our Lord and to Our Lady the glorious Virgin Mary?' On another occasion a fellow Basque who was a friend of his had spat at the word 'Jew' when the saint mentioned it. On this, Ignatius took him aside and said, according to his biographer, ' "Now, Don Pedro de Zárate, be reasonable and listen to me" – And he gave him so many reasons that he all but persuaded him to become a Jew'.[34] These incidents show that Ignatius had so far escaped the influence of the atmosphere in Spain as to become a deep and sincere spiritual Semite.

Like its founder, the Society of Jesus refused to associate itself with racialism. When in 1551 the Jesuits opened a college at Alcalá without the permission of Archbishop Siliceo, the latter issued an order forbidding any Jesuit to act as a priest without first being personally examined by him. It was no secret that the reason for this order was Siliceo's hostility to the presence of converso Christians in the college. Francisco Villanueva, rector of the college, wrote indignantly to Ignatius about this.

> It is a great pity that there seems to be nobody willing to leave these poor people anywhere to stay on earth, and I would like to have the energy to become their defender, particularly since one encounters among them more virtue than among the Old Christians and hidalgos.[35]

Among Spanish Jesuits, however, there were inevitably those who took their race seriously. The first Provincial of the Jesuits in Spain, Antonio de Araoz, was one of these. He impressed upon Ignatius the fact that Siliceo had promised to visit the order with great favours if it would only adopt a statute of limpieza. He also warned that the good name of the Society in Spain would be harmed by the knowledge that there were New Christians in its ranks. Despite this Ignatius refused to change his attitude. All through the controversy in Spain about the statutes of limpieza, and up to his death in 1556, he would not allow his order to discriminate against conversos, and when conversos did apply to enter its ranks he advised them to join the Company in Italy rather than in Spain. When talking of the limpieza cult he would refer to it as *el humor español* – 'the Spanish humour'; or, more bitingly on one occasion, *humor de la corte y del Rey de España* – 'the humour of the Spanish king and his court'.

Because of the opposition of the Jesuits, Siliceo conceived an ardent hatred of the order, and in this he was followed by other prominent members of the Spanish clergy and the Inquisition. All three Generals of the order after Loyola were firm in their opposition to the statutes. The immediate successor of Ignatius was Diego Laínez, General from 1558 to 1565. The fact that he was a converso aroused bitter opposition to his election from Philip II and the Spanish Church. In a letter to Araoz in 1560 Laínez denounced limpieza as *el humor o error nacional* (the national humour or error) and demanded total obedience from the Spanish Jesuits. His successor was a Spaniard of unimpeachable Old Christian blood – Francisco Borja, Duke of Gandia, famous to history as St Francis. Borja's position was so well known that he was victimized to the extent of having his work put on the Index of prohibited books. On one of his visits to Spain the prime minister of Philip II, the prince of Eboli, asked Borja why his Company allowed conversos in its ranks. Borja's retort was uncompromising:

> Why does the king keep in his service x and y, who are conversos? If His Majesty disregards this in those he places in his household, why should I make an issue about admitting them into the service of that Lord for whom there is no distinction between persons, between Greek and Jew, or barbarian and Scythian?[36]

By the 1590s, however, the Jesuits in Spain found that recruits were falling off as the whispering campaign initiated by its enemies succeeded in presenting the Society as a party of Jews. Moreover, by a process of selection the chief posts in the Spanish province were going to Jesuits who favoured the statutes. The result was the success of pressure for a modification to the constitution of the Society, and at the General Congregation held at Rome in December 1593 it was voted to exclude all conversos from membership in Spain. Against this dishonourable retreat the lone voice raised in protest was that of a Spaniard, Father Ribadeneira.[37] Due almost exclusively to his singlehanded efforts to keep the Society to the path laid down by Loyola, a reaction to the vote of 1593 took place in the order. This led to a modificatory decree in February 1608, by which all conversos who had been Christians for five generations were allowed to enter the Society. The 1608 decree was nominally only a concession, but in practice it involved the complete reversal of the decision of 1593, since most conversos in Spain had in fact been Christians for five generations, as a result of the compulsory conversions of 1492.

Though a few other sees followed Toledo in adopting limpieza, the statutes were never universally accepted in Spain. Melchor Cano appears to have criticized them in a paper of 1550, and another Dominican, Domingo Baltañas, attacked them in a book published in Seville in 1556.[38] In Rome, prominent Spaniards spoke openly against limpieza. This persuaded Diego de Simancas, Bishop of Zamora, to publish in about 1572[39] his *Defensio Statuti Toletani*, possibly the last substantial defence of the racialist doctrines of Siliceo. By the end of the sixteenth century a profound dismay at the consequences of limpieza had begun to penetrate the upper circles of society. In a society where the degree of racial admixture gave no guarantee against impure blood, inquiries into ancestry threatened the security of the noblest families. For one member of a family to be refused a post because of suspicion of impurity meant an automatic and sometimes perpetual stigma on the rest of the family. The practice of limpieza therefore threatened to expose the entire nobility to infamy.

At this point a revolutionary *crise de conscience* occurred in the very citadel of orthodoxy, the Inquisition.[40] From about 1580, when Cardinal Quiroga – friend of the Jesuits and a notable opponent of antisemitism – was Inquisitor General, serious doubts about the statutes were raised in the Holy Office. 'I was in the Council of the Inquisition in 1580', reports a subsequent Inquisitor General, Guevara, 'and saw this matter proceed very far, with the Council resolved to petition the king about it, and putting forward many pressing reasons.' Nothing more seems to have happened until 1598, when Philip II himself had second thoughts. The king, reports a later writer, 'was very attached to the statutes, but in the last days of his life, when experience had matured, he ordered a big committee to be set up specifically to discuss this matter, and all of them agreed with His Majesty that the statutes should be restricted to one hundred years', meaning that freedom from the taint of heresy for three generations should make any converso fit for office.

Because of the king's death, nothing came of the proposal, but the ground was prepared for the great attack on the statutes mounted by the noted Dominican theologian Agustín Salucio, whose *Discurso* on limpieza was published in 1599.[41] Salucio, then aged seventy-six (he died in 1601), felt that 'I could not be true to my conscience if I did not speak my opinion on so important a matter.' His book was supported by personal letters from the very highest authorities: the patriarch of Valencia, Juan de Ribera; the Archbishop of Burgos; the Duke of Lerma.[42] Taking his stand on the innumerable abuses committed in the process of limpieza proofs – false testimony, bribery, forgery, lies – Salucio protested that 'the scandals and abuses ... have provoked a secret war against the authority of the statutes'. 'It is said', he commented, 'that there is no peace when the State is divided into two factions, as it is now

divided almost in half, as in a civil war.' He presented two main
objections of principle to the statutes: they had outlived their purpose; and whatever good they achieved was outweighed by the
harm. 'It would be a great comfort to the assurance of peace in the
realm', he summed up, 'to restrict the statutes so that Old Christians
and Moriscos and conversos should all come to form one united
body, and that all should be Old Christians and in peace.'

This noble and historic work, testimony to a profound yearning
for racial and religious peace in Spain, caused an immediate crisis
in the Inquisition. The Suprema overruled the Inquisitor General
and banned the book. However, procuradores of the Cortes had
been sent copies of the *Discourse* by wily old Salucio, and they at
once insisted on debating the matter. On 11 February 1600 they
presented a memorial to the king, petitioning 'how important it is
to make a decision on this matter, because of the great offences
caused to God every day'. At the same time they set up a committee
to report on Salucio's paper. In a discussion paper sent by the Cortes
to the committee, they complained that 'in Spain we esteem a
common person who is *limpio* more than a hidalgo who is not
limpio'.[43] As a result, the memorial continued, there were now two
sorts of nobility in Spain, 'a greater, which is that of *hidalguía*; and
a lesser, which is that of limpieza, whose members we call Old
Christians'. Irrational criteria of purity had also come into existence:
swordsmen were reputed *limpios* and physicians were reputed Jews;
people from León and Asturias were called Old Christians and those
from Almagro conversos.

> All this is so absurd that were we another nation we would call ourselves
> barbarians who governed themselves without reason, without law, and
> without God . . .
>   Another evil effect is that because of rigorous genealogical proofs the
> State loses eminent subjects who have the talent to become great theo-
> logians and jurists but who do not follow these professions because they
> know they will not be admitted to any honours.

As a result, people of no rank and little learning had risen to high
posts in the country, while true and learned nobility had been
deprived of the chance to pursue their careers. Discrimination
against Jewish blood would only make the conversos become more
compact, defensive and dangerous; whereas in France and Italy the
lack of discrimination had allowed them to merge peacefully into
the community. The natural consequence of limpieza proofs would
be that those who were irrefutably *limpios* (and hence alone capable

of holding office) would soon be a tiny minority in the country, with the great mass of the people against them, 'affronted, discontented and ripe for rebellion'.

In the summer of 1600 the Duke of Lerma asked the new Inquisitor General, Cardinal Niño de Guevara, to report on Salucio's book and various other documents. In August Guevara sent the king an astonishing report,[44] which contradicted the views of the majority of the Suprema and praised Salucio as 'a very learned friar to whom the whole Catholic Church and particularly the Holy Office owe a great deal'. The split in the Inquisition was not resolved, and Salucio's book remained under ban. However, with so many eminent leaders of Church and State hostile to the statutes, the floodgates to public discussion had been opened. In about 1613 a New Christian of Portuguese origin, Diego Sánchez de Vargas, issued in Madrid an attack against the statutes. In 1616 the Madrid magistrate, Mateo López Bravo, complained in his *De rege* that for those excluded by the limpieza laws 'there remains no way of hope except the sowing of discord'. In 1619 Martín González de Cellorigo, now resident in Toledo and an official of the Inquisition, wrote a *Plea for Justice* on behalf of the New Christians: it was addressed to the Inquisitor General but not actually published.[45]

In about 1621 an inquisitor, Juan Roco Campofrío, Bishop of Zamora and later of Soria, wrote a *Discurso*[46] against the statutes. According to him, the proofs of limpieza were a source of moral and political scandal in the nation. The stigma of impurity had divided Spain into two halves, one of which was constantly warring against the other. The outrages and quarrels provoked by the statutes had been responsible for over 90 per cent of the civil and criminal trials in Spanish courts. The racialism of the statutes was wrong, for many conversos and Moriscos had been more virtuous than so-called Old Christians, and many of those brought to trial by the Inquisition had in fact been Old Christians and not Jews. The great danger, the inquisitor went on, was that the greater part of the population of Spain would soon be branded as impure, and the only remaining guarantee of Old Christian blood would be one's plebeian origin. The defection of the inquisitor from the traditional belief in limpieza represented only one of the many tracts written in this period against a cult that divided society against itself. López Bravo's strictures, for example, were repeated with approval by Fernández de Navarrete in 1626.

Though Lerma had been opposed to the statutes, he did little to change them. It was otherwise with Olivares, who came to power in 1621 at the accession of Philip IV. Olivares never made a secret of his hostility to limpieza. At his instigation, the Inquisition in 1622 issued perhaps the most remarkable document ever to proceed from the inner portals of the Holy Office.

Conceding that there were now few or no judaizers in Spain, the Suprema in this 1622 document argued that 'it follows that since what gave rise to the statutes has totally ceased, it would be civic and political prudence that at least the rigour of their practice should cease'. Denouncing the widespread perjuries and forgeries involved, the inquisitors said: 'nobody can doubt this if he sees what goes on today in every city, town or village, even in the testimonials for familiars in any little hamlet. No one could better inform Your Majesty of this abuse, from direct experience, than the Holy Office.' After analysing in detail the evils of the system of genealogical proofs, the Suprema went on to argue that Hebrews no less than Gentiles were members of Christ's Church, and that unity of all, without discrimination, was essential. In words that could have been written by Olivares himself, the Council of the Inquisition stated that its aspirations were exactly those of Philip IV:

> that your several kingdoms should act in conformity and unity for both good and ill, joining together in friendly equality, so that Castile should act with Aragon, and both with Portugal, and all of them with Italy and the other realms, to help and aid each other as though they were one body (fortunate enough to have Your Majesty as head). These considerations, so in keeping with God's intentions, are in large measure frustrated if there remain such odious divisions and such bloody enmities as those which exist between those held to be *limpios*, and those held to be stained with the race of Judaism.

In this favourable climate it was possible for the Junta de Reformación in February 1623 to decree new rules modifying the practice of limpieza.[47] One act (involving three positive proofs of limpieza in any one of the four lines of descent) was enough when applying for office and no others were needed when promoted or changing one's job. Verbal evidence was not admitted if unsupported by more solid proof, and 'rumour' was disallowed. All literature purporting to list the descent of families from Jews, such as the notorious *Libro verde de Aragón*, was ordered to be publicly destroyed and burnt. Although these measures aroused much opposition, they also released a flood of anti-limpieza writings which take their stand with the other literature that makes this reign a time of intellectual crisis in Spanish history. That the problem was appreciated in the highest circles is shown by the report given by one member of the Junta de Reformación, who claimed that limpieza was

> the cause and origin of a great multitude of sins, perjuries, falsehoods, disputes and lawsuits both civil and criminal. Many of our people, seeing that they are not admitted to the honours and offices of their native land, have absented themselves from these realms and gone to others, in despair at seeing themselves covered with infamy. So much so that I have been told of two eminent gentlemen of these realms who were among the greatest soldiers of our time and who declared on their deathbeds that since they were unable to gain entry into the orders of chivalry they had very often been tempted by the devil to kill themselves or to go over and serve the Turk, and that they knew of some who had done so.[48]

To question limpieza was to question the fundamentals of life as practised since the end of the fifteenth century. This ability to recognize the darker side of a social dogma was part of the crisis of conscience in mid-seventeenth-century Spain. Attitudes, however, were so deeply ingrained that legislation proved to be no solution. The reform of February 1623 was reconfirmed in March 1638 and ordered to be observed 'by all the councils, courts, Colegios Mayores and statute communities'. In fact, it remained a dead letter and was not observed by a single body outside the government and the Inquisition. The latter, not surprisingly, soon ceased to observe the reform. The controversy, therefore, continued well into the seventeenth century. The Inquisitor General in 1623 commissioned a further reasoned attack on the statutes by Diego Serrano de Silva, a member of the Suprema.[49] In 1632 a powerful and persuasive document against limpieza was published by Fernando de Valdés, rector of the Jesuit seminary in Madrid and a consultant for the Inquisition. Basing himself on Salucio's discourse but going further in his attack on the statutes, Valdés summed up: 'Let the final and strongest argument against the statutes be that our republic has lost its respect for them.' In 1635 the noted political writer Jerónimo de Zeballos, repeating arguments used by his predecessors, wrote his own *Discurso* against the practice of limpieza.[50]

From its inception in 1580, this impressive and astonishing campaign against the statutes of limpieza was led, at every stage, by Inquisitors General and officials of the Inquisition, aided by ministers of state such as Lerma and Olivares. There was an obvious contradiction in the Inquisition, which had done so much in its early history to discriminate against conversos, coming to their aid in the seventeenth century. Yet the Inquisition had, of course, been responsible neither for antisemitism nor for the statutes, and though it maintained its old ferocity against heresy it was content to connive at the systematic infringement of the limpieza rules by people of known Jewish origin.

It was a censor of the Inquisition, Francisco Murcia de la Llana, who in 1624 condemned both the racialism and the xenophobia of his contemporaries:

> Look into yourself [he addressed Spain] and consider that no other nation has these statutes, and that Judaism has flourished most where they have existed. Yet if any of your sons marries a Frenchwoman or a Genoan or an Italian you despise his wife as a foreigner. What ignorance! What overwhelming Spanish madness![51]

So thoroughly had the Inquisition cleansed Spain of heretical conversos by the beginning of the eighteenth century that the Jewish question, for all practical purposes, ceased to exist. The disappearance of the Jewish menace meant that antisemitism degenerated into an irrational prejudice with no roots in actual conditions. The 'Jew' became a myth, a legend – no more. Judaizers were a curious rarity in the second half of the eighteenth century. Yet the official apparatus of limpieza continued to function, more and more obviously at variance with right reason. It was this irrational nature of the statutes no less than their pronounced social effect that attracted the attention of the ministers of the crown. In 1751 José de Carvajal thought the treatise of Agustín Salucio so convincing that he ordered a copy of it to be made for himself;[52] and the Count of Floridablanca considered the penalties for impurity unjust because 'they punish a man's sacred action, that is, his conversion to our holy faith, with the same penalty as his greatest crime, that is, apostasy from it'.[53]

But it needed more than reforming ministers to abolish limpieza which, being part of the social system more than a religious issue, survived the abolition of the Inquisition. Official recognition of its need ceased with a royal order of 31 January 1835 directed to the Economic Society of Madrid, but up to 1859 it was still necessary for entrance into the corps of officer cadets. The last official act was a law of 16 May 1865 abolishing proofs of purity for marriages and for certain government posts.

The main effect of limpieza was obviously to divide Spanish

society into the 'ins' and 'outs'. Of this, the most vicious example was the treatment meted out to the conversos of Palma de Mallorca. As late as the mid-eighteenth century, 'although good Catholics, their sons were denied entrance to the higher ranks of the clergy, and their daughters to the religious orders. They were forced to live in a restricted area of the city, and the people calumniated them with the names *Hebreos*, *Judíos*, *Chuetas*. Guilds, army, navy and public offices were closed to them.'[54] Despite various efforts by the government and some clergy, discrimination continued up to the end of the nineteenth century. In 1858 they were still 'refused all public offices and admission to guilds and brotherhoods so that they were confined to trading. They were compelled to marry among themselves, for no one would contract alliance with them nor would the ecclesiastical authorities grant licences for mixed marriages.'[55] Happily this state of affairs was not common in peninsular Spain.

A less conspicuous but no less important result of limpieza was the perpetuation of the concept of 'honour' in its worst social sense. So far did purity of blood cease to have any connection with the Jewish problem that in 1788 we find Charles III's minister Aranda using the phrase *limpieza de sangre* in the sense of purity from any taint of servile office or trade, so that the synonymous term *limpieza de oficios* also came into existence by the end of the century.[56] Here we have the term used in a purely class context: the upper classes were pure and the lower were servile, the distinction being grounded on a racialist dogma whose origins had almost been forgotten. The net result was that the upper classes continued to maintain their (racial and class) purity by refusing to undertake any industry or employment that was beneath their honour and dignity. In this way an essentially mediaeval outlook was transmitted into the nineteenth century through the limpieza statutes.

8

Organization and Social Control

> We have corrected Thy work and have founded it upon miracle, mystery and authority.
>
> Dostoevsky, *The Brothers Karamazov*

The Spanish Inquisition, as we have seen, superseded entirely the mediaeval tribunal which had existed in the kingdom of Aragon since 1238. The new institution was in character and purpose of Castilian origin, and as such aroused substantial opposition in other parts of the peninsula. By the early sixteenth century, however, most of this opposition had been eliminated, and we are left with a centralized tribunal under Castilian control whose authority extended over all the realms of the Spanish crown. From its inception, the Inquisition was meant by Ferdinand and Isabella to be under their control and not under that of the pope, as had been the case with the mediaeval tribunal. Sixtus IV was surprisingly co-operative, and his bull of institution of 1 November 1478 gave the Catholic monarchs power not only over appointments but also, tacitly, over confiscations. The inquisitors were to have the jurisdiction over heretics normally held by bishops, but were not given any jurisdiction over bishops themselves. Subsequently the pope saw his error in granting independence to a tribunal of this sort, and enshrined his protest in a brief of 29 January 1482. At the same time he refused to allow Ferdinand to extend his control over the old Inquisition in Aragon.

Further conflict ensued with the bull issued by Sixtus on 18 April, denouncing abuses in the procedure of the Inquisition. Ferdinand, however, held firm to his policy despite opposition in Rome and Aragon, and his eventual victory was confirmed by the bull which on 17 October 1483 appointed Torquemada as chief inquisitor of the kingdom of Aragon. Earlier that year Torquemada had also received a bull of appointment as Inquisitor General of Castile. He was now therefore the only individual in the peninsula whose writ extended over all Spain, since even the crowns of Castile and Aragon were only personally and not politically united.

The Inquisition was in every way an instrument of royal policy, and remained politically subject to the crown. This, however, did not make it exclusively a secular tribunal. Any authority and jurisdiction exercised by the inquisitors came directly or indirectly from Rome, without whom the tribunal would have ceased to exist. Bulls of appointment, canonical regulations, spheres of jurisdiction – all had to have the prior approval of Rome. The Inquisition was consequently also an ecclesiastical tribunal for which the Church of Rome assumed ultimate responsibility.[1]

The central organization of the new tribunal was in 1483 vested in a council (Consejo de la Suprema y General Inquisición), and this body joined the other administrative councils whose existence had been confirmed at the Cortes of Toledo in 1480. Although Torquemada was the first Inquisitor General, the real founder of the Inquisition was Cardinal Mendoza, Archbishop of Seville and later of Toledo. It was this prelate, famous as a patron of Columbus, who set in motion the negotiations with Rome leading to the establishment of the Inquisition. Yet above him towers the shadow of Torquemada. The austere Dominican friar, who was prior of the convent of Santa Cruz at Segovia, left his indelible mark on the tribunal, and in 1484 Sixtus IV praised him for having 'directed your zeal to those matters which contribute to the praise of God and the benefit of the orthodox faith'.[2] Though of converso origin himself, he was the first to introduce a statute of limpieza into a Dominican house, his own foundation at Avila dedicated to St Thomas Aquinas.

The importance of Torquemada suggests that the Dominicans were controlling the new Inquisition as they had controlled the mediaeval one. In fact, though all the early appointments were of Dominicans, and Dominicans continued to play an important role,[3] only a minority of inquisitors were from the order: in Valencia, for instance, there were only six Dominicans among the fifty-two for whom details are available over the period 1482–1609.[4] A special privilege was obtained on 16 December 1618 when Philip III, at the request of the Duke of Lerma, created a permanent place in the Suprema for a member of the Order of Preachers, to be occupied in the first place by the then Inquisitor General, Aliaga.[5] By the seventeenth century and more especially in the eighteenth, Jesuits had become influential in the Inquisition.

Torquemada's importance is also misleading on another issue. Although the Inquisitor General may seem to have been a powerful individual, in practice his commission was often limited in authority, and renewable only after papal approval. Moreover, the pope frequently granted equivalent powers to other clerics in Spain, as in 1491 when a second Inquisitor General of Castile and Aragon was appointed for a brief time, and in 1494, when four bishops in Spain were promoted to this post at the same time that Torquemada held it. This plural headship of the tribunal continued to exist for political reasons. When Torquemada died in 1498 he was succeeded by Diego Deza, who in 1505 became Archbishop of Seville. It was not until 1504 that Deza became sole head of the Inquisition, because the bishops appointed under Torquemada continued to hold office up to that date. Queen Isabella died on 26 November 1504 and this led to a temporary separation of the kingdoms of Castile and Aragon, because of Ferdinand's quarrels with his son-in-law, Philip I of Castile. As a result, Ferdinand asked the pope to appoint a separate Inquisitor for Aragon. This occurred in June 1507 when Cisneros was appointed to Castile and the Bishop of Vic, Juan Enguera, to Aragon. The two posts remained separate until the death of Cisneros in 1518, when Charles I appointed Cardinal Adrian of Utrecht, Bishop of Tortosa and since 1516 Inquisitor General of Aragon, as Inquisitor for Castile as well. After this the tribunal remained under one head alone.

The Spanish Inquisition was based essentially on the mediaeval one. It is a crucial fact, which can easily be overlooked because of the wholly different conditions under which each tribunal came into existence. There was in reality no other precedent from which to work, and the Spanish inquisitors followed down to the last detail – in all aspects of arrest, trial, procedure, confiscations, recruitment of inquisitors, familiars and so on – the regulations that had been in use in thirteenth-century Languedoc and Aragon. As late as the reign of Philip II, the classic Aragonese manual of Eymeric could be accepted as a standard guide by its Spanish commentator, Francisco Peña.[6] There is no reason, therefore, to suggest that the Inquisition in the peninsula was peculiarly Spanish. Apart from some obvious differences, such as the transfer in Spain of authority over heresy from bishops to inquisitors, the Inquisition in the peninsula was simply an adaptation to Spanish conditions of the mediaeval French tribunal.

The first rules drawn up were those agreed upon in a meeting at Seville on 29 November 1484. Under Torquemada these rules were amplified in 1485, 1488 and 1498, and his successor Diego Deza added some articles in 1500. All these regulations were later known under the collective title of the *Instrucciones Antiguas*. They were unsystematic, had to be regularly modified, and led to variations of practice between the different tribunals. An organized, bureaucratic Inquisition emerged only with the issue in 1561 of the Instructions of Fernando de Valdés, in eighty-one clauses. These set out to achieve a thoroughly centralized organization, tight control by the Suprema and financial stability for the tribunals. A product of the crisis years after 1558, the Valdés Instructions gave the Holy Office a reputation for rigidity.[7] Subsequent modifications were collected and printed by Gaspar Isidro de Argüello at Madrid in 1627 and 1630 in a compendium called the *Instrucciones del Santo Oficio de la Inquisición, sumariamente, antiguas y nuevas*. This was followed by the comprehensive *Compilación de las Instrucciones del Oficio de la Santa Inquisición*, published at Madrid in 1667 by the Inquisitor General.[8]

The Council of the Inquisition (sometimes known for short as the Suprema) was presided over by the Inquisitor General. All authority exercised by inquisitors was at one time held to be by direct delegation from the pope, but later this was modified to the opinion that it was the Inquisitor General himself who delegated the papal powers. Growth of the Inquisitor General's power was modified by the increasing authority of the Suprema. The relationship between Suprema and Inquisitor General was never satisfactorily settled because they usually acted in concert and did not dispute supremacy, but there were several occasions when the Council proved that it was independent of and not subject to the Inquisitor. In the early seventeenth century the Suprema consisted of about six members, who usually met every morning and also three afternoons: the afternoon sessions, normally on legal business, were attended by two members of the Council of Castile. Correspondence was divided between two secretariats, one for 'Aragon'[9] and one for Castile. Members of the Suprema were appointed by the king alone, and the Suprema itself more often than not issued orders without any need to have the vote of the Inquisitor General. When divisions arose in the Council a decision was taken by majority vote, in which the vote of the Inquisitor General counted no more than that of another. In general, however, no clear rules for procedure were ever adopted and the authority of the Inquisitor General depended on circumstances and on his own character. One outstanding case, that of Fray Froilan Díaz, brought out clearly the extent to which the Inquisitor General could be expected to overrule the opposition of the Suprema.

Froilan Díaz, a Dominican who had been confessor since 1698 to the king, Charles II (1665–1700), was arrested in 1700 after various palace intrigues on the charge of having helped to cast a spell over the hapless king, known in Spanish history as el Hechizado, the bewitched. The prosecution was at the instance of the German queen and her friend Balthasar de Mendoza, Bishop of Segovia, who in 1699 had been appointed Inquisitor General. Díaz, who was an ex-officio member of the Suprema, was imprisoned while an investigation was made by five theologians who found that in fact there was no basis for a serious charge against him. Accordingly, in June 1700 all the members of the Council except Mendoza voted for Díaz's acquittal. Mendoza refused to accept the findings and ordered the arrest of the other members of the Suprema until they assented to the arrest of Díaz. At the same time he ordered the tribunal of Murcia to bring Díaz to trial. This the inquisitors did – and acquitted him. Mendoza thereupon ordered a retrial and kept Díaz in prison. Opposition to the actions of the Inquisitor General was by now universal. There was consequently wide support for the new French king, Philip V, when he discovered that Mendoza was politically opposed to the Bourbon dynasty and confined him to his see of Segovia. Mendoza now made the mistake of appealing to Rome, an act which was unprecedented in the whole history of the Spanish Inquisition. The crown immediately stepped in to prevent any interference from Rome, and finally in 1704 Díaz was rehabilitated and reinstated in the Suprema, while Mendoza was replaced as Inquisitor General in March 1705.[10]

The case proved to be the last important one in which the Inquisitor General attempted to assert his supremacy. Thereafter the preoccupation of the tribunal with administrative routine and censorship, rather than with great matters of state, involved fewer opportunities for personal initiative, and authority came more and more to reside in the Suprema and the machinery it controlled. More obscure prelates were also chosen as Inquisitor General, a significant example being the choice of the Bishop of Ceuta to succeed Mendoza in 1705.

The growth of the Suprema's authority led to greater centralization in the Inquisition, a process hastened in the seventeenth century as the volume of heretics, and therefore of business, diminished in the provincial tribunals. In the early days, as the case of Lucero showed, local autonomy could be carried to scandalous extremes. This situation was later remedied by more conscientious Supremas. At first cases were referred by provincial tribunals to the Suprema only if agreement could not be reached, or if the latter made a special order summoning a case before it. In the early 1530s, when it was felt that the Barcelona tribunal was showing excessive severity in suppressing a witch-craze in Catalonia, all sentences passed by it were required to be confirmed by the Suprema. The Barcelona inquisitors do not seem to have accepted interference from the centre, for the Inquisitor General in 1566 was obliged to examine their records and to denounce the irregularities and cruelties in the tribunal. From this time onwards greater attention was paid by the Suprema to the procedure and sentences of local tribunals, who were required after 1632 to send in monthly reports of their activities. By the mid-seventeenth century all sentences were required to be submitted to the Suprema before being carried out. With this, the machinery of the Inquisition reached its most complete stage of centralization. In the eighteenth century business became so rare that the tribunals became mere appendages of the Suprema, which initiated and executed all prosecutions.

The supremacy of the Council extended in particular to finances, and all the tribunals were expected to pay sums on demand to the central administration. At other times, more fortunate tribunals were expected to contribute to the expense of the less fortunate ones. In all this, the standard procedure of ecclesiastical organization was followed.

The tribunals of the Inquisition in their early days were itinerant: the Barcelona inquisitors, for example, celebrated autos de fe in Gerona and Tarragona. Inquisitions were set up wherever there seemed to be a need and political conditions permitted. In the first ten years the following tribunals seem to have been established:[11] 1482: Seville, Córdoba, Valencia, Saragossa; 1483: Jaén, Ciudad Real (moved to Toledo 1485); 1484: Barcelona, Teruel; 1485: Toledo, Llerena, Medina del Campo (moved to Salamanca 1488); 1486: Segovia, Lérida; 1488: Salamanca, Murcia, Alcáraz, Baleares, Valladolid (moved to Palencia 1493); 1489: Burgos, Cuenca, Osma; 1490: Avila; 1491: Calahorra, Siguenza, Jérez; 1492: León. This proliferation of tribunals became uneconomic once the number of judaizers decreased. In 1503, therefore, the five tribunals of León, Burgos, Salamanca, Avila and Segovia were suppressed and merged into the single vast tribunal of Valladolid. By 1507 there were only seven tribunals in Spain where in 1495 there had been sixteen. Several changes occurred in the sixteenth century, including the establishment of the tribunal at Granada in 1526. After two unsuccessful attempts, an Inquisition was finally set up in Galicia in 1574. The permanent tribunals of Spain, with dates of first establishment, were:[12]

Kingdom of Castile

Seville	1482	Cuenca	1489
Córdoba	1482	Las Palmas	1505
Toledo	1485	Logroño	1512
Llerena	1485	Granada	1526
Valladolid	1488	Santiago	1574
Murcia	1488	Madrid	1640

Kingdom of Aragon

Saragossa	1482	Barcelona	1484
Valencia	1482	Mallorca	1488

The location of the districts is shown in the map on page 141. It is evidence of the remarkable indifference of the Inquisition to other secular or ecclesiastical authority that its districts often crossed political frontiers: the territory of Orihuela in Valencia, for example, was put under the tribunal of Murcia; Teruel in Aragon was put under the tribunal of Valencia; Calahorra in Castile was put under the Navarrese tribunal of Logroño; and Lérida in Catalonia fell under the control of the tribunal of Aragon. The Inquisition was able to do this because its authority, unlike that of the crown, covered the whole of Spain regardless of frontiers. Portugal, for the period 1580–1640 when it came under the Spanish crown, did not have its Inquisition incorporated into that of Castile, and its tribunal

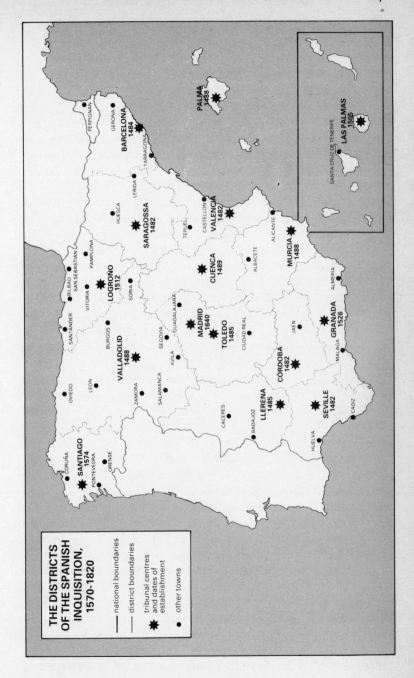

THE DISTRICTS
OF THE SPANISH
INQUISITION,
1570-1820

——— national boundaries
—— district boundaries
✸ tribunal centres
and dates of
establishment
● other towns

therefore functioned independently for a while. In 1586, however, Philip II had the Cardinal Archduke of Austria, who was governor of Portugal, nominated as head of the Portuguese Inquisition, so bringing the Portuguese tribunal more closely under Spanish royal control.

Each tribunal, according to Torquemada's Instructions of 1498, was to consist of two inquisitors ('a jurist and a theologian, or two jurists'), an assessor (*calificador*), a constable (*alguacil*), and a prosecutor (*fiscal*), with any other necessary subordinates. The number of personnel, as we shall see, grew rapidly. By the end of the sixteenth century the major tribunals of the peninsula had three inquisitors each.[13] Contrary to the image – still widely current – of inquisitors as small-minded clerics and theologians fanatically dedicated to the extirpation of heresy, it must be stressed that, in the sixteenth and seventeenth centuries at least, the inquisitors were an elite bureaucracy.[14] Because the Inquisition was a court, its administrators had to be trained lawyers: Diego de Simancas thought that 'it is more useful to have jurists rather than theologians as inquisitors'. Theological problems were normally left to the assessors to sort out. By the same token, inquisitors did not have to be clergy and could be laymen. All this shows that the inquisitors were in principle a bureaucracy not of the Church but of the State: they received their training in the same institutions that contributed personnel to the councils of state, corregidorships and high courts.

This conclusion is confirmed by what we know of the origins and careers of the inquisitors. An analysis of fifty-seven inquisitors of Toledo, from the period 1482–1598,[15] shows that all but two had degrees and doctorates based on the study of law at university, and that nearly half had been trained in the exclusive Colegios Mayores. Philip III in 1608 stipulated that all inquisitors must be *letrados*, or graduates in law. Making use of this legal background, many went on to serve in the high courts of the realm; for these, service in the Inquisition was merely a stepping-stone to a further career. In practice, of course, the bureaucracy of State and Church overlapped, so that although some inquisitors were laymen it was more useful to be in holy orders. Moreover, the ecclesiastical character of inquisitors was underlined by their dependence on canonries for income, and by the subsequent promotion of many to bishoprics.

The sparsity of tribunals, and their limited personnel, made it essential to seek additional help from members of the public. This was achieved through *familiars* and *comisarios*. The familiar was a common feature of the mediaeval Inquisition and was continued in the Spanish one. Essentially he was a lay servant of the Holy Office, ready at all times to perform duties in the service of the tribunal. In return he was allowed to bear arms to protect the inquisitors, and enjoyed a number of privileges in common with the other officials. To become a familiar was a high honour, and in the earlier decades of its history the Inquisition could boast of a high proportion of nobles and titled persons among its familiars. By the beginning of the sixteenth century the familiars were banded together in a brotherhood or *hermandad* known as the Congregation of St Peter Martyr, modelled directly on the associations founded by the mediaeval Inquisition after the murder of an inquisitor, Peter Martyr, in Italy in 1252. The comisario was normally a local parish priest who acted for the Inquisition on special occasions and also supplied it with information.

Familiars acquired notoriety in fact and in legend for acting as informers and spies, but this was never their real purpose. Comisarios were normally in a better position to supply information. Neither familiars nor comisarios, however, were meant to be spies, and the records of the Inquisition show clearly that the majority of denunciations were made not by them but by ordinary people – neighbours, acquaintances – in response to appeals made in the edicts of faith or simply as a result of personal conflicts. There was no need to rely on a secret police system, because the population as a whole was encouraged to recognize the enemy within the gates.

Since familiars were usually laymen[16] it was inevitable that jurisdiction over them in cases of crime should be claimed by the secular courts. Conflicts arose regularly over this, and it was only in 1518 that Charles v decreed that the cognizance by secular courts of criminal cases concerning familiars and other officials and servants of the Inquisition was contrary to its privileges. After this ruling the tribunal did not hesitate to protect even the humblest of its employees from the justice of the civil courts, a position which led to further friction and quarrels.

One solution to which the Inquisition agreed was a voluntary limitation of the number of familiars. The concordia of Castile in 1553 was devoted largely to defining the number of familiars and the jurisdiction of the civil courts; in all serious crimes secular justice was to hold good and the Inquisition was limited to the cognizances of petty offences only. Although this concordia remained in force until the end of the Inquisition, it was only partly successful, for disputes continued as before, and neither the secular nor the inquisitorial courts were concerned to observe its stipulation. In the fuero provinces the concession of new concordias became more frequent because they were even less observed than in Castile. Although Valencia received a concordia in 1554 by which the number of familiars was reduced and jurisdiction defined, it was found necessary in 1568 to issue a new one reinforcing the clauses of the earlier concordia and adding new rules. Even this was insufficient, to judge by a report of the Council of Aragon on 21 July 1632 which claimed that no peace or safety could be expected in Valencia unless there was a reform in the selection of familiars, since nearly all the crimes committed involved familiars who were sure to escape with impunity, relying as they did on the intervention of their protectors the inquisitors.[17]

In Aragon the struggle was even more pronounced because of the great pride taken in their constitutional liberties by the aristocracy of the realm. Here the question of familiars was not resolved till the concordia of 1568, which was the same as that issued in Valencia the same year. As in Valencia, however, the concordia was not enough to pacify the province, and disputes continued as before. It was only after 1646, when the Cortes of Aragon had passed as law measures which restricted the jurisdiction of the Inquisition, that some satisfaction was gained by the secular tribunals of the realm.

In Catalonia conflicts over familiars were nominally settled by a concordia made at the Cortes of Monzón in August 1512, but the Inquisition never really accepted this. Then in 1553 the Cortes ruled that no official exercising civil jurisdiction in Catalonia could be a familiar. Further disputes ended in the Inquisition proposing a concordia in 1568. This was violently opposed by the Catalans: the viceroy reported that 'all the courts, the Consellers, the Diputats and other judicial officers are determined to lay down their lives' rather than accept it. Small wonder that the Barcelona inquisitors reported that 'they will not be content until they have driven the Inquisition from this realm'.[18] Finally in 1585 it was agreed by the Inquisition at Monzón that 'familiars and officials of the Holy Office cannot be admitted to office in the courts or in public administration' in Catalonia – a unique concession.

The endless story of disputes over the numbers of familiars and problems over jurisdiction, has tended to overshadow the history of the familiars themselves. By creating a network of familiars within each tribunal district, the Inquisition was able to attach to its interests a large and possibly influential section of the local population. Because the number of familiars appointed was often excessive, successive concordias between State and Inquisition in both Castile and Aragon attempted to set ceiling figures. Thus the Castile concordia of 1553 suggested 805 familiars for Toledo, 554 for Granada and 1,009 for Galicia.[19] In reality the number of familiars might vary widely. In Galicia in 1611 there were a total of 388 familiars and 100 comisarios for the whole province (a ratio of one per 241 households in the population), but these officials were distributed through less than 6.4 per cent of the towns and villages – evidence of a very low level of contact between Inquisition and people.[20] In Valencia, by contrast, in 1567 there were as many as 1,638 familiars (a ratio of one for every 42 households).[21] Midway between them was the tribunal of Barcelona, which in 1600 had 815 familiars, or one per 110 households.[22]

The social standing of familiars was of paramount importance to the Inquisition, which attempted to recruit from the highest circles and the purest blood. In Galicia the policy seems to have succeeded in the trading areas, for the twenty-five familiars in Santiago were the wealthiest merchants in the city; but inland it was difficult to find suitable candidates. As a rule, members of the elite were happy to become familiars if this protected them from secular jurisdiction and gave them privileges of freedom from some types of taxation: in both Andalucia and Valencia gentry were a small but significant proportion of familiars.[23] In the predominantly rural society of those times, however, most familiars were inevitably peasant farmers (labradores). Virtually all familiars in Catalonia, for example, were labradores, with merchants as a significant proportion only in the seaports. In 1600 the average age of familiars in the diocese of Barcelona was forty-seven years, and most, even the merchants, were only of modest means. Thanks to the accord of 1585, in Catalonia no public officials could become familiars, so the latter post was neither prized nor respected. In 1632 the Inquisition was complaining that it had only five familiars in Barcelona, and all of lowly status.[24]

Although the network of familiars established a presence for the Inquisition, it did little else. It did not act as a form of social control: in Catalonia only about half the parishes in 1600 had familiars; in Valencia there were few in the Morisco towns where they were most needed, and in Galicia only a tiny fraction of towns had them.

Nor is it likely that a single familiar in a rural community would have risked his life to become a professional informer. In some areas familiars were openly discriminated against, if we may believe the inquisitors of Llerena, complaining in 1597 of 'the injuries which the corregidores, legal officials and town councils commit against the familiars of this Holy Office simply because they are familiars. This is certain, because a man can live in his village for twenty or thirty years without the officials doing anything to injure him, but as soon as he becomes a familiar they move against him, especially if there are conversos in the town council.'[25] The steady decline in the number of familiars in Spain suggests that the post, even with its privileges, was never popular. Between 1611 and 1641 in Galicia the number of familiars fell by 44 per cent: where previously they had existed in 226 villages, now they were to be found in only 108.[26] All the evidence shows that the Inquisition never built up an organizational apparatus of social control, and that its impact on the daily lives of most Spaniards was infrequent and marginal.

The most surprising aspect of the administration of the Holy Office is that it was never given a regular income on which to subsist. This was in part because it followed the model of the mediaeval Inquisition, which likewise never received a fixed source of revenue. The Spanish tribunal was from the first financed out of the proceeds of its own activities: confiscations were far and away the most important source.[27] Confiscation of property was the standard punishment prescribed by canon law for heresy. Ferdinand stated in 1485 that confiscations imposed in Spain were by order of the pope, so it would seem that the Church controlled the process, but in fact it was at first the secular authorities who carried out the confiscation. Only later did the inquisitors take over control. There were normally two stages to confiscations. At the first stage, upon the arrest of a suspect, his goods and income were 'sequestrated'. This could have terrible consequences and was much dreaded. The sequestrations were used to pay the costs of the prisoner in jail; if he were there long enough the money might all be used up, thus driving his dependants into poverty. In effect, therefore, a sequestration might amount to a confiscation. Confiscation proper, which occurred only at the second stage, resulted from a judicial verdict and was a regular penalty for major crimes. The process of sequestration is of enormous interest to historians, because the Inquisition made a practice of listing all the assets of the accused; not only, therefore, do the documents give us entire household inventories, but they also list thousands of books in private libraries, and the entire movable and immovable assets of famous people. Our best source for the fortune of the converso financier Fernando Montesinos, for example, is the inquisitorial breakdown of his assets made in 1654.[28]

The principal victims of confiscations were the conversos, whose notorious wealth must have stirred many an orthodox spirit. As Hernando del Pulgar wrote sardonically of the citizens of Toledo during a time of civil disturbances: 'What great inquisitors of the faith they must be, to be finding heresies in the property of the peasants of the town of Fuensalida, which they rob and burn!'[29] From the very first, then, the inquisitors were associated with confiscation of property, and it became common practice to imply, as Pulgar did, that the search for heretics was really a search for property.

The initial confiscations carried out by the Inquisition were very substantial indeed. Diego Susán, who led the plot in Seville in 1481 and was later burnt, was reputed to be worth nearly 30,000 ducats, and he was only one of 'many others, very prominent and very rich', to quote Bernáldez. In the words of a later chronicler of Seville, 'what was noticeable was the great number of prosecutions against moneyed men'.[30] In the years after this, great and wealthy converso families were ruined by even the slightest taint of heresy, for 're-conciliation' meant that all the culprit's property was confiscated and none of it was allowed to pass to his descendants, so that widows and children were often left without any provision. Whole families faced beggary and destitution because of the sins of one member only.

Not surprisingly, then, many ordinary Spaniards came to the conclusion that the Inquisition was devised simply to rob people. In 1483 after a regidor of Ciudad Real, the converso Juan González Pintado, was burnt for heresy, Catalina de Zamora was arrested by the Inquisition for asserting that 'this Inquisition is as much for grabbing property as for exalting the faith'. The unhappy conversos of Catalonia, protesting in 1510 against the technique of confiscations, complained that 'it is not goods that are heretics, but people'.[31]

In addition to the profits made at Seville, the Inquisition found that confiscations could be profitable elsewhere. During its brief one-year stay in the small city of Guadalupe in 1485, enough money was raised from confiscations by the tribunal to pay almost entirely for the building of a royal residence costing 7,286 ducats.[32]

In most of the cases we have on record, the money from confiscated property seems to have been largely disposed of by the Inquisition. What will probably never be clear, however, is what proportion of money went to the crown and what to the tribunal. Generalizations cannot be made from available examples. In 1676, to take one instance, towards the end of the last great and fruitful campaign of the Inquisition against the Portuguese judaizers resident in Spain, the Suprema claimed that it had obtained from the royal treasury confiscations amounting to 772,748 ducats and 884,979 pesos. These sums are extremely large for the period, and suggest that the crown was receiving a high proportion of confiscations. Yet if we look at the value of property confiscated on Mallorca after the alleged converso conspiracy of 1678 had been discovered, we find that the totals come to well over 2,500,000 ducats,[33] certainly the biggest single sum gathered in by the Inquisition in all the three centuries of its existence. Of this vast sum, however, it seems that the crown received under 5 per cent.

What happened to sums like these when they had been seized? Invariably judicial disputes arose over property. Debts of victims had to be paid, the expenses of officials and of court cases had to be met. The crown could claim a third, as had been customary. Some of the money was invested in *censos* and houses by the inquisitors. If we take the city of Lérida in 1487, the confiscations made there from converso property were assigned in part to the city council, to a religious order, to a hospital, and to various other needs, so that the Inquisition did not manage to control all the revenue available.[34] By a thousand different routes the money trickled out of the hands of the inquisitors. When the reason was not mismanagement, it was the sheer dishonesty of minor officials. Whatever the income from confiscations at any time, it is safe to assume that the tribunals did not grow appreciably wealthier, or at least did not keep up their temporary wealth for long periods.

After confiscations, there were three important sources of cash revenue. These were 'fines', which could be levied at any rate desired and were often used simply to raise money to cover expenses; and 'penances' (*penitencias*), which were more formal and were usually decreed at a solemn occasion such as an auto de fe; both fines and penances could, of course, be realized out of sequestrated property. Finally, there was the fairly small category of 'dispensations', when a punishment decreed by the Inquisition was commuted to a cash payment. Many with money were only too willing to pay for relief from the public shame of having to wear a sanbenito or penitential garment; others managed to escape service in the galleys by paying for dispensations. In 1497 the royal treasurer acknowledged receipt from the Toledo Inquisition of 6.5 million maravedis realized from dispensations, a very substantial sum for this early period.[35]

Why, during this phase of comparatively high income, was no provision made for a secure financial base? This may have been in part, as mentioned above, because the Spanish Inquisition was modelled on the mediaeval, which had no secure funds either. But we must also take into account the fact that the early Inquisition in Spain was an itinerant tribunal, created for an emergency and with no long-term plans, as the various Instructions of Torquemada show clearly. The Catholic Kings may well have thought of it as being no more permanent than that other useful organization of theirs, the Hermandad.

There were certainly no financial problems in the first years. Because the Inquisition, despite its ecclesiastical appearance, was an exclusively royal tribunal, all revenue from confiscations and fines went directly to the crown, which in turn paid out for the salaries and expenses of the inquisitors; under the Catholic Kings, the Holy Office was totally subject to the crown for finance. As late as 1540 the Suprema reported that orders for salaries of inquisitors in the crown of Aragon were always signed by the king and not by the Inquisitor General.[36] The crown, however, helped itself to so much inquisitorial income[37] that very soon it had to find extra money for salaries, and Ferdinand therefore turned to the Church. In 1488 the pope granted him the right to appoint inquisitors to one prebend (when vacant) in each cathedral or collegiate church, and the king made ten presentations that year.

Ferdinand had in fact endangered the financial position of the Inquisition, and under the absentee Charles v the Suprema slowly began to take control away from the crown. By the 1540s royal control was virtually nominal, and by the 1550s the Suprema was withholding details of confiscations from the king.[38] It was at this period that the Inquisition obtained its next secure source of revenue. Already, in 1501, the pope had granted to all the tribunals of Spain the income from specified canonries and prebends, but for several reasons this had never fully taken effect. Impressed by the struggles of the Inquisition against heresy within Spain in 1558-9, the pope in 1559 generously repeated the terms of the grant of 1501. From now on, aided by the income from ecclesiast-ical offices and from various financial agreements made with the Moriscos in the 1570s, the Inquisition became less dependent on the crown for survival.

The evolution from deficit to relative stability can be seen in the case of the tribunal of Llerena. In the early sixteenth century, with the profitable income from judaizers now virtually a thing of the past, most tribunals faced severe problems. The dangers of this situation were certainly in the mind of the anonymous converso of Toledo who in 1538 directed a memorial to Charles v: 'Your Ma-jesty should above all provide that the expenses of the Holy Office do not come from the property of the condemned, because it is a repugnant thing if inquisitors cannot eat unless they burn [*recia cosa es que si no queman no comen*].'[39] Unfortunately, this is exactly what the inquisitors of Llerena were forced to do. With no revenue coming in, they were obliged to go out and look for it. In 1550 the salaries of officials, amounting to 523,000 maravedis, could not be met by income from current fines, which brought in only 375,000 maravedis.[40] In July 1554 the inquisitor Dr Ramírez informed the Suprema that 'this Inquisition cannot subsist without going on a visitation[41] every year'. As remedies he proposed that one of the two posts of inquisitor be suppressed; that the post of receiver be dropped and the work given to the notary; that confiscations be looked after directly by the remaining inquisitor; and that further visitations be made to the diocese of Badajoz, which was promis-ingly full of suspicious people, so that 'with a bit of care there will be no lack of business whereby God our Lord will be served and the Holy Office be able to sustain itself'. By July 1572, with the new system of canonries, all this had changed. Two canonries, in Badajoz and Ciudad Rodrigo, now brought in 680,000 maravedis a year, and extensive confiscations from the wealthy family of Lorenzo Angelo in Badajoz raised income in 1572 to nearly two millions.[42]

For the next two centuries confiscations and canonries remained the chief direct sources of finance for each tribunal: two canonries, in Málaga and Antequera, provided the tribunal of Granada with 12.8 per cent of its income in 1573;[43] three canonries, in Córdoba, Jaén and Ubeda together provided 40 per cent of the income of the tribunal of Córdoba in 1578;[44] and four canonries – in Badajoz, Plasencia, Coria and Ciudad Rodrigo – provided 37.1 per cent of that of the tribunal of Llerena in 1611.[45] Without the regular annual income from these Church offices, the Inquisition would have gone bankrupt.

By their nature, confiscations and sequestrations could never bring in a reliable income: the vast majority of all those accused by the Inquisition were people of humble means, and the inquisitors would need to have had a regular annual turnover of hundreds of prisoners in order to get anything like a substantial revenue. Windfalls like the great persecution of Chuetas in Mallorca were exceptional. The normal picture is of tribunals trying desperately to find income for the costs of administration, prosecution, maintenance of prisoners, and the increasingly expensive autos de fe. The documentation is full of complaints by local inquisitors that they cannot provide either for themselves or for their prisoners.

The regular state of deficit in the tribunals can be illustrated by balancing their expenses against their income for the years 1618, 1671–8, 1705 and 1731:[46]

Inquisitorial budgets, 1618–1731
(—shows percentage excess of expenses over income; + shows same of income over expenses)

	1618	1671–8	1705	1731
Mallorca	−40.8	−60.8		−12
Logroño	−19	+11.5	−15.3	−19.8
Saragossa	−14.6	−21.8	−9	−48
Santiago	−36	−58	+0.2	−12
Toledo	−5.6	−25.9	−27.1	−55.8
Murcia	+14	−13.8	−43.1	−2.7
Barcelona	−11.7	−24.8	−14	−22.3
Cuenca	−28	−44.3	−56.4	−7
Granada	+3.2	−2.7	−27.3	−14.7

The figures leave no doubt that the Inquisition was in a parlous financial state. The continuous accounts of income and expenditure of the tribunal of Córdoba show us a persistent history of debt over three centuries: in 1578 expenses exceeded income by 14.6 per cent, in 1642 by 26.8 per cent, in 1661 by 33.8 per cent, in 1726 by 11.2 per cent.[47]

Why were the tribunals in constant debt? Quite apart from insufficient income, and the difficulties caused by the highest inflation rate in Europe, the problems of the Inquisition can be explained simply by the fact that bureaucracy was absorbing an enormous proportion of income. In 1498 Torquemada had suggested that each tribunal have two inquisitors and a small number of officials. By the late sixteenth century this concept of a modest establishment had disappeared for ever. Córdoba in 1578 had twenty-six officials, Llerena in 1598 had thirty;[48] the number in each case included three inquisitors. In Córdoba salaries consumed 75.6 per cent of income. In addition to this, each tribunal had to send a proportion of income to the Suprema, which had its own heavy expenses. The sum contributed by Córdoba to the Suprema in 1578 represented nearly a fifth of its costs. At this period the salaries of the Suprema bureaucracy were impressively high.[49] The Council spent 5.8 million maravedis a year on wages (the Inquisitor General got 1.5 million and each inquisitor over 700,000), compared with an average total wage bill for each of the bigger provincial tribunals of around 1.2 million. Local tribunals also had to finance special expenses such as the autos de fe: in the mid-seventeenth century, at a time when its normal annual income was around 3.5 million maravedis, Córdoba put on an auto (1655) which cost over two millions.[50]

This brings us to the most crucial source of inquisitorial income: censos, or investment income. We know that the Inquisition never became a great property-owning institution, and that the estates owned at the end of the eighteenth century were of modest value only; the tribunal of Seville, for example, owned a total of twenty-five rented dwellings and two small estates in 1799.[51] The Holy Office had never lacked the opportunity to become rich, but several factors hindered it doing so. Sequestrations and confiscations did not always produce their full values: against them had to be set the cost of maintaining prisoners, the debts already owed by those arrested and the claims of innocent dependent relatives. For example, when in 1760 a royal official in Santander was arrested, his sequestrated property was valued at 350,972 reales, but of this 36.6 per cent went to payment of his debts, 31.7 per cent to his heirs, and only the remaining 31.7 per cent to the Inquisition.[52] (The example is not necessarily typical: in all too many cases the Inquisition refused to pay creditors or family, and kept confiscated property for itself.) From the beginning, moreover, the crown had decided that the tribunal required cash rather than an accumulation of property. Confiscations were therefore put up for sale in the open market, and the cash obtained was invested, 'segund que el rey católico lo tenya mandado' (the reference, to King Ferdinand, was made in 1519).[53] Many tribunals were very lax in buying censos, and in 1579 the Suprema had to insist that as soon as one censo was paid off the cash must be reinvested in another. The need to have a steady income – one quite independent of the unreliable and irregular income from confiscations – was undoubtedly the main reason why by the sixteenth century most tribunals were investing heavily in censos. After the turmoil of the Morisco expulsions, for example, we find the Valencia tribunal in 1630 with 45,500 ducats invested in censals at 5 per cent, yielding an annual income of 2,275 ducats.

Censos, in short, became the regular cash source of the Inquisition. In 1573 no less than 74 per cent, and in 1576 80 per cent, of the income of the Granada tribunal came from censos and house rents;[54] in 1611, 63.3 per cent of the income of Llerena came from censos.[55] Everywhere the tribunals began to rely on investment income for survival. In the tribunals in Morisco territory the Inquisition was excessively vulnerable because most of the censos were on land worked by the Moriscos; events such as the Alpujarra risings or their eventual expulsion after 1609 were therefore disastrous, not simply because of the loss of the special payments made by the racial minorities but because most of the cash income, in censos and rents, came from Moriscos.

The Inquisition, in short, became a sort of savings bank through which money from various sectors of society – conversos, Moriscos, financiers – was reinvested. Since the inquisitors needed a regular cash flow rather than future benefits, lending was a fair business risk and preferable to any other economic activity (censos brought in 7 per cent in the late sixteenth century, arguably a higher rate of return than most other investments). Thus the Holy Office joined those other ranks of society whom González de Cellorigo was later (in 1600) to condemn for their devotion to the quick profit from censos, 'the plague and ruin of Spain'; and the later financial situation of the Inquisition depended more on fluctuations in the rate of interest than on confiscation of property.

Inevitably, individual inquisitors saw no reason why they should not also profit. Lea cites the cases of the Suprema president who was banished in 1642 for malversation of funds, and the inquisitor who died in 1643 allegedly leaving 40,000 ducats in gold and silver.[56] One may well suspect that some tribunals were richer than their financial statements suggested. Take, for instance, the tribunal of Toledo, which according to the table on page 151 had a permanent deficit balance. If this were really true, how does one explain the interesting case-history of the accountant of the Inquisition there, the priest Juan de Castrejana, who was born in poverty but who managed before his death in 1681 to buy up lands in his home town, endow a chapel and a hospital, lend money to his town council, buy investments in Madrid, set up a silk-manufacturing company and lend money to the silk merchants of Madrid?[57]

Quarrels of jurisdiction continued to plague the Holy Office long after its foundation. Before the organization of the papal Inquisition in the thirteenth century, the bishops of the Church had the principal jurisdiction over heretics. This episcopal power was not continued in the Spanish Inquisition, which claimed and maintained exclusive authority over all cases of heresy. Bishops still in theory retained their rights of jurisdiction, but in practice they seldom or never put the claim into effect. In January 1584 the Suprema informed the Bishop of Tortosa that the popes had given the Inquisition exclusive jurisdiction over heresy and had prohibited cognizance by others, but this claim was obviously false since in 1595 the pope, Clement VIII, informed the Archbishop of Granada that the authority of inquisitors in cases of heresy did not exclude episcopal jurisdiction.[58] These opposing pretensions led to frequent and serious quarrels between bishops and tribunals which were never satisfactorily settled.

Most of the religious orders were subject immediately to the papacy by their constitution, and were therefore generally free from episcopal jurisdiction. Since, however, the powers of the Inquisition derived from the papacy, the tribunals made every effort to bring the friars under their control in matters of faith. Some political rivalry entered into this question, because the first inquisitors, including Torquemada, were usually Dominicans and the Dominican order had won for itself a special position not only in the mediaeval Inquisition but also in the Spanish. Hostility between Dominicans and Franciscans led to the latter obtaining bulls from Rome to protect their privileges. Under Charles V the opposition crumbled. In 1525 the emperor obtained two briefs from the pope subjecting all friars in Spain to the Inquisition and its officers. This did not last long, for in 1534 and subsequently the pope restored to the Franciscans and other orders all the privileges they had previously enjoyed. The struggle went on intermittently until the beginning of the seventeenth century, when papal briefs of 1592 and 1606 decided entirely in favour of the Inquisition.

We have seen that the Society of Jesus, although founded and controlled by Spaniards, was met by hostility in the closed society of sixteenth-century Spain. Siliceo, the Archbishop of Toledo, showed particular hostility to the Jesuits; and the famous Dominican Melchor Cano led a vigorous series of campaigns, in which he denounced the *Spiritual Exercises* of St Ignatius as heretical and condemned the Society and all its works. Cano and Siliceo were only part of a wider campaign to discredit the Jesuit order.[59] One of the liberties questioned by the Inquisition was the Jesuit privilege of not having to denounce heretics to anyone but their own superior in the order. When in 1585 it was learned that the fathers of the Jesuit college at Monterrey in Galicia had been concealing the heresies of some of their number instead of denouncing them to the Holy Office, the latter acted immediately by arresting the provincial of Castile and two fathers from Monterrey. The Inquisition did not succeed in punishing its victims because the case was revoked to Rome in 1587, but the affair clinched its victory over the religious orders.

Only one class of people, the bishops, remained beyond inquisitorial jurisdiction. All others, from the highest nobles of the blood downwards, were liable to the authority of this tribunal which they unquestioningly supported for the greater part of its existence. Bishops could be tried only by Rome, a rule which had been upheld in the mediaeval Inquisition. In Spain, of course, the issue was of some importance, because of the high proportion of bishops who had converso blood. Among the earliest of those singled out for attack by the Inquisition was Bishop Dávila of Segovia, who entered his see in 1461. He had refused to allow the Holy Office into his diocese, and on being accused by the tribunal was summoned to Rome in 1490, in his eightieth year. Even more distinguished was Pedro de Aranda, Bishop of Calahorra and in 1482 president of the Council of Castile. He was summoned to Rome in 1493 and died there in disgrace in 1500. One of the most eminent bishops to suffer patent injustice was Hernando de Talavera, whose case we have already noted. But the most famous example of a clash between inquisitorial and episcopal authority, in a case which also involved royal and papal privileges, was that of Bartolomé de Carranza, Archbishop of Toledo.

Bartolomé de Carranza y Miranda was born in 1503 in Navarre, of poor but hidalgo parents.[60] At the age of twelve he entered the University of Alcalá, and at seventeen joined the Dominican order. He was sent to study at Valladolid where his intellectual gifts soon won him a chair in theology. In his early thirties he went to Rome to win his doctorate in the same subject, and returned to Spain famous. For a while he acted as a censor to the Inquisition, but refused all offers of promotion made to him. In 1542 he refused the wealthy see of Cuzco in America, and likewise rejected the post of royal confessor in 1548, and that of Bishop of the Canaries in 1550. He was twice sent to the sessions of the Council of Trent as a Spanish representative, in 1545 and 1551. He returned to Spain in 1553 and in the following year accompanied Prince Philip on his matrimonial journey to the England of Mary Tudor. There the ardent Carranza distinguished himself by the zeal with which he crushed heretics and purified the universities of Oxford and Cambridge, winning for himself the title of the Black Friar. He stayed in England from July 1554 to July 1557, after which he went to join Philip in Flanders. It was in May 1557 that Archbishop Siliceo of Toledo died. Philip immediately decided to give the post to Carranza, who refused the honour as he had refused all others. The king was adamant. Eventually Carranza said that he would accept only if ordered to do so. In this way the humble, devout and unambitious Dominican friar became the tenant of the most important see in the Catholic world after Rome.

Carranza was a parvenu in the ecclesiastical circles of Spain. His claims to Toledo were less than those of other distinguished prelates in Spain, notably Inquisitor General Valdés. Like Siliceo, he was a man of humble origins thrown into a rigidly aristocratic milieu. He had been nominated to the see while abroad without any effort by Philip to consult his Spanish advisers. Intellectually he was far inferior to his brother Dominican, Melchor Cano, a brilliant theologian who had always been Carranza's bitterest rival in the order. These among other factors were enough to raise up a host of enemies for the new archbishop. Only the weapon of attack was lacking. This was supplied by Carranza himself in his *Commentaries on the Christian Catechism* which he published in 1558 at Antwerp.

The *Commentaries* in themselves are now considered thoroughly orthodox in doctrine. The Council of Trent examined and approved the work, and numerous other distinguished theologians in Spain agreed with this; but there is no doubt that Carranza was a careless theologian. Phrases in his work were seized upon by hostile critics, notably Cano, and were denounced as heresy. The Archbishop of Granada called the *Commentaries* 'reliable, trustworthy, pious and Catholic'; the Bishop of Almería said the book 'contained no heresy and much excellent doctrine'. Yet Melchor Cano asserted that the work 'contains many propositions which are scandalous, rash and ill-sounding, others which savour of heresy, others which are erroneous, and even some which are heretical'. Led by Valdés, the Inquisition accepted Cano's opinion. Small wonder that Pope Pius v claimed, 'The theologians of Spain want to make him a heretic although he is not one!' If there were no actual heresies in Carranza, why was he looked upon with suspicion by his enemies? It is not enough to say that personal enmity loomed large, although this is true. Both Valdés and Cano detested Carranza. Another mortal enemy was Pedro de Castro, Bishop of Cuenca, who had entertained hopes of the see of Toledo, and his brother Rodrigo. Both these men, sons of the Count of Lemos, were aristocrats who resented the rise of men of humble birth to positions of influence. They were to play a key part in the eventual arrest and imprisonment of the archbishop.

Behind the personal enmities lay the fact that Carranza, for all his ardent Catholicism, was a liberal by Spanish standards. In 1530 as a student he had been twice denounced to the Inquisition for holding Erasmian views. At the Council of Trent he had supported the introduction of radical reforms in Church discipline. Later, during his imprisonment, his name was repeatedly linked with that of Reginald Pole, the Cardinal of England, another liberal who was looked upon in Spain as a heretic in Catholic clothing. What ruined Carranza was the Protestant crisis in Spain, which occurred at precisely the time of his elevation to the see of Toledo. Interrogation of Carlos de Seso and Pedro Cazalla resulted in detailed denunciations of the archbishop. On one occasion he was said to have told them he believed as they did; on another he was reported as saying, 'As for me, I don't believe in purgatory.' Preaching in London he was said to have used Lutheran terminology. The Inquisitor General carefully took note of all these testimonies. Still the Holy Office could not act against Carranza, for as a bishop he was answerable only to Rome. Valdés made urgent representations to Rome, and in January 1559 Pope Paul iv sent letters empowering the Inquisition to act against bishops for a limited period of two years, but both the prisoner and the case were to be referred to Rome. Valdés received the brief on 8 April 1559. On 6 May the fiscal of the

Inquisition drew up an indictment calling for the arrest of Carranza 'for having preached, written and dogmatized many heresies of Luther'. After much pressure Philip II gave his sanction on 26 June. On 6 August Carranza, expecting the blow to fall any day, was summoned to Valladolid by the government.

Fearing the import of the summons, Carranza set out but delayed the progress of his journey. On 16 August he was met by a Dominican colleague and friend from Alcalá who warned him that the Inquisition was searching to arrest him. Shaken by this, the archbishop continued his journey until four days later he reached the safety of Torrelaguna, just north of Madrid, where he met his friend Fray Pedro de Soto, who had come from Valladolid to warn him. But already it was too late. Carranza did not know that four days before his arrival the officials of the Inquisition had taken up their residence in Torrelaguna and were awaiting his coming. Carranza reached the little town on Sunday, 20 August. Very early in the morning of Tuesday 22 August the inquisitor Diego Ramírez and Rodrigo Castro (who was a member of the Suprema), together with about ten armed familiars, made their way up to Carranza's bedroom and demanded, 'Open to the Holy Office!' The intruders were let in, and an official addressed the archbishop, 'Your Honour, I have been ordered to arrest Your Reverence in the name of the Holy Office.' Carranza said quietly, 'Do you have sufficient warrant for this?' The official then read the order signed by the Suprema.

Carranza protested, 'Do the inquisitors not know that they cannot be my judges, since by my dignity and consecration I am subject immediately to the pope and to no other?' This was the moment for the trump card to be played. Ramírez said, 'Your Reverence will be fully satisfied on that account', and showed him the papal brief. All that day the archbishop was kept under house arrest and in the evening a curfew was imposed on the town. No one was to venture into the streets after 9 p.m. and nobody was to look out of the windows. In the silence and darkness that midnight the inquisitors and their prey were spirited out of Torrelaguna. On the night of 28 August Carranza was shuffled into the cells of the Inquisition in Valladolid. In the words of Lea, he 'disappeared from human sight as completely as though swallowed by the earth'.

Carranza was allotted two rooms in the prison cells. Here he was kept for over seven years, completely out of touch with the world outside. During the whole of his confinement he was not allowed any recourse to the sacraments. In human terms, the tragic story of the archbishop was just beginning; but politically the story was at an end. From now on Carranza ceased to matter as a human being and became a mere pawn in the struggle for jurisdiction between Rome and the Inquisition. He no longer counted in a controversy where the real issues had become the ambitions of individuals and the pretensions of ecclesiastical tribunals. Marañón observes that in this atmosphere of villainy there was at least one just man – Doctor Martín de Azpilcueta, known as Doctor Navarro, who sacrificed his career in Spain for the sake of defending the unfortunate archbishop faithfully and well at his trial.

The long negotiations between Rome and the Spanish authorities will not concern us here. Briefly, the papacy was concerned to claim its rights over Carranza and thereby to vindicate its unique control over bishops. Philip II saw the papal claim as interference in Spanish affairs and refused to allow the Inquisition to surrender its prisoner. Pope Pius IV in 1565 sent a special legation to negotiate in Madrid. Among the members of the legation were three prelates who later became popes as Gregory XIII, Urban VII and Sixtus V. These distinguished clerics failed to make the mission a success. As one of them wrote back to Rome:

> Nobody dares to speak in favour of Carranza for fear of the Inquisition. No Spaniard would dare to absolve the archbishop, even if he were believed innocent, because this would mean opposing the Inquisition. The authority of the latter would not allow it to admit that it had imprisoned Carranza unjustly. The most ardent defenders of justice here consider that it is better for an innocent man to be condemned than for the Inquisition to suffer disgrace.[61]

With the accession of Pius V to the papal throne in 1566, a solution came into sight. From his prison cell Carranza managed to smuggle a message out to Rome in the form of a paper bearing in his handwriting the words, 'Lord, if it be thou, bid me come to thee upon the waters' (Matthew XIV, 28). This was exactly what Pius intended to do. In July 1566 he ordered the Spanish authorities to send Carranza and all relevant documentation to Rome, under penalty of excommunication. The ageing archbishop reached Rome and was placed in honourable confinement in the Castle of Sant' Angelo. This second imprisonment lasted nine years. Pius V died in 1572 without having decided the case. His successor Gregory XIII finally issued sentence in April 1576. The verdict was a compromise, made no doubt in order to placate Spain. The *Commentaries* were condemned and prohibited and Carranza was obliged to abjure a list of 'errors', after which he was told to retire to a monastery in Orvieto. Meanwhile the papacy was to administer the vacant and wealthy see of Toledo. The sentence satisfied Philip and the Inquisition, whose authority would have suffered by an acquittal. It satisfied Rome, which had vindicated its sole authority over bishops; and, in a sense, it satisfied Carranza, who was not accused of any heresy despite the prohibition of his *Commentaries*, which was to remain in all the editions of the Spanish Index except the last one in 1790. Justice had been replaced by political compromise. Everything had been taken into consideration except the frail old man who, eighteen days after the papal verdict had been read over him, contracted an illness from which he died at 3 a.m. on 2 May 1576.

The Procedure of the Inquisition

'But I am not guilty', said K, 'it's a misunderstanding. And if it comes to that, how can any man be called guilty? We are all simply men here, one as much as the other'.

'That is true', said the priest, 'but that's how all guilty men talk'.

Franz Kafka, *The Trial*

The procedure of the Inquisition was founded on fear and secrecy. In his commentary on the fourteenth-century *Manual* of Eymeric, Francisco Peña in 1578 stated: 'we must remember that the main purpose of the trial and execution is not to save the soul of the accused but to achieve the public good and put fear into others'.[1] The public activity of the Holy Office was thus based on the premise, common to all disciplinary and police systems, that fear was the most useful deterrent. When the inquisitors began operations in a district they would first present their credentials to the local Church and secular authorities, and announce a Sunday or feast day when all residents would have to go to high mass, together with their children and servants, and hear the 'edict' read. At the end of the sermon or the creed, the inquisitor or his representative would hold a crucifix in front of the congregation and ask everybody to raise their right hand, cross themselves and repeat after him a solemn oath to support the Inquisition and its ministers. He would then proceed to read the edict.

In the early years this took the form of an 'edict of grace',[2] modelled on those of the mediaeval Inquisition, which recited a list of heresies and invited those who wished to discharge their consciences to come forward and denounce themselves or others. If they came forward within the 'period of grace' – usually thirty to

forty days – they would be reconciled to the Church without suffering serious penalties. The benign terms encouraged self-denun-
ciation. In Mallorca the first edict to be published brought in 337
conversos who denounced themselves. In Seville the edict filled the
prisons to overflowing. Only voluntary denunciation can explain
the extraordinary figures for Toledo: the number of penitents in the
city alone in 1486 was 2,400.³ As late as 1568 an edict of grace
in Valencia encouraged 2,689 Moriscos to denounce themselves.⁴

After about 1500, edicts of grace were usually replaced by 'edicts
of faith', which omitted the period of grace and instead invited
denunciation of those guilty of a detailed list of offences. In the
earlier period the heresies listed were principally Judaic or Islamic,
but as time went on further heresies were added; eventually by the
late sixteenth century the edict of faith was an extremely lengthy
and impressive document giving details of every conceivable offence, from Jewish and Muslim heresies to the errors of Lutherans
and alumbrados, and so on to popular superstitions, moral offences
and hostile attitudes to the Church and Inquisition.⁵ It must have
taken well over half an hour to read from the pulpit. A typical edict
contains the following passage inviting people to identify judaizers
in their midst:

> If you know or have heard of anyone who keeps the Sabbath according
> to the law of Moses, putting on clean sheets and other new garments,
> and putting clean cloths on the table and clean sheets on the bed on
> feast-days in honour of the Sabbath, and using no lights from Friday
> evening onwards; or if they have purified the meat they are to eat by
> bleeding it in water; or have cut the throats of cattle or birds they are
> eating, uttering certain words and covering the blood with earth; or have
> eaten meat in Lent and on other days forbidden by Holy Mother Church;
> or have fasted the great fast, going barefooted that day; or if they say
> Jewish prayers, at night begging forgiveness of each other, the parents
> placing their hands on the heads of their children without making the
> sign of the cross or saying anything but, 'Be blessed by God and by me';
> or if they bless·the table in the Jewish way; or if they recite the psalms
> without the *Gloria Patri*; or if any woman keeps forty days after childbirth
> without entering a church; or if they circumcise their children or give
> them Jewish names; or if after baptism they wash the place where the
> oil and chrism was put; or if anyone on his deathbed turns to the wall
> to die, and when he is dead they wash him with hot water, shaving the
> hair off all parts of his body ...

The fear engendered by the Inquisition is indubitable. We have
ample evidence of it in the mass flight of conversos from Andalucia

and Catalonia during the 1490s. Juan de Mariana reported the consternation among Spaniards when they found that 'they were deprived of the liberty to hear and talk freely, since in all the cities, towns and villages there were persons placed to give information of what went on. This was considered by some the most wretched slavery and equal to death.' The passage refers to professional informers, and to community set against community on the accidental basis of race. But denunciation and the weight of suspicion and hostility, were of course created within the community itself by its own response to the antisemitic campaign. Sermons and public exhortations encouraged a moral obligation to denounce both oneself and others. We have seen that in 1485 the rabbis of Toledo were asked to tell Jews to report judaizers. The Jewish and converso communities were split apart by such pressures. A particularly striking example of how rock-solid resistance to persecution could suddenly crumble, leading to betrayal and terror, is supplied in the great Chueta tragedy in Mallorca in 1678.[6]

Even where antisemitism was not the driving force, the atmosphere of denunciation and recrimination would have been 'equal to death' for those caught up in it. Petty denunciations were the rule rather than the exception. In 1530 Aldonça de Vargas in the Canary Islands was reported to the Inquisition for having smiled when she heard mention of the Virgin Mary. In 1635 Pedro Ginesta, a man over eighty years old, was brought before the tribunal of Barcelona by an erstwhile comrade for having forgetfully eaten a meal of bacon and onions on a day of abstinence. 'The said prisoner', ran the indictment, 'being of a nation infected with heresy [i.e. from France], it is presumed that he has on many other occasions eaten flesh on forbidden days, after the manner of the sect of Luther.'[7] Denunciations based on suspicion, therefore, led to accusations based on conjecture.

Some delations, of course, had nothing to do with heresy, as in the case of Alonso de Jaén, who was prosecuted in 1530 for urinating against the walls of a church; or in that of Gonzales Ruiz, who said to his opponent during a game of cards, 'Even with God as your partner you won't win this game.'[8] The self-denunciations were almost without exception occasioned by the fear that if one did not confess one would be denounced: for people in this frame of mind the edicts offered a welcome opportunity to unburden oneself of fear rather than of guilt. Lea cites the case of two husbands who in 1581 accused themselves of having asserted in conversation with their wives that fornication was no sin. The wives were summoned and confirmed the confessions. The only possible motive for the action taken by the husbands was fear that their wives would denounce them.[9]

The case is not unusual. The records of the Inquisition are full of instances where neighbours denounced neighbours, friends denounced friends, and members of the same family denounced each other. Many of these cases would have arisen through sheer malice or hatred. But there were others, more significant and terrible, where fear of denunciation alone became the spur to confession and counter-denunciation. The 'term of grace' had an important clause which set the seal on all this. To denounce oneself as a heretic was not enough to enable one to benefit from the terms of the edict of grace. It was also necessary to denounce all those accomplices who shared the error or had led one into it. The chain reaction set in process by this was highly effective in uprooting heresy. The price paid for such orthodoxy was a heavy one. It is possible to believe that only a small proportion of the population went about in perpetual fear of denunciation, and that the orthodox majority breathed openly and freely. But it was surely not entirely exaggeration for a converso writer of Toledo to claim in 1538 that

> preachers do not dare to preach, and those who preach do not dare to touch on contentious matters, for their lives and honour are in the mouths of two ignoramuses, and nobody in this life is without his policeman ... Bit by bit many rich people leave the country for foreign realms, in order not to live all their lives in fear and trembling every time an officer of the Inquisition enters their house; for continual fear is a worse death than a sudden demise.[10]

The equanimity with which many Spaniards accepted the violation of their personal thoughts and consciences brings one back with a start to the experience of the twentieth century. The problem arose out of the Inquisition. But the tribunal itself was only a weapon in the hands of a society that had surrendered part of its liberty to the voluntary purpose of excising from the heart of Spain all those who refused to conform to a specific set of values.

Because the holocaust years of the late fifteenth century were by no means typical of the atmosphere during the remaining three centuries of inquisitorial history, any emphasis on the fear induced by the tribunal must take account of the fact that over long periods there was no fear in the sense of universal anxiety. Individuals continued to fear the consequences of dissent (the licenciado Juan

López Batanero, priest and doctor of Alcázar de San Juan, was said in 1674 to have 'affirmed that simple fornication is no sin, and that he has papers with the arguments for this opinion, which he cannot now reveal *for fear of the Inquisition*, but after his death they can be published'[11]), and conversos continued to feel insecure; but Spaniards, then as later, were quite capable of coming to terms with an institution even if they did not like it. The everyday relationship between the Holy Office and the people will occupy us presently.[12]

For the first century of its existence the Inquisition went out to look for heretics rather than wait for them to be brought in, This was inevitable when tribunals were itinerant, but also continued when they were settled. The 1498 Instructions had laid down that 'the inquisitors go to all the towns where they have not received the oath of the general Inquisition'. In 1517 such visitations were to be once every four months, and by 1581 were required once a year. The purpose was to maintain an inquisitorial presence, though in practice, as we have seen from the case of Llerena, most of the effort was devoted to levying fines. In each town or village the inquisitors were to read the edict of faith and take testimonies; minor offences could be dealt with on the spot by a single inquisitor, but graver ones required consultation.[13] Visitations were invariably hated by the inquisitors.[14] Each visitation involved having to travel for long periods through difficult countryside and sometimes through territory in private jurisdiction where the authorities were hostile. Perhaps the only consolation was that the inquisitor, accompanied by a secretary and an *alguacil*, was undertaking real pastoral work. In his visitation of 1553 the inquisitor of Llerena went to twenty-five towns, and in that of 1554 to twenty-two; the former journey lasted six months and the latter four. In Galicia in 1569 and 1570 the visitations lasted eight months, but by the 1580s it was possible to cut the period down to three. In Toledo in 1541 and 1542 the period was ten months, but by the late century this had been reduced to four. Journeys had to be made in good weather and not in harvest time: the months chosen were therefore normally from February to July.

The many months spent travelling show that visitations were a vital part of the inquisitorial presence, and could take up almost half the time of an inquisitor. Moreover, in visitation years the majority of those penitenced might be out in the villages rather than in the tribunal itself, so that few actual trials would take place. Between 1552 and 1559 the tribunal of Llerena penitenced an average of 122 persons a year on visitations, and managed to get about 300,000 maravedis a year in fines. Against these gains were to be set the disadvantages that the offences punished were mostly petty and trifling; that the money raised was never sufficient even to cover salaries; that conflicts might arise between the inquisitor who stayed behind and the one who went visiting; and that business would pile up during absences (in 1590 the Llerena inquisitors refused pointedly to undertake a visitation, even though directed to do so by the Suprema, because of the urgent cases pending in the tribunal).[15] Not surprisingly, by the early seventeenth century visitations were seldom practised.

In any case, visitations palpably failed to impose fear of the Inquisition on the Spanish people. The sheer impossibility of one inquisitor being able with any degree of frequency to visit the vast areas involved meant that in practice, visits were restricted to larger centres of population from which fines might more easily be raised. Add to this the infrequency of visitations and the sedentarization of tribunals in the cities, and we get a picture of a rural Spain that was largely out of touch with the Inquisition. 'This valley', a correspondent wrote in 1562 from the Vall d'Arán in the Catalan Pyrenees, 'does not know the Holy Inquisition.'[16] The Galician countryside and villages never saw the Holy Office.[17] This gulf between the Inquisition and much of rural Spain was, however, even greater than appears at first sight. Faced by the temerarious appearance in their midst of an outsider demanding to know their private sins and public errors, the rural communities responded with their own wall of silence.[18] Was the inquisitor of Barcelona in 1581, Dr Caldas, simply being naive when reporting after his visitation that he was surprised at how few denunciations there were?[19] It had been ten years since the last visitation to the archdiocese of Tarragona. Yet after four months visiting twenty-three towns (including very large ones such as Igualada, Cervera, Tarragona and Vilafranca), Dr Caldas obtained no more than fifty-three denunciations.

The very nature of the denunciations in these and other Catalan towns leads irresistibly to the conclusion, not that villagers used the Inquisition to play off scores against each other, but that the rural communities solidly rejected the interference of the Inquisition. Five denunciations were against familiars; one involved alleged bestiality 'twelve years ago'; one was against a man for saying 'ten years ago' that simple fornication was no sin; one involved a woman having said thirty years before (she was now dead) that there was no heaven and hell. In town after town, in this and other visitations, there was silence. It is possible that the Catalans were different. Year after year in the 1580s the Barcelona tribunal kept apologizing to the Suprema for the tiny number of prosecutions: 'it is not negligence on our part that there are no more cases' (1586), 'we have made every effort, so that it is not negligence that there are no more cases' (1588).[20] The inquisitors reported in 1623 that edicts of faith were now seldom read in Catalonia.

> they produce few denunciations, and this year we were almost resolved not to publish the edict in this city, because for the last four years not a single person has come to the tribunal in response to the edicts. And in 1621 we visited the regions of Gerona and Perpignan, and even though it was ten years since the last visitation and both are large towns, there were only four or five denunciations, two of them trifling; and if we read the edicts every year the only fruit would be that people would lose their fear of and respect for the censures.[21]

There were undoubtedly parts of Spain where old scores were paid off when the inquisitors came to call: the high figure of 240 denunciations in the diocese of Burgos in 1541[22] may possibly have reflected tensions between Old and New Christians. But in compact and stable communities, where there were few or no minority groups to victimize, the Inquisition was pushed aside as an irrelevance. In Morisco areas the people were willing to denounce themselves under the terms of edicts of grace, but when edicts of faith were proclaimed their community solidarity made them mute.[23] Old Christians were no different: we have already encountered the Galician priest who begged his parishioners not to 'go telling things about each other or meddle in things touching the Holy Office'.

If the Holy Office welcomed denunciations, it often knew when to distinguish between the false and the true. In 1637 when Felipe Leonart, a needlemaker of French origin living in Tarragona, was unanimously denounced by his wife, son and daughter-in-law for Lutheranism, the tribunal very quickly realized that the charges had been made out of sheer malice, and suspended the trial after rejecting the accusations.[24] False-witness was not very frequent, if we take the example of the tribunal of Toledo, in which the 1,172 trials that took place between 1575 and 1610 contained only eight cases of perjury. Perjurers themselves were not treated with any severity commensurate with the ruin they brought upon their victims, though in some few cases they suffered burning, scourging and the galleys, which may have acted to dissuade false-witness for the future. More difficult to deal with were cases of pathological self-denouncers such as the French nun in a convent at Alcalá, Ursule de la Croix, who confessed to heresy and eating meat on Fridays. She was absolved for this, but confessed again to the same crimes. The second time she was reconciled and given a very light penance. When she decided to denounce herself for the third time in 1594, however, she was obligingly sent to the stake.[25]

The heavy reliance put upon denunciations raises the question of the trustworthiness of witnesses. In the Spanish Inquisition, unfortunately, witnesses were given more advantages than in any secular judicial tribunal, because their names were concealed. This concealment provoked widespread hostility, clearly expressed in the several Cortes held under Charles v, particularly that of Valladolid in February 1518. But the influence of Cisneros was thrown heavily against allowing the publication of witnesses' names, and the Inquisition retained its practice unaltered. The concealment of names often meant that when a charge was levelled against a prisoner it had to be phrased in general terms, so that the accused would not know from the occasion cited who the accuser might be. In other words, a prisoner would be kept entirely in the dark about the reasons for his confinement, and if accused in general terms of heresy he would have to rely entirely on his memory to decide which occasion had led to his arrest.

The necessity for concealment was justified by cases in which witnesses had been murdered in order to prevent them testifying. This, at least, was the argument of Cisneros. But, as a memorial from the city of Granada put it in 1526, the system of secrecy was an open invitation to perjury and malicious testimony.[26] This objection would not have been valid but for the fact that all denunciations were taken seriously, and that even if a man were later exonerated the evil brought on him by a slight and secret accusation was immense. When, for example, Doctor Jorge Enríquez, physician to the Duke of Alba, died in 1622, secret witnesses claimed that his body had been buried according to Jewish rites. The consequence was that all Enríquez's family, relatives and household were thrown into prison and kept there for two years until their acquittal for lack of evidence.

Judicially, the courts of the Inquisition were no worse and no better than the secular courts of the day. Faults existing in the procedure of the Holy Office would be no less evident in the royal courts where reforms were instituted by the famous Cortes of Toledo in 1480. The distinguishing feature of the Inquisition – its absolute secrecy – was the one which made it more open to abuses than any public tribunal. This secrecy was not, it seems, originally a part of the inquisitorial framework, and early records refer to public trials and a public prison rather than a secret one. But by the beginning of the sixteenth century secrecy became the general rule and was enforced in all the business of the tribunal. Even the various Instructions of the Inquisition, although set down in print, were for restricted circulation only and not for the public eye. What this necessarily involved was general public ignorance of the methods and procedure of the Inquisition – an ignorance which in its earlier period helped the tribunal by creating reverential fear in the minds of evildoers, but which in its later period led to the rise of fear and hatred based on a highly imaginative idea of how the tribunal worked. The Inquisition was therefore largely to blame for the unfounded slanders cast upon it in the eighteenth century or before. The natural outcome of this enforced ignorance is shown by the debates of the Cortes of Cadiz in 1813, on the projected decree to abolish the Inquisition. If the defenders of the tribunal relied on the argument of a mystical and mythical unity given to Spain by the Inquisition, its detractors relied almost completely on legendary misapprehensions about the entire structure and function of the institution.[27]

The outside world may have been kept uninformed, but internally the flow of information was almost impeccable. The administrative and secretarial apparatus of the tribunal took care to set down on paper even the most trifling business. Thanks to this, the Spanish Inquisition is one of the few early modern institutions about whose organization and procedure an enormous amount of documentation is available. In part the Inquisition, like any judicial court, needed paperwork in order to survive: the struggle to establish precedents and to keep written evidence of privileges forced officials to record everything.

Before an arrest took place, the evidence in the case was presented to a number of theologians who acted as *calificadores* to determine whether the charges involved heresy. If the calificadores decided that there was sufficient proof of heresy, the prosecutor or fiscal drew up a demand for the arrest of the accused, who was then taken into custody. Such at least were the rules. But in numerous cases arrest preceded the examination by calificadores so that all the preliminary safeguards against wrongful arrest were dispensed with. As a result, prisoners sat in inquisitorial gaols without any charge ever having been produced against them. This led the Cortes of Aragon in 1533 to protest against arbitrary arrest, as well as arrest on trifling charges. Zeal of officials and inquisitors alike often outran discretion, and we have cases in the tribunal of Valladolid in 1699 when several suspects (including a girl aged nine and a boy aged fourteen) had lain in prison for up to two years without any *calificación* having been made of the evidence against them. It should be noted, however, that when abuses like this came to the notice of the Suprema it invariably issued severe rebukes to the culprits.

Arrest was accompanied by immediate seizure of the goods held by the accused. An inventory was made of everything in the possession of the man or his family, and all this was held by officials of the Inquisition until the case had been decided. The inventories drawn up in this way are of great historical interest, since they allow us to see in minute detail exactly how the household of a sixteenth- or seventeenth-century family was run. Every item in the house, including pots and pans, spoons, rags and old clothes, was carefully noted down in the presence of a notary. In some cases these items were valued at the time of the inventory – an important measure because of the frequent need to sell the items to pay for the upkeep of a prisoner or his dependants. If a prisoner's case went unheard or undecided for years on end, the sequestration of his property involved real hardship for his dependants, deprived at one blow of their means of income and even of their own homes. For as long as the accused stayed in prison the costs of his upkeep were met out of his sequestrated property, which was as a rule sold piece by piece at a public auction.

Initially no provision was made for relatives during sequestration and the government had to intervene to help. In July 1486 Ferdinand ordered the tribunal in Saragossa to support the needy children of an accused man, Juan Navarro, out of the latter's property while the case was being heard. Others were not so lucky. There were instances of a rich prisoner's children dying of hunger and of others begging in the streets. These evils were finally remedied in the Instructions of 1561, which allowed the support of dependants out of sequestrations. This concession, already in practice but not codified in the mid-sixteenth century, came too late to save two generations of conversos from destruction of their property. Even after 1561, accused persons sometimes found little security for their property against dishonest officials, or against arbitrary arrest and lengthy trials.

The arrested person was usually spirited away into the prisons of the Inquisition, there to await trial. Of the various grades of prison kept by the tribunal, the most rigorous was the 'secret prison', meant particularly for the lengthy confinement of prisoners and not for temporary detainees awaiting trial. The Inquisition was fortunate in its choice of residences. In some of the largest cities of Spain it was allowed the use of fortified castles with ancient and reliable prison cells. The tribunal of Saragossa resided in the Aljafería; that of Seville in the Triana (in 1627 it moved to a site within the city); and that of Córdoba in the Alcázar.

In all these buildings the gaols were in a fairly good condition. This may explain why the secret prisons of the Inquisition were generally considered less harsh and more humane than either the royal prisons or ordinary ecclesiastical gaols. There is the case of a friar in Valladolid in 1629 who made some heretical statements simply in order to be transferred from the prison he was in to the milder one of the Inquisition. On another occasion, in 1675, a priest confined in the episcopal prison pretended to be a judaizer in order to be transferred to the inquisitorial prison. No better evidence could be cited for the superiority of inquisitorial gaols than that of Córdoba in 1820, when the prison authorities complained about the miserable and unhealthy state of the city prison and asked that the municipality should transfer its prisoners to the prison of the Inquisition, which was 'safe, clean and spacious. At present it has twenty-six cells, rooms which can hold two hundred prisoners at a time, a completely separate prison for women, and places for work.' On another occasion the authorities reported that 'the building of the Inquisition is separate from the rest of the city, isolated and exposed on all sides to the winds, spacious, supplied abundantly with water, with sewers well distributed and planned to serve the prisoners, and with the separation and ventilation necessary to good health. It would be a prison well suited to preserve the health of prisoners.'[28]

By contrast, in the sixteenth century the tribunal of Llerena was housed in a building it described in 1567 as 'small, old, poor and shabby', with only fifty-two cells, certainly not enough for the 130 prisoners it had that year.[29]

A more personal description of an inquisitorial prison is given by

a Portuguese who entered the cells of the tribunal at Lisbon in
1802. The picture resembles any Spanish inquisitorial prison:

> The gaoler who for greater dignity has the name of Alcaide, that is,
> keeper of the castle, addressed to me almost a little sermon, recommend-
> ing me to behave in this respectable house with great propriety; stating
> also that I must not make any noise in my room, nor speak aloud, lest
> the other prisoners might happen to be in the neighbouring cells and
> hear me, with other instructions of a similar kind. He then took me to
> my cell, a small room twelve feet by eight, with a door to the passage;
> in this door were two iron grates, far from each other, and occupying
> the thickness of the wall, which was three feet, and outside of these
> grates there was besides a wooden door; in the upper part of this was an
> aperture that let into the cell a borrowed light from the passage, which
> passage received its light from the windows fronting a narrow yard, but
> having opposite, at a very short distance, very high walls; in this small
> room were a kind of wood frame without feet, whereon lay a straw
> mattress, which was to be my bed; a small water-pot; and another utensil
> for various purposes, which was only emptied every eight days, when I
> went to mass in the prisoners' private chapel. This was the only oppor-
> tunity I had of taking fresh air during such a period, and they contrived
> several divisions in the chapel in such a manner that the prisoners could
> never see each other, or know how many were granted the favour of
> going to mass. The cell was arched above, and the floor was brick, the
> wall being formed of stone, and very thick. The place was consequently
> very cold in winter, and so damp that very frequently the grates were
> covered with drops of water like dew; and my clothes, during the winter,
> were in a state of perpetual moisture. Such was my abode for the period
> of nearly three years.[30]

The fact that the practice in inquisitorial prisons could be humane,
is sometimes interpreted falsely to show how benevolent the Inquisition was. What is undeniable is that the gaols were not dens
of horror. Prisoners were fed regularly and adequately from their
own purse on available food, particularly bread, meat and wine.
One fortunate prisoner in Toledo in 1709 managed to order for
himself in addition regular supplies of oil, vinegar, ice, eggs, choco-
late and bacon.[31] The expenses of all paupers were paid for by the
tribunal itself: at Las Palmas the money spent on the pauper
Catalina de Candelaría during her six-month stay in 1662 came to
154 reales. One of those who could afford to pay for themselves,
Isabel Perdomo, had to pay twenty-eight reales for her seven-week
stay in the same prison in 1674.[32] Apart from food, prisoners in
some tribunals were well cared for, this depending on their financial

resources. One Juan de Abel of Granada was granted in his cell the use of 'a mattress, a quilt, two sheets, two pillows, a rug, a blanket', and other items.[33] Even paupers were given slippers, shirts and similar items. Besides this, some comforts were allowed, such as the use of writing paper – a concession exploited to the full by Luis de León, who spent his four years in prison at Valladolid composing his great devotional treatise *Los Nombres de Cristo*.

There was, however, another side to the picture. Prisoners were cut off strictly from all contact with the world outside, and even within the prison were secluded from each other whenever possible. On finally leaving the gaol they were obliged to take an oath not to reveal anything they had seen or experienced in the cells: small wonder if this absolute secrecy gave rise to the most blood-curdling legends about what went on inside. A rule of the Spanish and the Roman Inquisitions was that detainees were denied all access to mass and the sacraments. One of the most notable sufferers in this respect was Carranza, whose trials must have been doubled by this heavy deprivation of spiritual comfort for the eighteen years of his imprisonment.

To balance the fortunate few who were treated kindly there are records of those who did not fare so well. John Hill, an English sailor captured in 1574 and imprisoned by the Las Palmas tribunal, complained of having to sleep on the floor with fleas, of lack of bread and water, and of being left all but naked.[34] These were standard complaints which could have been made of any other prison, secular or ecclesiastical. Other ordeals would include having to wear chains (which were not frequently used by the Inquisition), and being left interminably in unlit and unheated cells. In addition the Inquisition used two instruments to punish awkward prisoners: one was the *mordaza* or gag used to prevent prisoners talking or blaspheming; the other was the *pie de amigo*, an iron fork utilized to keep the head upright forcibly. Keeping in mind the general state of prisons in Europe as a whole down to relatively modern times, we may conclude with Lea 'that the secret prisons of the Inquisition were less intolerable places of abode than the episcopal and public gaols. The general policy respecting them was more humane and enlightened than that of other jurisdictions, whether in Spain or elsewhere.'[35]

The severities of prison life led to a regular death-rate which should be attributed not to torture (about which inquisitors were very careful) but to disease and relatively unhealthy conditions. As the Inquisitor General, Cardinal Adrian, observed in 1517, the prisons were meant for detention only and not for punishment. Inquisitors made it their special care to avoid cruelty, brutality and harsh treatment. The use of torture (inherited from the mediaeval Inquisition) was not looked on as an end in itself. The Instructions of 1561 laid down no rules for its use but urged that its application should be according to 'the conscience and will of the appointed judges, following law, reason and good conscience. Inquisitors should take great care that the sentence of torture is justified and follows precedent.'[36] At a time when the use of torture was universal in European criminal courts, the Spanish Inquisition followed a policy of circumspection which makes it compare favourably with other institutions. Torture was used only as a last resort and applied in only a minority of cases. Often the accused was merely placed *in conspectu tormentorum*, when the sight of the instruments of torture would provoke a confession.

Confessions gained under torture were never accepted as valid because they had obviously been obtained by pressure. It was therefore essential for the accused to ratify his confession the day after the ordeal. If he refused to do this, a legal pretext was invoked. As the rules forbade anyone to be tortured more than once, the end of every torture session was treated as a suspension only, and refusal to ratify the confession would be met with a threat to 'continue' the torture. Besides being compelled to confess their own heresies, victims were often also tortured *in caput alienum*, to confess knowledge of the crimes of others. Torture was used infrequently. Minor offences, which were the bulk of crimes tried by the Inquisition for most of its history, did not qualify for it. Lea estimates that in the Toledo tribunal between 1575 and 1610 about 32 per cent of those who qualified were in fact tortured.[37] Virtually all such cases involved heresy. Out of over four hundred conversos tried by the Inquisition at Ciudad Real in 1483–5, only two are known to have been tortured.[38] In the tribunal of Granada from 1573 to 1577, eighteen out of 256 accused were tortured – just over 7 per cent; in Seville from 1606 to 1612, twenty-one out of 184 were tortured – just over 11 per cent.[39] The incidence of torture in Valencia before 1530 seems to have been low; after 1530 about a third of those qualifying were tortured.[40] By the mid-eighteenth century torture had virtually fallen out of use in the tribunal, and finally in 1816 the pope forbade its use in any of the tribunals subject to the Holy See.

Torture was employed exclusively to elicit information or a confession, and was never used as a punishment. The scenes of sadism conjured up by popular writers on the Inquisition have little basis in reality, though the whole procedure was unpleasant enough to arouse periodic protests from Spaniards. At no time did the inquisitors resort to psychological methods or brain-washing, and their reputation for gratuitous cruelty is wholly without foundation. Torturers used were normally the public executioners who worked for the secular courts. Those required to be present at the proceedings were the inquisitors themselves, a representative of the bishop, and a secretary to record everything faithfully. Physicians were usually available in case of emergency. The basic rule to be observed was that the victim should suffer no danger to life or limb. In the vast majority of cases the rule was adhered to, but there are a few examples of victims who had their legs or arms broken because they persisted in refusing to confess. Even less in number are those victims who died as a result of torture. In such cases the inquisitors could comfort themselves that the victims died through their own obstinacy.

No distinctive tortures were used by the Inquisition: those most often employed were in common use in other secular and ecclesiastical tribunals, and any complaints of novel tortures would certainly refer to rare exceptions. The three main ones were the *garrucha*, the *toca* and the *potro*. The *garrucha* or pulley involved being hung by the wrists from a pulley on the ceiling, with heavy weights attached to the feet. The victim was raised slowly and then suddenly allowed to fall with a jerk. The effect was to stretch and perhaps dislocate the arms and legs. The *toca* or water torture was more complicated. The victim was tied down on a rack, his mouth was kept forcibly open and a *toca* or linen cloth was put down his throat to conduct water poured slowly from a jar. The severity of the torture varied with the number of jars of water used. The *potro*, which was the most common after the sixteenth century, involved being bound tightly on a rack by cords which were passed round the body and the limbs and were controlled by the executioner, who tightened them by turns of the cords at the end. With each turn the cords bit into the body and travelled round the flesh. In all these tortures it was the rule to strip the victims first. Both men and women were divested of all their clothes and left completely naked except for minimal garments to cover their shame.[41]

There seems to have been no age limit for victims, nor was there any limit on the torture. A victim would often have to undergo all the three tortures before he would confess. Less obdurate ones need only suffer one torture. While the Inquisition did not usually subject the very old and very young to torture, there are cases when tribunals apparently found this necessary. Women aged between seventy and ninety years are on record as having been put on the *potro*. In 1607 at Valencia a girl of thirteen was subjected to torture, but she seems to have been mildly treated since she overcame it without confessing.

Allowances were always made. In 1579 the inquisitors of Llerena informed the Suprema that 'all the clergy arrested for being alumbrados have been tortured and they haven't confessed anything, though it must be said that since several of them are very old and also ill and infirm from their long confinement, it has not been possible to torture them with the required rigour'.[42]

It was standard practice, which the Inquisition took over from secular courts,[43] to record all details of torture. A secretary noted every word and gesture during the proceedings, thus providing us with impressive if macabre evidence of the sufferings of victims of the Inquisition. Here are extracts from the official accounts of two tortures carried out in the sixteenth century. In the first is a woman accused in 1568 of not eating pork and of changing her linen on Saturdays.

> She was ordered to be placed on the *potro*. She said, 'Señores, why will you not tell me what I have to say? Señor, put me on the ground – have I not said that I did it all?' She was told to tell it. She said 'I don't remember – take me away – I did what the witnesses say'. She was told to tell in detail what the witnesses said. She said, 'Señor, as I have told you, I do not know for certain. I have said that I did all that the witnesses say. Señores, release me, for I do not remember it'. She was told to tell it. She said, 'Señores, it does not help me to say that I did it and I have admitted that what I have done has brought me to this suffering – Señor, you know the truth – Señores, for God's sake have mercy on me. Oh, Señor, take these things from my arms – Señor release me, they are killing me'. She was tied on the *potro* with the cords, she was admonished to tell the truth and the *garrotes* were ordered to be tightened. She said, 'Señor, do you not see how these people are killing me? I did it – for God's sake let me go.'[44]

Foreign heretics were submitted to the same procedure. Here is the case of Jacob Petersen from Dunkirk, a sailor aged twenty years, who was examined by the tribunal of the Canaries in November

1597. He was stripped and bound and given three turns of the cord.

> On being given these he said first, 'Oh God!' and then, 'There's no mercy';
> after the turns he was admonished, and he said, 'I don't know what to
> say, oh dear God!' Then three more turns of the cord were ordered to be
> given, and after two of them he said, 'Oh God, oh God, there's no mercy,
> oh God help me, help me!'[45]

After three more turns he confessed.

While these examples give us some insight into the agony of those who were tortured, it should be remembered that the procedure was often mild enough for very many to overcome it. A comparison with the cruelty and mutilation common in secular tribunals shows the Inquisition in a relatively favourable light. This in conjunction with the usually good level of prison conditions makes it clear that the tribunal had little interest in cruelty and attempted to temper justice with mercy.

Trial and Punishment

Qué maldita canalla!
Muchos murieron quemados,
Y tanto gusto me daba
Verlos arder, que decía,
Atizándoles la llama:
'Perros herejes, ministro
Soy de la Inquisición Santa'.

Calderón, *El Sitio de Breda*

Since the Inquisition usually arrested suspects only after the evidence against them seemed conclusive and had been approved by calificadores, the victim was naturally presumed guilty from the start and on him fell the onus of proving his own innocence. The sole task of the Inquisition was to obtain from its prisoner an admission of guilt and a penitential submission. If in the process of enquiry it was found that the evidence was false and the prisoner presumably innocent, he was immediately set free. The main task of the tribunal, however, was to act not as a court of justice but as a disciplinary body called into existence to meet a national emergency. In these circumstances, and considering the standards of justice prevailing at the time, the courts of the Inquisition were fully adequate for their task.

One of the peculiarities of inquisitorial procedure – and one which brought hardship and suffering to many – was the refusal to divulge reasons for arrest, so that prisoners went for days, months and even years without knowing why they were in the cells of the tribunal. Instead of accusing the prisoner, the inquisitors approached him and gave three warnings, over a period of weeks, to search his conscience, confess the truth and trust to the mercy of the tribunal.

The third warning was accompanied by information that the prosecutor intended to present an accusation, and that it would be wisest to confess before the charges were laid. The effect of this enforced ignorance was to depress and break down a prisoner. If innocent, he remained bewildered about what to confess, or else confessed crimes the Inquisition was not accusing him of; if guilty, he was left to wonder how much of the truth the Inquisition really knew, and whether it was a trick to force him to confess.

When, after the three warnings, the prosecutor eventually read out the articles of accusation, the accused was required to answer the charges on the spot, with no time or advocate to help him think out his defence. Any reply made in these circumstances could hardly fail to be incriminating. Only after this was permission given to enlist legal help for the defence.

One important concession made by the Spanish Inquisition, and not made by the mediaeval one, was that the accused could have the services of an advocate and a solicitor. This concession was written into the Instructions of 1484 and was generally upheld, though later modifications to the rule sometimes rendered the use of a lawyer farcical. In the earlier years of the Inquisition those accused could choose their lawyers freely, but the growing caution of the Holy Office later confined the choice to special lawyers nominated by the tribunal, so that by the mid-sixteenth century the prisoners' advocates or *abogados de los presos* were recognized as officials of the Inquisition, dependent upon and working with the inquisitors. This new class of lawyers was obviously distrusted by some prisoners, for in 1559 we have the case of a prisoner in Valencia telling his cell-mate that

> though the inquisitor might give him an advocate he would give him no one good but a fellow who would do only what the inquisitor wanted, and if by chance he asked for an advocate or solicitor not of the Inquisition, they would not serve, for if they went contrary to the inquisitor's wishes he would get up some charge of false belief or want of respect and cast them into prison.[1]

This does not mean that many *abogados de los presos* did not do their duty conscientiously. But they were hindered by the restrictions of the tribunal and by the subtle and dangerous task of defending the prisoner while condemning his heresy. Some special cases exist where the accused were allowed counsel of their own choice: one such was Carranza, who chose among others the distinguished canonist Martín de Azpilcueta to defend him.

When a prisoner was finally accused he was given a copy of the evidence against him in order to help him prepare a defence. This publication of the evidence was by no means as helpful as it might seem. In the first place, as we have seen, the names of all witnesses were suppressed. Even more important, all evidence which might help to identify witnesses was also suppressed. This meant that the prisoner was often deprived of any knowledge of the complete case against him. In this way the inquisitors were free to use as evidence information which had not been communicated to the accused. While this helped to protect witnesses against identification and recrimination, it sometimes crippled the defence. On this question the practice of the Suprema was not at first decided, but Valdés' Instructions of 1561 finally stipulated that any evidence liable to betray a witness could be omitted, and that only evidence contained in the publication was to be used in the case. This last regulation preserved the forms of justice.

The accused had several avenues of defence short of proving the complete falsity of an accusation. He could call favourable witnesses, disable hostile witnesses by proving personal enmity, or object to his judges, a process known as recusation. Several extenuating circumstances such as drunkenness, insanity, extreme youth, and so on, could also be pleaded. All these expedients were resorted to regularly, not always with equal success. In the great majority of trials before the Spanish Inquisition, defence consisted solely in the resort to witnesses, since this was the only way to get at the unknown sources of evidence.

The problem caused by anonymous witnesses was a serious one. We have the case of Diego de Uceda,[2] who was accused in 1528 of Lutheranism on the basis of a chance talk with a stranger on the road from Burgos to Córdoba. The suppression of all details of time and place in the published evidence led Uceda to imagine that the accusation arose from a talk some nights later at Guadarrama, and all his energies were spent vainly on proving that this latter conversation had been innocuous, while the real evidence against him went uncontradicted. Uceda decided to call witnesses in his favour: he had to wait six months before they could all be traced, and even then their depositions did not help to contradict the evidence. The resort to favourable witnesses was thus an unreliable and lengthy procedure.

Greater success could be had by disabling hostile witnesses. Felipe Leonart, whose case we have already noted, had no difficulty in

1637 in proving that accusations by his family had been made out of malice. Similarly, Gaspar Torralba of the village of Vayona, near Chinchón, gave in his defence in 1531 a list of 152 persons as his mortal enemies; most of the thirty-five witnesses against him happened to be on the list, and he was consequently let off lightly.[3] Pedro Sánchez de Contreras was accused at Logroño of blasphemy in 1669, but because he happened to be a corregidor he had full material evidence on all his enemies, men whom he had prosecuted for various crimes. He therefore handed the tribunal an enormous dossier with the criminal records of all his potential accusers; the case was dropped.[4]

Recusation of judges called for considerable courage, and was therefore not resorted to except where the prisoner could prove their personal enmity. Carranza was one of the few who succeeded in having his judges changed for this reason, though in the event it was of little help to him. Attempts to escape trial by pleading insanity or a wide range of other extenuating circumstances (drunkenness, grief) were also often made. The Inquisition could go to great lengths to establish the truth, and some of its attitudes may even be described as enlightened (witchcraft, as we shall see, was treated as a form of insanity). Drunkenness was cited as an excuse in the case of Andrés González, aged twenty when accused by the tribunal of Toledo in 1678 of blaspheming and swearing that 'he cared not for God or the Virgin', 'he did not believe in God', 'he believed in Mohammed'. As the story of his life unfolded before the inquisitors, they heard of his mother who had died when he was ten, and of his father who had remarried with a woman who beat Andrés and forced him to leave home. He had wandered in search of work until he came to Toledo, where he married a girl and worked partly as an agricultural labourer, partly as a carpenter's assistant. They were poor, and lived in the house of his wife's sister, where his hostile in-laws drove him to drink, which was when he was heard to swear; 'and when I quarrelled with my wife, her cousin and his wife, her sister and her sister's husband, all used to turn on me and beat me till the blood came to my teeth'.[5] The Inquisition sympathized, but banished him from the area for three years.

There was no formal trial, in the sense of a single act carried out in a single room within a set period of time. The trial was composed instead of a series of audiences at which the prosecution and defence made their respective depositions, and a series of interrogations carried out by the inquisitors in the presence of a notary. When both prosecution and defence had completed their duties the case was held to be concluded, and the time arrived for sentence to be pronounced. For this it was necessary to form a *consulta de fe*, a body consisting of the inquisitors, one representative of the bishop, and a few graduates in theology or law, known as consultors. A vote on the case was taken by this body. According to the Valdés Instructions of 1561, if the inquisitors and the episcopal representative agreed, their vote prevailed even against a majority of consultors; but if they disagreed, the case was to be referred to the Suprema. By the eighteenth century, however, centralization under the Suprema meant that few if any important decisions were made by provincial tribunals, and *consultas de fe* ceased to exist because all sentences were passed by the Suprema alone.

Such was the basic procedure. But it was of course open to abuse at every stage. The most important drawback from the prisoner's point of view was the impossibility of adequate defence. His advocate's role was limited to drawing up articles of defence which were presented to the judges: beyond this no argument or cross-examination was allowed. This meant that in reality the inquisitors were both judge and jury, both prosecution and defence, and the prisoner's fate depended entirely on the mood and character of the inquisitors.

One other drawback that affected most prisoners was the interminable length of trials. The classic case is that of Carranza, but others suffered no less. The inquisitors of Llerena in 1590, overwhelmed by successive denunciations of alumbrados, judaizers and Moriscos, reported the urgency of 'attending to the trials of the prisoners in this Inquisition, of whom there are over sixty, and some of them have been in prison up to seven years and many up to four years, and every day they present complaints that their affairs are being delayed so long'. As if this were not enough, they were just receiving denunciations made by an aggrieved Morisco of Hornachos against the rest of the town, 'and he is giving so much information that we believe he will take several years to finish'.[6] Other examples of delays include the case of Gabriel Escobar, a cleric in minor orders, who was arrested by the tribunal of Toledo in 1607 on a charge of illuminism, and died in prison in 1622 before his trial had finished. A Mexican priest, Joseph Brunón de Vertiz, who was arrested in 1649, died in prison in 1656 before his trial had even begun; he was eventually tried posthumously, con-

demned and burnt in effigy only in 1659.[7] These delays took a toll
not only of the years and health of a prisoner but also of his
sequestrated property, which was retained all this time to pay for
any expenses incurred.

Condemnation usually meant that the accused had to appear in
an auto de fe. This ceremony was held either in private (*auto particular*) or in public (*auto público*): it is the latter which has become
notorious as the *auto de fe*. The penalties passed by the Inquisition
were decreed at these ceremonies. As the range of punishment was
very broad, it would be helpful to give an analysis, based on recent estimates, of the offences dealt with. A preliminary count of
cases for the period 1540–1700 from nineteen tribunals – ten of
them (Saragossa, Logroño, Barcelona, Valencia, Mallorca, Sardinia,
Sicily, Mexico, Lima and Cartagena) representing the secretariat of
Aragon, and the remainder representing the tribunals of Castile
(but without Cuenca and Madrid) – shows the following total of
offences:[8]

	Aragon	Castile	Total	Percentage
Judaizers	942	4,065	5,007	10.2
Muslims	7,472	3,339	11,311	23.0
'Lutherans'	2,284	1,215	3,499	7.1
Alumbrados	61	88	149	0.3
Propositions	5,888	8,431	14,319	29.1
Bigamy	1,591	1,199	2,790	5.7
Solicitation	695	546	1,341	2.7
Against Holy Office	2,139	1,815	3,954	8.1
Superstition	2,571	1,179	3,750	7.6
Sexual	2,154	825	2,979	6.0
Other	93	—	93	0.2
Totals	25,890	23,202	49,092	100.0

The figures give us an extremely rough guide to the type of offences
tried by the Inquisition. There are important qualifications to be
made. The classification of offences is not that used by the Inquisition and should not necessarily be accepted as reliable. Moreover, the
impact of the Inquisition varied widely according to region, so that
general figures obscure vital differences. Because the Inquisition

also changed its emphasis from one period to another, it may be more informative to divide the activity of the tribunal into five main phases: (1) the period of intense anti-converso persecution after 1480 (2) the relatively quiet early sixteenth century (3) the great period of activity against Protestants and Moriscos, 1560–1614 (4) the seventeenth century, when most of those tried were neither of Jewish nor of Moorish origin (5) the eighteenth century, when heresy was no longer a problem. Unfortunately, statistics for the first and last of these periods are deficient. Though figures for the intervening phases are also very incomplete, a rough overall analysis, set beside the more reliable local data for Saragossa, Toledo and Galicia as given by Dedieu and Contreras,[9] will give a fair example of general evolution and regional variations.

The system of punishments can be grouped into four main classes. Accused were either acquitted ('absolved' or 'suspended'), penanced, reconciled or burnt (in person or in effigy). In the tribunal of Valencia, 3,075 of the trials in 1566–1609 concluded as follows: 44.2 per cent were penanced, 40.2 per cent reconciled, 2.5 per cent absolved, 9 per cent suspended, 2.1 per cent burnt in effigy, 2.0 per cent burnt in person.[10] In Galicia between 1560 and 1700, of 2,203 cases 18.5 per cent were absolved, 62.7 per cent penanced, 16.1 per cent reconciled, 1.9 per cent relaxed in effigy, 0.7 per cent relaxed in person.[11]

The number of acquittals, small as they were, meant an improvement on the mediaeval tribunal, which as a rule never acquitted. Outright acquittal, however, meant admitting an error, so it was common to suspend cases. Suspension was more to be feared than welcomed: it meant that the trial could at any time and under any provocation be renewed, and one remained thereafter technically under suspicion. From the sentence there was only a limited chance of appeal. In cases that ended in a public auto de fe, this was because the accused were not informed of their sentence until they were in the actual procession during the auto; by then it was too late to appeal. The delay in delivering a verdict would naturally heighten the suspense, fear and despair felt by prisoners. But when a man was sentenced to be relaxed he was always informed of his fate the night before the ceremony to give him time in which to prepare his soul for confession and repentance. Later in the history of the tribunal this information was given as much as three days in advance. In private autos there was much more opportunity to appeal after the sentence had been read out. In such cases the

		Percentages		
	Overall	Saragossa	Toledo	Galicia
Period II: 1540–59				
Judaizers	1.8	4.0	1.9	
Muslims	13.7	55.3	12.8	
'Lutherans'	4.2	6.2	1.87	
Propositions	52.0	7.7	55.5	
Bigamy	5.9	6.2	3.9	
Solicitation	0.02	0.0	0.07	
Against Holy Office	11.3	9.6	19.7	
Superstition	1.5	1.2	1.9	
Sexual and other	9.5	9.8	2.2	
Number of cases	4,182	481	1,346	
Period III: 1560–1614				(1560–99)
Judaizers	5.9	0.6	9.7	0.4
Muslims	31.6	56.5	12.9	0.2
'Lutherans'	7.7	8.8	6.8	6.3
Propositions	29.7	8.6	46.1	56.3
Bigamy	5.4	1.5	4.6	18.8
Solicitation	2.0	0.6	2.8	12.8
Against Holy Office	9.0	11.4	12.7	1.4
Superstition	3.8	1.2	1.5	1.9
Sexual and other	4.9	10.9	2.9	1.8
Number of cases	29,584	4,194	2,269	1,049
Period IV: 1615–1700				(1600–1700)
Judaizers	20.6	3.1	44.3	38.9
Muslims	9.0	2.4	2.5	6.7
'Lutherans'	7.6	10.2	2.4	12.7
Propositions	21.9	24.3	19.4	16.6
Bigamy	6.2	5.4	4.4	4.2
Solicitation	5.4	5.2	3.0	6.2
Against Holy Office	4.2	6.1	6.8	2.3
Superstition	16.7	21.0	11.9	10.4
Sexual and other	7.9	22.4	5.2	1.9
Number of cases	15,326	1,292	1,949	1,154

appeal always went to the Suprema, appeals to Rome not being encouraged.

To be penanced was the least of the punishments imposed. Those who did penance had to 'abjure' their offences: *de levi* for a lesser offence, *de vehementi* for a graver one. The penitent swore to avoid his sin in the future, and if he swore *de vehementi*, any relapse made him liable to severe punishment on the next occasion. Penitents were then condemned to penalties such as the sanbenito, fines, banishment or sometimes the galleys. 'Reconciliation' was in theory the return of a sinner to the bosom of the Church after due penance had been performed. In practice it was the most severe punishment the Inquisition could inflict, short of relaxation. All the penalties were heavier: in addition to the sanbenito, accused persons could be condemned to flogging and to long spells in prison or the galleys. In most cases confiscation of goods occurred, so that even if a prisoner escaped with a prison sentence of a few months, he came out an orthodox Catholic indeed but facing a life of beggary. An additional rule, frequently enforced, was that anyone backsliding after reconciliation was to be treated as a relapsed heretic and sent to the stake.

The sanbenito, a corrupt form of the words *saco bendito*, was a penitential garment used in the mediaeval Inquisition and taken over by the Spanish one. It was usually a yellow garment with one or two diagonal crosses imposed on it, and penitents were condemned to wear it as a mark of infamy for any period from a few months to life. Those who were to be relaxed at an auto de fe had to wear a black sanbenito on which were painted flames, demons and other decorative matter. Anyone condemned to wearing the ordinary sanbenito had to put it on whenever he went out of doors, a practice by no means popular in the first decades of the Inquisition. The order to wear a sanbenito for life should not be taken literally. As with sentences of perpetual imprisonment, the order was invariably commuted to a much shorter period at the discretion of the inquisitor. The chief criticism to be levelled against these garments is less the deliberate shame they were meant to cast on their wearers than the policy of perpetuating infamy by hanging them up in the local church *ad perpetuam rei memoriam*.

The imprisonment decreed by the Inquisition could be either for a short term of months and years, or for life, the latter usually being classified as 'perpetual and irremissible'. Neither sentence need involve actual confinement in a prison. By the Instructions of 1488 the inquisitors could at their discretion confine a man to his own house or to some other institution such as a convent or hospital, with the result that very many 'prisoners' served their sentences in moderate comfort. The main reason for this surprising concession was that the tribunals often lacked prison space when their cells were already full, and had to make do with alternatives. Prisoners made the most of this. In 1655 a report on the tribunal of Granada observed that prisoners were allowed out at all hours of the day without restriction, they wandered through the city and its suburbs and amused themselves at friends' houses, returning to their prison only at night; in this way they were given a comfortable lodging-house for which they paid no rent.[12] Another modification to the apparent stringency of inquisitorial decrees is that 'perpetual' imprisonment was almost never enforced. By the seventeenth century a 'perpetual' term rarely involved imprisonment for more than three years, if the prisoner was repentant, and 'irremissible' prison usually meant confinement for about eight years. Despite this the Inquisition continued to decree 'perpetual' sentences, probably because in canon law it was the custom to condemn heretics to life imprisonment. Incongruous sentences such as 'perpetual prison for one year' appear as a matter of course in inquisitorial decrees.

The galleys were a punishment unknown to the mediaeval Inquisition, and were devised for the new one by Ferdinand, who thereby found a cheap source of labour without having to resort to open slavery. This punishment was perhaps the most indefensible of any operated by the Spanish Inquisition, but was not frequently used; and victims were never sentenced to any period over ten years, in contrast to secular tribunals which then and later condemned prisoners to the galleys for life.[13] The galleys constituted an economical form of punishment. Tribunals were freed from the duty of maintaining penitents in their prisons, and the State was saved the need to hire rowers at some expense By the mid-eighteenth century the tribunal, like the State, ceased to use the galleys as a punishment.

A more common form of physical punishment was flogging. The use of the lash as chastisement was very old in Christian tradition, but under the Inquisition the punishment became very much more than chastisement. The penitent was usually condemned to be 'whipped through the streets', in which case he had to appear stripped to the waist – often mounted on an ass – and was duly flogged through the streets with the specified number of strokes by the public executioner. During this journey round the streets, passers-by and children would show their hatred of heresy by hurling stones at the victim. Women were flogged in the same way as men. Nor was there any limit on age, cases on record showing that girls in their teens and women of seventy or eighty were subjected to the same treatment. It was the general rule to prescribe no more than two hundred lashes for the accused, and sentences of one hundred lashes were very common.

These and other punishments were sometimes decreed separately, sometimes together. At the Granada auto on 30 May 1672 Alonso Ribero was sentenced to four years' banishment from the locality, six years in the galleys and a hundred strokes of the lash, for falsifying documents of the Inquisition; and Francisco de Alarcón was sentenced to five years' banishment, five years in the galleys, two hundred strokes of the lash and a money fine, for blasphemy.[14] Other penalties in the canon need little explanation. Exile or banishment from the locality was a common sentence for bad influences. Confiscations were exacted whenever possible. Of the several unusual punishments which at one time or another made their appearance in the Inquisition, it is worth noting the one dealt out in the Mexican Inquisition in December 1664 to a penitent who was smeared with honey, then covered with feathers and made to stand in the sun for four hours during an auto de fe.

The ultimate penalty was the stake. The execution of heretics was by the fifteenth century such a commonplace of Christendom that the Spanish Inquisition cannot be accused of any innovation in this respect. It had been the practice, hallowed by the mediaeval Inquisition, for Church courts to condemn a heretic and then hand him over, or 'relax' him, to the secular authorities. These were obliged to carry out the sentence of blood which the Holy Office was forbidden by law to carry out. In all this there was no pretence that the Inquisition was not the body directly and fully responsible for the deaths that occurred. It is consequently difficult to understand why apologists for the Inquisition have pretended that the tribunal bore no responsibilty at all. Its responsibility was so absolute that contemporaries like Hernando del Pulgar were in no doubt that to mitigate the severity of the tribunal, they must approach the Inquisitor General and not the secular authorities.

Two classes of people alone qualified for the stake – unrepentant heretics and relapsed heretics. The latter class consisted of those who, after being pardoned for a first serious offence, had repeated the offence and were adjudged to have relapsed into heresy. Those who actually died at the stake were only a small proportion of the victims listed in records as 'relaxed'. These unlucky few were always given the choice between repenting before the auto de fe reached its climax, in which case they were 'mercifully' strangled when the flames were lit; or remaining unrepentant, in which case they were roasted alive. The majority of those who were 'relaxed' were in fact burnt in effigy only, either because they had died or because they had saved themselves by flight. In the early years of the Inquisition, the large number of victims burnt in effigy is a guide to the volume of refugees escaping from the tribunal.

The proportionately small number of executions is an effective argument against the legend of a bloodthirsty tribunal. Nothing, certainly, can efface the horror of the first twenty holocaust years. Nor can occasional outbursts of savagery, such as overtook the Chuetas in the late seventeenth century, be minimized. But it is clear that for most of its existence the Inquisition was far from being a juggernaut of death either in intention or in capability. The figures given above for punishments in Valencia and Galicia suggest an execution rate of well under 2 per cent of the accused. It has been estimated that in the nineteen tribunals analysed above, the execution rate over the period 1540–1700 was 1.83 per cent for relaxations in person and 1.65 per cent for relaxations in effigy.[15] If this is anywhere near the truth, it would seem that during the sixteenth and seventeenth centuries less than three people a year were executed by the Inquisition in the whole of the Spanish monarchy from Sicily to Peru – possibly a lower rate than in any provincial court of justice. A comparison, indeed, of secular courts and the Inquisition can only be in favour of the latter as far as rigour is concerned. In 1573, for instance, the corregidor of Plasencia handed over to the Holy Office in Llerena a Morisco condemned by his jurisdiction to be hanged and quartered for allegedly smashing an image of the Virgin, but the Inquisition found the case unproven and set him free.[16] It must be remembered, of course, that although the death rate was low it was also heavily weighted against people of Jewish and Moorish origin. The relative frequency of burnings in the earlier years disappeared in the eighteenth century, and in the twenty-nine years of the reigns of Charles III and Charles IV only four people were burnt.[17]

The ceremony of an auto de fe has a literature all to itself. Among native Spaniards it began its career as a religious act of penitence and justice, and ended it as a public festivity rather like bullfighting or fireworks. To foreigners it always remained a thing of impressive horror and fear. Their journals and letters written while on tour in Spain reveal both amazement and disgust at a practice which was unknown in the rest of Europe. If reminded that the public execution of criminals in other countries was no better than the auto de fe they would no doubt have rejected any such comparison, since the one was motivated by 'justice' and the other by 'fanaticism'. Whatever the modern verdict, there is no doubt that autos were popular. Accounts, engravings and paintings show us that every function of this sort always had a maximum audience up to the beginning of the eighteenth century. Visitors would throng in from outlying districts when it was announced that an auto would be held, and the scene would invariably be set in the biggest square or public place available.

The elaborate and impressive staging of the proceedings, depicted clearly in paintings of the period, made for heavy expense and because of this public autos were not very frequent. Their frequency depended entirely on the discretion of individual tribunals, which sometimes tried to hold autos at least annually. Prisoners were carefully preserved for this most solemn occasion.

When enough prisoners had accumulated to make the holding of an auto worthwhile, a date was fixed for the event and the inquisitors informed the authorities of the municipality and the cathedral. One calendar month before the auto a procession consisting of familiars and notaries of the Inquisition would march through the streets of the town proclaiming the date of the ceremony. In the intervening month, all the preparations would have to be made. Orders went out to carpenters and masons to prepare the scaffolding for the occasion, and furniture and decorations were made ready. The evening before the auto a special procession took place, known as the procession of the Green Cross, during which familiars and others carried the cross of the Holy Office to the site of the ceremony. All that night prayers and preparations were made; then early next morning mass was celebrated, breakfast was given to all who were to appear in the auto (including the condemned) and a procession began which led directly to the square where the auto would be held.

There is available a contemporary account of the first auto de fe held at Toledo, on Sunday 12 February 1486, during which several hundred judaizers were reconciled to the Church. At this early epoch there was little or no emphasis on ceremonial, and the inquisitors were occupied solely with the task of reconciling large numbers of heretics quickly and efficiently.

All the reconciled went in procession, to the number of 750 persons, including both men and women. They went in procession from the church of St Peter Martyr in the following way. The men were all together in a group, bareheaded and unshod, and since it was extremely cold they were told to wear soles under their feet which were otherwise bare; in their hands were unlit candles. The women were together in a group, their heads uncovered and their faces bare, unshod like the men and with candles. Among all these were many prominent men in high office. With the bitter cold and the dishonour and disgrace they suffered from the great number of spectators (since a great many people from outlying districts had come to see them), they went along howling loudly and weeping and tearing out their hair, no doubt more for the dishonour they were suffering than for any offence they had committed against God. Thus they went in tribulation through the streets along which the Corpus Christi procession goes, until they came to the cathedral. At the door of the church were two chaplains who made the sign of the cross on each one's forehead, saying, 'Receive the sign of the cross, which you denied and lost through being deceived.' Then they went into the church until they arrived at a scaffolding erected by the new gate, and on it were the father inquisitors. Nearby was another scaffolding on which stood an altar at which they said mass and delivered a sermon. After this a notary stood up and began to call each one by name, saying, 'Is x here?' The penitent raised his candle and said, 'Yes.' There in public they read all the things in which he had judaized. The same was done for the women. When this was over they were publicly allotted penance and ordered to go in procession for six Fridays, disciplining their body with scourges of hempcord, barebacked, unshod and bareheaded; and they were to fast for those six Fridays. It was also ordered that all the days of their life they were to hold no public office such as *alcade*, *alguacil*, *regidor* or *jurado*, or be public scriveners or messengers, and that those who held these offices were to lose them. And that they were not to become moneychangers, shopkeepers, or grocers or hold any official post whatever. And they were not to wear silk or scarlet or coloured cloths or gold or silver or pearls or coral or any jewels. Nor could they stand as witnesses. And they were ordered that if they relapsed, that is if they fell into the same error again, and resorted to any of the forementioned things, they would be condemned to the fire. And when all this was over they went away at two o'clock in the afternoon.[18]

Two o'clock is the time of the midday meal in Spain. The inquisitors had therefore managed to get through 750 prisoners in one morning. This is a far cry from the dilatory pace, pomp and ceremony of later autos which went on well into the night and sometimes were continued the following day, as happened at Logroño in November 1610. The speed at Toledo in 1486 was probably a record, for after the 750 victims in February the tribunal managed to deal with nine hundred reconciliations on 2 April, 750 on 11 June, and nine hundred on 10 December, not to speak of two other autos on 16 and 17 August when twenty-seven people were burnt.

To contrast with the simplicity and efficiency of autos in the first years of the Inquisition, a good example is the grandiose auto held on 30 June 1680 in the Plaza Mayor of Madrid in the presence of the king and his court.

A usefully summarized version of the contemporary narrative of the auto was published in London in 1748 and goes as follows:

A Scaffold, fifty Feet in Length, was erected in the Square, which was raised to the same Height with the Balcony made for the King to sit in. At the End, and along the whole Breadth of the Scaffold, at the Right of the King's Balcony, an Amphitheatre was raised, to which they ascend by twenty-five or thirty Steps; and this was appointed for the Council of the Inquisition, and the other Councils of Spain. Above these Steps and under a Canopy, the Grand Inquisitor's Rostrum was placed so that he was raised much higher than the King's Balcony. At the Left of the Scaffold and Balcony, a second Amphitheatre was erected of the same Extent with the former, for the Criminals to stand in.

A month after Proclamation had been made of the Act of Faith, the Ceremony opened with a Procession,* which proceeded from St Mary's Church in the following order. The March was preceded by an Hundred Coal Merchants, all arm'd with Pikes and Muskets; these People furnishing the Wood with which the Criminals are burnt. They were followed by Dominicans, before whom a white Cross was carried. Then came the Duke of Medina-Celi, carrying the Standard of the Inquisition. Afterwards was brought forwards a green Cross covered with black Crepe; which was followed by several Grandees and other Persons of Quality, who were Familiars of the Inquisition. The March was clos'd by Fifty Guards belonging to the Inquisition, clothed with black and white Garments and commanded by the Marquis of Povar, hereditary Protector of the Inquisition. The procession having marched in this Order before the Palace, proceeded afterwards to the Square, where the Standard and the Green Cross were placed on the Scaffold, where none but the Dominicans stayed, the rest being retired. These Friars spent Part of the Night in singing of Psalms, and several Masses were celebrated on the Altar from Daybreak to Six in the Morning. An Hour after, the King and Queen of

---

* This procession took place on the eve, 29 June.

Spain, the Queen-Mother, and all the Ladies of Quality, appeared in the Balconies.

At Eight O'clock the Procession began, in like Manner as the Day before, with the Company of Coal Merchants, who placed themselves on the Left of the King's Balcony, his Guards standing on his Right (the rest of the Balconies and Scaffolds being fill'd by the Embassadors, the Nobility and Gentry). Afterwards came thirty Men, carrying Images made in Pasteboard, as big as Life. Some of these represented those who were dead in Prison, whose Bones were also brought in Trunks, with Flames painted round them; and the rest of the Figures represented those who having escaped the Hands of the Inquisition were outlawed. These Figures were placed at one End of the Amphitheatre.

After these there came twelve Men and Women, with Ropes about their Necks and Torches in their Hands, with Pasteboard Caps three Feet high, on which their Crimes were written, or represented, in different Manners. These were followed by fifty others having Torches also in their Hands and cloathed with a yellow Sanbenito or Great Coat without Sleeves, with a large St. Andrew's Cross, of a red Colour, before and behind. These were Criminals who (this being the first Time of their Imprisonment) had repented of their Crimes; these are usually condemned either to some Years' Imprisonment or to wear the Sanbenito, which is looked upon to be the greatest Disgrace that can happen to a Family. Each of the Criminals were led by two Familiars of the Inquisition. Next came twenty more Criminals, of both Sexes, who had relapsed thrice into their former Errors and were condemn'd to the Flames. Those who had given some Tokens of Repentance were to be strangled before they were burnt; but for the rest, for having persisted obstinately in their Errors, were to be burnt alive. These wore Linen Sanbenitos, having Devils and Flames painted on them, and Caps after the same Manner: Five or six among them who were more obstinate than the rest were gagged to prevent their uttering any blasphemous Tenets. Such as were condemned to die were surrounded, besides the two Familiars, with four or five Monks, who were preparing them for Death as they went along.

These Criminals passed, in the Order above mentioned, under the King's Balcony; and after having walked round the scaffold were placed in the Amphitheatre that stood on the left, and each of them surrounded with the Familiars and Monks who attended them. Some of the Grandees, who were Familiars, seated themselves on two Benches which had been prepared for them at the lowest Part of the other Amphitheatre. The Officers of all the other Councils, and several other Persons of Distinction, both Secular and Regular, all of them on Horseback, with great Solemnity arrived afterwards and placed themselves on the Amphitheatre towards the Right hand, on both Sides the Rostrum in which the Grand Inquisitor was to seat himself. He himself came last of all, in a purple Habit, accompanied by the President of the Council of Castile, when, being seated in his Place, the President withdrew.

They then began to celebrate Mass . . .

About Twelve O'clock they began to read the Sentence of the condemned Criminals. That of the Criminals who died in Prison, or were outlawed, was first read. Their Figures in Pasteboard were carried up into a little Scaffold and put into small Cages made for that Purpose. They then went on to read the Sentences to each Criminal, who thereupon were put into the said Cages one by one in order for all Men to know them. The whole Ceremony lasted till Nine at Night; and when they had finished the Celebration of the Mass the King withdrew and the Criminals who had been condemn'd to be burnt were delivered over to the Secular Arm, and being mounted upon Asses were carried through the Gate called Foncaral, and at Midnight near this Place were all executed.[19]

In this auto de fe eleven people abjured their errors and fifty-six were reconciled, two of them in effigy because they had died in the secret prisons. There were fifty-three relaxations, of which nineteen were in person, including a woman over seventy years old. The procedure at this auto represented the fully developed practice of the Inquisition. It can be seen that the burning of victims was not a part of the principal ceremony and took place instead at a subsidiary one, often outside the city, where the pomp of the main procession was absent. The central features of the auto were the procession, the mass, the sermon at the mass and the reconciliation of sinners. It would be wrong to suppose, as is commonly done, that the burnings were the centrepiece. Burnings may have been a spectacular component of many autos but they were the least necessary part of the proceedings and scores of autos took place without a single faggot being set alight. The phrase auto de fe conjures up visions of flames and fanaticism in the mind of the average Protestant reader. A literal translation of the phrase would bring us nearer to the essential truth.

The burning of a judaizer is described in detail in a contemporary narrative by an inquisitor of the auto held at Logroño on 24 August 1719. We enter the picture at the stage where the victim is already on the stake and a lighted torch is passed before his face to warn him of what awaits him if he does not repent. Around the judaizer are numbers of religious who

pressed the criminal with greater anxiety and zeal to convert himself. With perfect serenity he said, 'I will convert myself to the faith of Jesus Christ', words which he had not been heard to utter until then. This overjoyed all the religious who began to embrace him with tenderness and gave infinite thanks to God for having opened to them a door for his conversion. ... And as he was making his confession of faith a learned religious of the Franciscan Order asked him, 'In what law do you die?' He turned and looked him in the eye and said, 'Father, I have already told you that I die in the faith of Jesus Christ'. This caused great pleasure and joy among all, and the Franciscan, who was kneeling down, arose and embraced the criminal. All the others did the same with great satisfaction, giving thanks for the infinite goodness of God. ... At this moment the criminal saw the executioner, who had put his head out from behind the stake, and asked him, 'Why did you call me a dog before?' The executioner replied, 'Because you denied the faith of Jesus Christ; but now that you have confessed, we are brothers, and if I have offended you by what I said, I beg your pardon on my knees.' The criminal forgave him gladly, and the two embraced.... And desirous that the soul which had given so many signs of conversion should not be lost, I went round casually behind the stake to where the executioner was, and gave him the order to strangle him immediately because it was very important not to delay. This he did with great expedition.

When it was certain that he was dead, the executioner was ordered to set fire at the four corners of the pyre to the brushwood and charcoal that had been piled up. He did this at once, and it began to burn on all sides, the flames rising swiftly up the platform and burning the wood and clothing. When the cords binding the criminal had been burnt off he fell through the open trap-door into the pyre and his whole body was reduced to ashes.[20]

The ashes were scattered through the fields or on the river, and with this the heretic, whose conversion had brought him no temporal benefit, passed out of existence though not out of memory, for a sanbenito bearing his name would as a rule have been placed in the local church after his death. There was no age limit to victims meant for the stake: women in their eighties and boys in their teens were treated in the same way as any other heretics.

Because of the elaborate ceremony, autos often tended to be very costly. The auto held at Logroño on 18 October 1570 cost a total of 37,366 maravedis, most of which was spent not on the auto but on the feast of celebration held after it. This profligate expenditure was criticized by the Suprema and the cost of an auto held the following year on 27 December 1571 was cut down to 1,548 maravedis[21]. These costs may be compared with those of a larger tribunal, Seville, which in 1600 calculated that each of its autos cost over three hundred ducats (112,500 maravedis).[22] Itemized accounts of the expense on autos in the mid-seventeenth century give us an idea of where the money went in a period of rapidly rising prices. First, the tribunal of Seville.[23]

Seville *Auto de fe* of 30 January 1624

General expenses	28,076 maravedis
Benches, carpets, etc.	36,552
Cloth for sanbenitos	17,136
Candles	23,366
Advocates for criminals	26,520
Building of scaffolding	264,724
Total	396,374 maravedis

Seville *Auto de fe* of 29 March 1648

General expenses	84,184 maravedis
Painting of effigies, and clothing	37,400
Militia	10,200
Building of scaffolding	351,560
Meals for soldiers and effigy-bearers	21,148
Candles, shawls, hats	82,416
Bringing of accused from Córdoba	68,000
Meals	156,680
Total	811,588 maravedis

Even higher than these costs were those run by the tribunal of Córdoba for its auto on 3 May 1655.[24] The three largest items were:

Building of scaffolding	644,300 maravedis
Benches, cushions etc.	273,326
Meal for tribunal and its ministers	103,258

The total costs came to 2,139,590 maravedis, a staggering figure if those we have already cited are anything to go by.

The smaller tribunals, particularly those which could not profit from the presence of conversos and Moriscos, could seldom afford to have autos. This was regrettable, as an inquisitor of Barcelona commented in 1560, because 'I certainly think autos necessary to induce fear both among foreigners who come here, and among the people of this country who, claiming to be good Christians, all repeat that the Inquisition is superfluous here and neither does anything nor has anything to do'.[25] In Catalonia the Inquisition also had to put up with the fact that 'neither the viceroy nor the consellers normally attend autos' – clearly a blow to its prestige.[26] By the early seventeenth century public autos were rare in Barcelona. 'This Inquisition', the inquisitors explained to the Suprema, 'is unique in Spain in that it does not celebrate autos with the same pomp and decency as in other Inquisitions, and this Inquisition is very poor, so that what used to be done in public autos is now more conveniently done in some church.'[27] Nevertheless, there were tribunals which held autos de fe frequently, not only in the great repressions of 1480–1500 and the smaller anti-converso waves in 1650–80 and 1720–25, but also in apparently slack periods. We find, for example, the tribunal of Granada holding fifteen autos between 1549 and 1593, that of Murcia holding ten between 1557 and 1568, and that of Córdoba holding seven between 1693 and 1702.

By the eighteenth century the lack of victims and the rising cost of public ceremonies meant that autos de fe gradually fell into disuse. The new Bourbon king, Philip v, was the first Spanish monarch to refuse to attend an auto, which was held in 1701 to celebrate his accession to the throne. Later in 1720, however, he assisted at one. Philip's reign saw the end of mass persecution in Spain, and by the second half of the century only private autos were in use by the Inquisition. There is no need to attribute this to the growth of tolerance. The simple reason was that heretics had been successfully purged out of existence, so depriving the tribunal of combustible material for its fires.

Popular Culture
and the Counter Reformation

Rampart of the Church, pillar of truth, guardian of the faith, treasure of religion, defence against heretics, light against the deceptions of the enemy, touchstone of pure doctrine.

Fray Luis de Granada (on the Inquisition), *Sermon de las Caidas Públicas*

Although the Inquisition had been brought into existence specifically to combat the 'heretical depravity' of judaizers, it quickly came to concern itself with other offences, not least because judaizers were frequently accused of offences such as atheism, usury and bigamy (thus the Aragonese notary Dionis Ginot, burnt in effigy at Saragossa in 1486, was condemned for both Judaism and bigamy). Conversos were often accused of atheism, a perfectly credible accusation in view of the strange cultural situation in which many found themselves, living (in Pulgar's words) 'neither in one law nor the other'. If some were sceptical both of Judaism and of official Christianity, it is not surprising to find individuals like Alvaro de Lillo maintaining in 1524 that 'we are born and die and nothing more', or María de la Mota claiming that 'I'll look after myself in this world and you'll not see me badly off in the next.'[1] Both were tried by the Inquisition of Cuenca. As the Inquisition shifted its attention from conversos, it was to find that Epicurean sentiments like these were common among Old Christians as well. Indeed, what was particularly alarming was not simply that true religion may have been perverted by heresy, but that in many parts of Spain it could be doubted whether there was any true religion at all. It was this realization that moved one inquisitor to argue in 1572 that Galicia should have its own Inquisition:

> If any part of these realms needs an Inquisition it is Galicia, which lacks
> the religion that there is in Old Castile, has no priests or lettered persons
> or impressive churches or people who are used to going to mass and
> hearing sermons.... They are superstitious and the benefices so poor
> that as a result there are not enough clergy.[2]

'If the Holy Office had not come to this realm', a local priest wrote
later, 'some of these people would have been like those in England.'

Over much of Spain Christianity was still only a veneer. The
religion of the people remained backward, despite gestures of reform
by Cisneros and other prelates. It was still a period of vague theology, irregular religious practice, non-residence of both bishops and
clergy, and widespread ignorance of the faith among both priests
and parishioners. Over vast areas of Spain – the sierras of Andalucia, the mountains of Galicia and Cantabria, the Pyrenees of Navarre, Aragon and Catalonia – the people combined formal religion
with folk superstition in their everyday attempt to survive against
the onslaught of climate and mortality. The standard religious unit
was the rural parish, coinciding normally with the limits of the
village. Over four-fifths of Spain's population lived in this environment, beyond the reach of the big towns to which villagers only
went on market days to sell their produce. As religious reformers
and inquisitors quickly found out, the rural parishes were close-knit
communities with their own special type of religion and their own
saints. They were also hostile to any attempt by outsiders – whether
clergy or townspeople – to intrude into their way of life.

The Holy Office was far from being the only institution interested
in the religious life of Spaniards, and excessive attention to its activities can seriously distort the religious history of Spain. Already
by the late fifteenth century there had been three major channels
through which changes were being introduced into peninsular
religion: the reforms of religious orders, instanced on one hand by
the remarkable growth of the Jeronimite order and on the other by
the imposition of the reformist Observance on the mendicant
orders;[3] the interest of humanist bishops in reforming the lives of
their clergy and people, as shown for example by the synodal decrees of the see of Toledo under Alonso Carrillo and Cisneros;[4] and
the new literature of spirituality exemplified in García de Cisneros'
Exercises in Spiritual Life (1500).[5] As elsewhere in Catholic Europe,
the humanist reformers were well aware that theirs was an elite
movement which would take time to filter down into the life of the
people. Efforts were, however, being made by the orders: from 1518

the Dominicans were active in the remote countryside of Asturias. The principal impulse to popular missions came from the growth of the Jesuits in the 1540s. At the same time, several reforming bishops tried to introduce changes into their dioceses. It was an uphill task. In Barcelona, Francis Borja, at the time Duke of Gandía and Viceroy of Catalonia, worked hand in hand with reforming bishops but commented on 'the little that has been achieved, both in the time of Queen Isabella and in our own'.[6]

From the early century, nevertheless, a patient effort was made to christianize Spain. The immense confusion of jurisdictions presented a major obstacle: churches, monasteries, orders, secular lords, bishops, towns, the Inquisition – all disputed each other's authority. Not until Philip II in 1564 imposed the decrees of the Council of Trent in Spain, and forced bishops to hold diocesan synods and religious orders to reform themselves systematically, did a serious programme of change begin. From the 1540s at least, the Church authorities became concerned not only with the problem of converting the Moriscos but also with that of bringing the unchristianized parts of the country back into the fold. In Santiago in 1543 the diocesan visitor reported that 'parishioners suffer greatly from the ignorance of their curates and rectors'; in Navarre in 1544 ignorant clergy 'cause great harm to the consciences of these poor people'. Many rural parishes lacked clergy, particularly in Catalonia and the Basque country, where ignorance of the language made it difficult for priests to communicate with their flock.

The visitations of the inquisitors were complemented by those of diocesan and monastic visitors. In a sense their tasks did not overlap: bishops were primarily concerned with getting good clergy and decent churches; the Inquisition was concerned with getting orthodox worshippers. Jesuits made their own country into a mission field. 'This land', a canon of Oviedo wrote in 1568 to Borja, 'is in extreme need of good labourers, such as we trust are those in the Society of Jesus.' Another wrote in the same year: 'There are no Indies where you will suffer greater dangers and miseries, or which could more need to hear the word of God, than these Asturias.'[7] The mission field soon encompassed all of Spain: the Jesuit Pedro de León, who worked all over Andalucia and Extremadura, wrote that 'since I began in the year 1582, and up to now in 1615, there has not been a single year in which I have not been on some mission, and on two or three in some years'. The need was stressed by an earlier Jesuit, reporting on the inhabitants of villages near

Huelva: 'many live in caves, without priests or sacraments; so ignorant that some cannot make the sign of the cross; in their dress
and way of life very like Indians'.

What contribution did the Inquisition make to the christianizing
of Spain? The prosecution figures we have given on page 185 for
the period 1540 to 1614, though very incomplete, indicate beyond
doubt that whereas in the first phase of its history the tribunal had
been concerned almost exclusively with conversos, in the next century its attention was focused primarily on Old Christians. Nearly
two-thirds of all those detained by the Holy Office in this period
were ordinary Catholic Spaniards, unconnected with formal heresy
or with the racial minorities. We have already seen that Protestantism was no longer a serious threat and that virtually all those
arrested for the offence were foreigners. The new policy of the
Inquisition in directing its attention to Old Christians cannot be
viewed cynically as a desperate move to find sources of revenue:
the Old Christians who were prosecuted were invariably humble
and poor, and the tribunal's financial position was in any case
better after mid-century.

By its collaboration with the campaigns of bishops, clergy and
religious orders, the Inquisition contributed actively to the Counter
Reformation in Spain. It is doubtful, however, whether its contribution was as significant or successful as that of other branches of
the Church. We have already seen that the attempt to make a
direct impact through visitations was not fruitful. Because prosecutions in the Inquisition were initiated from below,[8] the tribunal
was in a peculiarly strong position to affect and mould popular
culture, and the volume of prosecutions in some areas may suggest
that it was carrying out its task successfully. The Holy Office, however, suffered from at least one major disadvantage: it was always
an alien body. Bishops, through their parish priests, were directly
linked to the roots of community feeling, and were able to carry out
a considerable programme of religious change based on persuasion.
The Inquisition, by contrast, was exclusively a punishing body; it
was operated, moreover, by outsiders, and though feared was never
loved; as a result, its successes were always flawed.

The biggest and perhaps the most important category of offences
dealt with by the tribunal in the sixteenth and seventeenth centuries was that covering 'propositions'. A 'proposition' was a verbal
offence, but the inquisitors were concerned less with the words than
with the intention behind them and with the implicit danger to

faith and morals. An immense range of themes was involved: at every stage the attempt was made to correct wrong belief (i.e. heresy) over such matters as sex, marriage, the theology of the Eucharist, miracles and so on. Blasphemy and 'simple fornication' were two dominant preoccupations.

Blasphemy, or disrespect to sacred things, was at the time a public offence against God and punishable by both State and Church; thus the Inquisition was only a small part of a big drive, which gathered force after the Council of Trent, to enforce respect for the sacred. In time, the tribunal gave the term a very broad definition, provoking protests by the Cortes of both Castile and Aragon: the Cortes of Madrid in 1534 asked specifically that cases of blasphemy be reserved to the secular courts alone. The Holy Office continued, however, to maintain its jurisdiction, punishing bad language according to the gravity of the context.[9] Blasphemous oaths during a game of dice, sexual advances to a girl during a religious procession, refusal to abstain from meat on Fridays, obscene references to the Virgin, wilful failure to go to mass: these were typical of the thousands of cases disciplined by the Inquisition. Anticlerical sentiments were also punished: among the accused we find Lorenzo Sánchez, notary in 1669 of the Inquisition, saying that 'tithes are ours, and the clergy are our servants, which is why we pay them tithes'. Active hostility to religion fell into the category of sacrilege, as in the case in 1665 of Francesc Dalmau, a farmer of Tarragona, who was accused of going into the pulpit fifteen minutes before mass began and preaching ridiculous and absurd things until the priest appeared; it was also said that he habitually left mass for the duration of the sermon and that he ridiculed Holy Week ceremonies.[10]

The disciplining of words and actions was time-consuming, and formed the principal activity of inquisitors during their visitations. In rural areas there was greater understanding shown to the reasons for irreligion: in Galicia in 1585, for example, the inquisitors admitted that doubts about the presence of Christ in the sacrament were widespread, but 'more out of ignorance than malice', and that questioning of the virginity of Mary was 'through sheer thickheadedness rather than out of a wish to offend'. They had the case of the man in a tavern who, when a priest present claimed to be able to change bread into the body of Christ, exclaimed in unbelief, 'Go on! God's in heaven and not in that host which you eat at mass!'[11] In Granada in 1595, a shepherd from the village of Alhama claimed not to believe in confession and said to his friends: 'What sort of confession is it that you make to a priest who is as much of a sinner as I? Perfect confession is made only to God.' The inquisitors concluded that 'he seemed very rustic and ignorant and with little or no capacity of understanding', and sent him to a monastery to be educated.[12] Rather than lightening its sentences because of the low degree of religious understanding in rural areas, the Inquisition in fact increased its punishments in order to achieve a greater disciplinary effect. Thus every type of expression – whether mumbled by a drunkard in a tavern or preached by an ignorant priest from the pulpit – that could be taken to be offensive, blasphemous, irreverent or heretical, was carefully examined by the Holy Office and acted upon. It was at the level of verbal offences rather than heretical acts that the Inquisition came most into contact with the ordinary people of Spain for the greater part of its history.

For those who were arrested instead of being simply penanced during a visitation, there was normally a close examination in the basic elements of belief.[13] Prisoners were asked to recite in Castilian the Our Father, Hail Mary, Credo, Salve Regina and the ten commandments, as well as other statements of belief. The interrogatory seems to have come into use in the 1540s, and provides excellent evidence of the extent to which ordinary Spaniards were instructed in the faith. An analysis of 747 interrogations from the tribunal of Toledo[14] shows that there was an appreciable improvement in knowledge of the essentials during the late sixteenth century: before 1550 only about 40 per cent of those questioned were able to repeat the basic prayers; by the 1590s this had risen to nearly 70 per cent. By the late seventeenth century levels of religious knowledge were impressively high, if we may trust the evidence from Toledo. Hundreds of accused from the lower classes and from rural areas enjoyed a basic knowledge of the prayers of the Church, and all were able to recite the Our Father and Hail Mary. Among the exceptions was Inés López, an illiterate fifty-year-old hospital nurse who in 1664 'crossed herself and recited the Our Father and Hail Mary well in Castilian, but did not know the creed, the Salve, the confiteor, the laws of God and of the Church, the articles of faith or the sacraments; the inquisitor warned her and ordered her to learn them, for she has an obligation to do so as a Christian'.[15]

The improvement in religious knowledge is not, of course, to be credited to the Inquisition. It was the teaching Church of the

Counter Reformation that set up schools, made sermons obligatory and enforced recitation of prayers at mass. However, even in its negative disciplinary role the Inquisition made a serious contribution to the evolution of Spanish religion. The censorship of the Holy Office has commonly been looked upon exclusively in its destructive aspect. It is therefore all the more important to emphasize its constructive and *formative* aspects. The Holy Office attempted to impose on Spaniards a new respect for the sacred, notably in art, in public devotions and in sermons.

Diocesan synods at Granada in 1573 and Pamplona in 1591 were among those which ordered the removal and burial of unseemly church images. The Inquisition, likewise, attempted where it could to censor religious imagery.[16] In Seville in the early seventeenth century it recruited the artist Francisco Pacheco to comment on the suitability of public imagery. Public devotions were generally under the supervision of the bishops, but here too the Inquisition had a role. It helped to repress devotional excesses, such as credulity about visions of the Virgin.[17] The celebration of pilgrimages and of fiestas such as Corpus Christi was regulated by the episcopate; but written works, such as the text of *autos sacramentales* – plays performed for Corpus – normally had to be approved by the Inquisition, creating occasional conflicts with writers. On the other hand, the tribunal steadfastly refused to be drawn into the debate over whether theatres were immoral and should be banned. It is well known that substantial Counter-Reformation opinion, especially among the Jesuits, was in favour of shutting theatres; and indeed they were shut periodically from 1597 onwards. But theatres were normally under the control of the Council of Castile, not of the Holy Office, and the only way the latter could express an opinion was when plays were printed. Even then it kept clear of the theatre, and the major dramatists of the Golden Age were untouched: no play by Lope de Vega, for example, was interfered with until 1801. When the Inquisition did tread into the field, by requiring expurgations (in the 1707 Index) in the Jesuit Camargo's *Discourse on the Theatre* (1689), it explained that the ban was 'until changes are made; but the Holy Office does not by prohibiting this book intend to comment on or condemn either of the opinions on the desirability or undesirability of seeing, reading, writing or performing plays'.[18]

The third significant area of activity was sermons. No form of propaganda in the Counter Reformation was more widely used than the spoken word, in view of the high levels of illiteracy. Correspondingly, in no other form of communication did the Inquisition interfere more frequently. Sermons were to the public of those days what television is to the twentieth century: the most direct form of control over opinion. The impact of the Holy Office on spoken sermons – among those denounced to it were sermons by Carranza and Fray Francisco Ortiz – was perhaps even more decisive than its impact on printed literature. Interference in the pulpit could on occasion be frankly political: the tribunal of Llerena in 1606 prosecuted Diego Díaz, priest of Torre de Don Miguel, for preaching (in Portuguese) that God had not died for Castilians;[19] and the tribunal of Barcelona in 1666 prosecuted a priest of Reus for having declared that 'he would prefer to be in hell beside a Frenchman than in heaven beside a Castilian'.[20] More normally, the problem consisted in preachers who got carried away by their own eloquence or who were shaky in their theology, such as the Cistercian Maestro Cortés who in 1683 put the glories of Mary above those of the Sacrament, or the priest in Tuy who on Holy Thursday told his flock that in the Sacrament they were celebrating only the semblance of God, whose real presence was above in heaven.[21]

A major sphere of inquisitorial activity was in sexual life. The bishops after Trent made extensive efforts in Spain to impose the new view of the sanctity of matrimony: in Barcelona after 1570, for example, licences to marry could not be issued without both parties being formally instructed in religion, and the bishops issued decrees against the common practice of young people living together after betrothal. The Inquisition, for its part, enforced post-Tridentine morality by attempting to stamp out the widespread conviction that 'simple fornication' was no sin, and also prosecuted various sexual offences including bigamy.

'Simple fornication', in early modern Spain, was voluntary intercourse between two unmarried adults.[22] The Inquisition took an interest in this and other sexual questions not because of the sexual act in itself but because of the implied disrespect for the sacrament of matrimony. In pre-Tridentine Spain, a low level of religious awareness and the persistence of traditional moral practices combined to produce far greater sexual freedom among all age groups than is commonly imagined. This was reflected in the remarkably widespread view that sex ('simple fornication') was not wrong if it broke no rules: by extension, concubinage was not wrong, nor was it wrong for an unmarried adult to have sex with a prostitute. The absence of sexual guilt was shared by laity and clergy alike. The inquisitors of Toledo were actively preoccupied with the problem, and from 1573 the Suprema encouraged other tribunals to pursue the matter. In Toledo prosecutions for simple fornication constituted a fifth of all prosecutions in 1566–70, a third in 1581–5, and a quarter in 1601–5.[23] Striking evidence that the imposition of the new morality was, in some measure, an imposition of urban rigour on rural laxity comes from Galicia, where propositions on fornication (such as that of Alonso de Meixide, who maintained 'that in his village it had never been a sin to have carnal intercourse between unmarried men and women') were more commonly found among the peasantry. This was so much the case that the inquisitors there explained in 1585 that 'the reason why we are less strict with fornicators is because we know from experience that most of those we arrest in these lands, where there is a great lack of doctrine especially in the rural areas, speak from stupidity and ignorance and not from a wish to commit heresy'.[24]

The Inquisition continued its sexual campaign with a drive against bigamy. Because the offence was normally punishable in civil and Church courts, there were constant protests against the Inquisition's interference. The Catalan concordia of 1512, for example, laid down that bishops alone should try bigamy cases unless heresy were involved. Since it was precisely the heresy rather than the crime that interested the Inquisition, it continued its activity despite repeated protests from the Cortes of Aragon. Some tribunals were more diligent than others in pursuing the offence: in general, a twentieth of cases tried by the Inquisition were for bigamy. From the mid-sixteenth century five years in the galleys became the standard punishment for men – a much lighter penalty than that meted out by secular courts. Women, no less than men, were frequent bigamists. Many did not feel they were committing wrong: when Francisco Cossio was arrested by the tribunal of Toledo in 1694, the evidence against him included a letter to his parish priest in which he said that 'it is true that marriage, in the opinion of those with whom I have discussed it, is valid; but in my case it was necessary to re-validate it in order to continue it'.[25]

The moral behaviour of clergy had preoccupied Church reformers through the centuries, and bishops were happy to obtain the cooperation of the Inquisition. Trent had placed clerical reform at the forefront of its programme: bishops defined the duties of priests strictly and cut back their public role (they could no longer, for example, go to taverns or wedding-feasts). It was inevitably easier to pass decrees than to enforce them, and clergy continued to use their privileged position to disport themselves, break the laws and seduce parishioners.[26] The Inquisition was particularly interested in the problem of solicitation during confession. The confession-box as we know it today did not come into use in the Church until the late sixteenth century, before which there was no physical barrier between a confessor and a penitent, so that occasions for sin could easily arise. The frequent scandals caused Fernando de Valdés in 1561 to obtain authority from Pius IV for the Inquisition to exercise control over cases of solicitation, which were interpreted as heresy because they misused the sacrament of penance. Though accused confessors were usually guilty it is quite clear that blame often lay with the confessant. Among curious cases of solicitation was that denounced by an elderly beata in Guisona (Catalonia) in 1581, against an itinerant Franciscan who 'told her she must accept the penance he imposed, and this startled her, and the friar said he had to give her a slap on her buttocks and he made her raise her skirts and gave her a pat on the buttocks and said to her, "Margarita, next time show some shame", and then he absolved her'.[27] In Valencia the parish priest of Beniganim was tried in 1608 for having solicited twenty-nine women, most of them unmarried, 'with lascivious and amorous invitations to perform filthy and immoral acts'.[28]

There were many cases of marginal sexuality in which the Inquisition also intervened, and which accounted for a twentieth of all cases prosecuted. Sodomy was the most significant.[29] Homosexuality in the middle ages was treated as the ultimate crime against morality, and the standard definitions of it refer to the 'abominable' or the 'unspeakable' crime. The usual punishment was burning alive or, in Spain, castration and stoning to death. Under Ferdinand and Isabella the punishment was changed to burning alive and confiscation of property. Since the old Inquisition had exercised jurisdiction over sodomy, the Spanish tribunal seems to have begun to do so; but on 18 October 1509 the Suprema ordered that no action was to be taken against homosexuals except when heresy was involved. Here a curious split in policy seems to have occurred, because although the tribunals of Castile never again exercised jurisdiction over sodomy, the Inquisition in Aragon now officially adopted powers over this very crime. On 24 February 1524 the pope, Clement VII, issued a brief granting the Inquisition of the realms of Aragon jurisdiction over sodomy, irrespective of the presence or absence of heresy. From this time onwards the Aragonese inquisitors kept their new authority, which they never gave up, despite the typical complaints raised by the Cortes of Monzón in 1533. Aragon was unique in this matter, for not even the Roman Inquisition exercised jurisdiction over sodomy. The punishment laid down by the law, and rigorously enforced by the State, was death by burning.

The Inquisition was equally harsh to sodomizers (whether of men or of women), but tended to restrict death by burning only to those aged over twenty-five. Minors, who were inevitably a high proportion among those arrested for this offence, were normally whipped and sent to the galleys. A certain liberality on the part of the Suprema can be seen in the fact that some death sentences were commuted, and mildness was also shown to clergy, who were always a high proportion of offenders. In cases studied by Bennassar for Saragossa in the late sixteenth century, the majority of those found guilty were either flogged and banished, or sent to the galleys; only a small number, about 15 per cent of those sentenced, were burnt. The treatment of bestiality was much harsher. This is surprising, considering that the inquisitors were well aware that the offence, was almost exclusively a rural crime, committed by solitaries of low intelligence: in Saragossa, twenty-three out of a sample of fifty-five found guilty were burnt, and another twenty-five sent to the galleys.

Though the Inquisition fulfilled a significant role in the Counter Reformation, it was only one and not necessarily the most important of the many forces active in both Church and State. For this very reason the role of the Inquisition in cases of witchcraft should not be exaggerated. In 1370 and 1387 the laws of Castile declared that sorcery was a crime involving heresy, for which laymen would be punished by the State and clergy by the Church. Well after the foundation of the Inquisition, jurisdiction over sorcery and witchcraft remained in secular hands: this is demonstrated by a decree of 1500 which ordered an investigation into sorcery but put the matter into the hands of corregidors and the civil courts.[30] The mediaeval Inquisition had likewise left such questions largely in secular hands, so that no change of policy was involved. By the early sixteenth century, when the Holy Office began enquiries into the heresy of witchcraft, repression of the offence was still normally in the hands of the State courts. The Inquisition's reluctance to interfere was motivated in part by doubts whether any heresy was involved. Certain types of popular superstition, 'sorcery', and the whole range of astrology, were ill-defined areas in which many learned men and clergy themselves dabbled. Astrology, for example, was on the university syllabus at Salamanca; but not until the late sixteenth century did the Inquisition, encouraged by the papacy, attempt to suppress it as a science; Quiroga's Index of 1583 followed Rome in banning occult arts and divination.[31] This move (which preceded Sixtus v's bull of 1585 against magic, *Caeli et terrae*) confirmed the tribunal's concern to wipe out alternatives to the truths of Counter Reformation religion.

The campaign against popular superstition was a broad one, marginal to the Inquisition's concerns in the sixteenth century but more significant in the seventeenth, when in some tribunals it accounted for a fifth of all prosecutions. Popular culture, especially in the rural areas, had always sought unorthodox cures to daily afflictions: villages had their wise men or wise women (*curanderos*) who could offer medicinal ointments, find lost objects, heal wounded animals, help a girl to win the affections of her loved one. Cures might take the form of potions, charms, spells or simply advice. It was a subculture that coexisted with and did not try to subvert official Catholicism, though in certain New Christian areas the Christian content of the spells was doubtful.[32] In rural areas the world of magic even entered the Church, with many clergy incorporating folk practices – rites, prayers, offerings, dances – into the normal liturgy. All this was stamped on firmly by reforming bishops, post-Tridentine clergy and the Inquisition.[33] In the process of contrasting the dark world of primitive superstition with the illuminated world of the gospel, unfortunately, preachers and learned men unduly simplified the forces at work and helped to create fears of 'witchcraft'.[34]

Magic and witchcraft were not treated as a major problem until the late fifteenth century. In 1484 Pope Innocent VIII issued the bull *Summis desiderantes* which first recognized witchcraft as a disease to be rooted out. Two German Dominicans, Kramer and Sprenger, were sent to deal with the superstition in north and central Germany. Two years later they issued their handbook, the *Malleus Maleficarum* (Hammer of Witches). In this impressive compilation of case-histories the Dominicans argued that, far from witchcraft being a delusion, it was a practice based on actual commerce with Satan and the powers of darkness, and that witches did in fact eat and devour human children, copulate with devils, fly through the air to their meetings or 'sabbats', injure cattle, raise up storms and conjure down lightning.[35] No book did more in its time to promote a belief it was allegedly fighting. The view of the *Malleus* was supported by subsequent decrees of popes and bishops. In Europe as a whole the witch-craze gained momentum,[36] but there was always an important number of theologians and bishops in both Italy and Spain who considered that talk of flying through the air and copulation with the devil was a delusion to be pitied rather than punished.

Mediaeval secular practice had been that witches should be burnt, and the Inquisition at first followed suit. The Saragossa tribunal burnt one in 1498, another in 1499 and three in 1500. In 1507, according to Llorente, the tribunal of Calahorra burnt thirty women for witchcraft.[37] From this time on, cases of witches were regularly reported, the first at Toledo being in 1513 and at Cuenca in 1515. At Cuenca the popular fear was fed by stories of children being found bruised and murdered, 'wherefore it is suspected they were wounded or killed by *xorguinos* and *xorguinas* (wizards and witches)'.[38] From 1520 edicts of faith in both Castile and Aragon began to add magic, sorcery and witchcraft to the list of offences implying heresy. However, the belief in the sabbat was still far from being accepted by learned opinion. At Saragossa in 1521 a theologian declared that the sabbat 'was a delusion and could not have occurred, so no heresy is involved'.

The Inquisition was not the only court concerned with prosecutions. In Navarre for most of the sixteenth century, witchcraft was examined not by the Inquisition but by the State: in 1525, for example, possibly thirty witches were burnt on the orders of the State prosecutor, licenciado Balanza of the Royal Council of Navarre.[39] As late as 1568 the Suprema ordered the tribunal of Barcelona to hand back to the episcopal court a case of 'incantations'; and in Navarre in 1596 (the case of the witches of Araiz) the local inquisitor ordered that 'it is agreed not to deal with these matters in the Holy Office', and the prosecution reverted to the Royal Council of Navarre. Here, then, were two important aspects of the role of the Inquisition in witchcraft: some inquisitors were sceptical of the reality of diabolic witchcraft, and the tribunal made no claims to exclusive jurisdiction.

The subsequent policy of the Inquisition arose out of an historic meeting held at Granada in 1526.[40] As a result of the persecution of witches by secular authorities in Navarre that year, Inquisitor

General Manrique delegated a committee of ten, which included the letrado Hernando de Guevara and the future Inquisitor General Valdés, to decide whether witches really did go to the sabbat. The discussion paper offered to the meeting stated that 'the majority of jurists in this realm have agreed that it is certain that witches do not exist', because of the impossibility of the acts they claimed to do. A vote was taken and a majority – six – of those present decided 'that they really go'; a minority of four, including Valdés and Guevara, voted 'that they go in their imagination'. The meeting also decided that since the homicides to which witches frequently confessed might well be illusory, they should be tried by the Inquisition and not handed over to the civil authorities; if, however, the authorities had proof of homicide, they should be free to act on their own account.

Many of those on the committee, including Guevara, were during those same weeks in Granada discussing the conversion of the Moriscos, and in general the committee was concerned more to educate the so-called witches than to chastise them. The Bishop of Mondoñedo, for example, suggested the following remedies: 'send preachers to those parts, to tell the people of the errors of the witches and how they have been deceived by the devil; the inquisitors and secular judges should proceed with caution; the monasteries of that region should be reformed'. One of the resolutions of the whole committee was that 'great care be taken to preach to them in their language', namely in Basque. The urgent need for rechristianization was noted subsequently by the theologian Alfonso de Castro in his *Adversus haereses* (1534), referring to 'Navarre, Vizcaya, Asturias, Galicia and other parts, where the word of God has seldom been preached. Among these people there are many pagan superstitions and rites, solely because of the lack of preachers.'

The persecution and execution of witches continued but the Holy Office, guided by the 1526 resolutions, played very little part in it. A witch persecution took place in Navarre in 1527–8[41] and an active role was played by the local inquisitor Avellaneda, but the judicial authority in charge was the Royal Council of Navarre, which apparently executed at least fifty witches. When further troubles occurred in Navarre in 1538 the then inquisitor, Valdeolitas, was instructed by the Suprema not to accept the confessions of witches literally, and to 'speak to the principal people and explain to them that the loss of harvests and other ills are either sent by God for our sins or are a result of bad weather, and that witches should not be suspected'. In 1550 the inquisitor of Barcelona,

Sarmiento, was dismissed for having executed witches without referring the cases to the Suprema.[42] Thus for most of the sixteenth century the Inquisition maintained an enlightened record. Joana Izquierda, tried before the Toledo tribunal in 1591, confessed to taking part in the ritual murder of a number of children. Sixteen witnesses testified that the children had in fact died suddenly, and that Izquierda was reputed to be a witch. What would in any other European country have earned Izquierda the death sentence, in Spain earned her nothing more than abjuration *de levi* and two hundred lashes.[43]

The only significant relapse from this good record occurred in 1610 in Navarre. The explanation for this must be sought not in Spain but in France. Just across the frontier, in the Pays de Labourd, the Bordeaux judge Pierre de Lancre had conducted a horrendous witch-hunt in the autumn of 1609, during which he executed eighty witches. The campaign supplied most of the material for his famous book on witchcraft, *Tableau de l'Inconstance* (1612). The Labourd executions sent a shiver of terror through the Navarrese valleys and created a witch-scare in Spanish territory that swept along with it the inquisitors of Logroño, one of whom was Alonso de Salazar Frias.[44] A great auto de fe was held in the city on Sunday, 7 November 1610, and so lengthy were the proceedings that the ceremony had to be continued into the following day. Of the fifty-three prisoners who took part in the auto, twenty-nine were accused of witchcraft and of these, five were burnt in effigy and six in person.[45] This extreme measure produced a reaction in the Suprema, which in March the next year deputized Alonso de Salazar Frias to visit the relevant districts of Navarre, carrying with him an edict of grace to invite the inhabitants to repudiate their errors. Salazar's mission was to be an epoch-making one. He began work in May 1611 and ended his labours in January 1612, but only on 24 March did he eventually present his report to the Suprema. During the time of his mission, Salazar declared, he reconciled 1,802 persons: of these, 1,384 were children between the ages of nine and twelve in the case of girls, and between nine and fourteen in the case of boys; of the others, 'several were old and even senile, over the age of seventy and eighty'. After close examination of all the confessions and evidence about murders, witch-sabbats and sexual intercourse with devils, Salazar came to his conclusion:

> I have not found the slightest evidence from which to infer that a single act of witchcraft has really occurred. Indeed, my previous suspicions

have been strengthened by new evidence from the visitation: that the evidence of the accused alone, without external proof, is insufficient to justify arrest; and that three-quarters and more have accused themselves and their accomplices falsely.

I also feel certain that under present conditions there is no need of fresh edicts or the prolongation of those existing, but rather that in the diseased state of the public mind every agitation of the matter is harmful and increases the evil. I deduce the importance of silence and reserve from the experience that there were neither witches nor bewitched until they were talked and written about.

Salazar's long memorial[46] was a victory, neither for humanism nor for rationalism, but quite simply for the laws of evidence. As a trained lawyer (*letrado*) he was interested less in the theological debate over the reality of witchcraft than in the material problem of having to arrest people on the basis of unsupported hearsay: 'there is no use in saying that the evidence for witchcraft is certain. Nobody doubts this.... The real question is: are we to believe that witchcraft has occurred in a case simply because the witches say so?'

Salazar's report was contested by his colleagues but finally accepted by the Suprema. He was helped powerfully by the fact that, as he himself pointed out, the Inquisition since 1526 had turned its face against the traditional death sentence for witches; that more and more *letrados*, rather than theologians, were becoming inquisitors; and that the best informed opinion in Spain was in favour of scepticism over the reality of witchcraft. Even before the mission to Navarre, the Inquisitor General had commissioned a report from the scholar Pedro de Valencia. In his report, dated April 1611,[47] Valencia was careful not to deny the reality of witchcraft, but his conclusions suggested that there was a strong element of mental sickness in the Navarre events, and that exceptional care must be taken to prove offences. 'The accused must be examined first to see if they are in their right mind or possessed or melancholic.' Their conduct 'is more that of madmen than of heretics, and should be cured with whips and sticks rather than with sanbenitos'. Finally Valencia advises that 'one must look for evidence, according to law, of an offence having been committed'.

On 29 August 1614 the Suprema issued authoritative instructions which were to remain the principal guide to the future policy of the Inquisition. Drawn up in thirty-two articles, the instructions adopted Salazar's scepticism towards the claims of witches, and advised caution and leniency in all investigations. Belated justice was done to the victims of the Logroño auto of 1610: their sanbenitos were not to be exposed, and no stigma was to attach to them or to their descendants. Although the Inquisition was still obliged to follow European opinion and regard witchcraft as a crime, in practice all testimony to such a crime was rejected as delusion, so that Spain was saved from the ravages of popular witch-hysteria and witch-burnings at a time when it was prevalent all over Europe.

The decision of 1614 benefited those accused but placed the Inquisition in an ambiguous position in theory and in practice: in theory, because it admitted that diabolism was possible but denied any single instance of it; in practice, because it became reluctant to intervene in witchcraft cases and often conceded jurisdiction to the civil authorities. The Inquisition reverted to its practice of not burning, but continued to prosecute all types of superstition with vigour: in many tribunals in the seventeenth century this was the largest category of offences after 'propositions'. Two cases from Barcelona show how the new attitude worked.[48] In 1665 the tribunal uncovered a group of middle-class diabolists who recited black masses, conjured up devils and beheaded a goat at one of their ceremonies: a priest in the group was suspended from holy orders for five years, and a surgeon was flogged and banished for the same length of time. In the same year Isabel Amada, a widow of Mataró, was denounced by shepherds who had refused to give her alms; within three days, they said, 'two of their mules and thirty sheep died, and the accused claimed that she had done it with the help of the devil'. She was set free by the inquisitors. Such lenient verdicts would have been unthinkable in other European countries.

Had all tribunals, Church and secular, behaved in this way, the prosecution of superstition would have become in Spain what the Inquisition intended it to be: a means of disciplining the people into orthodox Christianity. The control of much jurisdiction over witchcraft by the secular power meant, however, that – contrary to what is frequently affirmed – witches continued to be executed in Spain. In the kingdom of Aragon, for example, the civil authorities continued in full possession of their jurisdiction over witchcraft and the Inquisition seems to have made no more than token efforts to assert its claims. Indeed, more witches were tried before secular courts in Upper Aragon in the early seventeenth century than before the Inquisition.[49] Witches in Aragon were hanged, not burnt, by the civil courts, but the number of those executed is not known. In

Catalonia, likewise, executions continued: in the jurisdiction of Vic, forty-five witches were sentenced by the civil authorities in 1618–22.[50]

Traditional and 'closed' societies are normally distrustful of outsiders: in Counter-Reformation Spain the distrust was actively encouraged by the Inquisition. From 1558 the Lutheran scare was used as a disincentive against contact with foreigners, but it was ironic that in this very decade Spain's imperial expansion took thousands of Spaniards abroad and brought them into touch with the rest of Europe on a scale unprecedented in Spanish history. The imperial experience did nothing to change the attitude of the inquisitors, who continued to be distrustful of all contact with foreigners, and a common accusation levelled against many of their accused was that they had been to a *tierra de herejes*, which in inquisitorial parlance meant any country not under Spanish control.

Foreigners visiting the peninsula, particularly if disrespectful to aspects of Spanish religion (refusing to take off one's hat, for example, if the Sacrament passed in the street), were liable to arrest by the Inquisition. This happened so frequently that Protestant powers trading to Spain made it their primary concern to secure guarantees for their traders before they would proceed any farther with commercial negotiations. England, being a market for Spanish raw materials, secured easier terms than might have been expected. In 1576 the Alba-Cobham agreement settled the position of the Inquisition *vis-à-vis* English sailors. The tribunal was allowed to act against sailors only on the basis of what they did *after* arriving in a Spanish port. Any confiscation was to be confined to the goods of the accused alone, and was not to include the ship and cargo, since these did not usually belong to him. Despite the outbreak of hostilities between England and Spain over the Dutch question, the agreement of 1576 continued to hold good for at least two decades after.[51] When peace eventually came under James I, the agreement was incorporated into the treaty of 1604 which ended hostilities. The guarantee was again renewed after the war of 1624–30, in article nineteen of the peace treaty of 1630, which promised security to English sailors 'so long as they gave no scandal to others'. The proviso was not to Cromwell's liking. In 1653 he proposed to Spain a treaty of alliance which would have given Englishmen virtual immunity from the Inquisition. The relevant articles would have allowed English subjects to hold religious services openly, to use Bibles freely, to be immune from confiscation of property and to have some Spanish soil set apart for the burial of English dead. So great was his prestige that the Council of State was quite ready to concede the articles,[52] but the proposal was rejected because of the firm opposition of the Suprema, which refused to allow any compromise.

All properly baptized persons, being *ipso facto* Christians and members of the Catholic Church, came under the jurisdiction of the Inquisition. Foreign heretics, therefore, appeared from time to time in autos held in Spain. The burning of Protestants at Seville in the mid-1500s shows a gradual increase in the number of foreigners seized, a natural phenomenon in an international seaport. Of those appearing in the Seville auto of April 1562, twenty-one were foreigners – nearly all Frenchmen. The auto of 19 April 1564 saw six Flemings relaxed in person, and two other foreigners who abjured *de vehementi*. That of 13 May 1565 saw four foreigners relaxed in effigy, seven reconciled and three who abjured *de vehementi*. One Scottish Protestant was relaxed at the Toledo auto of 9 June 1591, and another, master of the ship *Mary of Grace*, at the auto of 19 June 1594.

The harvest reaped by the Inquisition was by now greater from foreign Protestants than from natives. In Barcelona from 1552 to 1578, the only relaxations of Protestants were of fifty-one French people. Santiago in the same period punished over forty foreign Protestants. These figures were typical of the rest of Spain. The details given by Schäfer show that up to 1600 the cases of alleged Lutheranism cited before the tribunals of the peninsula totalled 1,995, of which 1,640 cases concerned foreigners. 'Harvest' is the right word to use when we come to the plight of foreign merchants whose countries were hostile to Spain. Their crews were arrested, their ships seized and their cargoes confiscated. Of the two Englishmen relaxed at the great Seville auto of 12 December 1560, one, Nicholas Burton, was a ship's master whose cargo had been confiscated and whose losses, when added to the other confiscations levied at the auto made up the grand total of £50,000. Such at least was the report, and it certainly pointed to some profit having been made by the Inquisition.[53]

Foreign Protestants did not normally appear in autos de fe at the end of the seventeenth century, but the pressure on them continued, especially in the ports. Catalonia, for example, experienced the presence of foreigners in the form of sailors in the ports, soldiers in the foreign regiments of the Spanish army and French immigration across the Pyrenees. The Barcelona tribunal had regular numbers of 'spontaneous' self-denunciations from foreigners wishing to become Catholics: in the 1670s and 1680s there were about a dozen cases a year, often outnumbering those of native Spaniards, and in the record year 1676 no less than sixty-four foreigners came before the Inquisition there, renounced the heresies they had professed and asked to be baptized.[54] There were still unfortunate cases – such as the twenty-three-year-old Englishman who was arrested for public misbehaviour in Barcelona in 1689 and died in the cells of the Inquisition – but in general the Holy Office was both lenient and tolerant. It is significant that after the long war of the Spanish Succession from 1702 to 1714, when thousands of heretical (Huguenot, English and German) troops had been captured by Spanish forces on Spanish territory, not a single fire was lit by the Inquisition to burn out any heresy that might have entered the country.

The fate of foreigners who fell into the hands of the Holy Office may best be examined in the well-documented history of the tribunal in the Canary Islands. The Canaries were a regular port of call for Englishmen, not only for direct trade (in wines) but also because they were a convenient halt before the long voyage across the Atlantic to Spanish America and the South Seas. Between 1586 and 1596 in particular, English traders and sailors were subjected to severe persecution by the Spanish authorities, then at war with England. An auto de fe held at Las Palmas on 22 July 1587 included for the first time fourteen English seamen, one of whom – George Gaspar of London – was relaxed in person, being the only Englishman ever to suffer death in this tribunal. The next public auto, on 1 May 1591, included the burning of the effigies of four English seamen, two of whom had been reconciled in the previous auto. The auto de fe of 21 December 1597, apparently the last in which Englishmen appeared,[55] included eleven English sailors. This is not, of course, the total number of Englishmen who were captured by the Inquisition. The lists show that from 1574 to 1624 at least forty-four Englishmen were detained in the cells of the Canaries Inquisition. Many saved their skins by 'spontaneous' conversion: during the seventeenth century at least eighty-nine foreigners became Catholics in this way, and in the eighteenth century 214 did, of whom the English were a majority.[56]

The English sailors were particularly vulnerable to the Inquisition because many of them were old enough to have been baptized in

the true faith under Queen Mary, and young enough to have con-
formed without difficulty to the Elizabethan settlement. They were
consequently apostates and heretics, and as such not readily forgiv-
able by the tribunal.

Soon, however, a more realistic attitude towards foreigners began
to be shown by the Inquisition. When war broke out again in 1624
between England and Spain, the resident English were left unmolested, thanks to the inquisitors in the Canaries. Commercial
reasons were the main motive behind the anxiety of the authorities
not to persecute foreigners unnecessarily, and this moderate attitude seems to have encouraged the traders, for by 1654 the number
of Dutch and English residents in Tenerife alone was put at 1500.[57]
This happy state of affairs was almost immediately shattered by
Cromwell's clumsy aggression against Hispaniola in 1655. The
Spanish authorities undertook reprisals against the community of
English merchants in the peninsula, who, forewarned of the Hispaniola expedition, got out of the country before the blow fell.
Reports from tardy officials in charge of the reprisals were pathetic.
In Tenerife the confiscations 'in this island, in Canary, and in La
Palma are of small consideration'. In the port of Santa Maria 'there
was one Englishman, no more'. In Cadiz only the English Catholics
remained. In San Lucar 'they were so forewarned that nothing
considerable remains', and 'the majority of them and the richest
have sold everything and left with the English fleet'.[58] They eventually came back, as they always did. By that time Protestant merchants had little to fear from the wrath of the Inquisition, which
had grown to respect the existence of *bona fide* trading communities
where religion counted far less than the annual profit. To this
extent the Holy Office was moving out of an intolerant age into a
more liberal one.

The Last Days of the Conversos

The greatest crime held against them was not the sins they had committed but the profits they had acquired.

Menasseh ben Israel, *Esperança de Israel* (1650)

The large number of judaizing cases with which the Inquisition dealt in the early sixteenth century marked the end of the generation of Jews who had had direct acquaintance with the Mosaic law as taught before 1492. Anyone punished for judaizing in 1532 at the age of fifty would have been ten years old in 1492, probably just old enough to remember the Jewish environment and practice of his family. The terrifying holocaust of the early decades of the Inquisition effectively destroyed underground Judaism, as the figures show clearly: from 1540 to 1559 only 1.9 per cent of the 1,346 cases dealt with by the tribunal of Toledo concerned judaizers.

For the rest of the sixteenth century Spain was no longer conscious of a judaizing problem. In many sectors of public life, particularly in the early century, there was little discrimination against conversos: Samuel Abolafia, who returned voluntarily to Spain in 1499 and became a Christian as Diego Gómez, was happily integrated into Old Christian society despite a brush with the Inquisition.[1] Feeling against Jews showed itself more in prejudice than in persecution. Antisemitism obviously existed, but the discriminatory statutes of limpieza did not begin to gather force until after the statute of Toledo in 1547. Ironically, as antisemitism developed there were serious attempts to restrict its excesses. It became, for example, a common insult in Spain to call one's opponent a Jew; but the Inquisition tried to stamp on the practice. The aggrieved party could take his case to the Holy Office as the body best qualified to examine his family tree, disprove the accusation publicly, and thus uphold his 'honour'. By the 1580s, as the growing feeling against the doctrine of limpieza shows, antisemitic prejudice was itself being called into question. It was a key argument of Salucio that judaizers had almost totally disappeared from the realm, 'and although there are signs that some remain, it is undeniable that in general there is no fear or suspicion of them'. Other writers admitted that most conversos were now peaceful and reliable Christians. Diego Serrano de Silva in 1623 argued: 'we see by the experience of many years that families of this race are at heart thorough Christians, devout and pious, giving their daughters to convents, their sons to the priesthood ...'

There continued, of course, to be judaizers, but it is difficult to describe them as Jews, since their heresies owed more to strong family and community traditions than to active Jewish belief. Virtually all external signs of Judaism had disappeared. Circumcision was no longer practised, since children were liable to discovery; synagogues or meeting-places were no longer possible; the sabbath was normally not observed, though token observances might be made or observance even moved to a different day; the great festivals of the year were not celebrated, though there appears to have been a general preference to celebrate at least one – the fast of Esther; and many even learned to eat the forbidden foods since there was no better way of dissimulation. Judaizers of the late sixteenth and early seventeenth century were thus unrecognizable as Jews.[2] Those who clung fast to their identity, nevertheless, maintained an ineradicable faith in the one God of Israel, passed down from father to son the few traditional prayers they could remember, and used the Catholic Old Testament as their basic reading. It is very likely that the edicts of faith of the Inquisition, with their detailed description of judaizing practices, actually helped groups to remember old rites.[3]

Their daily lives continued to be fraught with danger. The struggle against proofs of limpieza was particularly onerous. In Fregenal de la Sierra (Extremadura) most of the town were conversos and therefore conveniently swore to each other's Old Christian credentials; the inquisitor reported that the people apparently believed sincerely that baptism made one automatically into an Old Christian. During an inquisitorial visit in 1576, he said, over four hundred false witnesses to proofs of limpieza were found, and 'most of those who go to America from this district are conversos'.[4] Higher up in elite society, where there was more contempt for limpieza, false testimonials were winked at and some conversos found little difficulty in making their way. The wealthy Márquez Cardoso family, for example, employed agents of Old Christian origin and noble rank to swear to their limpieza.[5] Day-to-day existence among the judaizers, however, brought occasional mishaps. In Madrid in 1632 the women in the family scolded a fifteen-year-old son for assisting at the Catholic mass: he ran weeping from the house and threatened to denounce them all to the Inquisition. It was the neighbours, unfortunately, who on hearing the noise and realizing what it was about, called the inquisitors. All the members of the family appeared before the Inquisition, and the father was burnt.[6]

The relatively undisturbed life of Spanish conversos was transformed from about 1600 by an influx of Portuguese conversos. Of the refugees who fled from Spain before and during 1492, a great number went to Portugal, swelling its Jewish community to about a fifth of the total population. Portugal did not yet have an Inquisition, so the trials now suffered by the Spanish exiles who had gone there were caused by the crown, the clergy and the populace. The permission which had been granted to Jews to reside (at the price of nearly a ducat a head) was limited to six months only, after which they were offered the same alternatives of conversion or expulsion. When the time was up the richer Jews bought themselves further toleration, but the poorer were not so lucky and many went into exile again, over the sea and across to Africa. The final imposition of conversion on the Jews in Portugal was modified in 1497 by the promise not to persecute conversos for a period of twenty years. Although the crown benefited from tolerating this wealthy minority, communal hatreds were soon stirred, and in 1506 Lisbon witnessed the first great massacre of New Christians. Despite such outbreaks, there was little official persecution until about 1530, so that the conversos in Portugal were flourishing undisturbed at precisely the time that their generation was being rooted out in Spain. In 1532 King João III determined to introduce an Inquisition on the Spanish model. The institution of this tribunal was delayed only by the powerful support commanded in Rome by the wealthy New Christians.[7] Eventually in 1540 the Portuguese Inquisition celebrated its first auto de fe; but its powers were still not fully defined, thanks to the vacillation of Rome and the enormous bribes offered periodically by the conversos. Only on 16 July 1547 did the pope issue the bull which finally settled the structure of an independent Portuguese Inquisition.

The introduction of a native Inquisition does not by itself explain what we are concerned with – the mass emigration of Portuguese New Christians back into Spain, which for many of them had been the land of their birth. In the three tribunals of the Portuguese Inquisition at Lisbon, Evora and Coimbra, there were between 1547 and 1580 only thirty-four autos de fe, with 169 relaxations in person, fifty-one in effigy and 1,998 penitents.[8] This activity, for a country with so large a percentage of Jewish descendants, is obviously restricted when compared to the activity of Spanish tribunals, and indicates that political conditions and political pressure had weakened the hands of the Portuguese inquisitors. The great change occurred only in 1580, when Philip II annexed Portugal and introduced an inquisitorial rigour which would have been possible only in a conquered country. In 1586 the Cardinal Archduke Albert of Austria, who was also governor of Portugal, was named Inquisitor General of the country, with the result that within nineteen years (1581–1600) the three Portuguese tribunals witnessed fifty autos de fe, in forty-five of which there was a total of 162 relaxations in person, fifty-nine in effigy and 2,979 penitents.[9] It is small wonder that by the end of the reign of Philip II the Spanish Inquisition was alarmed to discover within Spain the existence of a new threat, this time from the Portuguese who had fled from their own Inquisition.

The new trend is shown by the increase in judaizers at autos de fe. The auto at Toledo on 9 June 1591, at which the king was present, included twenty-seven judaizers, of whom one was relaxed in person and two in effigy; that at Granada on 27 May 1593 included over seventy-five judaizers; and one at Seville in 1595 included eighty-nine judaizers.[10] As the new century advanced, the preponderance of Portuguese judaizers became clear and undeniable. To take a few examples at random: in the auto at Córdoba on 2 December 1625, thirty-nine of the forty-five judaizers penanced were Portuguese, and the four relaxations were all of Portuguese; another auto there on 21 December 1627 included fifty-eight judaizers, all of them Portuguese, and Portuguese figured in all the eighteen relaxations, of which five were in person; an auto at Madrid on 4 July 1632 showed that seventeen of the forty-four victims were Portuguese, and similarly one at Cuenca on 29 June 1654 showed that eighteen out of fifty-seven were of the same nation; finally, the Córdoba auto of 3 May 1655 showed that three out of five judaizers relaxed were Portuguese, as were seven out of nine penanced, and that almost all the forty-three reconciled were of the same nationality.[11] The ebb of Castilian Jewry was replaced by a flood-tide of Portuguese New Christians who fed the flames and coffers of the Spanish monarchy.

The immigrants brought a new perspective into the life of the Inquisition, which now found that it had to struggle against the royal wish to tolerate such wealthy subjects as the Portuguese. Just after 1602 the Portuguese offered Philip III a gift of 1,860,000 ducats (not to mention enormous gifts to the royal ministers), if the crown would issue a general pardon to judaizers of their nation for all past offences. That the conversos could afford so great a sum is clear from their own admission that they were worth eighty million ducats all told. Royal penury gave way before such a magnificent offer, and application was made to Rome. The papal decree for a pardon was issued on 23 August 1604 and published on 16 January 1605; on the latter date the three Portuguese tribunals released a total of 410 prisoners.[12] By this astonishing agreement the Spanish crown revealed its own financial bankruptcy and its willingness to jettison religious ideals when the profits from a bribe exceeded those from confiscations.

This did not mean any more than a temporary respite in the work of the Inquisition, which resumed activity in both Portugal and Spain as soon as the terms of the pardon had been worked off. In Portugal particularly, the Inquisition resumed work with a thoroughness it had not shown in the old days, and when in 1628 the prelates of Portugal proposed new measures to be enforced against the New Christians, the latter paid Philip III another handsome sum, probably well over 80,000 ducats, to allow them to leave for Spain. The emigrants, however, left not only for Spain but also for foreign lands of the dispersion, so swelling the numbers of the communities in France, Holland and England. That such emigration was a grave loss to Spain was perfectly obvious to everyone, and it formed the basic problem discussed with the royal ministers by the Portuguese residing in Spain under Philip IV. A memorandum sent to the king by the New Christian merchants claimed that they were the financial mainstay of the crown, since their contribution lay in

> sending to the East Indies countless ships laden with merchandise, whose customs duties maintain the navy and enrich the kingdom; supporting Brazil and producing the machinery to obtain sugar for all Europe; maintaining the trade to Angola, Cabo Verde and other colonies from

which Your Majesty has obtained so many duties; delivering slaves to the Indies for their service, and journeying and trading from Spain to all the world. Finally, the New Christians are today in Portugal and Castile those who maintain commerce, the farming of the revenues to Your Majesty, and the agreements to supply money outside the realm.[13]

Because of emigration, they claimed, the advantages of their services were being lost, and Rouen, Bordeaux, Nantes and Florence were benefiting from it. The Spanish authorities were susceptible to this kind of argument, and to stories that the commercial powers – particularly Holland and, after Cromwell's day, England – were controlled by Jews. The Portuguese merchants must therefore be retained in the peninsula. This became easier after the first state bankruptcy of Philip IV's reign, in 1626: the losses suffered by the Genoese bankers created a vacuum into which Portuguese financiers moved, although not without great protests from contemporaries. One of these, the writer Pellicer de Ossau, in 1640 put his objections in this way:

It was thought that the evils brought about by the Genoese financiers could be cured by resorting to the Portuguese, for since they were at the time subjects of the crown, to make use of them would also benefit the crown. But this was only to go from bad to worse. For since most of the Portuguese merchants were Jews, fear of the Inquisition made them establish their main trading houses in Flanders and cities of the north, keeping only a few connections in Spain. The result was that far from Spain benefiting, most of the profits went to the Dutch and other heretics.[14]

The Count Duke of Olivares, prime minister of Philip IV, saw matters in quite a different light. He ignored any protests which might interrupt his plans to use Jewish finance to restore the fortunes of the monarchy, and the years of his ministry in Spain were those when converso bankers flourished most.

His modification of the statutes of limpieza in 1623 was the first public break to be made with official antisemitism. In 1634, and again in 1641, he is said to have opened negotiations with the exiled Jews in Africa and the Levant, to persuade them to return to Spain under guarantees which would reverse the evil consequences of their expulsion. The inspiration for such a radical and certainly unpopular policy is difficult to find, and it seems to have contributed eventually to the downfall of Olivares. With him went the end of all hopes to found a truly united Spain: united not in the narrow sense demanding expulsion of all racial and religious minorities, but in the broader sense envisaged in the Union of Arms – a commonwealth of equals, without the provincialism of fueros or the sectarianism of race.

In 1628 Philip IV granted the Portuguese financiers freedom to trade and settle without restriction, hoping thereby to win back from foreigners a section of the Indies trade. Thanks to this, the New Christians extended their influence to the principal trading channels of Spain and America. However successful they may have been in business, they could nevertheless not escape the consequences of their racial origin, and several of them had to suffer the rigours of the Inquisition. From the 1630s to the 1680s some of the wealthiest men in Spain were ruined in fame and fortune by the Inquisition. The Portuguese financiers among them were, in addition, tarnished by identification with their nation, which was in revolt against Madrid after 1640; and with the disgrace of Olivares in 1643 their last great protector disappeared.

In 1636 the Inquisition brought the financier Manuel Fernández Pinto to trial for judaizing. On one occasion during his career he had lent Philip IV the sum of 100,000 ducats. Now the tribunal extorted from him the enormous sum of 300,000 ducats in confiscations.[15] Even more prominent than Pinto was Juan Núñez Saravía,[16] whom we first meet as contributor, with nine other Portuguese financiers, to a loan of 2,159,438 ducats made to Philip IV in 1627. In 1630 Saravía was denounced to the Inquisition as a judaizer and protector of judaizers. No action was taken by the tribunal, which continued to accumulate evidence from France and America showing that, besides his religious errors, Saravía was also guilty of exporting bullion to his co-religionaries abroad and importing base money in its place. Early in 1632 Saravía and his brother Enrique were arrested, and after the usual delays of the Inquisition Juan was finally in 1636 put to mild torture under which he admitted nothing. He was condemned to abjure *de vehementi* and fined 20,000 ducats, appearing with his brother and other judaizers in the Toledo auto of 13 December 1637. From men of Saravía's standing the tribunal could expect to make large profits, and besides the fine on Juan it is estimated that his brother Enrique was condemned to confiscations which amounted to over 300,000 ducats. Juan Saravía was no doubt ruined by a case which had destroyed his good name and obliged him to fritter away five years in an inquisitorial prison, for he never makes any further appearance amongst the number of bankers who served the crown.

After 1640, as we have observed, the Portuguese financiers in Spain were in a difficult position, without a native country and without official support, particularly after the fall of Olivares. The wealthier among them were eliminated one by one. In 1641 a probable relative of Saravía called Diego de Saravía was tried by the Inquisition and suffered the confiscation of 250,000 ducats in gold, silver and coin.[17] In 1646 the aged financier Manuel Enrique was arrested and condemned, and in 1647 another financier not named in the records was tried at Toledo. The records bring out the close connections between victims. In 1646, for instance, the property of the wealthy financier Esteban Luis Diamante was sequestrated by the Inquisition. Diamante was a colleague in the banking firm of his brothers-in-law Gaspar and Alfonso Rodríguez Pasarino, of whom the latter was in prison accused of judaizing, while the former had saved himself by flight. Alfonso had a daughter named Violante who was married to the eminent banker Simon de Fonseca Piña, an astute and wealthy businessman who seems never to have come into conflict with the Holy Office. The property confiscated from the Pasarinos on this occasion probably exceeded 100,000 ducats.[18]

Apart from the wealthy few, there were whole families of ordinary conversos living in Madrid who suffered from the renewal of persecution. The 1650s saw the beginning of wholesale arrests and trials which turned into a reign of terror for the Portuguese converso minority in Spain. A contemporary living in Madrid in mid-century supplies us with a dramatic account of facts and rumours about arrests.[19] 'No one trusts the Portuguese financiers any more. They are going bankrupt and fleeing from the Inquisition. I have been assured that after the auto at Cuenca over two hundred families took to flight during the night. This is what fear can do' (22 August 1654). 'In Seville at the beginning of April four wealthy Portuguese merchants were seized at night by the Inquisition' (17 May 1655). 'The Cardosos have fled to Amsterdam, taking 200,000 ducats in wool and 250,000 in gold. It is said this was because the Inquisition wished to arrest them, and so they are in search of a land where one lives in greater freedom than in Spain' (2 June 1655). The wealthy Cardoso brothers, who administered taxes in several provinces, fled because a blackmailer had threatened to testify that they were judaizers unless they paid for silence. Faced with the possibility of having to prove their case against false testimony, 'they preferred to fly from punishment rather than remain in gaol until the truth was established' (29 May 1655). The diarist thought it a serious matter that lying witnesses should be able to ruin the lives of prominent men like these.

> The fact is that if it is the practice in the Holy Office, as they say it is, not to punish false witnesses because no one would denounce if they did so, then that is terrible and even inhuman, to leave the life, honour and property of one who may be innocent to the mercy of his enemies. Every day we see many people like this emerging from their travails after great sufferings and years of prison.

'On Monday the thirteenth at midnight the Inquisition seized fourteen Portuguese traders and financiers, in particular two tobacco merchants. These people sprout like mushrooms' (15 September 1655). 'Since last Saturday the Inquisition in Madrid has imprisoned seventeen Portuguese families.... In the street of the Peromostenses they are hurriedly building a prison big enough to hold all the people that fall every day into the trap. It is said for certain that there is not a Portuguese of high or low degree in Madrid who does not judaize' (18 September 1655). 'There is not a single tobacco merchant in Madrid whom the Inquisition hasn't arrested. The other day they took away two entire families, both parents and children. Many others are fleeing to France' (23 October 1655).

The condemnation of judaizers and the flight of wealthy fugitives brought about precisely the situation Olivares had attempted to avoid: bankruptcies among the trading classes of Madrid and other cities, leading to a collapse of confidence in some leading financiers and a consequent contraction in the size of the group of bankers on whom the crown could ultimately rely. Heads continued to roll. 'There has been an auto at Cuenca. Brito abjured *de vehementi*; he was condemned to the sanbenito, banishment and to pay 6,000 ducats. Montesinos met the same fate, but the fine was higher: 10,000 ducats. Blandon, 4,000. El Pelado, 300.... All were from Madrid and had lived years there; very rich men' (8 January 1656). Brito was the financier Francisco Díaz Méndez Brito, who was made to do penance here once, and was again at a later date imprisoned by the Inquisition. Montesinos was the banker and merchant Fernando de Montesinos Téllez, a prominent financier who at the age of sixty-six was imprisoned together with his wife Serafina de Almeida in 1654, by the Inquisition of Cuenca. Serafina was a cousin of the Cortizos family, whom we shall meet presently. Fernando was a man of enormous fortune. His assets at the time of his arrest amounted to 213,721,195 maravedis or 567,256 ducats; of this sum a substantial part was tied up in Amsterdam, so that his effective assets were put conservatively at 474,096 ducats. His household goods alone, worth 10,000 ducats, were a testimony to his affluence,[20] yet the Inquisition penalized the couple only, and left the fortune undisturbed. Fernando and Serafina were fined a total of 8,000 ducats. After this 'he went to Amsterdam to live there freely, terrified of being burnt if he returned. He left his sons behind, having given them all his property. It is said that they will send the property over there bit by bit, and then one day do the same as he' (22 November 1656). Montesinos, therefore, apparently returned to the open practice of Judaism in Amsterdam. But his sons, far from following his example, continued the family's financial services to the crown. The great deflation of 1680 began their ruin as bankers, and by the beginning of the eighteenth century they had gone into liquidation.

The liberal attitude of the Inquisition towards Montesinos' fortune was not dictated by unselfishness. The fact was that so many wealthy financiers were appearing before the tribunal that the government took alarm at the possible threat to the financial stability of Spain. On 7 September 1654 the Council of Finance (*Hacienda*) came to an agreement with the Inquisition that the latter was to attend only to the personal property of those accused, and that money which was involved in official contracts was to be dealt with by the former. The agreement had the virtue of differentiating between a financier and his firm. As a result we find that the imprisonment of principals such as Fernando Montesinos did not automatically lead to the dissolution of their business.

The auto de fe held at Cuenca on 29 June 1654 included among its victims the financier Francisco Coello, administrator of taxes in Málaga.[21] In 1658 Francisco López Pereira, administrator of taxes in Granada, who had once before been tried by the Inquisition of Coimbra in 1651, made another appearance before the tribunal in Spain but had his case suspended. Diego Gómez de Salazar, administrator of the tobacco monopoly in Castile and a fervent judaizer, was reconciled in the auto held at Valladolid on 30 October 1664, and almost all his family suffered condemnation in due course.

Among the most prominent conversos in mid-century was the financier Manuel Cortizos de Villasante, born in Valladolid of Portuguese parents.[22] His astuteness and financial dealings raised him to the highest ranks in the kingdom, and he had become by the end of his life a knight of the Order of Calatrava, Lord of Arrifana, a member of the Council of Finance and secretary of the Contaduría Mayor de Cuentas, the principal department of the treasury. All this occurred at a time when the statutes of limpieza were in full force. Suddenly, after his death in 1650, it was discovered that he had been a secret judaizer and had been buried according to Jewish rites. The discovery would normally have led to the ruin of his family, but their rank and influence saved them from disaster. Indeed, notwithstanding the strong suspicion that other members of the family were secret Jews, Manuel's son Don Sebastián was in 1657 appointed Spanish ambassador to Genoa; while another son, Don Manuel José Cortizos, continued his father's work as a financier of the crown, obtained the title of Viscount of Valdefuentes in 1668 and shortly afterwards that of Marquis of Villaflores. Throughout the reign of Charles II, Cortizos was second to none in the financial services he rendered the crown. In 1679, thanks to defaulting by his creditors, he was obliged to ask for a moratorium on his transactions, even though his assets were worth several million ducats.

Another tobacco administrator in a high social position, Luis Márquez Cardoso, was reconciled together with his wife at an auto in Toledo in November 1669. In August 1691 Simón Ruiz Pessoa, a leading Portuguese financier who had managed the customs duties of Andalucia from 1683 to 1685, was arrested by the Inquisition in Madrid. In 1694 Don Francisco del Castillo, a member of the Contaduría Mayor de Cuentas, born in Osuna and resident in Ecija, was arrested in Seville by the tribunal.

The most eminent Portuguese financier to suffer in this reign was Francisco Báez Eminente. He took no part in international exchange but restricted his considerable fortune to the administration of the customs duties of Andalucia, Seville and the Indies (the *almojarifazgos*), as well as provisioning the royal army and navy in Andalucia. During his term of administration in 1686 such severe measures were taken against smugglers that, according to one source, 'we came to experience what was held to be impossible in Cadiz, namely that there should be no smuggling'. Eminente was a member of the Contaduría Mayor, and in view of the fact that most of Castile's trade passed through Andalucia his work was of the highest importance to the crown, which he served, as the government later admitted, 'for over forty years with credit, industry and zeal that were well known'. Despite this long service and his advanced years, on 26 December 1689 he was suddenly arrested by the Inquisition in Madrid. His colleague Don Bernardo de Paz y Castañeda was arrested at about the same time. The arrests made no difference to the firm of Eminente, which had been handed over to his son Juan Francisco in April 1689, and continued successfully under him well into the next century.

Thus, once again in the seventeenth century, judaizers were the main preoccupation of the Inquisition: in the tribunal of Toledo they made up over 44 per cent of all cases.[23] Though the more active Judaism of the Portuguese brought new life to the practice of Jewish rites, most Iberian conversos remained cut off from the development of international Jewry. It is remarkable, for instance, that the millennarian movement of Sabbatai Zevi, which shook the entire Jewish world and found its ablest controversialist in the north African rabbi Jacob Saportas,[24] seems to have caused no tremor in Spain, even though the Inquisition was aware of the phenomenon and warned its tribunals to keep a watch at the ports for any unusual emigration of conversos. Likewise, there was no active development of Judaic thought in Spain. Isaac Cardoso (d. 1680), professor of Madrid and Valladolid and physician to Philip IV, left the country in 1648 and went to live as a Jew in Venice; here he published his *Philosophia libera* (1673), which was an exposition of atomist philosophy based on Gassendi and owed little to Judaism.[25]

A few individuals exiled themselves, but reluctantly: Enríquez Gómez, whose parents had been tried by the Inquisition, and who himself became a Jew in France, remained so attached to his native land – which alone provided him with the public for whom he could write – that he returned to Spain in 1650 and wrote for thirteen years in Seville under the pseudonym Fernando de Zarate. While abroad in Rouen in 1647 Gómez wrote the second part of his *Política Angélica*, a reasoned programme for reform of the Inquisition: he asked for the identification of witnesses, the suppression of confiscations, a ban on sanbenitos, and speedy trials. He reserved his harshest strictures for the practice of limpieza, which he called 'the most barbarous seed sown by the devil in Christendom.... Because of it the best families have left the realm; it has created thousands of godless, has injured neighbourly love, has divided the people and has perpetuated enmities.'[26] A more determined exile was Gaspar Méndez, who fled to Amsterdam, where he changed his name to Abraham Idana and in 1686 wrote a stinging attack on the Inquisition for 'using unheard-of tortures to force many to confess what they have *not* done, this being the cause why many who have been arrested and have entered the prisons without knowing anything other than that they are Christians, have come out as Jews. This is the reason why I left a country where such a tribunal holds sway.'[27]

Converso predominance in the autos is notable. In the Granada auto de fe of 30 May 1672 there were seventy-nine judaizers out of ninety victims, fifty-seven of them being Portuguese; the great Madrid auto of 30 June 1680 included 104 judaizers, nearly all Portuguese; and the Córdoba auto of 29 September 1684 included thirty-four judaizers (some of them cried out 'Moses, Moses' as they perished in the flames) among the forty-eight penitents.[28] Autos de fe after the 1680s show a definite decline from these numbers, indicating that the first generation of Portuguese conversos had been wiped out as surely as the native conversos had been at the beginning of the century.

A special exception to this decline of persecution must be noted in Mallorca, where the burnings erupted only in the second half of the century. Cut off as it was from the mainland, Mallorca followed a slightly different development from the rest of Spain. The mediae-val Inquisition had existed there since 1232 and the new tribunal was introduced only in 1488. Even before this, the island suffered from a Jewish problem which paralleled that on the mainland. The great massacres of 1391 were repeated here in riots in August 1391, and St Vincent Ferrer extended his proselytizing activities to the island in 1413. By about 1435 it was reckoned that the whole Jewish population had embraced Christianity, but as in Spain it was found necessary to introduce the Inquisition to root out the doubtful cases. The first autos de fe showed the existence of a real problem: in 1489 there were fifty-three relaxations of conversos, most of whom were burnt in effigy as fugitives. On 26 March 1490, after no less than 424 conversos had responded to the terms of clemency offered in an edict of grace, eighty-six conversos were reconciled; and on 31 May 1490 there were thirty-six relaxations and fifty-six reconciliations. Up to September 1531 every person relaxed in the Mallorcan Inquisition was Jewish, and the total number of relaxations to that date was 535.[29] By the 1530s the same phen-omenon that we have noted for peninsular Spain occurred: the number of converso victims declined sharply and a whole genera-tion of judaizers ceased to exist. Now, however, the Morisco problem took its place, aggravated by the fact that Morisco refugees from

Valencia often chose to flee to the Balearic islands. Mass reconciliations of Moriscos occurred in Mallorca from the 1530s, and the first nine relaxations took place in the auto of 10 July 1535. Between 1530 and 1645 there were ninety-nine Moriscos reconciled in Mallorca, twenty-seven of them in 1613 alone.[30] The corresponding absence of judaizers is shown by the fact that between 1535 and 1645 only ten people were relaxed, and of these seven were Moriscos. The absence of judaizers at this particular period, when they proliferated in Spain, is evidence that the Portuguese emigrants did not make their way to the Balearics in any numbers.

After a lull of well over a century, the storm burst eventually over the converso descendants – the Chuetas – in 1675, when a young man of nineteen years, Alonso López, was burned in the auto of 13 January.[31] With him were burnt the effigies of six Portuguese judaizers, indicating that persecution in the Spanish peninsula had at last driven this race out into the Mediterranean. Repercussions from this case led in 1677 to a general arrest of conversos, and by 1678 the Inquisition had arrested 237 of them on the charge of complicity in what seems to have been a genuine plot to assert their political and human rights. Now followed two great waves of devastation in 1679 and 1691. In the spring of the former year no less than five autos de fe were held in Mallorca, with a total of 221 reconciliations. As we have seen, the confiscations made at these autos reached a record total of well over 2.5 million ducats. Crushed by these events, the conversos waited ten years before they could stir again. In 1688 some of them, led by Onofre Cortes and Rafael Valls, attempted to recoup all in a plot which fell through and led directly to the four autos de fe held in 1691, at which thirty-seven prisoners were relaxed in person; those reconciled or burnt in effigy increased this figure to a total of eighty-six converso victims. After this great suppression, the conversos of Mallorca made no further attempt to improve their position. They remained a depressed community, subjected to calumny and discrimination, and continued like this into modern times.

Throughout Spain, then, the seventeenth century closed with a holocaust of conversos. The eighteenth century opened with a new dynasty and a new outlook on religion. Philip v seemed to mark the change to a new era by refusing to attend an auto de fe held in his honour at the beginning of the reign. With elimination first of the native judaizers and then of the Portuguese immigrants, it appeared that the converso problem had at last been solved. All this was delusion. Philip v grew to learn that he must live according to the customs of his subjects, and did not after this refuse to attend autos. The change of dynasty involved very little change in religious practices, and the persistence of judaizers in Spain was treated with severity as great as in the preceding century. A final wave of repression occurred in the early 1720s. Why it came so late, in a period when several people were beginning to consider persecution unjust, is difficult to say.

Certainly the situation for Spanish Jews was changing for the better, thanks in part to the capture of Gibraltar by the English in 1704 and its cession to England by the peace of Utrecht (1713). Spain laid down a condition 'that on no account must Jews and Muslims be allowed to live or reside in the said city of Gibraltar'. The English made no attempt to observe these discriminatory demands, and very rapidly the Jewish community grew. By 1717 there were three hundred Jewish families there, with their own synagogue, and by the nineteenth century Jews were a tenth of the population on the Rock.

Among the most significant conversos of the late century, and a man whose career aptly illustrates the strange mixture of tolerance and intolerance of those days, was Dr Diego Mateo Zapata.[32] Born of Portuguese parents in Murcia in 1664, Zapata was brought up by his mother as a secret Jew. In 1678 she was arrested, tortured and emerged in an auto de fe in 1681. His father was arrested on suspicion, but set free. Zapata went to the University of Valencia to study medicine, and then to Alcalá, where he was befriended by Francisco Enríquez de Villacorta, a doctor with Jewish origins. He moved to Madrid and, thanks to his connections, managed to prosper. In 1692 he was arrested in Madrid by the Inquisition on charges of Judaism, and spent a year in the cells of the tribunal at Cuenca; the prosecution was suspended, and he was released in 1693. In 1702 he was elected president of the Royal Society of Medicine in Seville. The early eighteenth century found him rich and successful in Madrid, in possession of a large library that included the works of Bacon, Gassendi, Bayle, Paracelsus, Pascal and other philosophers. In 1721 he was suddenly arrested, again on charges of Judaism, and appeared in an auto de fe in Cuenca in 1725, condemned to ten years' banishment and the loss of half his goods. He returned to active work in Madrid, helped to found the Royal Academy of Medicine in 1734, and died in 1745.

His posthumously published *Ocaso de las formas aristotélicas*

(Sunset of the Aristotelian Forms), which appeared in 1745, was a radical departure from his earlier devotion to the principles of Galen which still dominated orthodox medicine in Spain. Zapata shares with Dr Juan Múñoz Peralta the fame of being among the last men of medicine to suffer at the hands of the Inquisition.[33] Peralta was distinguished enough to have been physician to the king and queen in the War of Succession, and was subsequently summoned to Versailles to attend to Louis XIV himself. In 1700 he was elected first president of the Royal Medical Society of Seville. Tried and imprisoned by the Inquisition shortly before 1724, he never returned to practise as a royal physician.

The toll of judaizers in the 1720s was substantial. Although there were several important autos in 1720 in Madrid, Mallorca, Granada and Seville, the real wave of repression broke out in 1721 and stretched into the late 1720s. The peak years were 1722–3. Over the period 1721 to 1727, according to Lea, sixty-four of the autos that took place condemned a total of 824 judaizers, with over a hundred other victims.[34] If we take only the judaizing victims in Castile, it is possible to draw up a representative table for the years 1721–5. The number of relaxations (both in person and in effigy) is given in parentheses but is included in the total figures.[35]

	1721	1722	1723	1724	1725
Madrid	14 (5)	11		20 (9)	
Granada	48 (20)	48	108 (12)	38 (21)	27 (7)
Seville	38 (7)	82 (11)	35 (2)	41 (1)	10 (3)
Cuenca	31 (5)	18 (3)	1	8 (6)	10 (8)
Murcia		63 (1)	18 (1)	7 (2)	4
Córdoba	27	13 (4)	25 (8)	34 (8)	
Valladolid		14 (3)	2	5 (4)	5
Toledo		44 (11)	6 (1)		5 (1)
Llerena		17	11 (1)		14

Total: 902 (165)

From this table we can see that within these five years, in nine of the tribunals of Castile, over nine hundred judaizers were condemned to punishments ranging from burning at the stake for over 160 persons, to the more ordinary penalties of reconciliation and confiscation. To these figures we must add those for the other tribunals of the peninsula. In the years after 1725 the number of autos and of victims declined rapidly, and by mid-century the converso community had ceased to be a major religious issue. With this last great persecution the practice of Judaism in Spain crumbled and decayed. Cases were rare in the later eighteenth century, the last one to occur at Toledo being in 1756. Among more than five thousand cases coming before the tribunals between 1780 and 1820 when the Inquisition was suppressed, there were only sixteen cases of judaizing, and of these, ten were of foreigners while the remaining six were prosecuted only on suspicion.[36] The Jews had been to all appearances eliminated from Spain, the last prosecution of their race being the case of Manuel Santiago Vivar at Córdoba in 1818.

The presence of the Jew continued to be felt long after this date. So long as the doctrines of limpieza existed in Spain, racial distinction remained an obsession. It was the task of nineteenth-century liberals to wipe out the shame of racialism from their country's statute books. The Cortes of Cadiz in 1811 abolished limpieza in several fields, but the reactionary regime of Ferdinand VII in 1824 reinforced all the old regulations. Not until well into the nineteenth century were Spaniards allowed to take office in their own country regardless of their distant racial antecedents, and the liberal constitutions of the period made it their duty to set this down in writing. It was only under Isabella II in 1865 that limpieza was eventually made unnecessary for entry into offices of State.

All this did not mean a relaxation of antisemitism. When in 1797 the finance minister Pedro Varela resurrected the long-forgotten plans of Olivares and attempted to bring the Jews back into Spain, his suggestions were firmly rejected by Charles IV. As late as 1802 the crown was issuing threats against those of its subjects who were shielding Jews from the Inquisition. In 1804 a French Jewish merchant of Bayonne was molested by the tribunal, whereupon the indignant French ambassador intervened to say 'that the exercise of international rights ought not to depend on an arbitrary distinction about the religion in which a man was born and the religious principles he professed'.[37] The struggle continued into the opening decades of the twentieth century, where it merged into problems that are part of contemporary history.

To the new generation of Spaniards, Jews were the dark stain on the history of their country. Their shadow was everywhere present, yet they themselves were extinct. The only surviving memory of them was in the sanbenitos which foreign travellers report having

seen hung in churches in the peninsula up to well into the nineteenth century. But if the Inquisition could claim to have rid Spain
of the Jewish menace, it was still partly to blame for the bitter
legacy of antisemitism in the country. The political right wing in
nineteenth-century Spain adopted the Jew as its prototype enemy,
sometimes distinct from and sometimes identified with the free-
mason. The Jew, who had now become a myth and no more,
became identified in certain minds with all that was hostile to the
tradition represented by the Inquisition. To be a Jew meant not
being a Catholic, therefore not to be a Catholic meant being a Jew:
the result of this popular reasoning meant that 'Jews and free-
masons', 'Jews and Protestants' and 'Jews and foreigners' became
self-explanatory identifications. In the constant struggle waged by
the right wing to preserve Catholic Spain, all that was hostile and
sinister became personified in the Jew who was on the other side.
But this is a matter of myth, not of history, and does not concern
us directly. The aberrations of the nineteenth century found their
last heyday in the racist literature circulated in Spain during the
Second World War.

Speculation and curiosity still hang around the issue of Jewish
survivals in the nineteenth century. The question was put at its
most dramatic by George Borrow during his indefatigable travels
with the Bible round western Spain. In 1836 he was riding by
night on his *burra* through Old Castile, when about two leagues
before Talavera he fell into conversation with a figure making the
same journey on foot. Hardly had a few words been exchanged
than

> the man walked on about ten paces, in the same manner as he had
> previously done; all of a sudden he turned, and taking the bridle of the
> *burra* gently in his hand, stopped her. I had now a full view of his face
> and figure, and those huge features and Herculean form still occasionally
> revisit me in my dreams. I see him standing in the moonshine, staring
> me in the face with his deep calm eyes. At last he said –
>
>   'Are you then *one of us?*'[38]

In this way, in the middle of the nineteenth century, Borrow came
upon one of the few remaining communities of secret Jews in Spain.
The incident has been fiercely attacked by writers of all shades of
opinion, and there is little doubt that the speeches Borrow puts into
the mouth of his new friend Abarbanel verge on fantasy. Yet there
seems no reason to doubt that Borrow did meet Spaniards – as he

later met an ex-inquisitor – who testified to their personal experience of secret judaizers in the country. Several other travellers bear witness to the same phenomenon. The obvious difficulty is that it is impossible to locate or estimate the number of underground judaizers. Popular exaggeration would have affected Borrow as much as anyone else. One of his predecessors, Joseph Townsend, reports in 1787 after travelling through the country:

> Even to the present day both Mahometans and Jews are thought to be numerous in Spain, the former among the mountains, the latter in all great cities. Their principal disguise is more than common zeal in external conformity to all the precepts of the Church; and the most apparently bigoted, not only of the clergy, but of the inquisitors themselves, are by some persons suspected to be Jews.[39]

To some extent the existence of crypto-Judaism may be part of the arsenal of antisemitic propaganda, but it seems reasonable to believe that Borrow at least based his conclusions on genuine talks with genuine Jews. Whatever the truth of the matter, the fact remains that Judaism continued to be an issue in Spain long after the last heretic had died at the stake. On the one hand, there was a legacy of suspicion and fear based on antisemitism – the willingness to blame the secret and concealed enemy for all the evils of policy and history. On the other, there was a distinct atmosphere of racialism which has persisted into modern times. On both counts the Inquisition had some part to play and some responsibility to bear in the tragedy of a hunted people.

The Inquisition in Politics

> There is no vassal free of its power whom it does not treat as
> an immediate subordinate, subjecting him to its mandates,
> censures, fines and prisons; no casual offence or light incivility
> to its servants which it does not avenge and punish as a crime
> against religion.
>
> Report of the Royal Councils, 1696

The temporal privileges of the Inquisition were quite naturally subjected to criticism and hostility throughout its career. Since it possessed remarkable ecclesiastical and political powers, the tribunal
came regularly into direct conflict not only with the government
but also with Rome. These quarrels can usually be described as
concerning jurisdiction, but occasionally certain transcendent principles would be at stake, so elevating a simple issue of jurisdiction
into something much greater. With Rome the difference can be
traced back to the very beginning, simply because the Inquisition
derived its authority from the pope and was consequently governed
by papal regulations. Complaints against the tribunal could be best
dealt with if taken directly to the fount of authority, the pope. As
we have seen, the conversos did their best both in Castile and in
Aragon to obtain papal decrees to modify the rigour of the Holy
Office. This was a legitimate procedure, since the constitution of
the tribunal allowed appeals to Rome; and Rome was eager to
maintain its rights in the matter, not only to preserve control over
the courts of the Inquisition but also to preserve possible sources of
revenue, for the conversos paid liberally for any bulls granted by
the pope. But the Spanish monarchs, supported by the inquisitors,
refused to take cognizance of papal letters which openly contradicted the verdict of their courts. Ferdinand's famous letter to Sixtus

IV in May 1482 illustrates the firmness of the Spanish attitude. The vacillation of Rome before Spanish claims, and the contradictory policies followed by successive popes, made it possible in the end for the inquisitors to have things their own way. As early as 2 August 1483 Sixtus IV granted to the conversos a bull which revoked to Rome all cases of appeal, but only eleven days later he suspended this, claiming he had been misled. When his successor Innocent VIII tried to pursue a similar policy of issuing papal letters to appellants from Spain, Ferdinand stepped in and on 15 December 1484 issued a pragmatic decreeing death and confiscation for anyone making use of papal letters without royal permission.[1]

Papal policy continued to be intransigent well after this date, and the persistence of jurisdictional conflict is shown by Ferdinand's next decree of 31 August 1509, which in effect renewed the penalties of the 1484 decree. Under Charles V the papacy became more cautious, and Clement VII in 1524 and 1525 renewed the permission it had regularly (in 1483, 1486, 1502, 1507, 1518 and 1523) granted to the Inquisitor General to exercise appellate jurisdiction in place of the pope and to hear appeals which would normally have been directed to the Holy See. This did not mean that Rome had given up the right to hear appeals, and when papal letters again began to be issued Charles V in 1537 reinforced the decree of 1509.

On occasion Charles wrote to the pope himself, as in his letter of 4 May 1527 demanding the revocation of a papal brief issued to Luis Alvárez de San Pedro, 'imprisoned by the Holy Office'.[2] This firmness on his part assured a period of tranquillity in relations between Spain and Rome (without, of course, considering the military differences between the two, and the tragic sack of Rome by imperial troops in 1527), and in 1548 the pope again confirmed his unwillingness to interfere with the independent jurisdiction of the Spanish Inquisition. But under Philip II, and with the accession in 1555 of the bizarre Pope Paul IV to the see of Peter, conflicts between the two broke out with increased ferocity.

Although Rome did occasionally refer appeals back to Spain,[3] the Inquisition was more usually employed rejecting the claims made by holders of papal letters. This situation continued throughout the seventeenth century. But the Inquisition was not unduly concerned by difficulties with Rome, and even before the end of the sixteenth century we find the secretary of the Suprema asserting complacently that the Holy See had abandoned its claim to ultimate

jurisdiction over cases tried by the tribunal. Under Philip v the new
Bourbon dynasty tolerated no interference by Rome, and so continued the tradition of Philip II. Hostility under Philip v was aggravated by the exigencies of the international situation and by the
papal support given to the Archduke Charles, Habsburg pretender
to the throne of Spain. In 1705 papal decrees were forbidden in
Spain and all appeals to Rome prohibited. This assertion of 'regalism' was supported by most of the bishops and also by the
advocate-general Melchor de Macanaz in a famous memorandum
in 1713. With the advent of the Bourbons and their new extension
of power over the western Mediterranean, in both Spain and Italy,
a declining papacy had little opportunity to assert its old jurisdictional claims.

From the beginning, the tribunal was so closely allied with and
so dependent on the crown that later historians came to regard it
as a secular tribunal more than an ecclesiastical one. This argument was adopted especially by Catholic apologists who hoped to
disembarrass the Church of an unattractive chapter in ecclesiastical
history. There is a *prima facie* case for the argument. The crown
had absolute powers of appointment and dismissal of inquisitors,
power which Ferdinand employed whenever he felt it necessary. In
questions of administration, although decisions were in practice left
to inquisitors, the king was kept carefully informed. A letter from
Ferdinand to Torquemada, dated 22 July 1486, even shows the
king laying down regulations for sixteen detailed and minor points
such as the salaries of doorkeepers in the Inquisition; for any other
question, he tells Torquemada, 'see to it yourself and do as you
think fit'.[4] That the king did exercise control over the Inquisition is
shown by the protests of the earlier Cortes of the sixteenth century,
which all went to the crown for redress and reform. Ultimately, of
course, control rested on the fact that the tribunal was financially
dependent on the crown.

Since, as we have noted above (chapter 5), the Inquisition was
also an ecclesiastical tribunal, there were bound to be conflicts of
interest – some of which will be touched on presently – between its
secular and its ecclesiastical character. Much ink has been spent on
trying to define the true nature of inquisitorial authority.[5] The truth
is that the Inquisition itself always refused to define its own jurisdiction clearly, since that would have been to set clear limits to its
power. Though the question of jurisdiction over familiars, for example, had repeatedly been agreed upon through concordias, there

continued to be constant quarrels between civil courts and the Inquisition. As late as the seventeenth century an official of the Inquisition, discussing 'whether the jurisdiction that the Holy Office exercises over its lay officers and familiars is ecclesiastical or secular', came arbitrarily to the conclusion that 'this jurisdiction is ecclesiastical'.[6] In other words, secular courts could not try familiars. On the other hand, the Inquisition itself claimed the right to try laymen for non-ecclesiastical offences and for injuries done to its officers. At one and the same time, then, the Inquisition claimed to be exempt from secular authority but also claimed to be able to exercise secular authority. The problem of jurisdiction affected all authorities, in both Church and State, when questions of precedence were involved. Indeed, quarrels over precedence in public events were one of the most common causes of conflict. The inquisitors argued that because they represented both pope and king they were entitled to precedence over all other authorities, including bishops and viceroys. As a result, Church and city authorities would often refuse to attend autos de fe (the Chancillería of Valladolid refused to attend the great auto of 1559 for this reason), and in Barcelona the consellers as a rule never went to autos.

The problem, which continually infuriated other jurisdictions in Spain because in effect it gave the Inquisition unlimited authority in both ecclesiastical and secular matters, arose out of the peculiar dual nature of inquisitorial power. To confirm its claim of exclusive authority over its own officials, the tribunal always took refuge in the papal bulls it had been granted: neither the crown nor the Church courts, it argued, could go against these papal privileges. When critics pointed out that this therefore limited the Inquisition to being a papal and ecclesiastical tribunal, inquisitors were quick to retort that, on the contrary, the Holy Office was also a secular tribunal, exercising power delegated by the crown. Indeed, the crown always supported this pretension. On 18 August 1501 King Ferdinand issued a decree prohibiting one of his own corregidors from 'issuing a declaration saying that the Inquisition is of a different jurisdiction, because in fact it is all ours'. And on 9 December 1503 at Ocaña, Queen Isabella confirmed the dual jurisdiction of the Holy Office, saying that 'the one jurisdiction aids and complements the other, so that justice may be done in the service of God'.[7] Armed with these powers, the inquisitors were, of course, free to arrest royal officials in the name of royal authority, even when royal courts ruled against: in the sixteenth century, for instance, they arrested the corregidor of Murcia for disrespect, the *diputats* of Perpignan for insults and the vicar general of Saragossa for arresting a commissary, and they made the entire city council of Tarragona together with the dean and chapter of the cathedral attend mass as penitents with candles in their hands, to atone for not letting the inquisitors into their city when fleeing from a plague in Barcelona.[8]

Recent commentators have insisted that the Inquisition, thanks to its privileges and dual jurisdiction, served the interests of royal absolutism.[9] It was certainly an advantage to the king that over all the Spanish realms, half of which rejoiced in provincial liberties (fueros) which freed them effectively from royal control, the only tribunal to exercise unquestioned authority was the Inquisition, and because of this the crown was obliged to make use of it when all other methods of coercion failed. In 1507, for example, Ferdinand was pursuing the famous son of Pope Alexander VI, Cesare Borgia, into Navarre. Failing to secure his victim by any other means, Ferdinand persuaded the Inquisition to initiate proceedings against him for blasphemy, atheism and materialism. But death in battle cheated both the Holy Office and the King of Aragon of their prey. In subsequent years there were continual conflicts between the Inquisition and the secular authorities in the crown of Aragon. But there appears to be no evidence whatever that royal authority benefited from the situation.

The undoubted hostility of the Inquisition to the fueros was put plainly in a statement of 1565: 'there is no point in saying that [the actions of the Inquisition] are against the fueros and laws of the realm, since *the Holy Office is not subject to the fueros when these are out of step with the law*'.[10] In practice the inquisitors were careful not to overstep the limits of prudence, yet nothing could efface from the minds of the Aragonese the feeling that the Inquisition was an alien institution. Though the Catalan language appears to have been used generally in trials of the first few decades, for example, after the 1560s the rule was enforced that 'all the Inquisitions must follow a uniform procedure, and in matters of faith the Castilian language must be used'.[11] This was merely an administrative convenience, for there is massive evidence that the Counter Reformation was precisely the period when the ecclesiastical authorities did their utmost to promote knowledge of the Catalan and Basque languages; but the shadow of Castile remained.

In Valencia, conflicts with the Inquisition centred on familiars and Moriscos: in both matters the nobility contested inquisitorial jurisdiction. In Aragon the Cortes of Monzón in 1564 claimed that 'the inquisitors publish edicts on whatever they please and against everybody, on matters outside their jurisdiction, and against all the rules and laws of this kingdom. For many years now they have begun arresting many people who have not been nor are heretics, some for having quarrelled with servants of their familiars, others for debts and petty causes.'[12] The conflict between the Inquisition and the Aragonese elite arose in large measure out of the Morisco problem, but became broad-based and bitter: by 1566 the diputados of Aragon were demanding that 'the inquisitors should not be able to issue edicts without the approval of the ordinary'. By 1591, during the Antonio Pérez troubles, the rebels were demanding 'that there should be no Inquisition in Aragon, or if there is one the inquisitors and their ministers should not be Castilians'.

Catalonia, of all the realms, was notoriously the most hostile to the Inquisition. In 1566 the diputats of Perpignan arrested and imprisoned the officials of the Inquisition after a dispute: the diputat Mossen Caldes de Santa Fe led the prisoners through the city, the Inquisition later complained, 'to the sound of trumpets, and held celebrations and banquets as though he had gained a triumph and done something heroic'. The quarrel extended to Barcelona in 1568 when the Catalans refused to accept the concordia of that year. The persistent opposition of the Catalans to the pretensions of the Inquisition was never in theory successful: on the other hand, although the inquisitors scored in every skirmish, they never won the war.[13] In Catalonia the Inquisition was always a despised institution enjoying little more than the passive support of the elite and the people.

None of these conflicts was sought by the crown, and from none of them did the crown gain any advantage: it is therefore unconvincing to present the Inquisition as a tool used by the monarchy against the fueros. In a few moments of national crisis the Holy Office certainly played a role, but only a marginal one. When the revolution of 1640 broke out in Catalonia, for example, it was the Inquisitor General himself who suggested that his tribunal should begin proceedings against the rebels.[14] The Catalans drove out the Castilian Inquisition and in September 1643 re-established the old papal Inquisition. This was suppressed when Barcelona fell in 1652, and the Castilian tribunal was reintroduced in August 1653. During the war of the Spanish Succession from 1702 to 1714, when the provinces of Aragon broke away from Castilian tutelage, it was

the Inquisition that threatened censures against those guilty of treas-
onable opinions. An inquisitorial edict of 1706 ordered penitents
to denounce confessors who told them in the confessional that
Philip v was not the rightful King of Spain.[15] These measures were
in the realm of threat rather than action. The tribunal rarely took
any action which could even remotely be described as political, and
it would consequently be quite false to regard it as an instrument
of State. Philip II is said to have claimed on one occasion that
'twenty clerics of the Inquisition keep my realms in peace'.[16] This
flattering claim, repeated often by the Inquisition itself, certainly
referred to nothing more than religious peace, and there was no
possible ground on which the tribunal could maintain that it had
helped to keep the people of Spain subservient to the crown.

The first great case in which the Inquisition played a nakedly
political role was that of Antonio Pérez. In all its ramifications the
story of Antonio Pérez concerns matters of personal, national and
international intrigue and rivalry: it has been told repeatedly, and
at last definitively by Gregorio Marañón.[17] In 1571 Pérez became secretary of state to Philip II: two years later his patron and the chief
minister of Philip, Ruy Gómez, Prince of Eboli, died. Pérez thereby
obtained one of the most powerful posts in the monarchy and also
inherited leadership of the court faction formerly led by Ruy Gómez.
A contemporary observed that Pérez 'climbed so high that His
Majesty would not do anything save what the said Antonio Pérez
marked out for him. Whenever His Majesty even went out in his
coach, Antonio Pérez went with him. When the pope, my lord Don
Juan of Austria, or other lords required anything of the king, they
had recourse to Antonio Pérez and by his means obtained what they
solicited of His Majesty.' Another said, 'Great men worshipped him;
ministers admitted his superiority; the king loved him.'[18] Philip
depended for advice and policy almost entirely on this brilliant and
sinister young man of converso origin whose success enabled him
to live as a great lord and whose charm led him into an intimate
and still mysterious liaison with the Princess of Eboli, the beautiful
one-eyed widow of Ruy Gómez.

Ambition eventually led to Pérez's ruin. At the centre of the monarchy he held the king's secrets and controlled the money offered
by pretendants to favours. His long hand stretched as far as Flanders, where at that moment the king's half-brother, the famous Don
Juan of Austria, was acting both as governor and as pacifier of
rebellion. While claiming to sympathize with Don Juan's moderate

policy and keeping up a correspondence with his secretary Juan de Escobedo, to whom he entrusted several state secrets, Pérez also seems to have opened up negotiations with the Dutch rebels in order to promote his own interests. Eventually rivalry with Escobedo and distrust of Don Juan led Pérez to adopt a hostile attitude towards the two, and he began to influence Philip surreptitiously against his half-brother.

Philip's secret jealousy of the martial victor of Lepanto needed no encouragement. Suspicious of the way his plans for Flanders were being blocked by Madrid, Don Juan sent Escobedo to Spain in 1577 to make enquiries. On arriving at the court it became clear to Escobedo that Pérez had been playing a double game with his master and with the king. He began to look around for evidence to condemn the royal secretary. But Pérez had already managed to convince Philip that Escobedo was the malign influence in the affairs of Flanders and in the end he persuaded the king that the only solution was to eliminate Don Juan's secretary. Reasons of state supplied Philip with the necessary moral justification for judicial murder, and he gave his approval to any action Pérez might take. First poison was tried, but this failed. Then on the night of Easter Monday, 31 March 1578, hired assassins came up to Escobedo as he rode with a few friends through the narrow, dark streets of Madrid, and ran him through the body.

Popular rumour instantly pointed to Pérez as the assassin, and Escobedo's family, aided by Pérez's rival in the secretariat of state, Mateo Vázquez, demanded justice for the murdered man. Despite all the rumours, it is interesting to note that Cardinal Gaspar Quiroga, Archbishop of Toledo and Inquisitor General, 'did not hesitate to face public opinion by showing an ostentatious liking for Pérez and his group. On the day after the imprisonment of Pérez and La Eboli, when all Madrid singled them out as responsible for the crime, Don Gaspar visited Antonio's wife and children, and offered money to them, as also to the Princess's children.'[19] The imprisonment did not occur immediately. Philip was torn between covering up for Pérez, which would mean that he had approved of the murder, and punishing Pérez, a course which was even more dangerous because of what the latter was capable of revealing. At this juncture Don Juan died and his state papers were sent to Spain. On reading them Philip discovered that Pérez had deceived him and that his brother and Escobedo were guiltless of the imputations cast against them. Disillusion on the king's part grew into dislike and then into hatred.

He encouraged Mateo Vázquez in his attacks on Pérez, and then in 1579 summoned Cardinal Granvelle from abroad to become his chief minister. Pérez sensed the change in Philip's attitude, and prepared for flight. But on the night of 28 July 1579, the very day that Granvelle reached Madrid, Pérez and the Princess of Eboli were arrested.

It was not until June 1584 that the charges against Pérez were drawn up by the prosecutor. In these he was accused of selling posts, receiving bribes and betraying state secrets. The Escobedo affair was left aside as though it were irrelevant, a sure sign of the king's intervention. The investigation that followed led to Pérez being sentenced to two years' imprisonment and an enormous fine. He was still subjected to mild treatment, however, principally because he had in his possession state papers which incriminated the king. His refusal to surrender the papers led to firmer treatment by the government, and in 1588 an accusation of murder was presented against him. After two years of rigorous imprisonment, in February 1590 he was put to the torture and ordered to state the reasons which had made him advise the king to have Escobedo eliminated. His statement under torture produced an implicit confession of responsibility for Escobedo's death, but gave no concrete reasons for his advice to the king which had led to the assassination. Philip could now ease his conscience with the consideration that Pérez had misled him and therefore bore the sole guilt for the murder. All this time the Cardinal Inquisitor had continued to protect the secretary. He sent Pérez advice, guided the tactics of his defence, kept him informed of proceedings in the Royal Council, and knew of (and perhaps assisted in) his plans of escape to Aragon. Escape had now become necessary since all hope was lost after Pérez's confession. In April 1590, with the help of several highly placed friends, Pérez escaped from prison in Madrid and rode across country to the borders of Aragon.

There he was protected from the king's hand by the fueros. Once he had set foot in Aragon the crown of Castile was powerless to touch him. There was only one course open to Philip – to use the Inquisition to get at Pérez. And it was Quiroga, as Inquisitor General, who was forced to set in motion what Marañón calls the 'last and cruellest prosecution against his former friend'. Safe in Aragon, Pérez was lodged for his own security by the Aragonese authorities in the Justiciar's prison at Saragossa. From this vantage-point he began a campaign to win over Aragon to his cause. In Madrid, meanwhile, sentence of death was pronounced against him. Philip's recourse to the Inquisition encountered some difficulty at first, because it was necessary to find Pérez guilty of heresy before charges could be preferred against him. But the royal confessor, Father Chaves – who seventeen years before had taken part in the prosecution of Carranza, and who had repeatedly given Philip his spiritual approval for acts carried out in the name of *raison d'état* – now managed to find evidence of heresy in some of the more innocuous expletives used by Pérez. Of one sentence where Pérez wagered his word against God's nose, Chaves noted: 'This proposition ... is suspect of the Badian heresy which says that God is corporal and has human members'. Such nonsense was supported by other testimony, which ruled that Pérez's assumed intention to escape abroad from prison, in so far as it included a plan to escape across the Protestant state of Béarn, involved heresy because it implied consorting with heretics. Armed with these fabricated accusations, the Inquisition proceeded to move against Pérez.

On 24 May 1591 the inquisitors in Saragossa had Pérez transferred from the Justiciar's prison to their own in the Aljafería, after the Justiciar had been induced to sign a warrant for the removal. By now, however, Pérez's propaganda against the king had made him a popular hero in Saragossa, and no sooner had the news of the inquisitorial action been made known than a vast mob thronged the streets calling for Pérez's release and threatening the authorities. In the ensuing tumult the viceroy of Aragon, the Marquis of Almenara, received wounds from which he died a fortnight later. But Pérez was victoriously returned to the Justiciar's prison by the mob, which 'went all the way calling out, "Liberty!" And he cried out with them'.[20] The May riots were repeated on 24 September, when once again the Inquisition claimed jurisdiction over the prisoner and tried to remove him to the Aljafería. After this occasion, when Pérez was set free by the rebels in Saragossa, the whole political situation changed. The Inquisition had failed in its immediate purpose and a viceroy had been murdered by rebels harbouring a fugitive. Philip therefore resorted to armed force. In October 1591 Castilian troops entered Aragon, subdued Saragossa and executed the Justiciar and other rebels. Pérez fled abroad to Béarn, attempted an unsuccessful invasion in 1592 and then went into exile in France and England, still maintaining his campaign against Philip II. .What always remained transparently obvious was that there was no truth in the charge of heresy levelled by the Inquisition against Pérez, so much so that in 1607 Pope Paul v issued a brief absolving Pérez from these alleged charges. In 1611, the year of Pérez's death in Paris, the papal nuncio there certified that he lived and died a Catholic.

There is little evidence of the Inquisition being used for political purposes in the seventeenth century. The one outstanding case of Jerónimo de Villanueva, who enjoyed power and influence under Olivares and fell soon after his master, was based on legitimate charges arising out of the illuminism of the nuns of the convent of San Plácido.[21] The prolonged persecution of Fray Froilan Díaz, whom we have discussed already, concerned obscure issues which were neither religious nor political.

In Castile jurisdictional conflicts were no less serious than in the fuero provinces. Several times in the course of the seventeenth century the council of Castile urged the king to take action, notably in proceedings in 1620, 1622, 1631 and 1639, when the inquisitors were accused of 'enjoying the privilege of afflicting the soul with censures, life with adversity, and honour with exposure'.[22] It is significant that most of these protests occurred in the crisis years of the century,[23] when the statutes of limpieza and other aspects of policy were called in question. Opposition to the Inquisition in Castile was normally led by representatives of royal authority; by, that is, high courts, corregidors and government councils in Madrid. This confirms our previous conclusion that the tribunal was not significantly exploited in order to extend royal power. The few occasions when the crown made use of inquisitorial officials, in order to check smuggling at the frontiers or the distribution of false coin,[24] were marginal and temporary.

Endless clashes between the Inquisition and other Castilian courts reached a climax at the end of the seventeenth century.[25] The Chancillería of Granada, a supreme court of the realm, had been humiliated by the Inquisition in a dispute in 1623, but in 1682 it was caught up in yet another typically petty case over a secretary of the Inquisition who had ordered the arrest of a noisy neighbour. This time the city council, the archbishop and the Chancillería combined against the Holy Office with such effectiveness that the crown ordered the banishment until further notice of the inquisitors. At the same time the council of Castile protested energetically against the abuses committed by the Inquisition. The final straw came in 1696, when the Diputación of Catalonia entered into conflict with the inquisitor of Barcelona, Bartolomé Sanz y Muñoz, and complained that 'the disorders in this tribunal arise in part because the inquisitors are normally foreigners, from another province, who have no understanding of the temperament of our people'. Sanz was deported from Catalonia by royal order. As an immediate result, the government in Madrid set up a special committee consisting of two members from each of the six leading councils. On 12 May 1696 this body issued a damning report on the abuses of jurisdiction committed by the tribunal:

> There is no vassal free of its power whom it does not treat as an immediate subordinate, subjecting him to its mandates, censures, fines and prisons; no casual offence or light incivility to its servants which it does not avenge and punish as a crime against religion; not satisfied with exempting the persons and property of its officials from all public taxes and contributions, it even wishes to claim the immunity of not having criminals arrested in its houses; in the style of its letters it uses and affects ways to decrease respect for the royal judges and even respect for the authority of superior magistrates ...[26]

It then went on to prove that precedent fully favoured complete royal authority over the Inquisition in all matters not pertaining to faith. Although the report was not acted upon, the attitude of Philip v in the subsequent reign made it clear that he wished to subject the tribunal more closely to royal control, and regalism came to be the official policy of the State with regard to the Inquisition.

14

The Inquisition in History

O duro Oficio, quién te llama Santo?

João Pinto Delgado *Autobiografía* (1633–4)

During the eighteenth century the Inquisition became openly political in its hostility to the Enlightenment, and lost the little support
it had enjoyed among the progressive elite in Spain. In the epoch
following the French Revolution, one of the first acts of the French
regime that occupied Spain in 1808 was to abolish the Holy Office
on 4 December. The patriotic forces in the country were represented
at the Cortes of Cadiz (1810), which on 22 February 1813 also
decreed the abolition of the Inquisition, by a margin of ninety votes
against sixty. It was an act that provoked considerable opposition
from traditionalists, and on 21 July 1814 Ferdinand VII restored
the tribunal, but in name rather than in reality. Effectively the Holy
Office was now moribund. On 9 March 1820 the king was forced
by liberal opposition to abolish it yet again. The final decree of
suppression, issued by the government of Queen Isabella II on 15
July 1834, was little more than a formality. From this date the
Inquisition ceased to exist in the Spanish monarchy.

'In the present liberal state of knowledge', wrote Prescott in
1837, at the beginning of a chapter on the Inquisition in his *History
of the Reign of Ferdinand and Isabella*, 'we look with disgust on the
pretensions of any human being, however exalted, to invade the
sacred rights of conscience, inalienably possessed by every man.' A
later writer, conversant with an age where liberalism has repeatedly
been eclipsed and the human conscience consistently invaded and
perverted, would perhaps look on the Inquisition from a rather
different point of view. There is little justification for regarding the
tribunal purely as an instrument of fanatical intolerance, and the

Inquisition must consequently be treated not merely as a chapter in the history of intolerance but as a phase in the social and religious development of Spain. It would be difficult to prove that religious bigotry alone was responsible for the various events we have already outlined in this book. The intolerance of the Spanish Inquisition becomes meaningful only if related to a wide complex of historical factors, and the religious issue was not always the most prominent or relevant of these.

Foreign propaganda from the Reformation onwards was justified in insisting on the religious dimension. In England John Foxe warned his contemporaries that

> this dreadful engine of tyranny may at any time be introduced into a country where the Catholics have the ascendancy; and hence how careful ought we to be, who are not cursed with such an arbitrary court, to prevent its introduction.[1]

For Foxe and others the Inquisition was just another example of the evils of Rome, and in their works the tribunal was presented as the supreme institution of intolerance:

> When the inquisitors have taken umbrage against an innocent person, all expedients are used to facilitate condemnation; false oaths and testimonies are employed to find the accused guilty; and all laws and institutions are sacrificed to satiate the most bigoted vengeance.[2]

Protestant pens depicted the struggle of heretics as one for freedom from a tyrannical faith. Wherever Catholicism triumphed, they claimed, not only religious but civil liberty was extinguished. The Reformation, according to this interpretation, brought about the liberation of the human spirit from the fetters of darkness and superstition. Propaganda along these lines proved to be strikingly effective in the context of the political conflicts of the sixteenth century, and there were always refugees from persecution to lend substance to the story. As late as the mid-nineteenth century one of the best examples of such propaganda could be found in John Motley's brilliant history of *The Rise of the Dutch Republic*, first published in London in 1855. Motley adhered close enough to the truth to appear convincing, yet writing half a century after Llorente he could say this of the Spanish Inquisition:

> It taught the savages of India and America to shudder at the name of Christianity. The fear of its introduction froze the earlier heretics of Italy, France and Germany into orthodoxy. It was a court owning allegiance to no temporal authority, superior to all other tribunals. It was a bench

of monks without appeal, having its familiars in every house, diving into the secrets of every fireside, judging and executing its horrible decrees without responsibility. It condemned not deeds but thoughts. It affected to descend into individual conscience, and to punish the crimes which it pretended to discover. Its process was reduced to a horrible simplicity. It arrested on suspicion, tortured till confession, and then punished by fire. Two witnesses, and those to separate facts, were sufficient to consign the victim to a loathsome dungeon. Here he was sparingly supplied with food, forbidden to speak, or even to sing – to which pastime it could hardly be thought he would feel much inclination – and then left to himself till famine and misery should break his spirit. When that time was supposed to have arrived, he was examined. Did he confess and forswear his heresy, whether actually innocent or not, he might then assume the sacred shirt, and escape with confiscation of all his property. Did he persist in the avowal of his innocence, two witnesses sent him to the stake, one to the rack. He was informed of the testimony against him, but never confronted with the witness. The accuser might be his son, father, or the wife of his bosom, for all were enjoined, under the death penalty, to inform the inquisitors of every suspicious word which might fall from their nearest relatives. The indictment being thus supported, the prisoner was tried by torture. The rack was the court of justice; the criminal's only advocate was his fortitude – for the nominal counsellor, who was permitted no communication with the prisoner, and was furnished neither with documents nor with power to procure evidence, was a puppet, aggravating the lawlessness of the proceedings by the mockery of legal forms. The torture took place at midnight, in a gloomy dungeon, dimly lighted by torches. The victim – whether man, matron, or tender virgin – was stripped naked and stretched upon the wooden bench. Water, weights, fires, pulleys, screws – all the apparatus by which the sinews could be strained without cracking, the bones bruised without breaking, and the body racked exquisitely without giving up its ghost – was now put into operation. The executioner, enveloped in a black robe from head to foot, with his eyes glaring at his victim through holes cut in the hood which muffled his face, practised successively all the forms of torture which the devilish ingenuity of the monks had invented. The imagination sickens when striving to keep pace with these dreadful realities.[3]

Side by side with this presentation of the Inquisition as a threat to human liberty went a more practical consideration. The tribunal was looked upon as the great instrument of that enemy of the Protestant religion, Spain. Attacks on it, and stories of its horrors, became part of the machine of anti-Spanish propaganda in western Europe, where some Catholic powers, no less than Protestant, were beginning to dispute Spanish hegemony. In the Netherlands it was bruited about that Spain intended to introduce the Inquisition as a means of subduing the country.

In fact, the Netherlands already possessed an Inquisition of its own, which Philip II himself confessed was 'more merciless than the one here',[4] and the rumour was little more than a legend employed to discredit Spain and incite rebellion. William of Orange in his famous *Apologia* of 1581, written in reply to a decree outlawing him, turned the issue into a brilliant exercise in anti-Spanish propaganda. The execution of heretics, he claimed, was a natural occupation for bloodthirsty Spaniards: 'the brightness of the fires wherein they have tormented so many poor Christians, was never delightful or pleasant to mine eyes, as it hath rejoyc'd the sight of the Duke of Alba and the Spaniards'. Then came the unkind cut: 'I will no more wonder at that which all the world believeth: to wit, that the greatest part of the Spaniards, and especially those that count themselves noblemen, are of the blood of the Moors and Jews'.[5]

To a racially sensitive *hidalgo*, this was abuse indeed. A legend of Spanish cruelty and barbarism had to be created if Europe were to sympathize with the revolt of the Netherlands, and the Inquisition was the most natural choice of weapon. How effective such propaganda was, is shown by the universal fear in Protestant countries that Spanish or Catholic domination anywhere would result in the introduction of the notorious tribunal. During the religious wars in France, the Huguenots feared that Henry II, in concert with Philip II of Spain, planned to establish a native Inquisition. William of Orange and the Count of Egmont were so disturbed about this that they asked Cardinal Granvelle in 1561 to deny the report.[6] Yet apart from his Italian states Philip had little serious intention of exporting the Spanish Inquisition. Even in England, where he exercised some influence as husband of the queen, no steps were ever taken to introduce the tribunal. The truth was that most European countries already had their own machinery for dealing with heretics, and had no need for outside help. Besides this, the Spanish tribunal was not by nature a primarily anti-Protestant body, and would have needed substantial modification if introduced into some European states. Finally, the foreign policy of Philip II was by no means consistently anti-Protestant, so that the picture of Spain as a rabidly Catholic power distorts the reality of sixteenth-century international politics.[7]

The many pamphlets and works written since the sixteenth

century on the horrors of the Spanish Inquisition would require considerable space to be studied adequately: the picture they all paint can, however, be easily guessed. Perhaps the most important of all the propagandists was Reinaldo González Montano, a Spanish victim of and refugee from the Holy Office, who published abroad in Heidelberg in 1567 his *Sanctae Inquisitionis Hispanicae Artes aliquot detectae ac palam traductae*. The vivid style and imagination of its author made this book an immediate international success. It was translated into all the major languages of western Europe, went through several editions in various forms, and served as the basis for further literature on the subject. The year after its appearance it was translated into English by a government official and published with a dedication to the Archbishop of Canterbury, Matthew Parker. As time went on, the legend grew out of all proportion, thanks to the efforts of zealous Protestants to keep alive the cause for which their martyrs suffered. To a nineteenth-century edition of Foxe's *Book of Martyrs*, a certain Reverend Ingram Cobbin MA added the following account of the Inquisition, enlivening it with detailed falsehoods with which even Foxe had not sullied his original narrative. During the Napoleonic wars in Spain, the Reverend Cobbin assured his readers, the French liberating troops broke into the secret cells of the tribunal in Madrid:

> Here they found the instruments of torture, of every kind which the ingenuity of men or devils could invent. The first instrument noticed was a machine by which the victim was confined and then, beginning with the fingers, all the joints in the hands, arms and body were broken and drawn one after another, until the sufferer died. The second [was the water torture]. The third was an infernal machine, laid horizontally, to which the victim was bound; the machine then being placed between two scores of knives so fixed that by turning the machine with a crank the flesh of the sufferer was all torn from his limbs into small pieces. The fourth surpassed the others in fiendish ingenuity. Its exterior was a large doll, richly dressed and having the appearance of a beautiful woman, with her arms extended ready to embrace her victim. A semicircle was drawn around her, and the person who passed over this fatal mark touched a spring which caused the diabolical engine to open; its arms immediately clasped him, and a thousand knives cut him in as many pieces.[8]

To Spaniards such grotesque misrepresentation only proved that the outside world was interested, against all the facts, in preserving the Black Legend (*Leyenda Negra*) of an obscurantist, cruel and fanatical Spain. The Inquisition took its place beside all the other historical iniquities attributed to Spaniards – the wars of religion, the destruction of the American Indians, the expulsion of the Jews and Moriscos – and probably outdid them all in the volume of polemical literature through the centuries.[9]

No small part in this can be attributed to the Italians who, in their struggle against Spanish imperialism in Italy, gave an impetus to the Black Legend long before the Dutch revolt stirred the conscience of Protestant Europe.[10] It was in the Italian provinces of the Spanish crown that the greatest and most successful revolts against the Inquisition occurred. The risings of 1511 and 1516 in Sicily were caused partly by popular hatred of the tribunal's familiars. Ferdinand the Catholic attempted to introduce the Spanish Inquisition into Naples, which already had its own episcopal Inquisition, but effective protests blocked his bid. The issue did not subside, and both in 1547 and 1564 there were risings in the province because of rumours that the Spanish tribunal was going to be established. Similarly, in 1563 Philip II had to admit defeat when universal opposition greeted his attempt to replace the episcopal Inquisition in Milan by a Spanish one. Italian 'nationalism', and not any particular fear of the Spanish tribunal, was the driving force behind this hostility.

The same reason makes it sometimes difficult to accept Italian accounts of the Inquisition at face value, and the very valuable reports of the Venetian ambassadors share this defect: that they invariably depict the tribunal as a despotic body in control of a hypocritical nation. In 1525 ambassador Contarini claimed that everyone trembled before the Holy Office. In 1557 ambassador Badoero spoke of the terror caused by its procedure. In 1563 ambassador Tiepolo said that everyone shuddered at its name, as it had supreme authority over the property, life, honour and even the souls of men. In 1565 ambassador Soranzo reported that its authority transcended that of the king.[11] These accounts were far from being 'unbiased reports', as Lea claims them to be. They were subjective appraisals from which hostile undertones were seldom absent. Francesco Guicciardini, as Florentine ambassador to Ferdinand, was also representative of Italian opinion when he described the Spaniards as 'very religious in externals and outward show, but not so in fact'.[12] Almost the same words were used by the Venetian Tiepolo in 1563. Such hypocrisy in religion, taken hand in hand with the existence of the Inquisition, meant to Italians that the tribunal was created not for religious purity, but simply to rob the Jews. Some conclusion of this sort was certainly held by the prelates of the Holy See whenever they intervened in favour of the conversos. Moreover, the racialism of the Spanish authorities was scorned in Italy, where the Jewish community led a comparatively tranquil existence. As the Spanish ambassador at Rome reported in 1652:

> In Spain it is held in great horror to be descended from a heretic or a Jew, but here they laugh at these matters, and at us, because we concern ourselves with them.[13]

This lack of love between two leading Latin countries is of some importance because it shows that the tide of opinion in Europe was not confined to Protestant countries only, and that contemporary Catholic sentiment could also be added to the general attitude.

What did Spaniards themselves think of the Inquisition? There can be no doubt that the people as a whole gave their ready support to its existence. The tribunal was, after all, not a despotic body imposed on them tyrannically, but a logical expression of the social prejudices prevalent in their midst. It was created to deal with a problem of heresy, and as long as the problem was deemed to exist people seemed to accept it. The Inquisition was probably no more loved or hated than the police are in our time: in a society where there was no other general policing body, people took their grievances to it and exploited it to pay off personal scores. By the same token, it was on the receiving end of frequent hostility and resentment; but at every moment the inquisitors were convinced that the people were with them, and with good reason. 'It is only the lords and leading persons who wage this war against the Holy Office', they complained in Aragon in 1566, 'and not the people.'[14] At no time in *ancien régime* Spain – neither in the revolts of 1520 nor the urban risings of 1648 nor in any other act of social unrest – did the populace attack the Inquisition; only in March 1820 did they for the first time break into the tribunal's palaces, by now half-empty buildings from which a handful of startled prisoners were liberated.

This degree of support must not be misinterpreted. Both defenders and opponents of the Inquisition have accepted without question the image of an omniscient, omnipotent tribunal whose fingers reached into every corner of the land. The extravagant rhetoric on both sides has been one of the major obstacles to understanding. For the Inquisition to have been as powerful as suggested, the fifty or so inquisitors in Spain would need to have had an extensive bureaucracy, a reliable system of informers, regular income and the firm co-operation of the secular and ecclesiastical authorities. At no time did it have any of these. From what we have seen of the flimsy network of familiars, the financial difficulties of the inquisitors and the perennial conflicts with all other jurisdictions (especially in the fuero realms), we can conclude that the real impact of the Inquisition was, after the first crisis decades, so marginal to the daily lives of Spaniards that over broad areas of Spain – principally in the rural districts – it was little more than an irrelevance. Outside the major cities, there were towns which saw the inquisitors maybe once every ten years, or even once in a century. The people supported it, therefore, not because it weighed on them heavily and obligated them, but for precisely the opposite reason: it was seldom seen, and even less often heard. It has frequently been suggested that the survival of the proverb '*Con el Rey y con la Santa Inquisición, chitón!*' ('On the king and the Holy Office, not a word!')[15] is testimony to the power of the Holy Office to silence criticism. This suggestion not only betrays a curious belief that Spaniards are unable or unwilling to criticize those who rule over them: it is also unhistorical. The archives of the Inquisition contain thousands of cases of forthright criticism by ordinary Spaniards, not subversive radicals wishing to abolish the institution (though many did so wish) but ordinary citizens objecting to bullying familiars, greedy inquisitors and corrupt personnel. Very many Spaniards, neither of Jewish nor of Moorish origin, hated the Holy Office. Like any police system, it was not loved; but Spaniards felt that its continuation was a guarantee of true religion.

At every stage there was criticism and opposition, which varied in character from generation to generation. Early critics such as Pulgar and Talavera could remember the tolerant aspects of convivencia. Alonso de Virués subsequently also criticized intolerance and those 'who spare neither prison nor knout nor chains nor the axe; for such is the effect of these horrible means, that the torments they inflict on the body can never change the disposition of the soul'.[16] Juan de Mariana, a supporter of the Inquisition, criticized both forced conversion[17] and the belief in limpieza. By the eighteenth century, inquisitors like Abad y Sierra were convinced that fundamental changes in structure were needed. The important point is that there was no wholly unquestioning support, either at the popular or the elite level.

Contact with the outside world was one of the most potent causes of growing disillusionment with the Inquisition, as Catholics came to realize that coercion was not inevitable in religion. We have the opinion of a pharmacist arrested by the Inquisition at Laguna (Tenerife) in 1707. He is reported to have said:

> that one could live in France because there there did not exist the poverty and subjection that today exists in Spain and Portugal, since in France they do not try to find out nor do they make a point of knowing who everyone is and what religion he has and professes. And so he who lives properly and is of good character may become what he wishes.[18]

A generation later in 1741, another native of the Canaries, the Marquis de la Ville de San Andrés, echoed precisely the same sentiments when he praised Paris, where life was free and unrestricted, 'and no one asks where you are going, or questions who you are, nor at Easter does the priest ask if you have been to confession'.[19] In 1812 in the Cortes of Cadiz, the priest Ruiz Padrón, who had travelled in the United States and knew Benjamin Franklin, rejected the Inquisition on the grounds that it was unnecessary to the practice of the faith. This was the spirit that threatened to splinter the defences of the closed society. It was, in one way, an urge to freedom, but in another way it was a demand for justice. The fate of the Jews and Moors continued to be on the conscience of intelligent statesmen. When José Carvajal began to interest himself in the attacks directed by Salucio against the statutes of limpieza, his main preoccupation was 'the cruel impiety with which they have treated those who were outside the Catholic religion, barring all human doors of entry against them'.[20] This was in 1751. A similar approach was adopted by Jovellanos in 1798. For him the first blame to be laid against the Inquisition was on account of the conversos:

> From this arose the infamy that covered descendants of these conversos, who were reputed infamous by public opinion. The laws upheld this and approved the statutes of limpieza de sangre, which kept out so many innocent people not only from posts of honour and trust but also from entering churches, colleges, convents and even unions and trade guilds. From this came the perpetuation of hatred not only against the Inquisition but against religion itself.[21]

Jovellanos argued that the injustices committed against a whole section of society by the Inquisition now needed to be remedied. The tribunal had lost all theoretical justification for its existence, since the modern threat to religion came no longer from Jews and Moriscos and heretics but from unbelievers. Against these the tribunal would be of little avail, since its ministers were ignorant and incapable. The time had come to get rid of such a superfluous body, to right the injustices of history, and to restore to the bishops their old powers over heresy.

Despite this, Jovellanos and his other Catholic colleagues in the government and in the ranks of the nobility were not radical revolutionaries. Their desire for reform, for a change in the nature of society, was limited by the concern for stability. The Catholic liberals who opposed the Inquisition were unwilling to look too far. Jovellanos wrote to his friend Jardine: 'You approve of the spirit of rebellion; I do not. I disapprove of it openly and am far from believing that it carries the seal of merit.'[22] Because of this, the attitude of Catholics as such towards the Inquisition ceased to be of great consequence, and was lost among the waves of turbulence created by those whose hatred of the Holy Office was only part of their distrust of organized religion.

Because the Inquisition from its origins was a conflictive institution, its history has always been polemical. The rule of secrecy, unfortunately, gagged the mouths of its own spokesmen and aided those of its detractors, with the result that for its entire career the propaganda war was won effortlessly by its enemies. Foreign writing remained and to some extent still remains affected by the inevitable bias. The discovery of the riches of inquisitorial documentation, and its exploitation first by Llorente and then by Henry Charles Lea, has helped to restore the balance of information but has also created new dangers. Scholars are in danger of studying the Inquisition in isolation from all the other dimensions of State and society, as though the tribunal were somehow a self-explanatory phenomenon; as a result old misconceptions are being reinforced and the Inquisition is once again being assumed to have played a central role in religion, politics, culture and the economy. It is timely to recall Menéndez Pelayo's satire on those who have blamed the tribunal for all the ills of Spain.

> Why was there no industry in Spain? Because of the Inquisition. Why are we Spaniards lazy? Because of the Inquisition. Why are there bullfights in Spain? Because of the Inquisition. Why do Spaniards take a *siesta*? Because of the Inquisition.[23]

Undue concentration on the institution of the Holy Office, to the exclusion of other relevant factors, has been and continues to be perhaps the biggest single obstacle to understanding the phenom-enon. The economic problems of the country, for example, have been blamed on the Holy Office. The persecution of conversos and the expulsion of the Jews led, we are told, to the impoverishment and decay of Spain, and the destruction of its middle class. Religious persecution led to the decay of trade with Protestant powers and thus to a collapse in Spanish power and wealth. The absurdity of the first proposition has been touched on above (chapter 2). The truth about trade with foreigners, both Catholic and Protestant, is that it increased rather than declined during the lifetime of the Inquisition, which in any case never interfered in trade policy. Nor did the tribunal have any influence on industrial policy: foreign Protestant manufacturers were as a rule forbidden to settle in Spain, but numerous Flemish and other Catholic manufacturers were ac-tively encouraged, and it would be foolish to suggest that only the excluded Protestants were efficient.

It is more relevant to ask whether the Inquisition soaked up the wealth of the Spanish people, since in fact many contemporaries complained of the greed of inquisitors. The persecution of con-verso traders was without doubt harmful to certain cities. Under Charles II a Mallorcan noble in 1679 protested that the persecution of the Chuetas 'would result in the gravest damage to and destruc-tion of the commerce that used to exist in Mallorca'; in 1683 the city of Murcia complained of 'the scarcity suffered in this city from all the property of merchants, the houses and revenue confiscated by the Holy Office'; in 1694 Antequera claimed that 'the Inquisition had driven out considerable capital by castigating those who owned it'.[24] Even if local complaints like this could be substantiated, it would be difficult to prove any long-term damage; nor, indeed, did the Inquisition benefit, for by the eighteenth century it was an impoverished body.

There has been more dispute over the cultural impact of the Inquisition than over any other single issue. 'It would seem super-fluous to insist', argued Lea, 'that a system of severe repression of thought by all the instrumentalities of Inquisition and state, is an ample explanation of the decadence of Spanish learning and litera-ture.'[25] For the English Catholic historian, Lord Acton, the injury inflicted on literature by the Inquisition was 'the most obvious and conspicuous fact of modern history'.[26] Spanish condemnation has been even more uncompromising: nineteenth-century liberals were ready to blame every failure in Spanish history on the Inquisition.

These views, based on the belief that the Inquisition had omnipotent control over culture, are quite simply mistaken. Spanish literature was barely touched by the Indices of prohibited books, and the post-Renaissance theatre – which to the largely illiterate population was the most direct form of culture – was not at all affected. There was a whole world of literature in which the Holy Office never interfered, despite the promptings of Alvar Gómez de Castro and Juan de Mariana. The romances of chivalry which made up the staple reading of ordinary Spaniards at home and the campfire reading of adventurers on the American frontier – between 1501 and 1650 a total of 267 editions of chivalric novels were issued, two-thirds of them in the early sixteenth century[27] – were never proscribed, though often attacked. The vast riches of scholarship opened up by the imperial experience, during the Inquisition's great period, were never affected: the histories of Herrera, Oviedo, Díaz and Gómara, the natural history of Sahagún, the treatises on mathematics, botany, metallurgy and shipbuilding that flourished under Philip ii, never came within the ambit of the inquisitors.

The wholly absurd image of a Holy Office glowering over the intellectual labours of Spanish scholars, must be rejected in favour of the dull reality: after the thunderclap of the 1559 Index, which was directed mainly against vernacular piety, no attacks were mounted against Spanish literature and not one in a hundred Spanish writers came into conflict with the Inquisition. Indeed, long after the measures of 1558–9 Spain continued to have an active intellectual life based on a world experience vaster than that of any other European nation.[28] Spain's contribution to navigation, geography, natural history and aspects of medicine was highly valued in Europe, leading to some 1,226 editions of Spanish works of the period 1475–1600 being published abroad prior to 1800.[29]

There was, nonetheless, a decay in some aspects of creativity. By the beginning of the seventeenth century Mariana was explaining that he had translated his history from the Latin because there were now few who understood the language.[30] Scientific research declined. Much of this atrophy has been blamed on the Inquisition, whose Indices excluded much of European scholarship from the peninsula. Any argument, however, that tries to give credit to the Inquisition for Spain's cultural successes, or blame for its failures, errs because it begins from the false premise that the tribunal controlled all aspects of life and thought in the country. The central role of the tribunal in 1559 is extended through time to make it into an arbiter of all existence in Spain. The present study has argued that this is not only implausible, but impossible. In the lives of the majority of the Spanish population the Inquisition played a minimal role: from birth to death, the life-cycle of the Old Christian believer was tied to his parish and to the Church, not to the Holy Office.[31] Outside of 1559, the Inquisition played a marginal role in intellectual life: clashes with individuals outside that crisis period were normally connected with Judaism. By the eighteenth century, as shown by the confiscation of Mayáns' manuscripts and books,[32] the reactionary State rather than the reactionary tribunal was the chief threat to liberty. The Inquisition played no part in repressing science: not a single scientific study was ever in itself proscribed, and no Index ever banned Copernicus. Despite its hostility to the fueros and occasional forays into political life,[33] it was never an instrument of political repression: political controversy of every sort, from speeches in the Cortes (some of them directed against the Inquisition) to the writings of the arbitristas, continued to make Spain one of the freest countries in Europe. Its battle against foreign books was successful only when supported by the State, and did not wholly block the European contacts of the elite, who continued to have significant intercourse with the elites of Italy and the Netherlands.

The Inquisition, then, must be reduced to its proper dimensions in Spanish history: its significance can be grossly exaggerated if we rely only on its own documentation for information. It is, moreover, too often assumed that it had a special philosophy of its own; in reality, as the preceding pages have argued, the Inquisition was only a product of the society it served, and evolved in tune with that society. There were consequently many contradictions in its activity. The pro-Erasmian Inquisition of Manrique was precisely the instigator of the harsh phase of anti-Morisco measures, and the anti-limpieza Inquisition of Quiroga was the very tribunal that initiated the repression of Portuguese judaizers.

Once the facile use of the Inquisition as an explanation for all the good or ill in Spanish history has been removed, the challenge to explain the cultural evolution of Spain becomes sharper. The decay in the universities, for example, clearly owed little to the Inquisition. Theology fell into a rigid Thomist and scholastic mould. 'If they prove to me that my faith is founded on St Thomas', exclaimed El Brocense, 'I'll shit on it and find another!' But by the seventeenth century Aquinas and Aristotle were the unshakeable pillars of philosophy in Spain. Population decline played a part in the declining intake of Castilian universities, where matriculations reached their peak at around 1620 and declined continuously into the eighteenth century. No new universities were founded in Castile between 1620 and the early nineteenth century. As in all periods of economic recession, preference went to 'useful' rather than speculative studies and the lack of prospects in certain subjects effectively doomed them. By 1648 it was proposed at Salamanca to suppress the chairs of Greek, Hebrew, mathematics and other subjects; Greek and Hebrew had not been taught since the 1550s.[34]

For none of this can the Inquisition be blamed. In area after area of Spanish culture it is increasingly obvious that factors were at work which it would be grotesque to try and attribute to the Inquisition. Aware that it was unreasonable to castigate the tribunal for all Spain's failures, Juan Valera in 1876 asked whether it was not something in Spain's own character that was culpable. He identified the cause as religious fanaticism: 'a fever of pride, a delirium of vanity. ... We thought we were the new people of God, and confused religion with patriotic egoism. ... Hence our divorce and isolation from the rest of Europe.'[35] Subsequent historians likewise looked at the problem in global terms. Claudio Sánchez Albornoz saw the seeds of future conflict in the massive rejection by Spain of its Jewish and Arabic culture: 'we had no religious wars in the sixteenth century, but we have had them in the twentieth'.[36] The contradictions within Spain which had apparently been reconciled by the imposition of religious uniformity were to break out again. For Ramón Menéndez Pidal the reconciliation had never taken place, and there always existed a struggle – often mute, never suppressed – between Two Spains.[37] The interplay between African and European Spain, isolationist and international Spain, liberal and reactionary Spain, caused the tensions that explained the strife in Spanish history. The Two Spains followed 'the fated destiny of the two sons of Oedipus, who would not consent to reign together and mortally wounded each other'. Menéndez Pidal looked forward to an age when reconciliation would eventually occur, and reintegration would lead to unity of purpose in a tolerant society.

The Inquisition, by its very nature, had been opposed to a tolerant society. Its introduction by Ferdinand and Isabella brought an end to the society of convivencia and provoked relentless opposition from New Christians who recognized its capacity for evil. The problem did not, however, start with the Inquisition. For a generation before its introduction, the polarization of Spanish society between rival clans based on racial antecedents had threatened political stability. New Christians featured both as victims and as aggressors. Discrimination on grounds of race had also existed long before the Inquisition. The tribunal, therefore, created no new problems and merely intensified old ones. Christian conversos were able sincerely to support the activities of the Holy Office, but sought ways to mitigate its antisemitic tendencies and financial irregularities. This attempt at a compromise position turned out to be a costly illusion. The Inquisition helped to institutionalize the prejudices and attitudes that had previously been commonplace in society. Like all police forces that operate in secrecy and are not publicly accountable, it began to enjoy the arrogance of power. As the society of conflict developed, the Inquisition found itself at the centre of social tensions, but because its physical contact with the population was minimal it did not attract the hostility of Spaniards; indeed, the people accepted it because its punishments were directed not against them but against the scapegoats of society: heretics, foreigners, deviants. Outside the crisis years of the mid-sixteenth century, few intellectuals felt threatened; from Macanaz onwards many felt that the Inquisition could be rendered harmless if subjected entirely to the State. Not until the eighteenth century did the tribunal show itself to be clearly out of step with opinion in both Church and State.

Even when all explanations have been offered, the questions remain. How could a society as tolerant as Castile, in which the three great faiths of the west had coexisted for centuries and into which the mediaeval Inquisition had never penetrated, change its ideology in the fifteenth century, against the instincts of many great men in both Church and State? How could a clergy and population that had never lusted for blood except in war (Queen Isabella thought even bull-fighting too gory), gaze placidly upon the burning alive of thousands of their fellow Spaniards for an offence – prevarication in religion – that had never hitherto been a crime? How could the Spanish people – who alone among Europeans had in their tens of thousands broadened their vision by travelling the extent of Europe, traversing the oceans and opening up the New World – accept without serious opposition the mental restrictions proposed by the Inquisition? The preceding pages have tried to offer the elements of an answer, but it is in the nature of the inquisitorial phenomenon that no answer can match the complexity of the questions. Even today in the twentieth century, other nations have had and continue to have their Inquisitions: the human condition is subject to frailties that are not limited to any one people or faith and that regularly reverse the gains made in previous generations by 'civilization' and 'progress'.

Notes

Chapter 1: Introduction

1 Cited in Américo Castro, *The Structure of Spanish History* (Princeton 1954), p. 221.
2 *Ibid.*, p. 225.
3 Sverker Arnoldsson, *La leyenda negra: estudios sobre sus orígenes* (Göteborg 1960).
4 Both Américo Castro and his opponent in controversy Claudio Sánchez Albornoz, *España, un enigma histórico* (2 vols, 2nd edn Buenos Aires 1956), suggest Jewish origins for the Inquisition. No modern historian supports this view.
5 *Don Quixote*, book 1, chap. 28.
6 Guicciardini, *Opere* (Bari 1929–36), vol. IX, p. 130, 'Relazione di Spagna'.
7 Ramon Menéndez Pidal, *The Spaniards in their history* (London 1950), p. 131.
8 Américo Castro, 'Algunas observaciones acerca del concepto del honor en los siglos XVI y XVII', *Revista de Filología Española*, III (1916).

Chapter 2: The Great Dispersion

1 'La Biblia de Mosé Arragel de Guadalfajara', cited in Américo Castro, *The Structure of Spanish History*, p. 489.
2 For a general perspective see Salo Baron, *A Social and Religious History of the Jews* (17 vols, 2nd edn New York 1952).
3 So that one writer could later claim that the Sephardim (from *Sepharad*, the Hebrew for Spain) took no part in the execution of Christ in Palestine.

4 Abraham A. Neuman, *The Jews in Spain. Their social, political and cultural life during the Middle Ages* (2 vols, Philadelphia 1944), II, p.184.

5 See, for example, F. Cantera Burgos, *Sinagogas españolas* (Madrid 1955).

6 The written language of the Jews was *ladino* (Castilian in Hebrew script); their spoken language was Castilian ('judeo-espanyol').

7 Luis Suárez Fernández, *Documentos acerca de la Expulsión de los Judíos* (Valladolid 1964), p.18. Separateness was, of course, forced on the Jews; at the same time they, like any cultural minority, also preferred to live together.

8 Yitzhak Baer, *A History of the Jews in Christian Spain* (2 vols, Philadelphia 1966), II, pp.95–134; Philippe Wolff, 'The 1391 pogrom in Spain. Social crisis or not?', *Past and Present* 50 (1971), pp.4–18; Angus Mackay, 'Popular movements and pogroms in 15th century Castile', *Past and Present* 55 (1972).

9 Thought by some to derive from a word for 'pig'.

10 Américo Castro, *The Structure of Spanish History*, pp.474–91.

11 Neuman, *op. cit.*, II, p.217; see also Castro, *op. cit.*, pp.491–6; and Julio Caro Baroja, *Los Judíos en la España moderna y contemporanea* (3 vols, Madrid 1962), II, pp.162–90.

12 Castro, *op. cit.*, p.499.

13 Neuman, *op. cit.*, II, p.187.

14 Manuel Serrano y Sanz, *Orígenes de la Dominación Española en América* (vol. XXV, Nueva Biblioteca de Autores Españolas, Madrid 1918), pp.46–7.

15 Antonio Domínguez Ortiz, *Los conversos de origen judío después de la expulsión* (Madrid 1957), p.146.

16 M.A. Ladero Quesada, 'Los judíos en el arrendamiento de impuestos', *Cuadernos de Historia*, anexos de *Hispania* VI (1975), pp.417–39.

17 Andrés Bernáldez, *Memorias del reinado de los Reyes Católicos* (Madrid 1962), chap.CXII, p.256.

18 For example, P. León Tello, *Judíos de Avila* (Avila 1963); there are numerous other valuable recent works on the *aljamas*.

19 This seems to be the drift of the presentation in Baer, *A History of the Jews*. Since Baer, diligent Spanish scholarship has unearthed a mine of information on the Jews, which makes it essential to consult the Spanish translation of Baer (Madrid

1981), where the translator, José Luis Lacave, presents a splendid bibliography of recent research in Spanish and Hebrew.

20 Bernáldez, *op. cit.*, chap.XLIII, p.98.

21 Serrano y Sanz, *op. cit.*, pp.37–8.

22 A. Rodríguez Moñino, 'Les Judaisants à Badajoz de 1493 à 1599', *Revue des Etudes Juives* (1956), pp.73–86.

23 'Copia de los sanvenitos que corresponden a la villa de Aguilar de la Frontera', British Library Add. MS 21447 ff.137–9.

24 Pilar León Tello, *Judíos de Toledo* (2 vols, Madrid 1979); see the map facing p.368 in vol. I.

25 F. Cantera Burgos and C. Carrete Parrondo, 'La judería de Buitrago', *Sefarad* XXXII (1972), pp.3–87.

26 'La judería de Hita', *ibid.*, pp.249–305.

27 J. Cabezudo Astraín, 'La judería de Sos del Rey Católico', *ibid.*, pp.89–104.

28 P. León Tello, 'La judería de Avila durante el reinado de los Reyes Católicos', *Sefarad* XXIII (1963), pp.36–53.

29 Baer, *op. cit.*, II, pp.70–243.

30 Examples from Suárez Fernández, *Documentos*, p.16.

31 *Ibid.*, p.15.

32 *Ibid.*, p.33.

33 Fidel Fita, 'Nuevos datos para escribir la historia de los judíos españoles: la Inquisición en Jérez de la Frontera', *Boletín de la Real Academia de la Historia* XV (1889), pp.313–32.

34 Suárez Fernández, *op. cit.*, p.41.

35 *Ibid.*, p.20.

36 W.H. Prescott, *History of the Reign of Ferdinand and Isabella* (3rd edn, London 1841), p.269 n.1.

37 See, for example, Stephen Haliczer, 'The Castilian urban patriciate and the Jewish expulsions of 1480–92', *American Historical Review* 78 (Feb. 1973).

38 On the expulsion my view coincides with that of Maurice Kriegel, 'La prise d'une décision: l'expulsion des juifs d'Espagne en 1492', *Revue Historique* CCLX (1978), 49–90.

39 B. Netanyahu, *Don Isaac Abravanel, statesman and philosopher* (Philadelphia 1968), pp.54–6.

40 P. León Tello, *Judíos de Toledo*, I, p.347.

41 For the whole case, see Fidel Fita, 'La verdad sobre el martirio del Santo Niño de La Guardia', *Boletín de la Real Academia de la Historia* XI (1887), pp.7–160; H.C. Lea, 'El Santo Niño de La Guardia', *Chapters from the Religious History of Spain*

(Philadelphia 1890), pp.437–68; and Baer, *op. cit.*, II, pp.398–423.

42 Isidore Loeb, 'Le nombre des Juifs de Castille et d'Espagne', *Revue des Etudes Juives* XIV (1887).

43 Baer, *op. cit.*, II, 510 ff.

44 Bernáldez, *op. cit.*, chaps. CX, CXII.

45 Quoted in Lea, *A History of the Inquisition of Spain* (4 vols, New York 1906–8) I, p.143.

46 J. Gómez-Menor Fuentes, 'Un judío converso de 1498. Diego Gómez de Toledo (Semuel Abolafia) y su proceso inquisitorial', *Sefarad* XXXIII (1973), pp.45–110.

47 Suárez Fernández, *op. cit.*, p.41.

48 Bernáldez, *op. cit.*, chap. CXII, p.262.

Chapter 3: The Coming of the Inquisition

1 The document is discussed, for example, in Nicholas G. Round, 'Politics, style and group attitudes in the Instruccion del Relator', *Bulletin of Hispanic Studies* 46 (1969), pp.289–319.

2 José Amador de los Rios, *Historia social, política y religiosa de los Judíos en España y Portugal* (3 vols, Madrid 1875–6), III, p.242.

3 Including Pedro de la Caballería, author of the antisemitic tract *Zelus Christi contra Judaeos, Sarracenos et infideles.*

4 Cecil Roth, *The Spanish Inquisition* (London 1937), p. 30.

5 Luciano Serrano O.S.B., *Los conversos D. Pablo de Santa María y D. Alfonso de Cartagena* (Madrid 1942), pp.23–4.

6 Francisco Márquez Villanueva, 'Conversos y cargos concejiles en el siglo XV', *Revista de Archivos, Bibliotecas y Museos* 63, ii (1957), pp.504–40.

7 In several influential works Américo Castro has laid great stress on the converso ethic in Hispanic literature, but his interpretations have tended to exaggerate the relative role of conversos. For an entertaining critique see Eugenio Asensio, 'Notas sobre la historiografía de Américo Castro', *Anuario de Estudios Medievales* 8 (1972–3), pp.349–92.

8 F. Cantera Burgos and P. León Tello, *Judaizantes del arzobispado de Toledo habilitados por la Inquisición en 1495 y 1497* (Madrid 1969), pp. xi–xii.

9 Domínguez Ortiz, *Los conversos de origen judío*, pp. 217–19

10 Cf. Caro Baroja, *Los Judíos*, I, pp. 269–70.

11 *Ibid.*, ii, pp. 162–244.

12 Inquisition to Suprema, 28 Apr. 1579, Archivo Histórico Nacional, sección Inquisición (hereafter AHN Inq.) leg. 2704.

13 Published by Rodrigo Amador de los Rios in *Revista de España* cv–cvi (1885).

14 Printed in Caro Baroja, *op. cit.*, iii, pp. 287–99.

15 *Ibid.*, ii, p. 264.

16 For discussion of the controversy see below, chap. 7.

17 Benzion Netanyahu, 'Fray Alonso de Espina: was he a New Christian?' *Proceedings of the American Academy for Jewish Research* xliii (1976), pp. 107–65.

18 Haim Beinart, *Conversos on Trial. The Inquisition in Ciudad Real* (Jerusalem 1981), p. 20.

19 Eloy Benito Ruano, *Toledo en el siglo XV* (Madrid 1961), appendices 16, 18, 19, 22, 44.

20 Luis Delgado Merchán, *Historia documentada de Ciudad Real* (Ciudad Real 1907), p. 419.

21 Caro Baroja, *op. cit.*, iii, pp. 279–81.

22 Nicolás López Martínez, *Los Judaizantes castellanos y la Inquisición en tiempo de Isabel la Católica* (Burgos 1954), appendix iv, pp. 391–404.

23 Baer, *op. cit.*, ii, pp. 424–5.

24 Beinart, *Conversos on Trial*, p. 242, my italics. This statement is at variance with all the known facts. Among other commentaries on the relation between Jews and conversos, see I.S. Révah, 'Les Marranes', *Revue des Etudes Juives* (1959–60); and G. Nahon, 'Les marranes espagnols et portugais et les communautés juives issues du marranisme dans l'historiographie récente (1960–75)', *ibid.*, 136 (1977).

25 I.S. Révah was the leading proponent of the view, based on inquisitorial documentation, that most marranos were Jews: see G. Nahon, 'Les sephardim, les marranes, les Inquisitions peninsulaires et leurs archives dans les travaux récents de I.S. Révah', *Revue des Etudes Juives* 132 (1973). The view that the Inquisition papers are wholly untrustworthy is forcefully presented by E. Rivkin, 'How Jewish were the New Christians?' in *Hispania Judaica* (Barcelona 1980).

26 Benzion Netanyahu, *The Marranos of Spain from the late XIVth to the early XVIth century, according to contemporary Hebrew sources* (2nd edn New York 1973).

27 Francesco Carreras y Candi, 'L'Inquisició barcelonina, substi-

tuida per l'Inquisició castellana (1446–1487)', *Institut d'Estudis Catalans* anuari 1909–10, p. 163.

28 Francisco Cantera, 'Fernando de Pulgar y los conversos', *Sefarad* IV (1944).

29 Among the inquisitors was the Catalan Nicolau Eymeric, whose *Directorium inquisitorum* (1376) was first printed in 1503 and then issued at Rome in 1578 with a commentary by the Spanish theologian Francisco Peña. There is a useful abridgement by Louis Sala-Molins, issued in Paris (1973) and in Barcelona (1983) as *El manual de los inquisidores*. Earlier than Eimeric is the classic, dated 1323, by Bernard Gui, *Manuel de l'Inquisiteur* (2 vols, Paris 1926–7).

30 C. Carrete Parrondo, 'Los conversos jerónimos ante el estatuto de limpieza de sangre', *Helmantica* XXVI (1975), p. 101.

31 Tarsicio de Azcona, *Isabel la Católica* (Madrid 1964), p. 379.

32 The bulls of the early years are given in Bernardino Llorca S.J., *Bulario Pontificio de la Inquisición Española en su período constitucional (1478–1525)* (vol. XV, Miscellanea Historiae Pontificae, Rome 1949).

33 Azcona, *Isabel*, p. 387.

34 Hernando del Pulgar, *Cronica de los Reyes Católicos* (vols. V–VI, Coleccion de Cronicas Españolas, Madrid 1943), V, p. 337.

35 *Relación Histórica de la Judería de Sevilla* (Seville 1849), pp. 24–6.

36 Bernáldez, *op. cit.*, chap. XLIV, pp. 99–100.

37 Bernardino Llorca S.J., *La Inquisición en España* (Barcelona 1936), p. 79.

38 Bernáldez, *op. cit.*, chap. XLIV, p. 101.

39 Lea, *op. cit.*, p. 587, appendix X. For the struggle over the Inquisition of Seville in 1482 see Azcona, *Isabel*, pp. 402–3.

40 Lea, I, p. 233.

41 *Ibid.*, p. 590, appendix XI.

42 Carreras y Candi, 'L'Inquisició barcelonina', *op. cit.*, pp. 134–7.

43 The basic source for the early years of the Catalan Inquisition is the contemporary Pere Miquel Carbonell, in *Colección de documentos inéditos del Archivo de la Corona de Aragón* (Barcelona 1864–5), vols. XXVII–XXVIII.

44 Ricardo Garcia Cárcel, *Orígenes de la Inquisición española. El tribunal de Valencia, 1478–1530* (Barcelona 1976), p. 50.

45 *Ibid.*, p. 60.

46 Quoted in Juan Antonio Llorente, *Memoria Histórica sobre qual*

ha sido la opinión nacional de España acerca del tribunal de la Inquisición (Madrid 1812), pp. 90–91.

47 Lea, *op. cit.*, I, p. 247.

48 Antonio C. Floriano, 'El Tribunal del Santo Oficio en Aragón. Establecimiento de la Inquisición en Teruel', *Boletín de la Real Academia de la Historia* 86–7 (1925) and 88 (1926).

49 Previous murders of inquisitors, notably by the Cathars in 1243, had always provoked a severe reaction. Other assassinated inquisitors include Conrad of Marburg in 1233 and Peter of Verona in 1252.

50 Some aspects are touched on by Jordi Ventura, 'Els inicis de la Inquisició espanyola a Mallorca', *Randa* V (1977), pp. 67–116.

51 For these figures, Lea, *op. cit.*, I, pp. 167, 183, 267.

52 For Barcelona, Carbonell, *op. cit.*; for Valencia, Garcia Cárcel, *Orígenes*, p. 195.

53 Pulgar, *Crónica*, chap. 96, p. 336.

54 Bernáldez, *op. cit.*, chap. 44, p. 101.

55 Zúñiga, *Annales de Sevilla* (año 1524), p. 482. These figures may, of course, be exaggerated. A recent investigator has suggested that in fact between 1481 and 1524, only 248 were burnt: Klaus Wagner, 'La Inquisición en Sevilla (1481–1524)', in *Homenaje al Profesor Carriazo* (Seville 1973), vol. III.

56 Lea, *op. cit.*, I, pp. 169–70; also Fidel Fita, 'La Inquisición toledana', cited below.

57 Cf. Bartolomé Bennassar, *L'Inquisition Espagnole XVe–XIXe siècle* (Paris 1979), p. 34.

58 Garcia Cárcel, *Orígenes*, p. 174.

59 Luis de Páramo, *De origine et progressu officii Sanctae Inquisitionis* (Madrid 1598), p. 170. Widely differing figures are given by Lea, *op. cit.*, IV, p. 520; by Delgado Merchán, *op. cit.*, pp. 217–25; and by Fidel Fita, 'La Inquisición de Ciudad Real en 1483–1485', *BRAH* XX (1892).

60 Fidel Fita, 'La Inquisición toledana. Relacion contemporanea de los autos y autillos que celebró desde el año 1485 hasta el de 1501', *BRAH* (1887), pp. 289–321.

61 Lea, *op. cit.*, IV, p. 523. These figures are incomplete. For a fuller statistical picture of Toledo, we await the forthcoming work of Jean Pierre Dedieu.

62 Lea, *op. cit.*, I, pp. 592–611, appendix XII.

63 These figures cover only the cases where a verdict is known. The full total of accused was 2,354: see Garcia Cárcel, *Orígenes*,

p. 167. His figures, if correct, make it impossible to accept the data given by Lea, *op. cit.*, IV, p. 522.

64 Carbonell, *op. cit.*, n. 43.

65 Baruch Braunstein, *The Chuetas of Majorca. Conversos and the Inquisition of Majorca* (New York 1972), p. 182–3, appendix III.

66 W. de Gray Birch, *Catalogue of a collection of original manuscripts ... of the Inquisition in the Canary Islands* (2 vols, London 1903), I, p. xxiv.

67 Carreras y Candi, 'L'Inquisició barcelonina', *op. cit.*, pp. 160–61.

68 Jordi Ventura Subirats, *La Inquisición española y los judíos conversos barceloneses (siglos XV y XVI)* (Barcelona 1975), p. 9.

69 Garcia Cárcel, *Orígenes*, pp. 171–2.

Chapter 4: The Roots of Opposition

1 Llorca, *La Inquisición*, p. 166.

2 Llorente, *Memoria Histórica*, p. 37.

3 For pre-Inquisition trials in one city, see Beinart, *Conversos on Trial*, p. 78.

4 The un-Spanish nature of the Inquisition has prompted both Castro and Sánchez Albornoz (*op. cit.*, chap. I, n. 4) to attribute to it a Jewish origin.

5 Juan de Mariana, *Historia General de España* (Biblioteca de Autores Espanoles, vols. XXX–XXXI, Madrid 1950), XXXI, p. 202.

6 Jaime Vicens Vives, *Ferran II i la ciutat de Barcelona 1479–1516* (2 vols, Barcelona 1936), I, p. 376.

7 Miguel Avilés, 'Motivos de crítica a la Inquisición en tiempos de Carlos V', in J. Pérez Villanueva (ed.), *La Inquisición Española. Nueva Visión, Nuevos Horizontes* (Madrid 1980), p. 187. This volume is cited hereafter as *Nueva Visión*.

8 Mariana, *loc. cit.*

9 Vicens Vives, *Ferran II*, I, p. 382.

10 Biblioteca Nacional, Madrid, MS. 1517.

11 See Antonio Márquez, *Literatura e Inquisición en España 1478–1834* (Madrid 1980), p. 25, citing from a piece by Angel Alcalá; and Azcona, *Isabel*, pp. 399–401. Lucena was apparently made to recant in public in Córdoba.

12 'Baptizati invite non recipiunt Sacramentum nec characterem

baptismalem, sed remanent infideles occulti': Páramo, *op. cit.*, p. 165.

13 Sigüenza, *Historia de la Orden de San Jerónimo*, II, p. 306, cited in Caro Baroja, *Los Judíos*, p. 150, n. 61.

14 Hernando de Talavera, *Católica impugnación* (ed. Francisco Martín, introduced by F. Márquez Villanueva, Barcelona 1961), p. 68.

15 Llorca, *Bulario*, pp. 113–15.

16 Bernáldez, *op. cit.*, chap. XLIV.

17 H. Graetz, 'La police de l'Inquisition d'Espagne à ses debuts', *BRAH* XXIII (1893), pp. 383–90.

18 Beinart, *Conversos on Trial*, p. 134.

19 Luis Ramirez y las Casas Deza, *Anales de Córdoba*, in *Colección de documentos inéditos para la Historia de España* (Madrid 1895) vol. CXII, p. 279.

20 R. Gracia Boix, *Colección de documentos para la Historia de la Inquisición de Córdoba* (Córdoba 1982), pp. 86, 96, 103.

21 T. Herrero del Collado, 'El proceso inquisitorial por delito de herejía contra Hernando de Talavera', *Anuario de Historia del Derecho Español* (1969).

22 C. Fernández Duro, 'Vida y obras de Gonzalo de Ayora', *BRAH* XVII (1890), pp. 448, 450. The best documented account of the Talavera affair is by Tarsicio de Azcona, 'La Inquisición española procesada por la Congregación general de 1508', in *Nueva Visión*, pp. 89–163. Azcona calculates that Lucero burnt 277 persons in four autos, and that 160 others were opportunely freed from this impending fate.

23 Archivo General de Simancas (hereafter AGS), Patronato Real, Inquisición, leg. 28 f. 39.

24 Lea, *op. cit.*, I, pp. 211–12.

25 *Ibid.*, p. 211.

26 AGS Patronato Real, Inquisición leg. 28 f. 16.

27 Archivo Histórico Nacional, Madrid (hereafter AHN), Inquisición leg. 4724² no. 8.

28 Pascual Gayangos and Vicente de la Fuente, *Cartas del Cardenal Don Fray Francisco Jiménez de Cisneros, dirigidas a Don Diego López de Ayala* (Madrid 1867), p. 261.

29 Lea, *op. cit.*, I, p. 215.

30 Llorente, *Memoria Histórica*, pp. 119–31.

31 AGS Patronato Real, Inquisición leg. 28 f. 45.

32 Llorente, *Memoria Histórica*, p. 156.

33 Joseph Pérez, *La Révolution des 'Comunidades' de Castille* (1520–1521) (Bordeaux 1970), p. 509.

34 For all this see J.I. Gutiérrez Nieto, 'Los conversos y el movimiento comunero', *Hispania* 94 (1964), pp. 237–61; and Pérez, *op. cit.*, pp. 507–14, 549–52.

35 British Library, Egerton MS, 1832 ff. 37–40.

36 G. Colas Latorre and J.A. Salas Auséns, *Aragón en el siglo XVI. Alteraciones sociales y conflictos políticos* (Saragossa 1982), p. 505.

37 Pérez, *op. cit.*, p. 551 n. 117.

38 See below, chap. 8.

39 1528 prosecution of Gaspar Mercader, AHN Inquisición leg. 2155[1]; Badajoz, *ibid.*, leg. 2701.

40 Jaime Contreras, *El Santo Oficio de la Inquisición de Galicia* (Madrid 1982), p. 683.

41 AHN Inquisición libro 735 f. 349.

Chapter 5: 'Silence has been imposed'

1 Marcel Bataillon, *Erasmo y España* (Mexico 1966), p. 490.

2 The Vulgate Latin was set between the Hebrew and the Greek, like Christ crucified between two thieves, as one of the prefaces remarks.

3 Bataillon, *op. cit.*, p. 280.

4 *Ibid.*, p. 240. The basic document in the debate has been printed by M. Avilés, *Erasmo y la Inquisición* (Madrid 1980).

5 Bataillon, *op. cit.*, p. 277.

6 Cf. Melquiades Andrés, 'Pensamiento teológico y vivencia religiosa en la Reforma española (1400–1600)', in Ricardo García-Villoslada, *Historia de la Iglesia en España* (5 vols, Madrid 1980), vol. III, 2, especially pp. 343–5.

7 See Glossary.

8 Antonio Márquez, *Los Alumbrados. Orígenes y filosofía* (1525–1559) (Madrid 1980), prints the edict pp. 229–38. He restricts the use of the term *alumbrado* only to the Guadalajara group.

9 There is a splendid study by Angela Selke, *El Santo Oficio de la Inquisición. Proceso de Fr. Francisco Ortiz* (1529–1532) (Madrid 1968).

10 Lea, *op. cit.*, III, p. 415; John E. Longhurst, *Luther and the Spanish Inquisition: the Case of Diego de Uceda* 1528–1529 (Albuquerque 1953).

11 Baer, *op. cit.*, II, p. 275.

12 *Ibid.*, II, pp. 350–56; Julio Caro Baroja, *Las formas complejas de la vida religiosa* (Madrid 1978), pp. 197–201.

13 Cf. the comments of J.L. Novalín, discussing the views of Márquez, in Garcia-Villoslada, *Historia, op. cit.*, III, 2, pp. 153–4.

14 M. Ortega Costa, *Proceso de la Inquisición contra Maria de Cazalla* (Madrid 1978).

15 Isabel was released in December 1538; Alcaraz in February 1539. A late casualty of the alumbrado trials was the Old Christian Rodrigo de Bivar, chaplain to the Duke of Infantado, arrested in 1539 but released: see Alastair Hamilton, *El proceso de Rodrigo de Bivar* (1539) (Madrid 1979).

16 Juan de Avila, *Avisos y Reglas Cristianas sobre aquel verso de David: Audi, Filia* (ed. Luis Sala Balust, Barcelona 1963), p. 32.

17 On alumbrados in the later period, see below, p. 96.

18 Angela Selke, in *Bulletin Hispanique* 62 (1960).

19 There is a splendid account in Bataillon, *op. cit.*, pp. 438–70; the trial is printed by J.E. Longhurst in *Cuadernos de Historia de España* vols. XXVII–XXXII, XXXV–XXXVI (1958–60, 1962).

20 Marcelino Menéndez y Pelayo, *Historia de los Heterodoxos Españoles* (8 vols, Buenos Aires 1945. The first edition was in 1881), IV, p. 129.

21 The literature on Valdés has grown appreciably. See especially J.E. Longhurst, *Erasmus and the Spanish Inquisition: the Case of Juan de Valdés* (Albuquerque 1950); J.C. Nieto, *Juan de Valdés (1509?–1541)* (Michigan 1968); Marcel Bataillon, *Erasmo y el Erasmismo* (Barcelona 1977), pp. 245–85; and the extremely important article by Carlos Gilly, 'Juan de Valdés: Ubersetzer und Bearbeiter von Luthers Schriften in seinem *Diálogo de Doctrina*', *Archiv für Reformationsgeschichte* 74 (1983), pp. 257–305.

22 J. Goñi Gaztámbide, 'El impresor Miguel de Eguía procesado por la Inquisición', *Hispania Sacra* I (1948), pp. 35–88.

23 Cited in Lea, *op. cit.*, III, p. 419.

24 Bataillon, *op. cit.*, p. 490.

25 *Ibid.*, p. 545.

26 Augustin Redondo, 'Luther et l'Espagne de 1520 à 1536', *Mélanges de la Casa de Velázquez* I (1965), p. 133.

27 Ernst Schäfer, *Beiträge zur Geschichte des spanischen Protestantis-*

mus und der Inquisition im sechzehnten Jahrhundert (3 vols, Gütersloh 1902), vol. II.

28 J.I. Tellechea, 'Biblias publicadas fuera de España secuestradas por la Inquisición española en 1552', *Bulletin Hispanique* 64 (1962), pp. 236–47.

29 For Egidio and other 'Protestants' see Edward Boehmer, *Bibliotheca Wiffeniana: Spanish Reformers of two centuries, from 1520* (3 vols, London 1864–1904).

30 J.L. González Novalín, *El inquisidor general Fernando de Valdés* (2 vols, Oviedo 1968).

31 For a recent view of Egidio and Constantino see Alvaro Huerga, *Predicadores, alumbrados e Inquisición en el siglo XVI* (Madrid 1973).

32 See A. Gordon Kinder, 'Cipriano de Valera, Spanish reformer', in *Bulletin of Hispanic Studies* 46 (1969), pp. 109–19; and his *Cassiodoro de Reina* (London 1975). For the Seville community in general, see Schäfer, *op. cit.*, I, pp. 345–67; II, pp. 271–426.

33 Schäfer, *op. cit.* I, pp. 233–48; III, pp. 1–813.

34 Leonor de Vivero was the wife of Pedro de Cazalla of Valladolid: both had been patrons in 1520 of Francisca Hernández, and were related to Maria de Cazalla, the alumbrada of Guadalajara. Of the ten children of Leonor and Pedro, four were burnt by the Inquisition (the three priests Dr Augustín de Cazalla, Francisco de Vivero and Pedro de Cazalla, and their sister Beatriz de Vivero). Leonor's bones were exhumed, and the family house razed.

35 On Rojas and Seso see especially J.I. Tellechea Idigoras, *Tiempos recios. Inquisición y heterodoxias* (Salamanca 1977); and his 'El clima religioso español en 1559', in *El arzobispo Carranza y su tiempo* (2 vols, Madrid 1968), I, pp. 105–239.

36 J.E. Longhurst, 'Julian Hernández', and E. Droz, 'Note sur les impressions genevoises transportées par Hernández', *Bibliothèque d'Humanisme et Renaissance* 22 (1960), pp. 90–118, 119–32.

37 On the shock registered by many: Tellechea, *Carranza*, II, p. 241 n. 21.

38 AGS Patronato Real, Inquisición leg. 28 f. 37.

39 Lea, *op. cit.*, III, p. 571, appendix VIII.

40 Tellechea, *Carranza*, I, 147–8.

41 Schäfer, *op. cit.*, II, pp. 286–8.

42 Biblioteca Nacional, Madrid, MS. 9175 ff. 258–60.

43 On the Carranza case see below, pp. 155–60.

44 Schäfer, *op. cit.*, II, p. 107; and J.P. Dedieu in Bennassar, *L'Inquisition*, pp. 282–4.

45 Dedieu, in *ibid.*, pp. 281–8.

46 Letter to Suprema, 23 Oct. 1560, AHN Inquisición libro 730 f. 23.

47 Schäfer, *op. cit.*, II, pp. 1–106.

48 Four Spaniards were burnt in person in Valencia for Lutheranism, and eight in effigy: Ricardo Garcia Cárcel, *Herejia y Sociedad en el siglo XVI. La Inquisición en Valencia 1530–1609* (Barcelona 1980), pp. 335–41.

49 J.M. López Piñero, *Ciencia y Tecnica en la Sociedad española de los siglos XVI y XVII* (Barcelona 1979), pp. 141–4.

50 Mario Scaduto S.J., 'Laínez e l'Indice del 1559', *Archivum Historicum Societatis Jesu* XXIV, 47 (Jan.–June 1955).

51 In his *History*, III, p. 485, Lea had originally argued that the first Index came out in 1547. J.M. de Bujanda, *Index de l'Inquisition Espagnole* (Geneva 1984), pp. 58–63, shows convincingly that the first only came out in 1551.

52 *Tres indices expurgatorios de la Inquisición española en el siglo XVI* (Madrid 1952).

53 I.S. Révah, 'Un index espagnol inconnu', *Homenaje a Damaso Alonso* (3 vols, Madrid 1963), III, pp. 131–46. For the Indices in general see Heinrich Reusch, *Der Index der verbotenen Bücher* (2 vols, Bonn 1883–5). Also the apologia by Miguel de la Pinta Llorente, 'Aportaciones para la historia externa de los indices expurgatorios españoles', *Hispania* XII (1952), pp. 253–300.

54 Antonio Rumeu de Armas, *Historia de la Censura literaria gubernativa en España* (Madrid 1940), pp. 16–20. On the same subject, the apologia by Antonio Sierra Corella, *La censura de libros y papeles en España y los índices y catalogos españoles* (Madrid 1947).

55 Virgilio Pinto Crespo, *Inquisición y control, ideológico en la España del siglo XVI* (Madrid 1983) p. 56: in 1590–1605, out of 103 identifiable calificadores, forty were Dominican and fourteen Jesuits.

56 See the sharp protest by the seventeenth-century inquisitorial censor Murcia de la Llana when Rome banned a book by a Jesuit friend: 'it is incredible that a book should be totally

banned by Rome after circulating for many years among Spaniards without causing any offence', AHN Inquisición libro 1231 ff. 672–3.

57 J. Pérez Villanueva, 'Baronio y la Inquisición española', *Baronio Storico e la Controriforma*, Atti de convegno internazionale di studi, Sora, October 1979 (Sora 1982).

58 Cf. Márquez, *Literatura e Inquisición*, pp. 151–2, 233–5; and J.M. de Bujanda, 'La littérature castillane dans l'index espagnol de 1559', *L'Humanisme dans les Lettres espagnoles* (ed. A. Redondo, Paris 1979).

59 Justo Cuervo, 'Fray Luis de Granada y la Inquisición', *Homenaje a Menéndez Pelayo* (2 vols, Madrid 1899), I, pp. 733–43.

60 Candido de Dalmases SJ, 'San Francisco de Borja y la Inquisición española, 1559–1561', *Archivum Historicum Societatis Jesu* 41 (1972), pp. 48–135.

61 Cf. J.M. de Bujanda, 'Literatura e Inquisición en España en el siglo XVI', in *Nueva Visión*, pp. 579–92.

62 Pinto Crespo, *Inquisición y control*, p. 182.

63 Felix Asensio SJ, 'Juan de Mariana ante el índice quiroguiano de 1583–1584', *Estudios Bíblicos* XXXI (1972), pp. 135–78.

64 Pinto Crespo, *op. cit.*, p. 199.

65 'Dictamen de Jeronimo Zurita acerca de la prohibición de obras literarias por el Santo Oficio', *Revista de Archivos, Bibliotecas y Museos* VIII (1903), pp. 218–21. The authorship of this item has now been attributed to Alvar Gómez de Castro: see P.E. Russell, 'Secular literature and the censors: a sixteenth-century document re-examined', *Bulletin of Hispanic Studies* LIX (1982), pp. 219–25.

66 Asensio, 'Juan de Mariana', *op. cit.*

67 For the formative censorship of the Counter Reformation, see chapter 11, p. 204.

68 Quoted in Pinto Crespo, *op. cit.*, p. 104.

69 AHN Inquisición libro 1275 f. 123, 'sobre visitas de navios'.

70 *Ibid.*, libro 1233 f. 209.

71 *Ibid.*, leg. 2155[1].

72 *Ibid.*, leg. 4470[1] no. 3.

73 Quoted in Pinto Crespo, *op. cit.*, pp. 128–9.

74 AHN Inquisición leg. 4470[1] no. 3.

75 Cf. Christian Peligny, 'Les difficultés de l'édition castillane au XVIIe siècle', *Mélanges de la Casa de Velázquez* XIII (1977), pp. 257–84.

76 AHN Inquisición leg. 4517¹ no. 1.

77 Pinto Crespo, *op. cit.*, pp. 166–9, shows that not all the books were in fact burnt.

78 AHN Inquisición leg. 4470¹ no. 4; leg. 4517¹ no. 1.

79 M. Agulló y Cobo, 'La Inquisición y los libreros españoles en el siglo XVII', *Cuadernos Bibliográficos* 28 (1972), pp. 143–51.

80 Juan Antonio Llorente, *Histoire Critique de l'Inquisition d'Espagne* (4 vols, Paris 1817–18), I, pp. 343–5; Márquez, *Literatura e Inquisición*, pp. 40–42; Bataillon, *Erasmo y Erasmismo*, p. 164.

81 Fidel Fita, 'Los tres procesos de San Ignacio de Loyola en Alcalá de Henares', *Boletín de la Real Academia de la Historia* 33 (1898), pp. 422–61.

82 Candido de Dalmases, 'San Francisco de Borja y la Inquisición', *AHSI* 41 (1972), p. 64.

83 For Luis de León see, *inter alia*, Lea, *op. cit.*, III, pp. 149–62; Luis Alonso Getino O.P., 'La causa de Fr. Luis de León ante la crítica y los nuevos documentos históricos', *RABM* IX (1903) and XI (1904); *Colección de documentos ineditos* X–XI (1847).

84 Miguel de la Pinta Llorente, *Proceso criminal contra el hebraista salmantino Martín Martínez de Cantalapiedra* (Madrid 1946), p. 392.

85 B. Rekers, *Benito Arias Montano (1527–1598)* (London 1972), chap. III. There is not the slightest bit of evidence to support the suggestion, made by A. Sicroff, *Les controverses des statuts de 'pureté de sang' en Espagne du XVe au XVIIe siècle* (Paris 1960), pp. 269–70, that Montano was of converso origin. Likewise, it is quite incorrect to say that 'the whole of Montano's work was prohibited' by the Inquisition (Rekers, *Montano*, p. 68). See on this J.A. Jones, 'Pedro de Valencia's defence of Arias Montano: the expurgatory indexes of 1607 (Rome) and 1612 (Madrid)', *Bibliothèque d'Humanisme et Renaissance* 40 (1978), pp. 121–36.

86 *Colección de documentos ineditos* XLI (1862), pp. 316, 387.

87 Gregorio de Andrés, *Proceso inquisitorial del Padre Sigüenza* (Madrid 1975).

88 Antonio Tovar and Miguel de la Pinta Llorente, *Procesos inquisitoriales contra Francisco Sánchez de las Brozas* (Madrid 1941), p. xliv.

89 Américo Castro, 'Erasmo en tiempo de Cervantes', *Revista de Filología Española* XVIII (1931), pp. 364–5.

90 *Ibid.*, p. 366.

91 Miguel de la Pinta Llorente, *La Inquisición Española y los problemas de la Cultura y de la Intolerancia* (Madrid 1953), pp. 152–3.

92 Cited in Márquez, *Literatura e Inquisición*, p. 83.

93 The date is 1556 and not 1566 as given in several sources. Some authors also confuse this Núñez with Hernán Núñez, 'el Pinciano'.

94 Enrique Llamas Martínez, *Santa Teresa de Jesus y la Inquisición Española* (Madrid 1972), p. 99; see also Francisco Márquez Villanueva, *Espiritualidad y Literatura en el siglo XVI* (Madrid 1968), pp. 145–52, 179–86.

95 Alvaro Huerga, *Predicadores, alumbrados e Inquisición en el siglo XVI* (Madrid 1973); *ibid.*, *Los Alumbrados de Baeza* (Jaen 1978); *ibid.*, *Historia de los Alumbrados (1570–1630)* (2 vols, Madrid 1978).

96 I.S. Révah, 'Un pamphlet contre l'Inquisition d'Antonio Enriquez Gómez', *Revue des Etudes Juives* CXXI (1962), pp. 81–168; Márquez, *Literatura*, pp. 113–20.

97 Though there is a high probability that he may have been one, there is no direct proof that Rojas was a converso: see the pertinent comments by Márquez, *Literatura*, pp. 46–8. The imaginative work by Stephen Gilman, *The Spain of Fernando de Rojas: The Intellectual and Social Landscape of 'La Celestina'* (Princeton 1972) is based on slender historical evidence.

98 Miguel de la Pinta Llorente and J.M. de Palacio y de Palacio, *Procesos inquisitoriales contra la familia judía de Juan Luis Vives* (Madrid 1964).

99 See items cited in note 94 above.

100 Menéndez Pelayo, *Heterodoxos*, v, p. 482.

101 Márquez, *Literatura*, pp. 189–200.

102 A. Paz y Meliá, *Papeles de Inquisición: catálogo y extractos* (2nd edn Madrid 1947), pp. 23, 69, 71.

103 'Las obras de caridad que se hazen tibia y flojamente no tienen mérito ni valen nada': *Quixote, op. cit.*, II, p. 36. See A. Castro, 'Cervantes y la Inquisición', *Modern Philology* 27 (1929–30), pp. 427–33.

104 Márquez, *Literatura*, pp. 168–9.

105 For some later writers, such as Esteban Villegas (d. 1669), whose work was in part destroyed by the Inquisition, see Márquez, *op. cit.*, pp. 89–91.

106 But contrast the opinion of J.M. López Piñero, *Ciencia y Tecnica*

en la Sociedad española de los siglos XVI y XVII (Barcelona 1979), p. 143.

Chapter 6: The End of Morisco Spain

1 For Valencia see E. Ciscar and R. García Cárcel, *Moriscos i Agermanats* (Valencia 1974). For conversions, see the documents in H.C. Lea, *The Moriscos of Spain: their conversion and expulsion* (London 1901), pp. 409–14.

2 A. Redondo, *Antonio de Guevara (1480?–1545) et l'Espagne de son temps* (Geneva 1976).

3 Chapter on 'demografía morisca' in A. Domínguez Ortiz and Bernard Vincent, *Historia de los Moriscos* (Madrid 1978).

4 M.A. Ladero y Quesada, *Los Mudéjares del reino de Castilla en tiempo de Isabel I* (Valladolid 1969).

5 Cf. J. Caro Baroja, *Los Moriscos del Reino de Granada* (Madrid 1957).

6 Louis Cardaillac, *Morisques et Chrétiens. Un affrontement polémique (1492–1640)* (Paris 1977). The best modern account of the culture of the Moriscos is the superb study by Anwar G. Chejne, *Islam and the West: the Moriscos* (New York, Albany 1983).

7 Domínguez Ortiz and Vincent, *op. cit.*, chap. 5; also R. Benítez and E. Ciscar, 'La Iglesia ante la conversión y expulsión de los Moriscos', in García-Villoslada, *Historia de la Iglesia*, IV, pp. 255–307.

8 Cardaillac, *op. cit.*, p. 35.

9 M.S. Carrasco Urgoiti, *El problema morisco en Aragón al comienzo del reinado de Felipe II* (Madrid 1969), p. 149.

10 J. Contreras, 'La Inquisición de Aragon: estructura y oposición (1550–1700)', *Estudios de Historia Social* I (1977), pp. 113–41.

11 Mercedes García-Arenal, *Inquisición y moriscos. Los procesos del Tribunal de Cuenca* (Madrid 1978), p. 84.

12 Helen Nader, *The Mendoza family in the Spanish Renaissance* (New Brunswick 1979), p. 187.

13 For a guide to the extensive literature, see Domínguez Ortiz and Vincent, *op. cit.*, chap. 2.

14 García-Arenal, *op. cit.*, pp. 11, 23, 39.

15 J. Contreras, 'Las Causas de Fe en la Inquisición española: 1540–1700. Análisis de una estadística', Simposium Interdisciplinario de la Inquisición Medieval y Moderna, Denmark (Sept.

1978), pp. 20, 37, 40. This study is available in English in G. Henningsen and J. Tedeschi (eds), *The Inquisition in Early Modern Europe: Studies in Sources and Methods* (De Kalb, Illinois 1985).

16 García-Arenal, p. 39; J.M. García Fuentes, *La Inquisición en Granada en el siglo XVI* (Granada 1981), pp. xxxiii–xxxiv.

17 Bishop of Tortosa to Inquisitor General Cardinal Espinosa, from Onda, 28 July 1568, AHN Inquisición leg. 2155[1].

18 Carrasco Urgoiti, *op. cit.*, p. 148.

19 Luis García Ballester, *Medicina, ciencia y minorías marginadas: Los Moriscos* (Granada 1977).

20 Cardaillac, *op. cit.*, p. 100.

21 B. Vincent, 'Los moriscos del reino de Granada después de 1570', *Nueva Revista de Filología Hispánica* xxx (1981), pp. 594–608.

22 Tulio Halperín Donghi, 'Los Morisques du royaume de Valence au xvie siècle', *Annales* 1956; *ibid.*, 'Un conflicto nacional en el siglo de oro', *Cuadernos de Historia de España* (Buenos Aires), xxiii–xxiv (1955) and xxv–xxvi (1957).

23 A. Hess, 'The Moriscos: An Ottoman fifth column', *American Historical Review* 74 (1968–9).

24 Fernand Braudel, *La Mediterranée et le Monde mediterranéen à l'epoque de Philippe II* (Paris 1949), p. 591.

25 Luce López-Baralt, 'Crónica de la destrucción de un mundo: la literatura aljamiado-morisca', *Bulletin Hispanique* 82 (1980), pp. 16–58.

26 On taqiya see, *inter alia*, Peter Dressendörfer, *Islam unter der Inquisition. Die Morisco-Prozesse in Toledo 1575–1610* (Wiesbaden 1971), p. 131.

27 *Ibid.*, p. 64 n. 171.

28 Dario Cabanelas, 'Intento de supervivencia en el ocaso de una cultura: los libros plumbeos de Granada', *Nueva Revista de Filología Hispánica* xxx (1981), pp. 334–58.

29 Biblioteca Nacional, Madrid, ms. 721 f. 39–46.

30 In reality Morisco growth, in Valencia at least, was already falling off: James Casey, 'Moriscos and the depopulation of Valencia', *Past and Present* 50 (1971).

31 Domínguez Ortiz and Vincent, *op. cit.*, chap. 9.

32 British Library, Egerton ms. 1151 f. 323, 336. Cf. Pascual Boronat, *Los Moriscos españoles y su expulsion* (2 vols, Valencia 1901), ii, pp. 657–61.

33 AHN Inquisición leg. 4671¹.

34 On Cervantes' views see F. Márquez Villanueva, *Personajes y temas del Quijote* (Madrid 1975).

35 Boronat, *op. cit.*, II, pp. 196–7; F. Janer, *La condición social de los moriscos de España* (Madrid 1857), pp. 114, 116.

36 Boronat, *op. cit.*, II, pp. 68–93.

37 Henry Kamen, *La España de Carlos II* (Barcelona 1982), p. 487.

38 García Cárcel, *Herejía y Sociedad en el siglo XVI. La Inquisición en Valencia 1530–1609* (Barcelona 1980), p. 102.

39 For the emigration in general, Henri Lapeyre, *La Géographie de l'Espagne morisque* (Paris 1959); for the exiles to Africa, Martine Ravillard, *Bibliographie commentée des Morisques* (Algiers 1979).

40 Contreras, 'Estadística', *op. cit.*, p. 50.

41 AHN Inquisición leg. 5126¹.

Chapter 7: Racialism and its Critics

1 It is impossible to accept the view, given most currency by Américo Castro, that exclusivist concepts of honour were Jewish in origin: see B. Netanyahu, 'Américo Castro and his view on the origins of the *pureza de sangre*', Proceedings, *American Academy for Jewish Research* XLVI–XLVII (1979–80), pp. 397–457.

2 I.S. Révah, 'La controverse sur les statuts de pureté de sang. Un document inédit', *Bulletin Hispanique* 73 (1971), p. 265.

3 Sicroff, *Les controverses des statuts*, pp. 36–41.

4 Juan de Torquemada, *Tractatus contra Madianitas et Ismaelitas* (ed. N. López Martínez, Burgos 1957).

5 Sicroff, *op. cit.*, pp. 41–62.

6 Alonso de Oropesa, *Luz para conocimiento de los Gentiles* (ed. Luis A. Díaz y Díaz, Madrid 1979).

7 See above, chap. 3.

8 B. Cuart Moner, 'Los Estatutos del Colegio de San Clemente', in E. Verdera y Tüells (ed.), *El Cardenal Albornoz y el Colegio de España* (6 vols, Bologna 1979), IV, pp. 602–3.

9 Domínguez Ortiz, *Los conversos de origen judío*, pp. 58–9.

10 AHN Inquisición libro 497 f. 22–3.

11 C. Carrete Parrondo, 'Los conversos jerónimos ante el estatuto de limpieza de sangre', *Helmantica* XXVI (1975), pp. 97–116.

12 Sicroff, *op. cit.*, p. 96 ff.

13 'Sobre el Estatuto de limpieza de la Sancta Iglesia de Toledo', Biblioteca Nacional, Madrid, MS. 13267 f. 278.

14 'La contradicion hecha por algunas dignidades y canonigos de la Santa Iglesia de Toledo', *ibid.*, MS. 1703 f. 1–17.

15 Sicroff, *op. cit.*, p. 138 n. 184.

16 Philip II was told that 'the pope spoke ill of the Spanish statutes and said they were against canon law'; cited Sicroff, *op. cit.*, p. 143.

17 For example as in Bennassar, *L'homme espagnol*, p. 178.

18 Lea, *op. cit.*, II, 287.

19 Cited Sicroff, *op. cit.*, p. 94 n. 125.

20 Cf. Domínguez Ortiz, *Los conversos de origen judío*, pp. 59–73.

21 Fray Agustín Salucio, *Discurso sobre los estatutos de limpieza de sangre* (Cieza 1975 edn.), p. 2.

22 All these cases are documented in Lea, *op. cit.*, II, pp. 300–306.

23 Caro Baroja, *Los Judíos*, II, pp. 304–5.

24 AHN Inquisición libro 497 f. 50.

25 Narciso Hergueta, 'La Inquisición de Logroño. Nuevos datos históricos', *BRAH* XLV (1904), pp. 422–39.

26 Cf. the case in Valencia in 1691 cited in Kamen, *Carlos II*, p. 267.

27 AHN Inquisición leg. 1586 no. 8.

28 Quoted in Tellechea, *Carranza*, II, p. 241 n. 21.

29 Rojas was the son of the Marquis of Poza.

30 Tellechea, *Tiempos recios*, p. 53.

31 Marcel Bataillon, 'Honneur et Inquisition', *Bulletin Hispanique* XXVII (1925), pp. 15–17.

32 For Servet, there is a recent study by Angel Alcalá, *Miguel Servet: Restitución del Cristianismo* (Madrid 1980).

33 R.W. Truman and A. Gordon Kinder, 'The pursuit of Spanish heretics in the Low Countries: the activities of Alonso del Canto, 1561–1564', *Journal of Ecclesiastical History* 30 (1979), pp. 65–93.

34 Eusebio Rey, 'San Ignacio de Loyola y el problema de los "Cristianos Nuevos"', *Razón y Fe* 153 (1956), pp. 178–9.

35 Sicroff, *op. cit.*, pp. 272–3.

36 Eusebio Rey, *op. cit.*, p. 190. For hostility to the Jesuits, see Antonio Astraín S.J., *Historia de la Compañía de Jesús en la Asistencia de España* (7 vols, Madrid 1902–25), vols. I–III.

37 It has been argued that Ribadeneira was of converso origin: see Jose Gómez-Menor, 'La progenie hebrea del padre Pedro de Ribadeneira S.I.', *Sefarad* xxxvi (1976), pp. 307–32.

38 Domínguez Ortiz, *Los conversos de origen judío*, pp. 43–5.

39 The second edition was 1575.

40 Most of what follows is to be the subject of a documented article now in preparation.

41 There is a modern edition: see n. 21 above.

42 Lerma was at the time Marquis of Denia. The letters are in Biblioteca Nacional, Madrid, MS. 17909/5.

43 'Papel que dio el Reyno de Castilla a uno de los Sres Ministros de la Junta diputada para tratarse sobre el Memorial presentado por el Reyno a S.M. con el libro del Pe Mro. Salucio', Biblioteca Nacional, Madrid, MS. 13043 f. 116–27.

44 Printed by Révah, 'La controverse sur les statuts', *op. cit.*, from a late copy. My source is the original.

45 I.S. Révah, 'Le plaidoyer en faveur des "Nouveaux-Chrétiens" portugais du licencié Martín González de Cellorigo (1619)', *Revue des Etudes Juives* cxxii (1963), pp. 279–398.

46 'Discurso de un Inquisidor hecho en tiempo de Phelipe Quarto sobre los estatutos de limpieza de sangre de España, y si conviene al servicio de Dios, del Rey y Reyno moderarlos', Biblioteca Nacional, Madrid, MS. 13043 f. 132–71.

47 Domínguez Ortiz, *Los conversos*, pp. 103–8.

48 *Ibid.*, appendix iv (e), p. 233.

49 A version of his paper is in *ibid.*, pp. 243–4.

50 *Ibid.*, pp. 245–7.

51 'Discurso político del desempeño del Reyno', printed in Caro Baroja, *Los Judíos*, iii, pp. 318–20.

52 Carvajal to Joseph de Luyando, 28 Sept. 1751, Biblioteca Nacional, Madrid, MS. 13043 f. 130.

53 Domínguez Ortiz, *Los conversos*, p. 129 n. 14.

54 Baruch Braunstein, *The Chuetas of Majorca*, p. 123.

55 Lea, *op. cit.*, ii, p. 314, citing Tomás Bertrán Soler, *Un milagro y una mentira* (Valencia 1858).

56 Domínguez Ortiz, *Los conversos*, p. 130.

Chapter 8: Organization and Social Control

1 See chap. 13 below for a further discussion.

2 Lea, *op. cit.*, i, p. 174.

3 As we have seen, most theologians employed by the sixteenth-century Inquisition were Dominicans.

4 García Cárcel, *Los orígenes*, p. 135; *Valencia 1530–1609*, p. 127.

5 AHN Inquisición libro 1275 f. 169.

6 Nicolau Eymeric and Francisco Peña, *Le manual des inquisiteurs* (ed. Louis Sala-Molins, Paris 1973).

7 For a favourable view of the Instructions see J.L. González Novalín, 'Reforma de las leyes … del Santo Oficio durante la presidencia … de Fernando de Valdés (1547–1566)', in *Nueva Visión*, pp. 211–17.

8 AHN Inquisición libro 497.

9 In fact, for Aragon, Italy, Navarre and America.

10 Lea, *op. cit.*, ii, pp. 168–78.

11 I here follow J. Contreras and J.P. Dedieu, 'Geografía de la Inquisición española: la formación de los distritos 1470–1820', *Hispania* 40 (1980), pp. 37–93; but their information should be balanced against the exhaustive listing in Lea, *op. cit.*, i, pp. 541–55.

12 Again, the dates are derived from Contreras and Dedieu. It is possible to offer alternative dates, depending on what one means by the 'establishment' of a tribunal.

13 Toledo had four: see R. Pérez-Bustamante, 'Nóminas de inquisidores', in *Nueva Visión*, p. 261.

14 Cf. J. Caro Baroja, *El señor inquisidor y otras vidas por oficio* (Madrid 1970), pp. 20, 31.

15 By Dedieu, in Bennassar, *L'Inquisition espagnole*, pp. 84–5.

16 Regulations of 1560 and 1573 required that they be married, peaceable and *límpios*, with a minimum age of twenty-five: Lea, *op. cit.*, ii, pp. 275, 279.

17 Lea, *op. cit.*, i, 447.

18 Report of 13 May 1628, AHN Inquisición leg. 2155[1].

19 The totals were claimed by the Inquisition itself. There is thus no reason to doubt their veracity, as is done by Contreras, *Galicia*, p. 77.

20 *Ibid.*, pp. 90–92.

21 R. García Cárcel, 'Numero y sociología de los familiares de la Inquisición valenciana', *Nueva Visión*, pp. 277–8.

22 AHN Inquisición leg. 2155[2].

23 Cf. García Cárcel, 'Numero y sociología', *op. cit.*, p. 279. In Valencia and Granada the Inquisition also appointed Moriscos as familiars.

24 Lea, *op. cit.*, I, p. 416. For familiars see also Bennassar, *L'Inquisition espagnole*, pp. 97–102.

25 Inquisitors to Suprema, 24 June 1597, AHN Inquisición leg. 2707[1].

26 Contreras, *Galicia*, pp. 90–92, 129–30.

27 H. Kamen, 'Confiscations in the economy of the Spanish Inquisition', *The Economic History Review* XVIII, 3 (1965), pp. 511–25.

28 AHN Inquisición leg. 4971[1].

29 Hernando del Pulgar, *Los claros varones de España y las treinta y dos cartas* (Madrid 1747), letter 24, p. 252.

30 Diego Ortiz de Zúñiga, *Annales de Sevilla* (Madrid 1677), año 1480, p. 389.

31 Haim Beinart, *Records of the Inquisition of Ciudad Real* (3 vols, Jerusalem 1974–5), I, p. 391; Ventura, *La Inquisición española y los judíos conversos*.

32 Fidel Fita, 'La Inquisición en Guadalupe', *BRAH* XXIII (1893), pp. 283–8.

33 AHN Inquisición leg. 4776–9.

34 Pedro Sanahuja O.F.M., *Lérida en sus luchas por la fe* (Lérida 1946), p. 162.

35 Lea, *op. cit.*, II, p. 403.

36 Lea, *op. cit.*, I, p. 329.

37 Ferdinand, according to a chronicler, apparently got ten million ducats from confiscations: Lea, *op. cit.*, II, pp. 367, 371.

38 Lea, *op. cit.*, I, p. 330–31.

39 Miguel Avilés, 'Motivos de crítica', in *Nueva Visión*, p. 191.

40 AHN Inquisición leg. 2700.

41 For visitations, see chap. 9.

42 AHN Inquisición leg. 2702.

43 *Ibid.*, leg. 4760[1].

44 *Ibid.*, leg. 4723[3].

45 Cited in J. Fernández Nieva, *La Inquisición y los Moriscos extremeños (1585–1610)* (Badajoz 1979), p. 87.

46 For 1618, from García Cárcel, *Valencia 1530–1609*, p. 177; for 1671–8, from AHN Inquisición leg. 4994[1]; for 1705, from Archivo General de Simancas, section Gracia y Justicia leg. 622; for 1731, from Lea, *op. cit.*, II, appendix.

47 AHN Inquisición leg. 4723[3].

48 *Ibid.*, leg. 4723[3]; Fernández Nieva, *op. cit.*, p. 16.

49 'Memoria de los salarios que tienen', AHN Inquisición libro 1232 f. 205–9.

50 AHN Inquisición 4724¹ expediente 1.

51 Kamen, 'Confiscations', *op. cit.*, p. 524.

52 AHN Inquisición leg. 4597².

53 Cited in Lea, *op. cit.*, II, p. 433.

54 AHN Inquisición 4760¹; also M. Isabel Pérez de Colosia Rodríguez and Joaquín Gil Sanjuan, *Málaga y la Inquisición (1550–1600)*, no. 38 of *Jabega* (Málaga) 1982, p. 13.

55 Fernández Nieva, *op. cit.*, p. 87.

56 Lea, *op. cit.*, II, pp. 438–9.

57 Kamen, *Carlos II*, pp. 360–61.

58 Lea, *op. cit.*, II, p. 8.

59 Astraín, *Historia de la Compañía*, vols. I–III.

60 My account is based on Menéndez Pelayo, *op. cit.*, V, pp. 9–82; Gregorio Marañón, 'El proceso del Arzobispo Carranza', *BRAH* CXXVII (1950), pp. 135–78; and Lea, *op. cit.*, II, pp. 48–86. Authoritative work on the personalities and context of the Carranza case has been produced by J.I. Tellechea Idigoras; see especially the bibliography to his *Carranza*, I, pp. 23–6.

61 Marañón, 'El proceso', *op. cit.*, p. 145.

Chapter 9: The Procedure of the Inquisition

1 Cited by Bennassar, *L'Inquisition espagnole*, pp. 105–6.

2 Seville Instructions of 1484, clauses 1–5.

3 Baer, *Jews*, II, p. 343; Lea, *op. cit.*, I, pp. 169–70.

4 García Cárcel, *Valencia 1530–1609*, p. 192.

5 A useful edict of faith of 1624 is printed in Miguel Jiménez Monteserín, *Introducción a la Inquisición española* (Madrid 1980), pp. 503–35.

6 Angela Selke, *Vida y muerte de los Chuetas de Mallorca* (Madrid 1980).

7 *Records of the Spanish Inquisition, translated from the original manuscripts* (Boston 1828), p. 27.

8 W. de Gray Birch, *Catalogue of a collection of original manuscripts ... of the Inquisition in the Canary Islands* (2 vols, London 1903), I, pp. 103, 112.

9 Lea, *op. cit.*, II, p. 99.

10 Avilés, 'Motivos de crítica', in *Nueva Visión*, p. 190.

11 AHN Inquisición leg. 218 no. 20, case of 1674–6.

12 Below, chap. 11.

13 'La orden que ha de guardar el inquisidor que huviera de salir a visitar de la Inquisicion de Llerena', AHN Inquisición libro 1229 f. 168–79.

14 In what follows, the evidence for Llerena comes from AHN Inquisición leg. 2700; for Toledo, from J.P. Dedieu, 'Les Inquisiteurs de Tolède et la visite du district. La sédentarisation d'un tribunal (1550–1630)', *Mélanges de la Casa de Velázquez* XIII (1977), pp. 235–56; for Galicia, Contreras, *Galicia*, pp. 476–511.

15 AHN Inquisición leg. 2706[1] no. 33.

16 *Ibid.*, libro 730 f. 108.

17 Contreras, *Galicia*, p. 488.

18 Cf. García Cárcel, *Valencia 1530–1609*, p. 190: 'la respuesta al edicto fue casi siempre silenciosa'. He shows that visitations in 1589 and 1590 brought in only sixteen and thirty-eight denunciations respectively, p. 189.

19 'Memoria de las villas y lugares que visito el Dr Juan Alvarez de Caldas', AHN Inquisición leg. 2155[1].

20 *Ibid.*, libro 731 f. 10, 23.

21 Inquisitors to Suprema, 15 July 1623, *ibid.* leg. 2155[2].

22 Cited in Dedieu, *op. cit.*, p. 253. High figures for arrests normally meant a find of heretics: e.g. the Llerena tribunal arrested 130 judaizers in Badajoz in 1567.

23 García Cárcel, *Valencia 1530–1609*, p. 191.

24 *Records of the Spanish Inquisition*, pp. 78–113.

25 Lea, *op. cit.*, II, p. 572.

26 AGS Patronato Real, Inquisición leg. 28. Cf. Lea, *op. cit.*, I, pp. 585–6.

27 *Discusion del proyecto de decreto sobre el Tribunal de la Inquisición* (Cadiz 1813).'

28 *Colección de documentos ineditos* CXII, pp. 264–5, 270.

29 AHN Inquisición leg. 2701.

30 'Extracts from a narrative of the Persecution of Hippolyto Joseph da Costa Pereira', printed in the English version of Philip Limborch's *The History of the Inquisition* (London 1816), pp. 521–30.

31 Miguel de la Pinta Llorente, *Las cárceles inquisitoriales españolas* (Madrid 1949), p. 115.

32 Birch, *Canary Islands*, I, pp. 367–8.

33 Pinta Llorente, *Las cárceles*, p. 102.

34 Birch, *op. cit.*, I, p. 235.

35 Lea, *op. cit.*, II, p. 534.

36 AHN Inquisición libro 497 f. 45–6.

37 Lea, *op. cit.*, III, p. 33.

38 Beinart, *Conversos on Trial*, p. 120.

39 Bennassar, *L'Inquisition espagnole*, pp. 115–16.

40 García Cárcel, *Valencia 1530–1609*, p. 199.

41 The *potro* was virtually the only torture used in the seventeenth century by the Inquisition. A detailed account of torture methods at that epoch is given in AHN Inquisición libro 1226 f. 605–9.

42 Inquisitors to Suprema, 1 Apr. 1579, AHN Inquisición leg. 2704.

43 For a case of 1648 in a secular court, see F. Tomás y Valiente, *El derecho penal de la monarquía absoluta (siglos XVI–XVIII)* (Madrid 1969), pp. 414–17.

44 Lea, *op. cit.*, III, p. 25.

45 Birch, *op. cit.*, I, pp. 381–2.

Chapter 10: Trial and Punishment

1 Lea, *op. cit.*, III, p. 46.

2 See above, chap. 5, p. 67.

3 Lea, *op. cit.*, III, p. 68.

4 AHN Inquisición leg. 1679 no. 3.

5 *Ibid.*, leg. 37 no. 1.

6 To Suprema, 2 May 1590, AHN Inquisición leg. 2706[1] no. 33.

7 Lea, *op. cit.*, III, p. 79.

8 Contreras, in *Nueva Visión*, p. 370. The cases counted are 'causas de fe'. This table is given only to provide a rough guide, and no conclusions whatever can be drawn from it. Dr Contreras admits that the cases not logged account for at least 25 per cent more, and that the omission of Cuenca and Madrid seriously distorts the figures for Castile. I can add that there are omissions and errors in the listed figures, and that a significant part of activity, the 'causas criminales', is left out altogether.

9 All the data that follow are reproduced from Dedieu's chapter in Bennassar, *L'Inquisition espagnole*, pp. 29–31; and from Contreras, *Galicia*, p. 467. The overall figures are the work of Contreras and not of Dedieu. The figures for 'alumbrados' given

in Dedieu are added to those for 'Protestants' or 'Lutherans', itself a loose and unreliable grouping. For Toledo see Dedieu, 'Les causes de foi de l'Inquisition de Tolède (1483–1820)', *Mélanges de la Casa de Velázquez* XIV (1978), pp. 143–71.

10 García Cárcel, *Valencia 1530–1609*, p. 212.

11 Contreras, *Galicia*, p. 550.

12 Lea, *op. cit.*, III, p. 156.

13 In reality, even in state tribunals 'life' meant a maximum of ten years: see Kamen, *Carlos II, op. cit.*, pp. 266–7.

14 Biblioteca Nacional, Madrid, MS. 9475.

15 For some other figures, see García Cárcel, *Valencia 1530–1609*, p. 214; and Bennassar, *L'Inquisition espagnole*, pp. 118–19.

16 Letter of 11 May 1573, AHN Inquisición leg. 2703.

17 Llorente, *Histoire Critique*, IV, p. 92.

18 Fidel Fita, 'La Inquisición Toledana. Relación contemporanea de los autos y autillos que celebró desde el año 1485 hasta el de 1501', *BRAH* XI (1887), pp. 294–6.

19 *An authentick Narrative of the origin, establishment and progress of the Inquisition* (London 1748), pp. 35–9. The original account is Joseph del Olmo, *Relación Histórica del Auto General de Fe que se celebró en Madrid este año de 1680* (Madrid 1680).

20 Fidel Fita, 'La Inquisición de Logroño y un judaizante quemado en 1719', *BRAH* XLV (1904), pp. 457–9.

21 Jose Simón Díaz, 'La Inquisición de Logroño (1570–1580)'; *Berceo*, I (1946), p. 100.

22 AHN Inquisición leg. 4696².

23 *Ibid.*, leg. 5047³.

24 *Ibid.*, leg. 4724¹ no. 1.

25 Inquisitor to Suprema, 23 Oct. 1560, AHN Inquisición libro 730 f. 23.

26 21 Nov. 1560, *ibid.*, f. 26.

27 13 Aug. 1622, *ibid.*, leg. 2155².

Chapter 11: Popular Culture and the Counter Reformation

1 J. Caro Baroja, *Las formas complejas de la vida religiosa (Religión, sociedad y caracter en la España de los siglos XVI y XVII)* (Madrid 1978), p. 197, citing from S. Cirac Estopañán, *Registro de documentos del Santo Oficio de Cuenca y Sigüenza* (Cuenca 1965).

2 Contreras, *Galicia*, pp. 461, 463.

3 Cf. J. García Oro, *Cisneros y la reforma del clero español en tiempo de los Reyes Católicos* (Madrid 1971).

4 José Sánchez Herrero, *Concilios Provinciales y Sínodos Toledanos de los siglos XIV y XV* (La Laguna 1976).

5 For a survey of the literature see Melquiades Andrés, in García-Villoslada, *Historia de la Iglesia*, III-2°, pp. 337 ff.

6 The unfortunate destruction of all my research notes makes it impossible to give references for this and other quotations in this chapter.

7 J.L. González Novalín, 'Religiosidad y reforma del pueblo cristiano', in García Villoslada, *Historia de la Iglesia*, III-1°, pp. 351–84, gives a good summary of the missionary problem in Spain.

8 As in rural England: see K. Wrightson in *Journal of Peasant Studies* 5 (1977), p. 43.

9 For good discussions see Dedieu, in Bennassar, *L'Inquisition espagnole*, pp. 241–68; Contreras, *Galicia*, pp. 554–65, 654–62.

10 All cited cases are from Kamen, *Carlos II*, pp. 476–86.

11 Contreras, *Galicia*, pp. 561, 667.

12 J.M. García Fuentes, *La Inquisición en Granada en el siglo XVI* (Granada 1981), pp. 445–6.

13 Cf. Kamen, *Carlos II*, p. 480–81.

14 J.P. Dedieu, '"Christianisation" en Nouvelle Castille. Catéchisme, communion, messe et confirmation dans l'archevêché de Tolède, 1540–1650', *Mélanges de la Casa de Velázquez* XV (1979), pp. 261–93.

15 AHN Inquisición leg. 79 no. 24 f. 38.

16 V. Pinto Crespo, 'La actitud de la Inquisición ante la iconografía religiosa', *Hispania Sacra* XXXI (1978), pp. 285–322.

17 William A. Christian Jr., *Apparitions in Late Medieval and Renaissance Spain* (Princeton 1981).

18 R. Maria de Hornedo, 'Teatro e iglesia', in García-Villoslada, *Historia de la Iglesia*, IV, p. 330.

19 Isabel Testón and Mercedes Santillana, 'El clero cacereño durante los siglos XVI al XVIII', *Historia Moderna, Actas de las II Jornadas de Metodología y Didáctica de la Historia* (Cáceres 1983), p. 466.

20 AHN Inquisición libro 735.

21 *Ibid.*, leg. 217 no. 12; Contreras, *Galicia*, p. 561.

22 Any other sort of fornication, of course, implied an offence; for

example, involuntary intercourse was rape, and between married adults it was adultery.

23 Dedieu, in Bennassar, *L'Inquisition*, p. 327.

24 Contreras, *Galicia*, pp. 628–30.

25 AHN Inquisición leg. 24 no. 7.

26 For the scandalous life of the clergy in Coria in 1591 see A. Rodríguez Sánchez, 'Inmoralidad y represión', *Historia Moderna. Actas etc.* (Cáceres 1983), pp. 451–62.

27 AHN Inquisición leg. 2155¹.

28 García Cárcel, *Valencia 1530–1609*, p. 285.

29 For an excellent survey, see Bennassar, *L'Inquisition*, chap. x.

30 Lea, *op. cit.*, iv, p. 183.

31 *Ibid.*, p. 193.

32 Morisco sorcery was an undeniable dimension of belief in relevant areas: García Cárcel shows that twenty-one out of sixty-seven accused of superstition in Valencia in 1530–1609 were Moriscos: *op. cit.*, p. 249. On Morisco magic see also J. Caro Baroja, *Vidas mágicas e Inquisición* (2 vols, Madrid 1967), i, pp. 49–52.

33 For the European context of Counter Reformation reform, see Peter Burke, *Popular culture in early modern Europe* (London 1978).

34 A general study (which unfortunately omits Spain) is R. Kieckhefer, *European Witch Trials. Their Foundations in Popular and Learned Culture, 1300–1500* (London 1976).

35 *Malleus Maleficarum* (ed. Montague Summers, London 1948).

36 For the European context see, for example, H. Kamen, *European Society 1500–1700* (London 1984), chap. 8.

37 Llorente, *Histoire Critique*, ii, p. 43.

38 S. Cirac Estopañán, *Los procesos de hechicerías en la Inquisición de Castilla la Nueva* (Madrid 1942), p. 196.

39 F. Idoate, *Un documento de la Inquisición sobre brujería* (Pamplona 1972), p. 13.

40 Not, as Novalín (*Valdés*, p. 63) has it, in 1525; nor, as Caro Baroja claims (*Vidas mágicas*, ii, p. 60), in 1529. The notes of the meeting are in AHN Inquisición libro 1231 f. 634–7: 'Dubia quae in causa praesenti videntur'. There is a copy in the Bodleian, Oxford, MS. Arch. Σ. 130. Cf. Lea, *op. cit.*, iv, pp. 212–14.

41 The Basque events emboldened Fray Martín de Castañega, *Tratado de supersticiones* (Logroño 1529) to explain that women

were more likely than men to be witches because they were, among other things, 'more talkative than men and cannot keep secrets'.

42 Lea, *op. cit.*, IV, pp. 218–19.

43 *Ibid.*, p. 223.

44 On Salazar Frias and the Navarre context, see Gustav Henningsen, *The Witches' Advocate, Basque Witchcraft and the Spanish Inquisition* (Reno, 1980); and J. Caro Baroja, *Inquisición, Brujería y Criptojudaismo* (Barcelona 1974), pp. 183–315, which adds important dimensions to his *Las brujas y su mundo* (Madrid 1961).

45 Biblioteca Nacional, Madrid, MS. 718 f. 271.

46 For the memorial see Henningsen *op. cit.*; also Lea, *op. cit.*, IV, pp. 231–4.

47 'Acerca de los cuentos de las bruxas. Discurso de Pedro de Valencia', AHN Inquisición libro 1231 f. 608–29.

48 *Ibid.*, libro 735.

49 Angel Gari, 'Variedad de competencias en el delito de brujería en Aragón (1600–1650)', *Argensola* xx, 85 (1978), p. 198; also his 'La brujería en Aragón', *I Congreso de Aragón de Etnología y Antropología* (1979), pp. 27–44.

50 A. Pladevall, *Persecutió de les bruixes a les comarques de Vic a principis del segle XVII* (Barcelona 1974).

51 Albert Loomie S.J., 'Religion and Elizabethan commerce with Spain', *Catholic Historical Review* (Apr. 1964), pp. 30–31.

52 Consulta of Council of State, 31 March 1653, AGS Estado leg. 2528.

53 Lea, *op. cit.*, III, p. 447.

54 AHN Inquisición libro 735 f. 176.

55 L. de Alberti and A.B. Wallis Chapman (eds), *English Merchants and the Spanish Inquisition in the Canaries* (Royal Historical Society publications vol. xxiii) (London 1912), p. 80 n. 1.

56 F. Fajardo Spinola, *Reducciones de protestantes al catolicismo en Canarias durante el siglo XVIII: 1700–1812* (Gran Canaria 1977), pp. 48, 51.

57 Alberti and Chapman, *op. cit.*, p. x.

58 AGS Estado leg. 2981.

Chapter 12: The Last Days of the Conversos

1 J. Gómez-Menor Fuentes, 'Un judío converso de 1498. Diego Gómez de Toledo (Semuel Abolafia) y su proceso inquisitorial'. *Sefarad* XXXIII (1973), pp. 45–110.

2 Cf. Caro Baroja, *Judíos*, I, pp. 404–31.

3 I.S. Révah, 'Les Marranes', *Revue des Etudes Juives* (1959–60), p. 54.

4 Licenciado Montoya to Suprema, 11 Jan. 1581, AHN Inquisición leg. 2705[1] no. 21.

5 Caro Baroja, *Judíos*, III, p. 51.

6 *Ibid.*, I, pp. 465–6.

7 Lea, *op. cit.*, III, 239 ff.; A. Herculano, *História da origem e estabelecimento da Inquisiçao em Portugal* (3 vols, Lisbon 1907), I, pp. 228–86.

8 Lea, *op. cit.*, III, p. 259.

9 *Ibid.*, pp. 265–6.

10 Biblioteca Nacional., Madrid, MS. 721 f. 127–31; Llorente, *Histoire Critique*, II, p. 400; Lea, *op. cit.*, III, p. 267.

11 Bodleian Library, Oxford, Arch. Σ. 130 no. 8; Gaspar Matute y Luquín, *Colección de los Autos generales i particulares de Fe celebrados por el Tribunal de la Inquisición de Córdoba* (Córdoba 1840), pp. 65, 127; Biblioteca Nacional, Madrid, MS. 718 f. 375, MS. 6751 f. 53.

12 Lea, *op. cit.*, III, pp. 267–70.

13 Elkan Adler, 'Documents sur les Marranes d'Espagne et de Portugal sous Philippe IV', *Revue des Etudes Juives* XLIX (1904), pp. 63–5.

14 Caro Baroja, *Judíos*, II, pp. 56–7.

15 *Ibid.*, II, p. 59.

16 A. Domínguez Ortiz, 'El proceso inquisitorial de Juan Núñez Saravía, banquero de Felipe IV', *Hispania* 61 (1955).

17 Caro Baroja, *Judíos*, II, pp. 68–131.

18 The accounts of the firm are in AHN Inquisición leg. 5096[2].

19 The source is Barrionuevo's *Avisos*.

20 The Montesinos accounts are in AHN Inquisición leg. 4971[1].

21 Biblioteca Nacional, Madrid, MS. 718 f. 375.

22 This and the other cases that follow are taken from Kamen, *Carlos II*, pp. 489–91.

23 For an analysis of judaizers in Galicia, see J. Contreras, 'La Inquisición en Galicia y la minoría conversa. Un análisis so-

ciológico del judaizante gallego', *Estudios de Historia Social* 20–21 (1982), pp. 429–45.

24 For Sabbatai, see Gerschom Scholem, *Sabbatai Zevi: the mystical Messiah 1626–1676* (Princeton 1973).

25 Y.H. Yerushalmi, *From Spanish Court to Italian Ghetto. Isaac Cardoso: a Study in Seventeenth-Century Marranism and Jewish Apologetics* (New York 1971).

26 Révah, 'Un pamphlet ... d'Antonio Enríquez Gómez', *Revue des Etudes Juives* CXXI (1962), p. 149.

27 Maxim Kerkhof, 'La "Ynquisición de Luzifer y visita de todos los diablos" ', *Sefarad* XXXVIII (1978), p. 320.

28 Biblioteca Nacional, Madrid, MS. 9475; Jose del Olmo, *Relación*, *op. cit.*; Matute y Luquín, *op. cit.*, p. 210.

29 *Inquisición de Mallorca. Reconciliados y Relajados 1488–1691* (Barcelona 1946), pp. 201–75.

30 *Ibid.*, pp. 109–99.

31 For what follows, see Braunstein, *The Chuetas*.

32 J.B. Vilar Ramírez, *El Dr Diego Mateo Zapata (1664–1745)* (Murcia 1970).

33 For both Zapata and Peralta see A. Domínguez Ortiz, *Hechos y figuras del siglo XVIII español* (Madrid 1973), pp. 159–91.

34 Lea, *op. cit.*, III, p. 553.

35 This table is based on *Spanish Tracts 1683–1725* (British Library 4625 g. 1); *Relaciones de Autos de Fe, 1721, 1722, Madrid* (B.L. 4071 bb⁴³ 1–15); *Autos de Fe* (B.L. 4071 i. 3); and Matute y Luquín, *op. cit.*

36 Lea, *op. cit.*, III, p. 311.

37 G. Desdevises du Dézert, 'Notes sur l'Inquisition espagnole au dix-huitième siècle', *Revue Hispanique* VI (1899), p.490.

38 *The Bible in Spain* (London 1930 edn), p. 155.

39 *A journey through Spain in the years 1786 and 1787* (3 vols, London 1792), III, p. 84.

Chapter 13: The Inquisition in Politics

1 Lea, *op. cit.*, II, p. 110.

2 Biblioteca Nacional, Madrid, MS. 718 f. 38; also f. 3–4 and f. 8, for letters in 1518 and 1519.

3 In *ibid.*, f. 108–10, 'Remisiones de causas hechas por los summos Pontifices a la Inquisizion de España', are examples of

twenty-one appeals thus referred back between 1569 and 1608.

4 Lea, *op. cit.*, I, pp. 567–9, appendix I.

5 An excellent recent survey is F. Tomás y Valiente, 'Relaciones de la Inquisición con el aparato institucional del estado', in *Nueva Visión*, pp. 41–60.

6 AHN Inquisición libro 1262 f. 138–47.

7 *Ibid.*, libro 1275 f. 232.

8 'Justicias reales castigados por el Sancto Officio', *ibid.*, f. 1–8.

9 Bennassar, *L'Inquisition*, p. 373: 'L'Inquisition, arme absolue de la monarchie'; A. Domínguez Ortiz, 'Regalismo y relaciones Iglesia-Estado en el siglo XVII', in García-Villoslada, *Historia de la Iglesia*, IV, pp. 113–21.

10 Cited in Carrasco Urgoiti, *Problema morisco*, p. 151. My italics.

11 García Cárcel, *Valencia 1530–1609*, p. 318.

12 Carrasco Urgoiti, *op. cit.*, p. 142.

13 'Exemplares de haverse mandado borrar de libros de Audiencias y Consejos cedulas dadas contra el estilo de la Inquisición', AHN Inquisición libro 1275 f. 203, is taken up almost wholly with conflicts with Barcelona.

14 J.H. Elliott, *The Revolt of the Catalans* (Cambridge 1963), p. 456.

15 Biblioteca Nacional, Madrid, MS. 2569.

16 Quoted thus in Sánchez Albornoz, *op. cit.*, II, p. 563. Lea, *op. cit.*, IV, p. 250 quotes it as four clerics.

17 Gregorio Marañón, *Antonio Pérez.* (*El hombre, el drama, la época*) (2 vols, Madrid 1947). For quotations I use the one-volume English edition of 1954.

18 *Ibid.*, pp. 11, 13.

19 *Ibid.*, p. 53.

20 *Ibid.*, p. 276.

21 Lea, *op. cit.*, II, pp. 133–57.

22 Menéndez Pelayo, *op. cit.*, VI, p. 56.

23 Cf. Kamen, *Spain 1469–1714*, chap. IV.

24 Domínguez Ortiz, in *Historia de la Iglesia*, IV, p. 115.

25 What follows is drawn from Kamen, *Carlos II*, pp. 364–9, where full references are given.

26 'Consulta que hizo la Junta que mando formar el Señor Rey Don Carlos 2° a Su Magd para reformar abusos de Inquisición', Biblioteca de la Real Academia de la Historia, Est. 23, gr. 5 a B no. 129 ff. 308–52.

Chapter 14: The Inquisition in History

1 Foxe, *The Book of Martyrs* (London 1863 edn), p. 153.
2 *Ibid.*, p. 154.
3 London 1912 edn, p. 165.
4 M. Dierickx S.J., 'La politique religieuse de Philippe II dans les anciens Pays Bas', *Hispania* XVI (1956), p. 137.
5 *An Apology or Defence of William the First of Nassau, Prince of Orange*, a translation in *Phenix* XIII (1707), pp. 497, 530.
6 J.W. Thompson, *The Wars of Religion in France* (New York n.d.), p. 12.
7 Henry Kamen and Joseph Perez, *La imágen internacional de la España de Felipe II* (Valladolid 1980).
8 *The Book of Martyrs*, p. 1060.
9 William S. Maltby, *The Black Legend in England* (Durham N.C. 1971).
10 Sverker Arnoldsson, *La leyenda negra: Estudios sobre sus orígenes* (Göteborg 1960).
11 Cf. Lea, *op. cit.*, IV, p. 514 quoting the *Relazioni Venete*, serie I.
12 'Relazione di Spagna', Guicciardini, *Opere*, IX, p. 131.
13 Miguel de la Pinta Llorente, *Aspectos históricos del sentimiento religioso en España* (Madrid 1961), p. 37.
14 Carrasco Urgoiti, *Problema morisco*, p. 156.
15 Gonzalo Correas, *Vocabulario de refranes* (Madrid 1924), p. 124.
16 Llorente, *Histoire Critique*, II, pp. 14–15.
17 *Historia General de España*, (Biblioteca de Autores Españoles vol. XXX, p. 256), book 26, chap. 13.
18 Birch, *Canary Islands*, II, p. 905.
19 Quoted in Vicens Vives (ed.), *Historia Social y económica de España y América* (5 vols, Barcelona 1957), IV, p. 247.
20 Carvajal to Luyando, 28 Sept. 1751, Biblioteca Nacional, Madrid, MS. 13043 f. 130.
21 Jovellanos, 'Representación a Carlos IV sobre lo que era el Tribunal de la Inquisición', in *Obras* (Biblioteca de Autores Españoles vol. 87, Madrid 1956), 5, pp. 333–4.
22 Jean Sarrailh, *L'Espagne eclairée de la seconde moitié du 18e siècle* (Paris 1954), p. 317.
23 Menéndez Pelayo, *La Ciencia Española* (Madrid 1953 edn), pp. 102–3.
24 Kamen, 'Confiscations', *op. cit.*, p. 523.
25 Lea, *op. cit.*, IV, p. 528.

26 Lord Acton, *Essays on Church and State* (London 1952), p. 393.

27 Maxime Chevalier, *Lectura y Lectores en la España del siglo XVI y XVII* (Madrid 1976).

28 For another elaboration of this argument see Kamen, *Spain 1469–1714*, p. 191.

29 López Piñero, *Ciencia y Tecnica*, pp. 147–8.

30 Prologue to *Historia General de España*.

31 Cf. the picture given in Christian, *Local religion in Sixteenth-Century Spain* (Princeton 1981), and in C. Lisón Tolosana, *Belmonte de los Caballeros* (Oxford 1966).

32 Antonio Mestre, *Ilustración y Reforma de la Iglesia. Pensamiento político-religioso de don Gregorio Mayáns y Siscar (1699–1781)* (Valencia 1968), p. 143.

33 It was used against Olivares: his *Nicandro* was ordered to be seized. It also indulged in petty censorship: the 1640 Index ordered a reference to 'rey tirano' in a work to be altered: 'quítese *rey* y póngase *capitán*': see Domínguez Ortiz, in *Historia de la Iglesia*, IV, p. 115.

34 See R.L. Kagan, *Students and Society in Early Modern Spain* (Baltimore 1974).

35 'Del Influjo de la Inquisición y del fanatismo religioso en la decadencia de la literatura española', *Disertaciones y Juicios literarios* (Madrid 1878), p. 107.

36 *España, un enígma historico*, II, p. 563.

37 *The Spaniards in their history*, pp. 204–45.

Glossary

alfaquis	Muslim clergy who ministered to the Moriscos in Spain.
aljama	Arabic word for the ghetto in which Moors or Jews lived apart from their Christian neighbours. The Castilian words were *juderia* (for Jews) and *moreria* (for Muslims).
alumbrado	An illuminist, one of the groups of mystics who minimized the role of the Church and of ceremonies.
anusim	Hebrew term for the conversos.
arbitrista	A writer who drew up *arbitrios* or proposals for economic and political reform.
auto de fe	Religious ceremony, usually public, at which those tried by the Inquisition had their sentences decreed.
beata	Woman who dedicated herself to a solitary religious life, within or without a religious order.
calificadores	Experts, usually theologians, who assessed the evidence collected by the Inquisition and determined whether heresy was involved.
censos	(called *censals* in the Catalan lands) Annuities drawn from loans made to individuals or to public bodies.
Chancillería	The Castilian high courts in Valladolid and Granada; other high courts were called *audiencias*.
Comuneros	Those who took part in the 1520 revolt of the Comunidades in Castile.
consellers	Catalan term for city councillors, applied in particular to the city councillors of Barcelona.

conversos	Christianized Jews and their descendants; the term could also be applied to converted Muslims.
convivencia	'Living together', a term applied to the coexistence within mediaeval Spain of the three faiths – Christian, Islamic and Jewish.
corregidor	Crown-appointed civil governor in main Castilian towns.
Cortes	The parliament of each realm in Spain, consisting normally of three estates. By the sixteenth century the Castilian Cortes consisted in practice of only one estate, representing eighteen towns.
Diputación	In the Crown of Aragon, standing committee of the Cortes, with members appointed from each estate. In Barcelona the Diputación was also known as the Generalitat. The members of the Diputación were called *diputados* in Aragon, *diputats* in Catalonia and Valencia.
fueros	Laws and privileges of the non-Castilian provinces of Spain.
Germanías	'Brotherhoods', the union of the rebels in Valencia under Charles v.
hermandad	System of 'brotherhood' practised by some Castilian towns as a form of police force.
letrado	University graduate in law, the backbone of the upper levels of Church and State bureaucracy.
licenciado	University graduate; the term was often used to denote status.
limpieza de sangre	Purity of blood; freedom from any taint of semitic blood.
maravedi	Small Castilian coin used as basis of accounting in the early sixteenth century. There were thirty-four maravedis in a *real*, and 375 in a ducat.
Marrano	Abusive word, of obscure origin, applied to conversos.
Mozárabes	Christians living under Muslim rule.
Mudéjares	Muslims living under Christian rule.
procurador	A representative of the towns in the Castilian Cortes.

regidor	Town councillor.
sanbenito	The 'saco bendito' or sacred cloth, a penitential garment imposed by the Inquisition to bring shame on the wearer.
taqiya	'Dissimulation', the tactic of conformism permitted in certain conditions to Muslims living under an alien faith.

Index